RADICAL PLAY

A book in the series

Radical Perspectives:

A *Radical History Review* book series

Series editors:

DANIEL J. WALKOWITZ, New York University

BARBARA WEINSTEIN, New York University

Radical Play

ROB GOLDBERG

Revolutionizing Children's Toys in 1960s and 1970s America

Duke University Press Durham and London 2023

© 2023 Duke University Press. All rights reserved
Printed and bound by CPI Group (UK) Ltd, Croydon, CR0 4YY
Project Editor: Michael Trudeau
Designed by Aimee C. Harrison
Typeset in Garamond Premier Pro and ITC Avant Garde
by Westchester Publishing Services

Library of Congress Cataloging-in-Publication Data
Names: Goldberg, Rob, [date] author.
Title: Radical play : revolutionizing children's toys in 1960s and 1970s
America / Rob Goldberg.
Other titles: Radical perspectives.
Description: Durham : Duke University Press, 2023. | Series: Radical
perspectives | Includes bibliographical references and index.
Identifiers: LCCN 2022048891 (print)
LCCN 2022048892 (ebook)
ISBN 9781478025115 (paperback)
ISBN 9781478020134 (hardcover)
ISBN 9781478027102 (ebook)
Subjects: LCSH: Toys—United States—History—20th century. | Black
dolls—United States—History—20th century. | War toys—Social aspects—
United States. | Play—Social aspects—United States. | Toys—Political
aspects—United States. | Parenting—Political aspects—United States. |
Children—United States—Social life and customs—20th century. | BISAC:
HISTORY / Social History | SOCIAL SCIENCE / Ethnic Studies / American /
African American & Black Studies
Classification: LLC GV1218.5 .G65 2023 (print) | LCC GV1218.5 (ebook) |
DDC 790.1/33—DC23/ENG/20230228
LC record available at https://lccn.loc.gov/2022048891
LC ebook record available at https://lccn.loc.gov/2022048892

Cover photograph by the author.

In loving memory of my father,
Edwin Goldberg

Contents

Acknowledgments

I could not have written this book without the help of so many kind people. I first want to thank the many archivists, librarians, and curators who generously shared their collections and expertise. Carol Sandler and Tara Winner of The Strong welcomed me during my two weeks in Rochester and gave me an unforgettable special tour of the museum's vast holdings. Karen Kukil of the Sophia Smith Collection at Smith College helped me find precisely what I needed. Barbara Whiteman gave me an eye-opening tour of her incredible collection at the Philadelphia Doll Museum. Anne Yoder and Wendy Chmielewski of the Swarthmore College Peace Collection kindly made sure that I turned up every document related to toys. Allen Merry and Karen Kirsheman of the Free Library of Philadelphia went out of their way to track down sources on my behalf. Rukshana Singh, then of the Southern California Library for Social Studies and Research in Los Angeles, helped me access a small yet crucial collection without having to fly across the country. Helmut Knies of the Wisconsin Historical Society sent me a huge box of documents that turned out to be a gold mine. And Nick Okrent at the University of Pennsylvania's Van Pelt Library always patiently fielded my questions, helping me find whatever I was looking for (as well as what I didn't know I was looking for!). I also want to recognize the research staff at the New York Public Library's General Research Division and Science, Industry and Business Library; the Thomas J. Dodd Research Center, University of Connecticut at Storrs; and the Department of Special Collections at the UCLA Charles E. Young Research Library.

I interviewed many people by phone or in person over the course of researching this book. I am grateful to everyone who shared their stories, knowledge, and perspectives (and, in many cases, their archives) with me. Speaking to them was a highlight of this process. Thank you to Bette Benedict, David Crittendon, Karen Donner, Russ Ellis, Kirk Hallahan, Phil Hatten, Margaret Kannenstine, Myron Kaplan, Liz Krisel, Allenna Leonard, Merry Loomis, the late Nicki Montaperto, Michael Mouchette, Howard Neal, Letty Cottin Pogrebin, Pat Powers, Richard Register, Richard Reiss, the late Victoria Reiss, the late Saul Robbins, Jesse Rotman, Barbara Sprung, Francis Turner, Barbara Ulmer, and Ron Weingartner.

The generous support of several institutions was crucial. I benefited immensely from the Benjamin Franklin Fellowship at the University of Pennsylvania. Grants and awards from Penn's Department of History, the Business History Conference, the Center for Ethical Business Cultures at the University of St. Thomas, and the Center for Material Culture Studies at the University of Delaware also helped support my work. Saint Ann's School provided much-needed tuition assistance in the final stretch; a special thanks goes to Bob Swacker, Melissa Kantor, and Vince Tompkins.

Working with Gisela Fosado and Ale Mejía, my editors at Duke University Press, has been a delight from the moment I submitted my proposal. I feel lucky to have benefited from their expertise, and I thank them for their kindness and patience. Two anonymous readers commented on the manuscript with remarkable generosity, giving me pages of constructive feedback that I gratefully put to use. And thanks to series editors Barbara Weinstein and Danny Walkowitz for their enthusiastic support at the very beginning.

Sarah Igo, Ben Nathans, Tom Sugrue, and Mike Zuckerman played crucial roles in this book's original formulation and development. I also want to acknowledge the formative influence of Mary Frances Berry, Phoebe Kropp, Lisa Mitchell, Barbara Savage, and Barbie Zelizer, whose rigorous seminars and inspired teaching made me see history and the historian's responsibilities in a new light. Walter Licht helped me imagine this book in its earliest form. I am grateful for his guidance, enthusiasm, and friendship all these years.

I owe Kathy Peiss a special debt of gratitude. As I worked on the book, I often heard her voice in my head, asking me tough questions, telling me to trust my readers, pressing me to stand by my claims. I can't imagine a more wonderful mentor. I clearly landed in Philadelphia at the right time. Five years earlier, I arrived at the Saint Paul's School summer program, also at the right time, for it was there that I met another extraordinary mentor, David Serlin. I could not have finished this book, let alone started it, without his editorial genius and caring friendship all these years. He has taught me so much, about artifacts and history and life itself. Even longer ago, Andy

Bush and Deborah Dash Moore teamed up for a legendary course (and conversation) that I'm still thinking about. I continue to feel lucky to have been their student.

Many friends and colleagues took time to contribute to the ideas in this book. Elise Burton, Anne Conway, Brian Deimling, Yolanda Hester, Stephen Higa, Selah Johnson, Michal Lemberger, Emily Lordi, Amanda Robiolio, Stephanie Schragger, and Nicole Myers Turner all generously read and commented on parts of the manuscript at various stages, offering eye-opening suggestions and perspectives I hadn't considered. Lisa Kapp is one fabulous editor and friend; I can't imagine where this project would be without her input from the beginning. I have been in conversation with Tshepo Masango Chéry since the first week of grad school; her warmth and her wisdom, on writing history and making a life, mean so much to me. Thanks to Amy Ogata and Susan Weber for inviting me to participate in Bard Graduate Center's 2015 symposium, "Toys and Childhood: Playing with Design." My fellow panelists at OAH, CAA, SHCY, and BHC meetings gave me valuable food for thought as I tested new ideas. Matthew Kaplan was kind enough to invite me to his toymaking seminar. G. Giraldo pieced the poster together. Denny Renshaw shared his great visual eye. Much appreciation goes to my old colleagues in the Department of History at Saint Ann's School for years of support and camaraderie. And to my new colleagues at Germantown Friends School, thank you for the friendliest of welcomes into the community.

Other friends kept me going, more than they know, including Eric Anglès, Karega Bennett, Reed Black, Dave Bromwich, Lisa Caldes, Paige Cowett, Jesse Dillon, Deborah Dobski, Laurie Duchovny, Seth Endo, Jennie Hahn, Erica Kelley, Jesse Kohn, Jesse Langille, Bri McDonnell, Chris Mellon, Jenny Reckrey, Noah Rothbaum, Lydia Pecker, Liz Prescott, Meredith Tenhoor, and Robert Wood. Patty Brotman always asked me about my progress, and Jim Mullahy encouraged me to think deeply about the way I used images. Daniel Goldberg helped me picture the book years ago. My brothers, Joe and Paul, are always there for me. And I'm thankful for the support of all the other family in my life—whether their last name is Goldberg, Light, Glassman, Mandel, Yusba, Burba, Steinberg, Nickerson, Brotman, Lang, or Williamson. I deeply miss my father-in-law, Bob Brotman, who loved history and carried books on the American Revolution wherever he went.

Jan Goldberg, my *bashert*, understands play like no one I have ever met. She has shown me so much. I'm eternally grateful for all she gave, and gave up, so that I could finish this book, and for the joy and love she brings to our kids and our life together. Minny and Misha have grown up playing with Rhonda,

Derry Daring, and the other toys I write about. I thank them for reminding me that, while toys are good to think with, they're even better to play with. May they never stop playing!

Finally, this book is dedicated to my parents, Ed and June Goldberg, who created a loving, musical home where I always felt I could be myself. While my dad did not live to see this book in print, I can still hear the joyful shout he let out when I told him over the phone that I had gotten a book contract. He continues to be a guide to me in all I do. So does my mom. She also happens to be a meticulous editor, reading over nearly every page of the final draft. I love her very much.

Introduction

Victoria Reiss's home in 1960s New York City was a tolerant one when it came to her sons' play, with one exception: no war toys. To Reiss, a white Barnard College graduate and mother of three boys who was active in New York's peace movement (among other progressive causes), toy machine guns were symbols of war's horrors and little else; if her sons wanted to play war with sticks, that was different. But house rules end at one's doorstep. Reiss could expect the local toy store to stock war toys, but when her family pediatrician did too—a small arsenal in his waiting room, amid the puzzles and dolls—she had had enough. As the escalating US war in Vietnam began to occupy Reiss's attention, she made her private struggle against war toys public. As the cofounder and leader of Parents for Responsibility in the Toy Industry and, later, cofounder of the Public Action Coalition on Toys, Reiss staged pickets against toy guns outside the annual Toy Fair and gave awards to shops that agreed not to stock them. From the doctor's office to the toy industry headquarters, Reiss used toys to raise uncomfortable questions about war's everyday acceptance, not in isolation from the peace movement but as her own contribution to the cause.[1]

Lou Smith, meanwhile, came to toys by way of other movements transforming America in these years: civil rights and Black Power. From the Harlem office of the Congress of Racial Equality, to the Freedom Summer Project in Mississippi, to Los Angeles after the 1965 Watts Rebellion, Smith, who was Black, worked to improve the lives of his fellow Black Americans and overhaul the system that denied them equality. In the late 1960s, Smith was leading Operation Bootstrap, a unique self-help organization in South LA that set up small businesses as training sites for local men and women, when he went searching for a large corporation to participate in the program. It was the nearby toy manufacturer Mattel, the largest toy company in the world, that answered his call. With Mattel's support, Smith and his colleagues founded Shindana Toys, with Smith as president. Employing the local Black community and putting politics into every phase of the toymaking process, Shindana revolutionized the practices of dollmaking. Thanks to Smith and his colleagues, all activists-turned-toymakers, the popular Black liberation slogan "Black Is Beautiful" would for the first time be translated into the world of children's toys.[2]

As it turns out, second-wave feminism had its toymakers too. In the early 1970s, Barbara Sprung, a white schoolteacher and graduate student at Bank Street College, began a part-time job for the Women's Action Alliance that changed her life and the lives of countless others. The women's movement had begun to challenge the traditional gender and sex norms in the toy business—and Sprung joined them. Bridging the teachings of child development with her existing feminist commitments, Sprung helped found the new field of nonsexist early childhood education and assigned toys a key role in the curriculum. When she couldn't find representational toys that met her socially progressive specifications—women and men in all roles, racial diversity, a variety of family structures—she followed in the footsteps of earlier progressive educators and, with the help of the Milton Bradley Company, made them herself. To Sprung, the prototypes she developed were not just for new toys but prototypes for a new society.[3]

What can these stories tell us about the meanings Americans attached to toys in the 1960s and 1970s? What led Reiss, Smith, Sprung, and other activists across the era's movements against war, racism, and sexism to see toys as useful tools for social change? And, finally, how did the industry make sense of, manage, and participate in this unique moment of consumer dissent and activist toymaking? In answering these questions, *Radical Play* locates a definitive moment in the production of American children's culture when the toy industry was tested, challenged, and ultimately transformed by the progressive social visions of the age. In the years between the assassination of John F. Kennedy in 1963 and the election of Jimmy Carter in 1976, the antiwar, civil rights, and feminist movements brought their political concerns to Toyland, turning toys into vehicles for protest and reform. As the United States escalated the conflict in Vietnam, members of the two leading women's peace groups launched an unprecedented war on war toys. In the years following the April 1968 assassination of Rev. Dr. Martin Luther King Jr., Black Power community organizers and white racial liberals revitalized the Black freedom tradition of using dolls for racial uplift and anti-racist education. And in the 1970s, white women leaders from the most influential organizations of liberal feminism attacked the toy industry for its rampant stereotyping and exclusions related to gender, race, and family structure. As the examples of Smith and Sprung attest, some of these activists went beyond protesting into the arena of production itself. By the end of the 1970s, the combined efforts of these different advocates for change had both altered what was on retailers' shelves and reshaped the interpretation of toys in American culture.

But they did not accomplish this alone. In fact, no one did more to facilitate these efforts to transform American toys and childhood than the corporate toy industry itself. In the 1960s and 1970s, that industry's leaders were almost entirely white and disproportionately Jewish, as had been the case for decades; indeed, most of the major companies I write about in the following pages were founded or cofounded by Jews and, at least during this era, led by Jewish executives (often one of the founders), including Lionel, Ideal, Fisher-Price, Hasbro, Mattel, Creative Playthings, Kenner, and Remco.[4] In addition, while female executives ran three of the era's leading toy firms—Ruth Handler of Mattel, Lynn Pressman of Pressman Toy Corporation, and Min Horowitz of Gabriel Industries—the toy business as a whole was still largely male; the gendered term *toy man*, long used by and for professionals at all levels of the trade, was still part of industry speak. As I show, these toymakers engaged their era's social movements in diverse ways, using the tools of their trade. Some companies expressed their solidarity with activists' concerns through the creation of new products, like a liberated fashion doll, or by incorporating the language of antiwar or civil rights protest into their advertising. Others held press conferences to share their burgeoning social consciousness and apologize for past practices. One company president even left the industry's powerful trade association in protest of the association's failure to adopt a unified stance against war toys. And in a few remarkable instances, companies initiated and financed partnerships with the activists themselves. Such actions not only transformed their critics into allies, in some cases preemptively, but also empowered them to become toy entrepreneurs themselves. In the process, these toymakers created a new type of dialogue with the society around them and a theoretical win-win situation: an opportunity for producers and protesters alike to each achieve a kind of victory in the toy department. Starting in the 1960s, new groups outside the industry sought the right and the opportunity to participate in the business of children's toys. Through the public contestation and surprising collaborations that ensued, the cultural changes of the 1960s and 1970s took shape in the form of toys.

Toymakers may not have understood or articulated what they were doing as "politics," yet it was. By incorporating messages of peace or racial equality into their latest toys and marketing campaigns, they helped advance the movements' goals of translating the sixties imagination into children's culture.[5] Of course, the opposite was also true: when toymakers ignored the calls to integrate the doll shelves or pushed back against demands to eliminate sexist stereotypes, they were using their power not merely to foreclose that imagination but to preserve the white supremacist, heterosexist vision of society that had long reigned in the toy industry. When a toy salesman reacted to a 1964 public demonstration against war toys with the quip "I wonder what these dames let their boys play with? Dolls?" he was not just making a joke; he was showing his commitment to a traditional conception of white masculine identity development that the substitution of a (boy's) toy gun with a (girl's) doll threatened to disrupt.[6]

○

The politicization of play in the 1960s and 1970s rested on a series of new historical developments that redefined the status of children's toys in American life in the decades after World War II. By the time the first major mobilizations around toys erupted in the mid-1960s, American parents faced a fundamentally different and all-encompassing consumer culture of children's toys from what they knew in their own youth. Starting in the 1950s and continuing into the next decade, large-scale structural changes radically changed how the industry did business. Thanks to new mass-production techniques and new and cheaper plastics, as well as the rise of discount stores and the more efficient model of direct distribution they enabled, the toy business could offer a larger volume and variety of toys at historically low prices. Discount stores bought wholesale, cut out the traditional middleman role of the wholesaler (or jobber) in selecting toys, and removed the sales clerks. As prices dropped, these practices also reshaped the landscape of toy shopping. Toy departments of upscale department stores, independently owned toy shops, and variety retailers remained important venues for toy buying, but they also were increasingly displaced by new toy discount mart chains such as Toys "R" Us, founded in 1957.[7]

If these trends built a new suburban consumer landscape of shopping centers and malls, the 1950s toy industry was also now able to reach potential shoppers at home. While radio had been around since the 1930s, the birth of televised advertising took that ability to a whole new level: TV not only allowed manufacturers to reach consumers in the comfort of their living rooms but also provided an opportunity for them to visually demonstrate a product rather than just telling the family about it. By the early 1960s, when nine out of ten Americans had at least one TV in their home, televised marketing had been adopted by every major manufacturer with dreams of national sales. Moreover, with the advent of children's programming hours on the networks, advertisers could now target children directly, bypassing the mothers who had historically mediated the industry's relationship to the child consumer. This new age of child marketing, combined with the consolidation of an industry establishment made up of highly diversified national corporations hustling brand-name goods, helped create a more uniform consumer culture of play across the country.[8] This uniformity would play a key role in the campaigns against war toys and other controversial items. For one, recognizable brands meant that toy reformers across the country could effectively target particular companies in their protests. Meanwhile, the new level of standardization in what children played with made it possible to imagine a transformation of children's socialization on a national scale.

The child-centered culture of the postwar United States also helped under-write the politicization of playthings. On one level, this was not entirely new so much as another phase in what historians have shown was a long-standing trend in American family life: the adoption of the normative child-rearing ideals of the educated white middle class. Yet it would be hard to overstate the extent to which the new social conditions of postwar life intensified the child-centeredness of American society, including the extraordinary upturn in the birth rate from roughly 1946 to 1964. Coming less than a decade after the nation had gone from the depths of the century's worst economic slump into a physically and emotionally draining foreign war, the baby boom, writes media scholar Lynn Spigel, "created a nation of children who became a new symbol of hope."[9] "More than ever," historian Howard Chudacoff explains, "parents put children at the center of their culture."[10] Such an approach, of course, was facilitated by the economic prosperity of the 1950s, which was more widely (if not equitably) shared than any other time in the nation's history. If typical Americans exercised their new purchasing power with unprecedented spending on discretionary goods, in the context of child-centered family life, at least, few types of goods were understood to be more worthy of these dollars than toys.

That these developments supplied special fuel for the new toy-industrial complex was not lost on social observers. "Child-centeredness is necessary . . . to our toy economy," wrote anthropologist Jules Henry in his popular 1963 book, *Culture against Man*. "Take away child-centeredness from the toy business and it would be back in the nineteenth century."[11] With it, the toy economy swelled: between 1951 and 1961, retail toy sales in the United States increased by 120 percent, reaching $1.7 billion.[12] But it was not merely that toys were something fun to buy for the kids, or even something with which to bribe or spoil them. It was also the case that toys moved to the center of the new normative ideal of intensive consumerist child-rearing at a moment when the expanding fields of social and developmental psychology were reshaping how experts and their parent readers thought about what made for a healthy childhood, including what kinds of toys would best support it.

A large part of this was a midcentury shift in the professionals' definition of childhood well-being, as older concerns about physical health in a prevaccine age gave way to a new postscarcity preoccupation with psychological health, cognitive growth, and personality formation. Historian Leila J. Rupp has described the situation well, writing that "the 1950s brought a new emphasis on the quality of child-rearing, including . . . a popularized Freudian notion of the crucial importance of a child's first years, and the emergence of a new corps of child-rearing experts . . . who warned of the dire consequences of anything less than full-time attention from a mother for her children's well-being."[13] Whereas previously only the Freudians looked at early childhood, now virtually all of the human and behavioral sciences turned their attention to the child as a subject of study in the 1950s, especially when it promised to help solve thorny social problems like racial prejudice or the potential for homegrown fascism, as prominent intellectuals like anthropologist Margaret Mead and sociologist David Riesman believed it did.[14] By the early 1960s, the so-called cognitive revolution in psychology would be underway, with sweeping new pronouncements on the importance of the preschool years for all future learning. The new psychology not only popularized developmental theory as never before; it also directly inspired a wave of new federally funded programs as diverse as Head Start (1964) and the pioneering public television show *Sesame Street* (1969).[15]

As for attitudes about play, the emphasis on the first few years of life only added to the heightened anxiety over toy selection that came with so much focus on the child along with the potentially confusing abundance of choices in the aisles.[16] This focus helps explain why Dr. Benjamin Spock, the most famous child-care adviser of the period, devoted three of his magazine columns exclusively to toys in the period 1961–64 alone—this after not a single piece on toys in the previous decade and a relatively short section on the topic in his best-selling *The Commonsense Book of Baby and Child Care* (1946).[17] The noted psychologists Ruth M. Hartley and Robert M. Goldenson likewise left no question as to the high stakes of toys in their own guidebook, *The Complete Book of Children's Play* (1957): "When we buy toys, we are investing as surely as when we buy stocks, and the commodity we are investing in may be more important than shares in a concern."[18] Such heightened awareness about toys' importance in the lives of children was not lost on the industry. According to a 1964 editorial in the venerable trade magazine *Playthings*, nothing was more crucial to future sales than "awareness of the tremendous increase in the number of college-educated mothers, young women who approach the task of selecting toys for their youngsters in a much more thoughtful and sophisticated manner than was the case with most mothers a generation ago.... Many ... have taken wide-ranging liberal arts, child-psychology, and home economics courses as important parts of their curricula.... They're more aware of the function of toys in the development of their children along physical, psychological, and social lines."[19] But perhaps the toymaker A. C. Gilbert Jr., reflecting on the same cultural trend in *Playthings* just a couple of years earlier, said it best: "Who is not toy-conscious today?"[20]

Such toy-consciousness would continue to fuel the industry's remarkable growth, but it also would be responsible for the most embattled decade in the history of the trade. During the 1960s and 1970s, Americans involved in diverse social justice movements, from peace to Black Power to women's liberation, would tap into these new discourses on toys and play as well as older ones. As people engaged in trying to change the world, however, it was in the spirit of their age to ask a very different set of questions from those of mainstream experts: What are these toys teaching the young about the world around them? What are toys teaching them in terms of values to live by? Some looked with fresh eyes at their own kids' playthings. Some studied consumer catalogs and investigated the local toy aisles. Others revisited their own toy memories, recalling how few dolls or promotions featured anyone who looked like them; how it felt to be excluded from the industry's polished image of white American childhood; and how much the toy landscape hadn't changed since. The closer they looked, the more they felt that the only values that the toy industry was communicating were those of the status quo.

○

Three goals drive this book. One is to expand our understanding of 1960s and 1970s progressive and radical politics by returning the reform of children's media culture, seen here as a contested process involving a wide range of social, political, cultural, and industry actors, to a more prominent place in the narrative.[21] I see toys as central to a new politicized parenting discourse of "progressive parenting," an ideology first developed by psychologically oriented activist parents and left-leaning child experts in the 1930s and 1940s that combined the teachings of Sigmund Freud and progressive education with the social justice politics of the Popular Front.[22] Largely relegated to families on the left during the heyday of Popular Front culture, progressive parenting reemerged in the 1960s and 1970s with a new emphasis on bringing the commercialized world of children's popular culture in line with left-liberal values. These projects took a variety of forms, from the advent of watchdog groups such as the Council on Interracial Books for Children and Feminists on Children's Media to the development of innovative multimedia products like the award-winning 1972 record album *Free to Be... You and Me*, which was financed by the Ms. Foundation for Women. Together, they revised the fields of children's material and visual culture to be more racially and ethnically diverse; less bounded by conventional gender, sex, and family stereotypes; and consciously committed to fostering understanding and empathy around issues of identity, equality, and justice.[23] As I show, the efforts across different activist communities to transform the world of toys, starting in the early 1960s and reaching its height a decade later, would be a key aspect of this child-centered cultural movement and, arguably, one of the chief factors in propelling the new politics of parenting into the liberal mainstream.

A second goal of the book is to place business and the culture industry at the center of our understanding of the era's familiar cultural upheaval and spirit of dissent.[24] Consumer pressure, public protest, and critical shifts in American attitudes about war, race, and gender during the 1960s and 1970s provoked major changes in the toy industry's relationship to the world outside its institutional walls. One of them was that toymakers were forced to publicly reckon with, perhaps for the first time, their status as entrepreneurs of ideology—as producers of values and not just products. But perhaps the most surprising new development was that the proponents of a more socially conscious toy trade came not only from the ranks of political groups and child advocates but also from within the industry. Manufacturers, advertisers, and industry boosters alike consciously blurred the line between organizing markets and fostering movements. In doing so, they became the willing accomplices to their critics.

Finally, this book makes the claim that toys produced for children not only illustrate cultural change but also help shape it. Accordingly, I treat cultural objects that are often relegated to collectors' guides as historical subjects in their own right. A doll named Barbie has a role in this story, but it is a minor one compared to dolls with less familiar names such as Baby Nancy and Derry

Daring. For decades now, historians of consumer culture have drawn on the work of symbolic anthropologists to study the histories of a variety of cultural things, including toys and other childhood objects, and the different ways people have used them to construct identities and social relations.[25] Taking as a guiding premise Mary Douglas and Baron Isherwood's definition of consumption as "the very arena in which culture is fought over and licked into shape," this book aims to underscore the importance of both the fights over meanings and the objects of struggle themselves—the actual shapes into which culture is licked.[26] By analyzing the material culture of toy design alongside other artifacts of promotion and merchandising such as toy packages, I show how the various debates, exchanges, and interactions between pressure groups, manufacturers, marketers, and experts in the 1960s and 1970s remade the forms as well as the meanings of American children's culture.

○

"In the postwar years—the nearly two decades between the end of World War II and the assassination of John F. Kennedy—a cluster of powerful conservative norms set the parameters of American culture," writes historian Andrew Hartman.[27] Those norms, which together make up what Hartman has called "normative America," encompassed some of the most enduring ideologies of patriarchy, white supremacy, and heteronormativity: everything from the belief that women should be married and out of the workforce, to a patriotic faith in American exceptionalism, to an idealized projection of the national character that left out its singular racial and ethnic diversity.[28] With Barbie dolls and Burp Guns at the top of its best-seller list on the eve of the sixties, the American mass-market toy industry was essentially in the business of reproducing it all, in miniature. Could the world of toys be not just remade but repurposed for the goals of the 1960s and 1970s left, such as countering pro-military values, dismantling anti-Black racism, promoting a more egalitarian, unisex vision of human potential? At different times and in different ways, activists from across the era's radical cultural and political mobilizations said yes and set to work to transform the business of toys. To their surprise, the toy industry joined them.

Parenting for Peace

On the morning of March 9, 1964, the offices and sales rooms of the Toy Center complex in Midtown Manhattan were bustling with activity, as toymakers from virtually every US company prepared for their most anticipated day of the year: the opening of the weeklong American Toy Fair, the industry's annual tradeshow since 1903. If the Toy Fair had always been important to the business, in recent decades it had emerged as a make-or-break event for what had become a nearly $2 billion consumer industry. In floor after floor of manufacturers' showrooms, retail buyers from around the country and the world—including owners of small toy shops, buyers for national discount chains and department stores, and regional wholesalers—browsed, inspected, and judged the commercial prospects of the newest product lines. If they liked what they saw, they placed orders, effectively determining a significant share of their inventory for the months to come. The toys that generated the most buzz and sales at the Toy Fair frequently went on to become the year's best-selling items.

The Toy Center, founded in 1925, was originally not a place but an organization—a promotional agency, headquartered inside the famous Fifth Avenue Building in Manhattan's Flatiron District, whose chief mission was to transform that office building into "a concentrated central point for the toy industry."[1] Over the course of the 1930s and 1940s, the agency's officers, all of them toy executives, did just that. In fact, they carried out their mission so successfully that the Fifth Avenue Building, with its iconic street clock at the entrance, soon acquired a second name among New Yorkers: the Toy

Building. By 1946, the Toy Building housed (according to a Toy Center publication) "the sales rooms of a majority of the leading manufacturers and sales agents"; the offices of the Toy Manufacturers of the U.S.A., Inc. (TMA), the industry's trade association; and a host of club-like amenities for its member manufacturers and visiting dealers, including a barber shop, restaurant, and massage parlor.[2] By the 1960s, the Toy Center organization had extended its management operations beyond the Toy Building to another large office tower on the corner of the next block to the north; thanks to the fully enclosed pedestrian bridge connecting it to the Toy Building at the ninth floor, toymakers could travel throughout the new Toy Center complex without having to go outside or cross a street (see figure 1.1). Meanwhile, the Toy Building's owners decided to stop renewing leases for occupants unaffiliated with the toy business, bringing the original dreams of the Toy Center founders closer to reality.[3]

It was also during the post–World War II years that the TMA decided to take advantage of the industry's extraordinary geographical concentration of manufacturers and hold the annual Toy Fair on site. Yet even the Toy Center's two interlinked buildings were soon insufficient at Toy Fair time to contain all the new products, not to mention the throngs of toy buyers and dealers, that accompanied the industry's postwar boom. And so, the TMA had begun taking over the nearby New Yorker Hotel to house additional Toy Fair showrooms. With ten thousand visitors expected over the course of the week, the 1964 event was certainly going to require it.[4]

Among the thousands who came by subway or taxi to the Toy Fair's opening day was a group of six white women, some with young children in tow.[5] Unlike everyone else who arrived that morning, however, they never went in. For they were not there to place orders but to protest. Identifying themselves to the press as representatives of a newly formed coalition called Parents Against the Encouragement of Violence, they had come to publicly oppose the industry's recent proliferation of toy guns and other so-called war toys—a category that included everything from plastic grenades to miniature tanks and soldiers—in department stores, supermarket aisles, and television commercials (see figure 1.2). "Parent, Parents, we ask you ... please don't give our children toys of violence," stated the yellow printed handbills they gave out to everyone entering the buildings or walking by. "We're troubled about the effects of toy guns and weapons on children—are you? We're troubled at the climate of violence all around us—are you? ... Before our children grow up to accept violence as just part of life ... THINK! DON'T BUY! DON'T GIVE!"[6] Nothing like this had ever happened before. As toymakers and buyers

1.1. By the 1960s, the vast majority of US toy manufacturers leased showrooms and/or office space in one of the Toy Center's two linked buildings in New York City. The one known by the industry as the Toy Building is on the left. Advertisement from *Playthings*, February 1958. Courtesy of Todd Coopee.

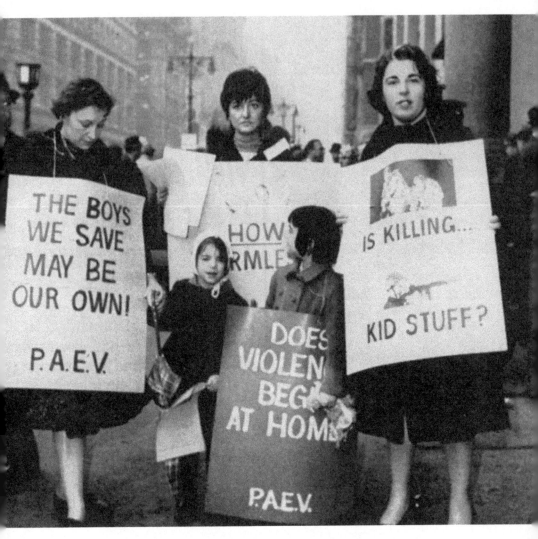

1.2. A group of women calling themselves Parents Against the Encouragement of Violence protests war toys outside the annual Toy Fair in New York City in early March 1964. Photograph from *Toy & Hobby World*, April 4, 1964.

entered the Toy Fair buildings that morning, they were met by demonstrators, not salespeople, holding picket signs that read "Let's Disarm the Nursery." More of an invitation than an objection, the slogan reflected the protesters' hopeful conviction that consumers and manufacturers could perhaps find common ground.[7]

The Toy Fair protest was just one manifestation of a national movement of anti–war toy action committees that had coalesced in the months after the November 1963 assassination of President John F. Kennedy. While a number of civic and religious groups would participate in the era's reinvigorated campaigns against war toys, most of the organizational momentum and leadership came from two national organizations: Women's International League for Peace and Freedom (WILPF), the oldest female-led peace organization in the country; and Women Strike for Peace (WSP), the youngest, and whose members were responsible for organizing the event.[8] In the months that followed the Toy Fair demonstration, the combined initiatives of WILPF and WSP would flower into the largest and most concerted agitation over toys in US history. As one element of that agitation, WILPF and WSP activists in New York City would make the picketing of the Toy Fair an annual tradition for the rest of the decade.

The intersecting identities and commitments of WSP and WILPF women made them uniquely suited and primed for the job of taking on a largely male-dominated industry and publicizing their cause far beyond pacifist quarters. They were advocates for nuclear disarmament and internationalism. They were mothers and consumers on behalf of children. They were disproportionally from the educated classes, well versed in child development and psychology, and socially and professionally connected to some of the most prominent liberal reformers, intellectuals, and experts of their day. Through toys, they would unite the moral priorities of the postwar antinuclear movement with the social conscience of progressive parenting, a politicized child-rearing model that combined the social justice, interracialist, and internationalist orientation of the 1930s and 1940s Popular Front with both Freudian psychology and progressive education's belief in the power of play.[9] "Play is serious business," stated Dr. Spock in *The Commonsense Book of Baby and Child Care*.[10] In the early 1960s, the women's peace-and-justice movement would give Spock's wisdom, trusted by millions, a new political twist.[11]

The case against war toys reflected a variety of ideological stances and intellectual sources, ranging from pacifism to the social sciences to early childhood theory. From the peace movement, activists brought their ardent moral aversion to the military as an institution and symbol, an aversion intensified by the arms race. From developmental and social psychology, they brought a commitment to scientific child-rearing in the name of producing what postwar experts called the healthy personality. And from the "progressive education" movement, they seized on a half century of writings on using carefully directed childhood play, along with the right set of toys, to cultivate creative, democratic citizens; according to adherents of this developmental model, highly realistic war toys overdetermined children's all-important fantasy play, impoverishing their imaginations and limiting the development of creativity.

The movement against war toys was also a product of its specific historical moment in the Cold War, a moment defined by militarized civil defense drills and the brush with nuclear annihilation brought on by the October 1962 Cuban missile crisis. In the eyes of the era's toy reformers, the nuclear age's threat to humanity required the popular rejection of militarism not only in the streets but also in the home. While the white middle-class nuclear household was often invoked as the first line of patriotic defense against the perceived menace of Soviet Communism, this particular group of middle-class women alternatively staged the home as a demilitarized zone, articulating a radical vision of how parents and children might relate to the political and existential threats of the era. In doing so, they repurposed the patriotic terms of postwar domesticity—that is, the appeal to scientific motherhood, the reliance on psychological experts, the centrality of consumer goods to the American Way of Life—to shatter, rather than fortify, the Cold War consensus.[12] Joining the politics of peace to the politics of parenting in an era when good childhoods became inextricably tied to good toys, they set the terms for the politicization of play for a long time to come.

○

Organized opposition to war toys was not exactly new in the spring of 1964. Concerns about this perennially popular class of playthings were as old as the peace movement itself, and usually coincident with surges in pacifist activity. In the nineteenth century, the American Peace Society had protested them, as had the Department of Peace and Arbitration within the Women's Christian Temperance Union (WCTU).[13] After World War I, and the subsequent birth of the modern toy industry, the newly formed US section of the worldwide WILPF (founded in 1919) took over leadership on the issue; in one early campaign of 1922, the Palo Alto, California, branch called for toy manufacturers and parents to "Disarm the Nursery."[14] In the four decades that followed, anti–war toy activities became a recurring, if also "sporadic and localized," part of WILPF's peace-education programming, rising and falling alongside spikes in toy-gun production and shifting political winds.[15]

Yet, for all these efforts, which were at times joined by like-minded groups such as the Society of Friends (Quakers), criticism of war toys at the dawn of the 1960s was largely relegated to pacifist quarters. Even within the WILPF National Office, which had probably spent more time and energy than anyone else on the issue over the years, activists were not yet ready to make unequivocal claims for what toys did or didn't do to children. A WILPF pamphlet titled *Junior Disarmament*, published around 1960, revealed as much when it stated that "the first thing that can be said about toys, good or bad, is that they are less important than they seem."[16] Their genuine concerns about children's moral and political socialization notwithstanding, few in the broader antiwar and nuclear disarmament movement—and even fewer outside of it—were likely to rank toys among the most pressing problems of war and peace in the post-Hiroshima era. That would soon change, not because child psychologists came to new conclusions about toys' significance in children's emotional, intellectual, or moral development but because activists did. By the decade's end, the same WILPF National Office responsible for *Junior Disarmament*'s relatively cautious position on toys would assert that "toys, the learning tools of childhood, are literally a life and death matter."[17] Nor would they be alone in framing the impact of toys in such weighty terms.

What changed and when? What convinced these activists in the 1960s that war toys were perhaps *more* important than they seem? And why did so many people, including influential child-rearing experts and even major toy manufacturers, not only begin to listen to these old arguments with new interest and concern but also, as we shall see, join the anti–war toy crusade?

○

One of the first sparks in this new chapter of toy activism was ignited when Mary Ellen Fretts, state president of Ohio WILPF, wrote to her organization's National Board in Philadelphia in October 1963. Sharing what she described as widespread concern among Ohio women over the "new crop" of war toys in the national marketplace, Fretts was curious to know whether "the National Board might help us to organize and popularize some sort of concerted action which might strike at the entire problem of childhood education through toys." She continued: "It seems like a difficult project since all manufacturers will sell as long as the public will buy; yet perhaps it can begin in neighborhoods and then go directly to the headquarters of toy-making, with protests and constructive criticisms."[18] One month later, Fretts's call for concerted action was circulated to peace educators around the country when Bess Lane, the new chair of WILPF's National Committee on Childhood Education, sent a memorandum to branches nationwide. "The Childhood Education Committee of WILPF is working on a project for which we are seeking help from the membership," Lane stated. "The project is called (temporarily) *Operation War Toys*. We are eager to provide some help in this area because of our own concern and the concern of large numbers of parents over the number, kinds and availability of 'death-dealing' weapons for children." After quoting liberally from the recent letters she had received, Lane closed by expressing her "[hope] that each of us will find the time and the opportunity to do something, however small, to help change the trend from the emphasis on violence in toys to an emphasis on those toys that may lead to constructive ways of living and learning."[19]

At almost exactly the same time, members of the country's other female antiwar organization, WSP, began contacting their group's leadership with similar concerns. "The step from atomic weapons to toy guns is not really a very large one," wrote Rita Morgan to WSP cofounder Dagmar Wilson in December 1963, and "the connection should be made clear."[20] Three months later, the organization's national newsletter, *Memo*, printed a letter from a member of Oakland WSP calling for a national effort: "We are anxious to reach [WSP] all over the country," she wrote, "urging them to write to manufacturers . . . and local toy dealers . . . to emphasize that we will not buy where we see extreme war toys displayed."[21]

The announcement of Operation War Toys and WSP's own parallel initiative met with an outpouring of interest from members of both groups—some of whom were active in the two at once. As news of the WILPF campaign spread through memos, phone chains, and word of mouth, Childhood Education Committees in branches across the country—including Ann Arbor, Minneapolis, and Buffalo—commenced a new era of anti–war toy protest and outreach. Meanwhile, the national office's Childhood Education Committee created the organization's first Subcommittee on War Toys, as if to indicate to members nationwide that this was not a fleeting campaign. And while WSP activists did not benefit from having an established education wing, local chapters swiftly formed special toy action committees, including groups in San Francisco, Los Angeles, New York, Philadelphia, Detroit, and Cambridge. Two WSP members also founded an information clearinghouse to distribute campaign news, educational resources, and activist tools for citizens who wished to get involved in the anti–war toy opposition. Within a few months of the initial calls to action, the combined forces of WSP and WILPF had accomplished a great deal. They had spawned a nationwide network of toy activists, built the basic elements of a shared movement apparatus, and integrated their campaigns into the existing structure of their organizations.

The urgency of these calls to organize and the scope of their activities were unprecedented. At a time when WILPF was working on African American civil rights and WSP was just coming out of its successful lobbying campaign for a nuclear-weapons testing ban and turning its attention to the growing US military presence in Vietnam, the turn to children's play, often seen as trivial, might seem out of place. Yet to the women spearheading this new movement, like Rita Morgan, US militarism found expression in multiple forms, large and small, and they were all of a piece. To wage a battle against the nuclear arms race yet not speak out against what WILPF leader and sociologist Elise Boulding dubbed "the toy race"—her name for what she and others perceived as the competition among toymakers to make the most death-dealing pretend weapons—was to neglect the role of culture in producing citizens who either accept or refuse their nation's military belligerence.[22]

Several converging factors, commercial as well as political, help explain the eruption of protest at this particular moment, not to mention the sense of urgency that energized it. For one thing, the "new crop" of war toys described by Mary Ellen Fretts and others was a bumper one, indeed. In December 1963, the *New York Times* reported that the toy trade "had produced a larger than usual assortment of toys with a military appearance."[23] The character was shifting too. As one writer observed in the *New Republic* in December 1962, "the emphasis is on achieving a nuclear capability," this two months after the Cuban missile crisis.[24] Some manufacturers were boasting about such investments, like the official from Aurora Plastics Corporation who claimed his company's "output of military and naval equipment could supply all of NATO's needs and then some."[25] Likewise, Mattel's Guerrilla Gun Set, introduced in 1963, shrewdly played off the latest developments in the Kennedy administration's policy of "limited war" in Southeast Asia. According to an item in the trade press, the set included "everything needed for make-believe guerilla warfare," from a machine gun and camouflaged poncho to a green beret, which had just become the official headgear of US Army Special Forces the previous year (hence the nickname the "Green Berets").[26] As one Mattel ad stated, "It's just like the outfit used by real jungle fighters."[27] So was Transogram's new Combat Medical Kit. As a promotion summed up the newly militarized landscape of play, "This year the toy business has turned khaki . . . and we're always 1A"—the military draft's code for immediate availability—"when it comes to marching ahead."[28]

Another expansion into contemporary history—or perhaps the future—was the Johnny Seven O.M.A. toy, introduced by Topper Toys at the 1964 Toy Fair and one of the most commercially successful toy weapons in history. The time-honored toy-gun formula may have reached its own new frontier in the Johnny Seven. In the context of make-believe war play, the Johnny Seven arguably offered the most potentially destructive handheld toy weapon ever produced. "O.M.A.," an acronym that stood for One-Man-Army, was an accurate characterization of this life-sized plastic rifle that could be disassembled to produce seven distinct weapons: grenade shooter, anti-tank rocket, armor-piercing shell, anti-bunker missile, repeating rifle, tommy gun, and automatic pistol (see figure 1.3). The Johnny Seven, declared Topper, "makes all other toy guns obsolete."[29] In one of the product's many full-page promotions in the trade press, the president of Deluxe Reading (Topper's parent company) made the bold claim that the Johnny Seven was not imitating the Department of Defense's weapons technology; rather, he argued, it

1.3. The Johnny Seven O.M.A. (1964), Topper Toys. From the 1966 Topper Toys catalog. Courtesy of Francis Turner.

was anticipating it! Referring to news reports of recent Pentagon efforts to develop a multipurpose gun not unlike the Johnny Seven, he claimed that Topper "was the innovator, coincidental as it might appear."[30] It would be hard to find a better example of what critics described as "extreme war toys."

Interestingly, however, the most visible shift of the early 1960s was not toward the realm of sci-fi military fantasy or nuclear annihilation but to the recent past of World War II. In the early 1960s, as a decorated war hero entered the White House, the battlefields and military outposts of the European and Pacific theaters of World War II swept popular culture, nowhere more prominently than in network TV.[31] "World War Two is being fought all over again, fictionally, on television, and the individual heroics are capturing juvenile imaginations in a big way," stated a toy industry observer in *Playthings* in April 1963.[32]

It was a decisive break, with major consequences for the business of toy firearms. For the entire decade of the 1950s, the genre of "adult westerns," such as *Gunsmoke* (1955–75) and *Bat Masterson* (1958–61), had dominated network primetime programming. In fact, the 1959 weekly lineup featured thirty-one different westerns, seven of which were ranked in the Nielsen Ratings' top ten.[33] Yet between 1962 and 1967, the networks shifted gears, becoming home to a dozen new shows about World War II, including *Combat!* (1962–67) and *McHale's Navy* (1962–67); by 1964, only seven of the thirty-one westerns of 1959 remained.[34] If the westerns had inspired record sales of "Wild West"–themed six-shooter cap guns and holster sets in the latter half of the 1950s, the shift on living room TV screens to the Pacific and European theaters had a similarly outsized impact.

In response, the nation's biggest suppliers of toy guns and battle regalia updated the historical period and style appropriately. Manufacturers known for their western six-shooter pistols and rifles, such as the Daisy Manufacturing Company, began to augment their arsenals with modern automatic-weapon toys. For instance, it would have been hard for anyone in the toy aisle not to see the stark contrast between Daisy's traditional back-country shotgun air rifles and its new Daisy Paper-Popper—hailed by the company as a "submachine gun design ... [with] a light-action trigger which makes handling easy for any youngster from 3 up."[35] Meanwhile, other toy-gun makers were dramatically expanding their arsenals. Marx Toys was typical. Between 1962 and 1963, the industry's largest company increased its assortment of military-style automatic toy rifles from two to ten. By the time it released its spring 1964 catalog, the company had tripled that number, devoting eleven pages of its catalog to guns, most of them based on recent models used by US soldiers.[36]

The military category also witnessed the introduction of war toys that no one had seen before, the most significant of which was Hasbro's new (and initially controversial) twelve-inch posable soldier doll named G.I. Joe: America's Moveable Fighting Man. The original G.I. Joe doll line included four different molded plastic male soldier dolls, each one dressed in a meticulously designed scale uniform of a different division of the Armed Forces. The newest and most influential addition to the military lineup for 1964, G.I. Joe not only was an instant commercial success but also launched the boys' market genre of "action figures"—a clever merchandising sleight of hand by Hasbro, which feared that the cultural association of dolls with girls and femininity would threaten the success of G.I. Joe among its target audience.[37]

Trade advertisements and industry enthusiasm tell only one part of the Kennedy-era militarization of children's play, however. With industry observers reporting that wartime heroics were capturing juvenile imaginations as never before, toy marketers made unprecedented efforts to feed those imaginations with a steady diet of TV advertisements for their plastic grenade and pistol products. For the toy world's "turn to khaki" was facilitated by what appears to have been the largest advertising push on any single toy category in the trade's history, to which the advent of TV promotion just a few years earlier was fundamental. In 1963–64, toy marketers began unleashing a barrage of new war-toy commercials on the major TV networks. One typical ad, for the Gung Ho Commando set made by Marx Toys, featured little boys suited up in camouflage fatigues, armed with machine guns, grenade mortars, and knives, exuberantly snake-crawling through the woods in search of an unnamed enemy.[38] As Marx told buyers in its 1964 catalog, the company had increased the number of ad minutes on network TV by 50 percent from the previous year.[39] That year Mattel similarly assured readers of *Playthings* that its Guerrilla Booby Trap, the latest addition to the Guerrilla Play Set, was "backed with a big TV schedule."[40]

Unsurprisingly, to toymakers and children alike, all these newfangled weapons required that kids be properly outfitted to play the part. In the trade press, Halco boasted of the "new outfit for the military-minded youngster," while another toymaker urged buyers to "cash in on the tremendous demand for Military and Jungle outfits" by purchasing "The No. 1 Suit of the Year!"[41] The latter was Herman Iskin & Co.'s Jungle Fighter Outfit, a camouflage fatigue set with leaf-covered helmet that, according to the company's ad copy, was voted number one "by the people who count—the grandmothers, grandfathers, mothers, fathers, children and buyers of America."[42]

That may be true. Independent industry sales figures from the time are hard to find, but self-reporting about the 1963 marketplace suggests that the toy-makers at Iskin were right about the heightened enthusiasm for military toys among the people who count. Nichols Industries reported a nearly 50 percent increase in 1963 sales from the previous year.[43] Remco Industries, which produced the "Monkey Division" line of weapons and combat sets that could be seen on TV commercials nationwide, similarly celebrated 1963's "Record-Breaking Sales-Makers."[44] The next year would be an even bigger one for war toys, with the two newest items—the Johnny Seven O.M.A. and G.I. Joe doll line—among the five best-selling toys in 1964 of any category.[45]

Broader structural changes in the business and landscape of toys also shaped the public reception of war toys. First, the recent widespread adoption of child-directed TV marketing meant that children now received manufac-turers' appeals to the fun of pretend killing in the comfort of their homes, bypassing the parents completely (so long as the TV remained on). Mean-while, new trends in the retail landscape—namely, the increasing turn to discount stores and supermarkets for brand-name toy sales—help explain the heightened anxiety and frustration in the letters quoted earlier. The issue of where the new war toys were being sold, not just what they looked like, was a significant concern. When one WILPF member wrote to her group's national office in October 1963 to express her interest in mobilizing an anti–war toy effort, she emphasized that it was not just the military toys that incensed her but the fact they were being sold "even at the supermarket."[46] A couple of years earlier, WILPF's Elise Boulding had expressed a similar sentiment in the liberal weekly *Saturday Review*. "The day this fall when a prominent shelf in our local A & P was invaded by a toy missile base ... was the moment of truth for me," Boulding stated. "It is no longer possible to remain silent."[47]

As the WSP picketers declared their opposition to war toys outside the Toy Center buildings during the 1964 Toy Fair, a panel of wholesalers was convened inside to predict the categories with the "greatest sales potential" for the year ahead: military toys came in second on the list to educational toys, with dolls ranked third.[48] While the protesters and the industry were of different minds when it came to the value of war toys, all parties seemed to believe that the nation was witnessing the birth of a new military-toy in-dustrial complex. With hindsight, it is clear the toy business could not have picked a worse time in which to swell the nation's retailers and TV commercial breaks with this assortment of military guns and other war toys. Ironically, at the exact moment the industry was doing so, the US peace movement was on the cusp of its most significant resurgence since World War I. And most crucial to this story, invigorating the reconstructed movement of the late 1950s and early 1960s—a movement concerned above all with ending the nuclear arms race, born out of a conviction that Cold War militarism constituted a threat to all humanity—was a growing legion of mostly white, middle-class women activists, some of them movement veterans, some entering protest politics for the first time. Many of them were married mothers of young children, and many were already involved in approaching the creation of a more just, demilitarized society through childhood education. In other words, thousands of the toy industry's ideal consumers—women with families and disposable income—were not just demonstrating against the arms race but leading the charge.

○

The early sixties was not the first time that women activists were at the forefront on issues of peace and internationalism. The founding of WILPF in the crucible of World War I had helped establish the centrality of women's leadership in the antiwar and antimilitarist movement in the United States, not to mention around the world, throughout the interwar years. But the postwar decades were unkind to women agitators for peace, a term the leaders of WILPF had always defined broadly to include traditional concerns like disarmament and antimilitarist education as well as the causes of civil liberties (especially in campaigns to resist the new regime of Civil Defense orders) and racial equality (this was a moment of violent white backlash to Black civil rights activism). No factor was more devastating than the harm done by the Second Red Scare, when FBI purges of suspected communists and fellow travelers enveloped not only the State Department but political and cultural organizations across the spectrum of the US left. By the end of the 1950s, anticommunist activities had destroyed a recent addition to left-wing women's social activism, the Congress of American Women, leaving WILPF—beset by internal conflicts over red-baiting and dwindling membership—to continue the women's peace-and-justice movement virtually on its own.[49] It was in this volatile context that tens of thousands of middle-class women, most of them mothers and many of them self-identified housewives, swelled the numbers of the peace movement—and its historically important women's sector—as it reconstituted itself to campaign against the nuclear arms race.

On November 1, 1961, an estimated fifty thousand women, including first-time activists and members of established groups like WILPF and the National Committee for a Sane Nuclear Policy (SANE), joined in a "Women's Strike for

Peace"—a day of rallies and marches and letter-writing events in cities and towns across the United States. The goals were to focus national attention on the dangers of nuclear fallout and to press newly elected President Kennedy to halt the testing of nuclear weapons by the United States and the Soviet Union. These events, described by historian Amy Swerdlow as "the largest female peace action in the nation's history," drew national coverage in mainstream media; soon after, a national organization of chapters and regional offices was informally knit together by participants.[50] Within a year, Women Strike for Peace could boast of more than sixty local chapters and offices in ten cities, a few of which used the name Women for Peace (WFP) or Women's International Strike for Peace (WISP).[51] The broad support for WSP across the spectrum of the postwar liberal left, from middle-class moderates with minimal organizing experience to longtime leaders of WILPF (many women would remain active in both groups) and veterans of the thirties Popular Front, was one of the most visible signs that the era's peace movement, long seen as a home for militant pacifists and war resisters, was acquiring broad legitimacy in the American mainstream.[52] It was from the ranks of these "nuclear pacifists"—historian Paul Lyons's name for "those who came to believe that the threat of nuclear confrontation made world peace a moral imperative"—that the WSP toy campaigns drew their leaders and foot soldiers.[53]

If WILPF's reinvigorated interest in toys had a long history to draw on from within its branch-based childhood education committees, one of the key reasons WSP activists were apt to turn their attention to toys so soon after the group's founding was the centrality of children and child-rearing to their moral and political consciousness from the start. According to Swerdlow, who was also a founding member of New York WSP, women who joined the organization were "the kind of women . . . whose devotion to children extended far beyond their own."[54] This belief makes sense given that the organizers' impetus for the original mobilization in November 1961 centered on concerns about dangerous chemical fallout from nuclear testing that was finding its way into the commercial milk supply, and thus children's bodies. In WSP's view, children were being treated as collateral damage in an irrational, dangerous, and macho Cold War political game among male world leaders that threatened human existence. To counter this trend, it was women's special responsibility, they contended, as socially defined caretakers of the next generation, not only to speak out but also to work to redirect human civilization toward a more peaceful, democratic path.[55] While WSP would take a strong position on the Vietnam War and other US policies, it presented its opposition to the nuclear arms race as nonideological, motivated by universal values of safeguarding children and life on earth. Given this child-centered politics, the turn toward toy disarmament was only fitting.

○

If the convergence of the early 1960s war-toy boom and the resurgence of women's peace-and-justice protest underwrote the coordinated launch of national anti–war toy campaigns at the tail end of 1963, the particular timing of that launch is also crucial. For no single event intensified the sense of urgency among the activists of WSP and WILPF more than the assassination of President Kennedy on November 22 of that year—the very moment the industry's pre-Christmas marketing blitz began. A number of the letters published in *Memo* testify to the strong links this particular group of activists drew between Kennedy's peace agenda and their own. For Naomi Marcus, Kennedy's murder had given her "painful reason to reflect on the causes and the results of violence."[56] Rose Della-Monica wrote about how the assassination had prompted "about 15–20 of us . . . to meet to discuss what could be done effectively to counteract the trend toward . . . the acceptance of violence as a game, even a way of life."[57] "Why can't we use the assassination of our president to drive home the lesson of the danger of this kind of toy?" asked Rita Morgan, in her letter to Dagmar Wilson.[58]

For WSP's Tamora Furnish, Kennedy's assassination proved a tragic end to a particularly terrifying and violent year, from the near nuclear holocaust of the Cuba crisis in the fall of 1962 to the backlash against the insurgent southern civil rights movement throughout 1963, most infamously in Birmingham, Alabama—where young Black demonstrators were attacked by police dogs and firehoses in May and four Black girls were murdered in a church basement in September. Not long after Kennedy was shot, Furnish, who six months later would organize WSP's National Peace Education Clearing House, published a fiery call to action in a local Chicago newspaper: "Dogs are turned on human beings. Murder is prevalent in headlines and on TV. Homes are bombed in the North. Children in church are killed in the South. . . . We rely on nuclear weapons 'to secure our way of life.' And finally, our young and vital President is killed by an assassin's bullet. . . . We need to question the violence of our lives. We can start with our children since they are the future."[59] To that end, she concluded, "I recommend a large scale movement to demand that the toys of peace replace the toys of war in our society." To Furnish, like so many who would join the anti–war toy campaigns, the social problems of anti-Black terror, militarism, and gun violence were to be fought not only in the streets and the courts and Congress—fronts where WILPF and WSP continued to work during this period—but also in the home, where the nation's future citizens were introduced to the society's values, for better or worse.

Furnish and the others also had special reason to see Kennedy's death as a loss for their larger cause. In the eyes of many in WILPF and WSP, the Democrat's 1960 election, coming on the tails of Republican Dwight Eisenhower's two-term reign, was a hopeful sign of change in the US position on the world stage. Feeding into this optimism, in his first year in office Kennedy had publicly challenged the Soviet Union at the United Nations Assembly "not to an arms race but to a peace race," and before his murder he had taken steps—with a great deal of pressure from the nuclear disarmament movement—to achieve that goal.[60] The most significant came in August 1963, when Kennedy secured the movement's minimum demand by signing the Limited Test Ban Treaty with Russia, which guaranteed an end to oceanic and atmospheric testing of nuclear weapons.[61] On top of that partial victory for the movement— many activists in WSP and other groups had wanted total disarmament—it was just weeks before his death that Kennedy, during an interview with several women's magazine editors, encouraged women to "get into whatever groups they feel reflect their judgment as to how things ought to be done" and work for "peace in their communities."[62] Coming off the test ban treaty and these words of encouragement, the assassination was a devastating blow to the women of the peace movement. The San Francisco WSP Toy Committee would soon pay tribute to their slain president's vision of a "peace race" when they invoked the words and spirit of his most famous exhortation, drawn from his first inaugural address, at the top of a flyer they handed out at demonstrations: "Ask . . . what you can do for your country."[63] Joining their campaign against war toys, in this view, was presented as an act of patriotism and civic duty, on a par with the Peace Corps and other Kennedy initiatives.

As the historian Michael Sherry has noted, "many Americans in the 1960s forged powerful emotive associations between the deaths of leaders and other death. . . . Leaders' deaths were not isolated events, but the most visible threads in a bloody fabric of violence; not death contained by national purpose, but death run amok."[64] In the shadow cast by Kennedy's murder over the period's surge of liberal moral idealism, of which WSP's birth was just one manifestation, the penetration of the new military-toy industrial complex into the lives of many WSP and WILPF activists seemed to only enhance this sense of death run amok. And in an era when parents were widely encouraged to use consumerism to rear good citizens, the reform of toys gave them something uniquely tangible and accessible to transform in their ongoing efforts to create a more just future world.

○

Not long after the first Toy Fair protest announced the movement to both the industry and the public at large—two syndicated articles on the event had appeared in scores of national and regional newspapers—Sarah Ramberg's first memo as head of WILPF's new Subcommittee on War Toys shared a list of "What Can Be Done" with branches across the country.[65] Over the course of the following months and years, the new toy action groups of WILPF, along with WSP chapters, employed virtually every tactic that she suggested and then some, and not just during the Christmas shopping season. If the business of toys had moved closer to a year-round industry, activists knew they had to make their voices heard year-round as well. Rejecting the confrontational tactics employed by radical pacifists like the War Resisters League, the anti–war toy campaigns adopted a style of activism that the sociologist John Lofland has called "polite protest." The "paradox of polite protest," Lofland writes, is that even while such protest is "marked by a remarkable degree of genteel civility, restraint, and even affability," it is often driven by "idealistic and radical goals."[66] The movement's mix of traditional petitions and protests with more playful pageantry would make for a lively publicity strategy, one that explains their remarkable success drumming up attention across mainstream print and television media.

The campaigns drew broadly from the tactical playbook of generations of consumer and civil rights activists in the hope that they might, in the words of Barbara Ulmer, a leader in both WILPF and WSP during this era, "materially shake [the toy industry's] confidence that we, a sizable portion of 'the public' really want our children growing up with a plastic grenade in one hand and a burp gun in the other."[67] The threat of a consumer boycott was one means to achieve that goal. In newsletters, pamphlets, and flyers, toy activists across the country urged their fellow citizens not only to stop buying war toys but also to formally register their dissent through letters and phone calls— contact information was often provided—to the "major munitions makers of the toy industry," as one WILPF member colorfully described the targets of their protest.[68] Media publicity was also a major part of their outreach work. Toy groups successfully landed numerous radio and TV interviews, shared their concerns in local and national press through countless letters to the editors, and successfully lobbied newspaper reporters to cover their actions and run feature stories on the issue.[69]

Meanwhile, the campaigns applied pressure to areas of the trade closer to home. One strategy was to invite unwanted publicity to local retailers by handing out flyers and talking to shoppers at downtown department stores and suburban shopping centers; while the days before Christmas were understood to be a key time to reach consumers and garner attention from local TV news crews, many campaigns picketed outside their local toy shops at other times of the year as well. Not surprisingly, the events that received the most media coverage were the ones that featured activists in festive costume: the December 1965 demonstration outside Macy's department store in Midtown Manhattan, where WSP's Pat Murray donned a Santa Claus suit; and the March 1966 Toy Fair picket, where members of Parents for Responsibility in the Toy Industry (PRITI), a recently formed New York City coalition of WSP and WILPF members, dressed up like Mary Poppins, the beloved fictional nanny of books and film.[70]

Under the leadership of Victoria Reiss, PRITI's longtime chairperson, the group would become well known in the movement for its playful, attention-grabbing activism.[71] With its Dove of Good Practice Award, PRITI also brought its public relations savvy to one of the more conventional backdoor tactics suggested by the toy campaigns: meeting with store owners and managers to convince them to stop selling military-themed playthings. The Dove Award was a certificate in the form of a six-inch-square sticker. Featuring a white dove holding a fig leaf in its beak, on a black background, the sticker was meant for display on a storefront window, as a sign of the retailer's solidarity with the anti–war toy campaigns. Below the image was a single line of text directed at prospective customers: "This Store Does Not Sell War Toys" (see figure 1.4).[72] Rather than have PRITI hand out the Dove Awards, however, Reiss called for local activists to present the seals themselves and offered tips on how to turn the award ceremony into a full-fledged media event that would benefit both the business and the campaigns. By the end of 1966 alone, Doves had been awarded to eleven stores in the New York area as well as one national variety store chain with two hundred branches across the country—each of which received its own sticker for its front entrance.[73]

Toy reformers proved to be a wellspring of unconventional tactics. One activist shared with WILPF's national office what she described as a "(fairly hostile) idea which I may use if they keep selling megadeath along with holiday groceries. I would fill the shopping cart up with all the stuff I need to buy—including frozen foods—then abandon it in the store with a note of protest . . . and walk out. If several women are aroused enough to do this at weekly intervals, it could become quite a nuisance."[74] Activists labored to become a nuisance in other imaginative ways. For instance, Seattle WSP suggested to readers of the national newsletter that they tear out toy-weapon

1.4. The anti–war toy group Parents for Responsibility in the Toy Industry (PRITI) advertises its Dove of Good Practice Award in a peace-movement newsletter. Advertisement from *The Toy*, no. 5 (Winter 1966–67): 8. Author's collection.

advertisements in popular magazines and return them to their source with a note of dissent—a tactic reminiscent of 1930s consumer campaigns that sent back bread labels to businesses in protest of unfair pricing. "As a method of protest," they explained, "this serves two ways; first, as a symbol of the rejection of this type of toy; second, as a graphic boycott since one cannot order from pages one does not have."[75] Other publicity tactics included bumper stickers with anti–war toy slogans and "pre-Christmas cards" urging recipients to boycott war toys in their holiday shopping.[76]

Sarah Ramberg's original list of actions had also encouraged leaders to draw on "Special Talents" to publicize the cause. "What hidden (or well-known) talents lie among your members?" she wanted to know, offering up "a skit for puppets or amateur dramatic groups" or "song or take-off folksingers might popularize" as examples. "Pete Seeger might put music to good words," she suggested, hoping to mobilize the popularity of Seeger's socially conscious brand of folk music among middle-class leftists and liberals during these years.[77] A founding member of the Almanac Singers who had been blacklisted in the 1950s for his Communist Party affiliations, Seeger did not add an anti–war toy ballad to his oeuvre of topical songs (as protest songs were known at the time). But one of his fellow musicians in the era's leftist folk music revival—in fact, the very composer whose song "Little Boxes" had helped him return to the national spotlight when he recorded it in 1963—did.

It was fitting that Malvina Reynolds, the sharp-tongued troubadour for justice, would be the one to take up the anti–war toy torch in the summer of 1964, and not just because she was a WSP supporter. For the decision to sing out against war toys in a new song called "Playing War," a rousing call for an all-family boycott of the war-toy business, seemed to perfectly align her long-standing antiwar politics (which dated back to her own childhood, when her parents opposed World War I) with her radical faith in children's capacity to understand the injustices of the world and call them out in kind. In time, Reynolds would become known as one of the era's wittiest and most prolific composers of children's songs, building a catalog that included "Magic Penny" and "Morningtown Ride." Before that, however, with only one recorded album to her name, "Playing War" placed her in a long tradition of progressive cultural programming for kids.

"There's a nameless war in Vietnam / There's wars in many lands / And my little boy in our back yard / Has a tin gun in his hand" was how the first verse began, and each verse was followed by this refrain: "I say no and the kids say no / We're playing war no more."[78] For Reynolds, a lifetime leftist who had performed at fundraisers for former vice president Henry Wallace's

1948 presidential run on the Progressive Party ticket and, in the 1950s, had penned a column for the Communist Party's West Coast newspaper *People's Daily World*, the struggle here, too, was one in which business exploited the people: toy companies ("the toymakers in Buffalo / are getting my boy set to go") and toy dealers and retailers ("the buyers in the department store / are getting my boy ready for war") were shamelessly preparing children to imagine themselves as future soldiers, simply to make a buck.[79]

"Playing War," with its chorus evoking the well-known African American spiritual "Down by the Riverside (Ain't Gonna Study War No More)," was apparently never recorded. But *Memo* published the lyrics and musical notation and encouraged WSP members to learn the "great new song."[80] While it would be the only musical contribution to the campaigns by one of their own, WSP and WILPF literature did occasionally feature rhyming verse that mimicked the style of an ad jingle—like this one, which appeared in the newsletter of the Peace Education Clearing House: "When you're doing any shopping / And you're picking out the toys / Please remember that your choices / Will be building girls and boys."[81] But what did that really mean? Aware that many parents might not assign the same developmental and political significance to toys and play that they did, activists worked to change that situation. Complementing their protests with an unprecedented parent-education initiative, they set out to shape popular understandings of toys and move parents closer to "playing war no more."

○

"It is up to us," wrote WILPF's Sarah Ramberg to her colleagues in 1964, "to educate parents and potential purchasers all across the country on the effects of different kinds of toys."[82] Accordingly, the letter-writing campaigns, boycotts, and publicity stunts directed toward the toy industry and retailers were accompanied from the start by extensive research and educational outreach efforts, designed to enlighten the public to the particular dangers of war toys and the critical importance of toy selection in general. In fact, Bess Lane's original memo about Operation War Toys in late 1963 called for WILPF members to help "collect ... pertinent material on the subject of war toys and games," including magazine articles and any studies "or research, in the field of war toys or games, showing their effect on a child's interests, attitudes, and social and emotional development."[83] Over the months that followed, activists solicited and collected expert-written articles and official statements from prominent friends and associates in the fields of pediatrics and child psychology. They created the Peace Education Clearinghouse to store what they collected, and soon launched a new national newsletter, the *National Peace Education Bulletin*, to make their findings more widely available to peace-movement colleagues. Meanwhile, they organized toy fairs and panels of experts, lectured to nursery-school teachers, and gave interviews on local TV and radio on toys. The South Suburban Minneapolis WILPF branch even put together an elaborate "study and action kit on toys of violence"—an informational packet filled with recent articles, statements by prominent experts, a bibliography pertaining to war toys and child psychology, and ideas for activism—for the National Childhood Education Committee.[84] The professed aim of these efforts was to help create a more coherent picture of how toys affected the growing child, a picture that they believed would ultimately support their view. Of course, they also had an agenda. Embracing the central faith of progressive educators and other children's cultural workers since the early twentieth century that "childhood play...represented...perhaps the most fundamental aspect of education," they updated the rulebook of "progressive parenting"—a politically conscious, psychologically oriented child-rearing ethos popular among leftist parents in the 1930s and 1940s—for a new consumer-oriented culture of play.[85]

One of the first steps in helping parents separate the good from the bad in playthings was to clarify the movement's position on war toys. Unlike the social panic over comic books in the 1950s, in which critics often suggested that the books actually caused juvenile delinquency or violent behavior, it was rare to hear toy reformers suggesting that cap guns or plastic soldiers caused aggressive behavior of any kind.[86] Rather, the chief concern was their impact on the child's formation of values. Bess Lane of WILPF spoke for many:

> Parents are asking what so much absorption with shooting, wounding, killing, is doing to the development of values in children. We do not know the whole answer, but we do know that when children receive as gifts small telephones, printing presses...they get the feeling of participating in adult activities.... It is reasonable to assume, then, that when children are given atomic cannons, jet bombers, nuclear submarines, flame throwers, they will enjoy the same feeling of identification with grownups. Perhaps the greatest danger of war toys is the habituation of children to the idea that war, nuclear destruction, is an acceptable grownup game.[87]

Lane's analysis of "the greatest danger of war toys" was echoed throughout the campaigns' literature, usually with a similar fluency in modern psychological concepts of personality formation. "Conditioning such as war games and war toys can make war seem acceptable in a time when war is no longer feasible," wrote Barbara Ulmer.[88] One WILPF branch put it more bluntly: "A toy from his parent is an endorsement of an idea. Give Tim a bazooka and you are saying to him, 'Ah well, war is a part of life.' You'll probably be a soldier someday and kill real people."[89]

The problem with this analysis was that most child-rearing experts and psychologists of the time saw war toys quite differently, reflecting the dominance of Freudian theory at midcentury. The notion that aggression and hostility were natural was a hallmark of Freud's contribution to modern conceptions of healthy personality development. Following this principle, the widely accepted view of childhood professionals was that toy weapons helped rather than harmed a child's growing psyche by providing a positive, therapeutic outlet for those aggressive impulses. During World War II, for instance, a pamphlet published by the US Labor Department's Children's Bureau not only stated that "belligerent play is often a safety valve for children" but also included guns and soldiers among its suggestions for handmade toys that parents and children could craft during the wartime toy-manufacturing pause.[90] Likewise, in the 1950s the editors of the venerable *Parents* magazine encouraged toy guns as a way to vent anger and frustration, even claiming that boys needed them.[91] Such positive endorsements of war toys help explain why that same magazine bestowed its "Commendation" seal on Mattel's best-selling Burp Gun (a Thompson submachine gun) and why *Good Housekeeping* handed its coveted "Guarantee Seal" to Ideal Toy Co. for its Atomic Cannon.[92]

The prevalence of these notions in popular thinking about toy guns is dramatically illustrated by the case of Dr. Milton I. Levine—a pediatrician, parenting advice columnist, and clinical professor at New York Hospital-Cornell Medical Center.[93] So convinced was Levine of the psychological value of pretend violence, he had a stock of toy firearms in the waiting room of his office for kids to play with while they waited for their check-up.[94] Curiously enough, Levine's young patients included the sons of PRITI chair Victoria Reiss. Reiss openly questioned the place of war toys in a pediatrician's office, but, as she recalled in an interview, Levine stood strong in his Freudian faith in their benefits. Such enthusiasm for war toys by trusted child-rearing institutions and experts, then, was not just an abstract, theoretical position but had practical, everyday implications that parents like Reiss had to regularly negotiate.

It is important to note that WSP and WILPF toy activists didn't disagree with Freud's theory of catharsis so much as disagree with its popular application vis-à-vis toy guns. That is, war play was okay in itself, so long as it came "naturally" from the child's imagination (as the theory held) and not a highly realistic, manufactured toy weapon. Writing in the pacifist Quaker magazine *Friends Journal*, WILPF's Sarah Ramberg was probably reflecting the views of many in the movement when she asked, "What do they (or I) mean by a 'war toy'? A baseball bat and vocal 'ack-ack-ack' make a very satisfactory machine gun. Many a skillet lid and stick have served time as shield and sword. A fist and finger will double for a pistol at a moment's notice. Does this mean that since children spontaneously play at killing we should give combat outfits or toy blockbusters for Christmas?"[95] Barbara Ulmer of WSP seemed to agree, urging the readers of *Memo* to remind parents that children "needing to work out their aggressions can do so just as easily with a punching bag."[96] The New York Toy Committee seconded that recommendation when it listed punching bags as one of the ways to "help a child develop into a healthy adult" without resorting to toy weapons.[97]

Probably no one had done more to authorize the dominant view on pretend violence than Dr. Benjamin Spock, the pediatrician who, in the post–World War II decades, became the most famous child-rearing expert of his time. It was Spock, after all, whose 1946 manual, *The Commonsense Book of Baby and Child Care*, had translated Freud's ideas into common wisdom and propelled them into mainstream parenting culture in the late 1940s and 1950s; in fact, by the early 1960s, *The Commonsense Book of Baby and Child Care* was the best-selling book in the United States after the Bible, having sold eighteen million copies and gone through more than fifty printings.[98] For Spock, the cultivation of "well-adjusted citizens" depended on the proper channeling of aggressive impulses.[99] Accordingly, toy gunplay wasn't just a valid way to "sublimate" normal aggression but a vital, even joyful one. As Spock explained, "He's having fun with the *idea* of killing."[100] Spock's popular column in *Ladies' Home Journal*, read by millions of mothers every month since the early 1950s, reinforced this view, as did *Dr. Spock Talks with Mothers* (1961), his most recent publication at the time of the anti–war toy campaigns. In the latter, Spock directly addressed parental concerns while reassuring readers that pretend gun killing was at once natural and beneficial to healthy emotional growth, a "safety valve for hostility."[101] "Some conscientious parents get [gunplay] turned around," he stated, adopting a soothing tone that suggested he understood such concerns, even if he believed they were misguided. "They try to discourage [it] . . . fearing that it might lead to gangsterism or brutality in adult life, whereas it really represents, at this stage, a way station in the progress toward civilization."[102] One can imagine the special disappointment of WILPF activists to encounter such an optimistic take on war toys—a boon to humanity rather than a threat—from Dr. Spock. This is not just because an endorsement from Spock would have been a huge boost for the campaigns but also because he was an official supporter of WILPF, having joined its Sponsor Board alongside some of the most prominent humanitarians, intellectuals, and philanthropists of the time.[103]

Yet even outside his ties to WILPF, there were few prominent child-rearing experts in the 1960s as well suited—or as likely—as Spock was to unite the parental and the political. During the late 1940s and 1950s, Spock had established his place in American parenting culture by prescribing reason, respect, and compassion in the home rather than the traditional child-care advice of discipline and moralizing; by encouraging parents to democratize family life and allow children to express their opinions and desires at a young age, Spock's style soon earned the title of "permissiveness."[104] At the same time, Spock's commitment to liberal politics grew stronger, supported by the ties he had forged with the left-wing intellectual circles of 1940s New York City; during the war years, for example, Spock had contributed his particular expertise to the short-lived newspaper *PM*, a hotbed for Popular Front politics.[105]

He soon began capitalizing on his popularity and wholesome public image as guardian of children and friend of mothers to shape not just family affairs but national and international ones. In the late 1950s, Spock appeared in campaign ads for Democratic presidential candidate Adlai Stevenson and, in 1960, for John F. Kennedy's successful presidential run. In the early 1960s, he also began taking public positions on major global issues, the nuclear arms race in particular. In 1962, Spock joined the national board of SANE, and the following year he became a cochairman.[106] Meanwhile, Spock's political activities seemed to be exerting a notable effect on his professional life during these years. His affiliation with the world of women's magazines is illustrative. Starting in the early 1950s, Spock had contributed a monthly parenting column to *Ladies' Home Journal*, one of the oldest and most mainstream of the mass-circulation women's magazines known as the glossies. Although Spock had long kept politics out of his advice columns, he was nonetheless dismissed for his political views, which were seen as (and probably were) out of step with the average mother.[107] Thus, the year Spock joined the national board of SANE was also the year he moved his column to *Redbook*, which catered to a younger and more liberal demographic of affluent white women and mothers.

These developments in Spock's professional work and identity help explain why Helen Rand Miller of San Francisco Women for Peace's new Anti-War Toy Committee wrote to Spock for advice in April 1964, just as the WSP and WILPF campaigns were mobilizing across the country. "Dear Dr. Spock," she began, like hundreds of thousands of other parents who had reached out to the famous pediatrician since the late 1940s, "I have hesitated to intrude upon your thinking, but I cannot withstand my friends who will demand, 'Why didn't you write to Dr. Spock?'...As you undoubtedly know Women Strike for Peace and the Women's International League for Peace and Freedom are working on war toys. But how to work effectively?"[108] Yet Miller also had another reason for writing. As she explained, she had actually written her own article against war toys and was wondering if Spock could use his influence at *Redbook* to get the piece published in its pages.[109] If Miller was mistaken in the assumption that Spock's antiwar politics would naturally translate into antiwar toy politics, contradicted as it was by everything Spock had written about the subject up to this point, her inquiry turned out to be quite prescient.

As Spock explained in a response letter to Miller a few weeks later, he had, quite coincidentally, just submitted a new column to his editor that not only revised but reversed his long-standing position on the matter. It was slated for publication later in the year. "To make a long story short," Spock wrote, "I said [previously] that it is normal for boys to express their aggressiveness through war play...and that it takes more than war play to make a militarist....However, I now believe that unrestricted war play...can coarsen children's standards of behavior to a degree. I also believe now that parents should actively teach their children the need to seek peace. On both these counts it would be good to eliminate war toys."[110]

Yet Spock stopped short of prohibition. As he explained to Miller, "conscientious, sensitive, peace-loving parents can tell their children why they don't want to buy them war toys and they can have some influence on toy manufacturers and toy stores," but those parents should "not *forbid* war play or *forbid* their children to buy their own pistols because their children would be likely to be the most peace loving anyway. The future delinquents and war-mongers are not the children whose parents would have the slightest interest in restricting war play."[111] While parents might use toys to symbolically communicate their values, Spock seemed to be suggesting, it was bad parents, not bad toys, that made violent or militaristic children.

Six months after Spock and Miller's exchange, millions of women opened up the November 1964 issue of *Redbook* to see Spock's latest column, titled "Playing with Toy Guns." The piece was significant for what it did say and what it did not. Introducing his new perspective, Spock proceeded with caution, as if to reassure readers that he had not adopted the crude behaviorism of earlier critics of children's popular culture. "I'd still explain to a mother that I don't think playing with toy pistols or viewing Westerns will themselves produce real delinquency or belligerence or militarism in a well-brought-up child," he wrote. "But nowadays I'd give her much more encouragement in her inclination to guide her son away from mock violence than I would have in the past."[112] In rejecting any causal link between make-believe gun battles and the real thing, he echoed the WILPF and WSP line: "It is not that pistol play... will lead to war or that the absence... will prevent war. It is attitudes that are crucial."[113] As in previous writings, Spock again drew a line between toy guns and civilization, but this time he turned the argument around: parents could help build "a more stable and civilized national life" not by encouraging war toys but by rejecting them.[114] And while he acknowledged that "depriving American boys of toy pistols, rifles, helmets, uniforms" would be "tampering with precious traditions," he appeared to believe it was worth it, albeit with exceptions.[115]

For while at one point Spock stated that "if all the parents of America became convinced and agreed on a toy-weapons ban on the first of next month, this would be ideal from my point of view," his opposition to war toys came with some important caveats.[116] Not only did the act of prohibiting war toys from the home turn them into a forbidden fruit that intensified children's desire for them, he said; there also were other social and emotional needs that needed to take precedence over parental politics. First, while Spock encouraged "peace-loving" parents to openly communicate their personal opposition to toy guns, he insisted that the gift of "a toy pistol or combat helmet" from a family member—Spock gave the example of an uncle—should never be confiscated. As Spock confessed, "I myself wouldn't have the nerve to take it away."[117] While the sentiment here can be interpreted in several ways—as an appeal to the necessary etiquette of gift giving, or perhaps as a lesson in putting family before politics—the comment could hardly have been more consistent with the era's popular stereotype of a Spock-inspired home: not just child-centered but child-dominated.

Another underlying goal of the original *Baby and Child Care*—and one that reflected Spock's progressive politics—was the cultivation of a more democratic household that empowered children to make their own decisions, including ones that were unpopular among their parents.[118] Reflecting that concern, Spock advised, "If when he was seven or eight he decided he wanted to spend his own money for battle equipment, I wouldn't forbid him."[119] One can also detect Spock's emphasis on peer acceptance in the making of a well-adjusted person.[120] Just as *Baby and Child Care* recommended that every child should "have the same allowances and privileges of the other average children in the neighborhood," regardless of parental objection to that standard, the long-term goal of the healthy personality required that even the most pacifistic mothers allow their children toy guns "if all their friends are pistol toters."[121] To prohibit them "would amount to carrying the issue unnecessarily far."[122] In laying out real-life situations where toy gunplay was either permissible or excusable, and at no point renouncing his Freudianism, Spock tried to reconcile what seemed to be his personal desire for a new era of progressive parenting with toys with the hallmarks of his famous approach to healthy development.

Despite his reservations and even ambivalence, the toy campaigns took Spock's revised position for all it was worth. Less than a week after Helen Rand Miller received Spock's response in April, her Anti-War Toy Committee quoted it in a protest letter to the Sears department store in downtown San Francisco.[123] *Memo* published the correspondence as well, making Spock's updated advice available to the campaigns six months before the *Redbook* column was published. "We thought you would be interested," wrote *Memo*'s editors, in what was clearly an understatement.[124] Going forward, WSP activists would frequently name Spock's November 1964 *Redbook* article in lists of references for concerned parents, while WILPF activists continued to write to Spock requesting new statements for their publicity material, requests that he always obliged.[125] But if the toy campaigns embraced Spock's encouragement of their effort, it was perhaps their desire for a more unequivocal statement from America's best-known child-care adviser that led one group of WSP activists to slightly bend the truth about what he had said, in their favor. "Dr. Benjamin Spock recommends that parents ban toy weapons if they want to bring up good citizens," stated a flyer produced by New York WSP the following year.[126] This was not exactly true, but it wasn't exactly false either. Activist mothers of the peace movement had looked to Dr. Spock for guidance in public life as well as private; with the issue of war toys, the two finally converged.[127] Over the next few years, a growing number of eminent psychologists and parental advisers would begin following Spock into the political arena by publicly coming out against war toys. In doing so, they expressed their belief that the political culture of the future could be transformed through the parenting culture of the present.[128]

o

While Benjamin Spock had accepted the movement's most basic proposition—that the problem with war toys was their impact on values and attitudes—the peace educators of WILPF and WSP also found war toys wanting for another reason: in their opinion, they simply weren't good toys.

"We will buy no war toys; we want our children to have good toys," asserted the San Francisco Anti-War Toy Committee in its letter to Sears.[129] But what did that mean? Speaking to a suburban Philadelphia audience that had come out for a special 1965 panel discussion on war toys organized by Germantown WILPF, Elizabeth Polster, the organization's national president in the mid-1960s, gave one answer. It wasn't just the perceived glorification of gunfights and intercontinental ballistic missile (ICBM) launches that made war toys a bad choice for play, said Polster; it was also that "war toys are simply poor toys in that they have a limited use. A tank is a tank, and nothing else; but blocks can be used to represent all sorts of things."[130] Polster's critique of overly structured representational toys, and preference for blocks and other "creative toys" (as she called the genre of nonrepresentational toys), reflected a set of assumptions about toys and learning with deep roots in both progressive education and upper-middle-class parenting ideology. The use of toys in progressive pedagogy stretched back at least to the early nineteenth-century German educator Friedrich Froebel, founder of the kindergarten and a major inspiration for the romantic views of children's innate goodness and curiosity that dominated the progressive education movement in the twentieth century. Believing play was crucial to the spiritual and intellectual life of the child, Froebel developed his own play materials, which he called "gifts," and made them central to the kindergarten program. In the early twentieth century, as progressive education grew in stature and key progressive contributions to modern schooling—such as group work, field trips, and attention to social and emotional development—found a home in the public-school mainstream, its leading theorists and practitioners seized on the possibilities of toys to foster creative play. For instance, the socialist educator Caroline Pratt organized her experimental Play School (later renamed City and Country School), founded in 1914, around what she called "creative pedagogy," and used her own original wooden unit blocks—soon to be a mainstay of early childhood institutions—as its centerpiece. Harriet Johnson, Pratt's colleague at the Bureau of Educational Experiments and another member of the New York radical educational circle, likewise promoted nonrepresentational playthings like blocks as a hallmark of the progressive classroom. Alongside the educator and children's author Lucy Sprague Mitchell, Pratt and Johnson helped lay the groundwork for Bank Street College, the first teacher's college to place progressive tenets—and specialized play materials—at the center of the curriculum.[131]

While the 1920s and 1930s saw the birth of several new national manufacturers, including Playskool, that specialized in early childhood–oriented "educational toys"—a loose, often ambiguous term that usually referred to nonrepresentational, multiuse playthings, as opposed to the type of science toy that taught specific concepts—such products were "little more than a fixture of progressive preschools and kindergartens, the emblem of a cult of 'good parenting' in an educated sector of the American middle class," writes the historian Gary Cross.[132] Yet that soon began to change in the late 1950s, when, in the wake of the Soviet Sputnik satellite's launch, US cultural anxieties about Russian technological success coalesced around education. Cold War educational fever swept not only high schools and higher education but also the field of early childhood learning. Indeed, worries over whether American children were becoming smart enough to compete in the international arena helped mainstream a set of assumptions about the capacity of educational toys to boost cognitive growth and cultivate creativity, the singular intellectual trait that, as the historian Amy F. Ogata has shown, had become as much of a middle-class parental obsession in the postwar years as it was a preoccupation of educational researchers.[133]

By the early 1960s, educational toys had become synonymous with cognitive enrichment and the promotion of creative play in early childhood institutions and parenting guides alike.[134] "Good toys have other values just as important as the teaching of adult skills and attitudes," wrote Dr. Spock in a 1963 column. "They provide outlets for turbulent feelings and they foster true creativity."[135] Following progressive wisdom, Spock recommended wooden blocks as the single most important staple of the child's toy box. Yet for all the investment in these ideas about good toys by educators, parents, and experts, there was very little research about play, much less toys, to support any of it. In 1967, the developmental psychologist Brian Sutton-Smith published a literature review of play research in *Young Children*, the journal of the National Association for the Education of Young Children. "The view that something is learned by play and games has long been a staple assumption of the 'play way' theory of education," wrote Sutton-Smith. "The difficulty with the [existing] studies," he went on, "is that we cannot be sure whether play merely expresses a preexisting cognitive status of the subjects or whether it contributes actively to the character of that status. That is, is the play constitutive of thought or merely expressive of thought? More simply, does the player learn anything by playing?"[136]

Despite the relative absence of scientific evidence, the activists of WILPF and WSP said yes—taking progressive educational wisdom on toys as an article of faith. Outreach materials show striking familiarity with and acceptance of what Sutton-Smith skeptically dubbed "the play way." "PLAY IS SERIOUS

BUSINESS. Play is a child's world. What he learns at play, he is learning about life," stated the South Suburban Minneapolis WILPF in its widely distributed study and action kit.[137] Likewise, a flyer produced by WILPF's National Childhood Education Committee asserted that "PLAY IS THE CHILD'S KEY TO TOMORROW!" while suggesting, in its imagery, that playing with blocks prepared children to build modern cities, whereas playing with war toys taught them to bomb cities to rubble (see figure 1.5).[138] The WSP chapters were similarly steeped in these ideas. "Remember, toys are teachers," stated a Philadelphia WSP pamphlet; "like sunshine and milk and vitamins, toys are to grow on."[139] The campaigns' particular understanding of "good toys," a term they used interchangeably with "creative toys," "challenging toys," and "constructive toys," was also reflected in the toy companies they endorsed and promoted in their outreach literature. In fact, activist recommendations centered on a handful of brands that during the 1940s and 1950s had come to occupy an honored place in the high-investment child-rearing approach of the professional or upper middle class.[140]

On virtually every such WILPF or WSP list of approved companies, usually alongside educational toy firms such as Childcraft and Child Guidance, was

1.5. Flyer by the National Childhood Education Committee, Women's International League for Peace and Freedom, November 1965. From the US Women's International League for Peace and Freedom Records. Courtesy of the Swarthmore College Peace Collection.

Creative Playthings. Founded in 1945 by Frank Caplan, a former WPA youth worker and former teacher at Caroline Pratt's City and Country School, and Bernard Barenholtz, who attended the progressive Teacher's College at Columbia University before joining the nonprofit sector, Creative Playthings, writes Ogata, "packaged and sold progressive educational theory in the form of toys."[141] While Caplan and Barenholtz began their success by catering to nursery- and elementary-school teachers trained in those principles during its early years, during the 1950s the company began garnering critical attention in fine art circles for its highbrow aesthetic appeal. With high-profile collaborations with the Museum of Modern Art, it attained a crossover status unseen in the toy business, then or since.[142] Through selective placement of ads in middle- and upper-middle-class magazines such as *Parents*, the *New Yorker*, and the Black-oriented *Ebony*, by the 1960s Creative Playthings had established itself as a favorite brand of well-educated, well-off parents who had imbibed the progressive educators' preferences for nonrepresentational toys, often made of wood, over the easily breakable plastic ones advertised on television and frequently tied to comic and movie characters. The trade magazine *Toys and Novelties* perhaps said it best when it observed that the company's primary appeal lay in "the psychological understanding of children implied in its products, with resulting benefits to parents seeking more in their children's toys than amusements."[143]

With Frank Caplan at the helm as president and spokesperson, that meant no war toys. Caplan himself publicly denounced the companies who did manufacture them as "psychiatric numbskulls." "Kids have a great deal of pent-up energy," he said, echoing Sarah Ramberg and others. "They can express it in a number of ways.... Why take the easiest way out and give them guns?"[144] In fact, it appears Caplan pulled his company out of the TMA (the industry's trade association) for failing to urge any restraint in war-toy production.[145] Needless to say, it would have been hard to find a company more educationally and politically compatible with the anti–war toy movement's vision of healthy play.

No wonder the campaigns cultivated something of a special relationship with the company. They not only promoted Creative Playthings to parents as a nonviolent alternative, with PRITI handing out its first Dove Award certificate to the Creative Playthings flagship store in New York City; they also mobilized the company's resources (including its promotional materials and personnel) as if it were the anti–war toy movement's own research division. One 1964 WILPF flyer, for instance, reproduced a page from the most recent Creative Playthings sales catalog titled "What Is Play?"—treating it with the authority of a child psychology textbook.[146] Likewise, a bibliography on toys and play distributed by the South Suburban Minneapolis WILPF named the Creative Playthings catalog as an authoritative source alongside articles by renowned psychologists and pediatric researchers.[147] Feelings of respect, it seems, were mutual, for the activists' use of a catalog morphed into a kind of partnership between the campaigns and the company. When Germantown WILPF organized its panel on the psychological effects of war toys in 1965, members invited a representative from Creative Playthings to share the stage with its other expert guest, Ruth Middleman, an experienced social worker and lecturer at the University of Pennsylvania.[148] Some might have questioned the decision to bring in someone from a for-profit company to speak objectively on the subject, but such was Creative Playthings' reputation by then that concerns of that kind probably did not trouble the organizers and may not have even crossed their minds. They believed there was value in having Creative Playthings on their side, and the people at Creative Playthings appeared to feel the same way.

Like the campaigns' preferred spots for protests and handing out flyers (high-end department stores rather than discount chains) and suggestions for edifying non-toy activities (such as subscriptions to science magazines), their choice of Creative Playthings as the standard bearer of good toys assumed a context of affluence that reflected the mix of economic privilege and access to educational capital that define the upper middle class.[149] Not only was Creative Playthings one of the most expensive brands in the market, with prices far out of reach of most Americans, but it also took steps to ensure exclusivity within the college-educated comfortable classes, from its retail structure to sales practices. In the 1950s, the company had only two stores of its own, in New York and St. Louis, mainly selling its goods directly to teachers by mail catalog. Buoyed by growing public clamor for toys that claimed to provide cognitive enrichment, it added storefronts in Chicago and Los Angeles, and in 1964 opened the first of its franchised seasonal Holiday Shops inside what Norbert Nelson, the firm's retail sales director, emphasized were "carefully selected department stores."[150] In fact, "avoidance of low-quality promotional outlets" was understood as part of the company's success.[151] Yet even the quality department stores were not free to promote and sell Creative Playthings toys as they would any other products, for the company required them to hire specialized, college-educated staff to manage the Holiday Shops and asked that the hosting store arrange a separate register to ring up consumer purchases. At a moment when the 1964 Civil Rights Act had just prohibited racial discrimination at the register, it was more than ironic (and potentially self-defeating) to see the self-consciously progressive Creative Playthings take such deliberate steps to segregate its business by class, down to the exchange of bills.[152] By promoting Creative Playthings, the anti–war toy campaigns not only gave Caplan free advertising; they also bolstered the company's expensive and exclusive vision of creative play in ways that may have narrowed the appeal of their cause.[153] Of course, activists served to gain from the relationship too. By investing the company's products with political meaning, they can be said to have made peace with the toy business.

The early-sixties mass mobilization against the nuclear arms race, observed the historian Charles DeBenedetti, was much more than a single-issue campaign; it was an attempt "to redefine American values and institutions."[154] Thanks to the women's peace-and-justice movement that helped lead the charge, children's toys became an important part of that effort. Through ardent protest and educational outreach, WILPF and WSP activists added a new dimension to the liberal sensibility of their time, imbuing the everyday practices of what the sociologist Allison J. Pugh calls "childrearing consumption"—the use of consumer goods to carry out parenting goals— with their particular vision of the pacifist imagination.[155] Assigning toys a key role in the practices of progressive parenting, they launched a new chapter in the US politics of play.

No War Toys

In December 1965, the toy editor of WSP's *National Peace Education Bulletin* offered this telling description of the anti–war toy movement at mid-decade: "The response this year to even the mildest sort of protest against toys of violence has been one of the most startling things in my experience," she wrote. "It is with a joyous 'awe'—and exhaustion—that this section of the BULLETIN is assembled. Letters have come in daily from across the nation, from completely diverse groups and individuals who feel that the educational direction of our children MUST NOT be left to toy manufacturers with financial motives."[1] Other WSP and WILPF members must have felt a similar awe that winter, and through 1966, when such sentiments began to regularly surface in the pages of national newspapers and magazines, and not only around Christmas. From glossy women's magazines like *Ladies' Home Journal* and liberal weeklies like the *New Republic*, to countless regional and national newspapers, the battle over war toys was headline news as well as the subject of features and editorials by leading social observers.[2]

In a sign that the issue had entered the public consciousness, that it had touched a national nerve, even the funnies, the syndicated comic strips that appeared in hundreds of daily newspapers across the country, took up the debate, including two of America's favorites. "The toy makers have begun disarmament talks," says a man to his wife as he sits in front of the television set watching the news, in a November 1965 *Grin and Bear It* comic by Lichty. "Now that's good news," she responds, "if they really mean it."[3] A month later, the character of Daisy Mae, wife of the poor white Appalachian antihero

Li'l Abner in Al Capp's satirical *Li'l Abner* comic, seemed to agree. Looking anxiously at the pile of war toys under the Christmas tree, Daisy Mae asks her husband, "Has Santa forgot this holiday is s'posed to celebrate *peace* on earth?" Flying through the sky in the next panel is Santa Claus himself. "Ah hain't forgot," Santa says, adopting the exaggerated hillbilly dialect of *Abner*'s fictional town of Dogpatch, "but mah toymakers has!"[4]

"There is no doubt," stated Libby Frank, WILPF National Childhood Education Committee chair, in her 1966 annual report, "that the Peace women of WILPF and Women Strike for Peace brought [the war-toy issue] out into the open and made it a legitimate topic for discussion."[5] It is hard to dispute Frank's analysis; WILPF and WSP clearly led the way. And yet the emergence of the war-toy debate as a full-blown public controversy during the mid to late 1960s was also a product of several new historical developments, some without obvious connections to toys, including the US escalation of the Vietnam War, the blossoming of the counterculture, a revolution in consumer advertising, and the assassinations of two of America's most prominent progressive figures, Martin Luther King Jr. and Robert F. Kennedy. While WSP and WILPF campaigns had reached wide audiences in cities and towns across the country in 1964 and 1965, the war-toy issue would come to resonate with an ever-growing number of Americans as the decade wore on. To the surprise and delight of the women's peace-and-justice movement, some of the nation's leading toymakers would be among them.

○

Starting in 1965, the widening US war in Vietnam became both a new catalyst and a context for interrogating the traditional acceptance of war toys in American children's culture. The February launch of a devastating US aerial bombing campaign, Operation Rolling Thunder, followed by the commitment of ground troops that summer was a first step in that direction, for it ignited a nationwide antiwar mobilization unseen since World War I. As the war eclipsed the antinuclear struggle among the priorities of liberals and leftists, a growing number of anti–Vietnam War critics—including the mass of young people across the country embracing the cultural radicalism of the new counterculture—discovered in the mass consumption of war toys an unusually potent and accessible symbol for their nation's uncritical embrace of military power and its consequences. In this sense, the Vietnam War's radicalization of the peace movement also initiated a new phase in the struggle against war toys, in which older activists of the middle-class women's groups and young radicals would find common ground. Nowhere did this take flight as it did in the beach towns of greater Los Angeles, where a new activist organization would draw on the symbols and style of an emergent countercultural ethos to expand the existing vision of creative, antiwar play.

The countercultural spirit was flourishing in the state of California in the mid-sixties, despite voters putting Republican Ronald Reagan, a socially conservative hawk who opposed civil rights legislation, in office as governor. While California countercultures drew mostly from the white middle classes, they encompassed a broad and often contradictory mix of ideological positions and lifestyles: beatnik artists and bohemians in Venice Beach; disaffected surfers in La Jolla; anarchist experiments in communal living and mutualism in the Bay Area, such as the Diggers; and the particular world of hippies, rock music, and drugs that defined San Francisco's Haight-Ashbury district.[6] The political commitments of these communities varied considerably, too, although the onset of the Vietnam War made politics harder to avoid and would blur the line dividing the New Left, led by Students for a Democratic Society (SDS), and the cultural radicals. It is thus a mistake to dismiss the influence of antiwar politics—or, for that matter, the influence of the larger vision of participatory democracy, egalitarianism, and authenticity usually associated with SDS—on the meanings and practices of cultural dissent and experimentalism in California and elsewhere.[7] Indeed, many young Americans discovered in the culture of antiwar protest itself a unique arena for enacting alternative values.[8] Richard Register, founder of the Santa Monica–based organization No War Toys (NWT), was one of them.

Register was an unlikely toy reformer—not a middle-aged, college-educated professional, married with children, but a twenty-one-year-old artist living in Santa Monica, searching for meaning and the next phase of creative work. Nor was it the growing toy arsenal in the stores or the recent toy arms advertising blitz that set Register on his crusade. As he explained in an interview, two events were "pivotal in the decision" to launch NWT.[9] The first was in July 1964. Driving through the Los Angeles neighborhood of Westwood, Register passed a young boy who, armed with a toy machine gun and dressed from head to toe in a soldier's outfit, was snake-crawling through the grass of his front yard. As Register recalled the scene, front lawns throughout the neighborhood were decked out with American flags, probably to mark the July Fourth national holiday. Seeing the child play war in this sea of stars and stripes immediately turned his mind to the growing US engagement in the Vietnamese civil war, which, while not headline news until the end of the year, was becoming a serious concern in antiwar circles. Was there any connection, Register wondered at the time, between this child's play and the nation's violence in other lands? "And so, in the back of my mind," explained Register, recalling the exact moment, "I was asking, 'Where does this whole attitude that allows people to kill one another and even get systematic about it come from?'"[10]

Sometime after that, Register was visiting with a friend, the artist Norman Zammitt, who had recently traveled to the Soviet Union.[11] In recounting his travels, Zammitt told Register that America's Cold War rival, traumatized by the death of twenty million of its people in World War II, had made the prohibition of war toys national policy. Although the story turned out to be apocryphal—state-run manufacturers did produce war toys in the USSR, though never on a large scale—the idea that the same country vilified by US leaders as the most aggressive and imperialistic nation on earth had taken a stand against toy weapons was a powerful one; combined with the image of the boy playing soldier, it was all Register needed to envision the task before him.[12] It was at that moment, he recalled, when "I decided to take off two years of my life doing my artwork, sculpture at the time, to focus on this, to see if I could get donations and become a full-time person at it."[13] In the spring of 1965, Register rented an office with the money from the sale of two sculptures and started NWT, the first grassroots advocacy group founded expressly to "improve the society through its toys."[14] Operating out of that office space—dubbed the No War Toys Coffeehouse—the group would transform the conversation on war toys in both style and substance while helping enlist all new audiences in the cause.[15]

It did not take long for Register, who assumed the position of NWT chairman, to hear about the anti–war toy initiatives being organized by the Los Angeles–area chapters of WILPF and WSP; soon enough, they became his "two biggest allies."[16] To be sure, Register had a lot in common with the existing campaigns. Like the activists of WILPF and WSP, he opposed war toys on the grounds that they communicated a distorted, unrealistic message about the world to children. As he saw it, there was a "lie implicit in all war toys and play killing among children. Killing is permanent; you can't get up and go home afterwards."[17] Moreover, like Bess Lane and other toy activists, Register did not go so far as to attribute the acceptance of militarism to playthings alone. But he clearly believed that children's first toys conditioned their moral and political development, and that toy guns and tanks had only one lesson to impart. "War toys are only a step," he wrote, "but the first step in this indoctrination to accept war."[18]

No War Toys also echoed the women's toy campaigns in describing itself as "a non-profit, non-political organization that seeks to eliminate war toys and replace them with creative toys."[19] If the language here reflected Register's familiarity with the discourse of creativity and educational playthings, his commitment to that particular vision of good toys was also reflected in his public endorsement and promotion of Creative Playthings as one of the few toy companies that parents could trust. Perhaps nothing expressed that trust so clearly as the "Toy Exchange" that NWT organized with Caplan's company at the Creative Playthings store in Los Angeles in 1966. At the event, conceived as a way to get rid of the war toys that kids already had in their homes while also incentivizing it, every child who handed in a toy gun received a Creative Playthings toy to replace it.[20] Register also shared the campaigns' faith in psychological expertise. Less than a year into the project, he had recruited several prominent academics and intellectuals to lend their name to the official NWT sponsors' board, including the psychiatrist Erich Fromm, the popular author and influential theorist of the Frankfurt School; the developmental psychologist Jerome Kagan of Harvard University, author of a recent college textbook on personality psychology; and the psychiatrist Jerome D. Frank of Johns Hopkins Medical School, an early leader of the recently founded antinuclear organization Physicians for Social Responsibility.[21] Yet Register wasn't satisfied to pick from a grab bag of general theories from Freud and others to support his opposition to war play. After all, NWT came out of a larger quest to answer fundamental questions about human creativity and aggression: whether the right kind of nurture and upbringing could help cultivate the former, while keeping the latter in check.

The timing of Register's quest could not have been better. The previous decade had witnessed a flowering of research into the psychology of creativity, with "as many creativity studies published between 1950 and 1965 as there had been in the previous two hundred years."[22] Those studies, like Register's questions, were the outgrowth of a widespread belief at midcentury that the science of psychology could provide solutions to the most pressing political problems of the time. And no problem preoccupied psychologists and sociologists of the immediate postwar period more than the rise of Nazi fascism in 1930s Germany. Could psychology help explain why German citizens appeared so susceptible to Nazi indoctrination? The most important attempt to answer this question was *The Authoritarian Personality* (1950). Authored by a distinguished team of psychologists and social theorists, including Else Frenkel-Brunswik and Theodor Adorno (both of them Jewish refugees from Europe), the book advanced a theory of personality that gained wide currency across the behavioral sciences in these years: that Adolf Hitler's rise to power and ability to maintain it had depended on German culture's cultivation of a particular character type, which the authors labeled the "authoritarian personality." The authoritarian personality, to the theorists, was a protofascist one, a mind characterized by submissiveness to authority and conformity; a society of authoritarian personalities created fertile ground for fascism to grow and find popular support. By contrast, the scholars argued, the cultivation of cognitive traits such as independence of thought, critical judgment, and creativity—three of the core qualities that constituted what the authors named the "democratic personality"—would foster fascist Germany's antithesis. If the United States wished its citizens to uphold cherished norms such as freedom of expression, pluralism, and racial tolerance, it needed to cultivate democratic personalities.[23] Creativity, then, was good for democracy.

The Authoritarian Personality launched a new era of research into social psychology's implications for world problems, and among the group of intellectuals at the forefront of this work was Dr. Frank X. Barron. In 1959, Barron earned his PhD in psychology from the University of California at Berkeley and then stayed on to work at the campus's influential Institute of Personality Assessment Research, known as IPAR. In the early 1960s, Barron left Berkeley for Harvard, where he assisted the cognitive psychologist Timothy Leary in the Harvard Psychedelic Research Project, including Leary's famous LSD studies, and taught a course for college freshmen titled "Psychological Problems of Disarmament."[24] Like many of the researchers who came out of IPAR, Barron also saw the possibilities of applying psychological research to the most pressing political issues of his time. In 1963, Barron published the book that would establish his reputation as a leader in the field of creativity research, *Creativity and Psychological Health: Origins of Personal Vitality and Creative Freedom.* "A new synthesis was, in fact, in the making in psychology," Barron wrote about those years, "a new way of looking at creativity not just in science, not just in art, even not just in personal relationships, but as a universal generative principle in Nature, from the burning of the sun to a child learning to speak."[25] With his notion of creativity as a "universal generative principle," Barron was just the authority Richard Register was looking for to support his program for NWT.

Through his reading of Barron's writings as well as the work of other psychologists, Register began to formulate his own working theory of individual and social transformation through play. He agreed with Barron's central insight that while children naturally possess both creative and destructive impulses, the creative energies needed to be encouraged if they were to overcome the urge to destroy.[26] This is why it is not all that surprising that Register not only got in touch with Barron during this period but also successfully enlisted the noted psychologist to contribute to one of his many NWT initiatives: a short-lived line of creative toys.[27] Although "it is well accepted that adult attitudes and personalities are formed mainly in childhood," wrote Register in a pamphlet about the line, which he cofounded with two NWT supporters with experience in business, "no company has connected toys to the later reality and purposively set about to improve the society through its toys and inform the public about creative and destructive play and its implications."[28] As he envisioned it, his would be the first. Just as WILPF and WSP focused on parental education as part of their activism, each of Register's new toys would include "an authoritative article by a behavioral scientist" inside the package.[29] In 1968, Register introduced his first (and, it seems, only) "toy" under the newly incorporated NWT brand: an unusual coloring book that opened from either the front or the back, and included blank pages for drawing as well as original drawings meant to inspire a child's writing.[30] The books apparently sold well in art museums.[31] But it was not just the kids who got something in the book's package; following Register's plans, parents did too: a printed article with the weighty title "Vitality or Violence," contributed by Dr. Frank Barron. "Surely the lesson at last is plain," Barron wrote in the piece, that "we must try to give our children the opportunity to turn their imagination towards the creative rather than the destructive in their play. If play is rehearsal, let the rehearsal be for happier times."[32]

Register was a creative publicist in other ways. With the help of a small cohort of active NWT members, between 1965 and the decade's end he would use NWT as a vehicle for a variety of initiatives to engage and challenge the public to take toys and play seriously. One of the most significant was *The Toy*, an oversized newspaper that functioned as the NWT newsletter from 1965 through 1967. It was edited by Register, who also wrote most of the articles, and "printed whenever possible" (as the header stated), funded as it was by local advertising. Friends also contributed to the editorial process, lending their skills for illustrations and photography. Resembling many of the underground papers of the time, each issue of *The Toy* was jam-packed with original editorials and announcements, reports on NWT activities and updates on the larger anti–war toy movement, photographs and cartoons, reprinted excerpts from expert-authored articles on topics like the psychology of violence and the meaning of play, and reproductions of the latest advertisements for war toys from companies such as Hubley and Hasbro. *The Toy* also advertised, for a nominal donation, NWT's wide-ranging activist merchandise: T-shirts, sweatshirts, buttons, posters (drawn by Register), and rubber stamps printed with the group's logo: a simple smiley-face line drawing that Register created, before it became a ubiquitous cultural image in the 1970s.[33] The publication would serve as one of the key strategic and information hubs of the anti–war toy movement as it reached a crescendo in the second half of the sixties.

As the underground paper and do-it-yourself ethos of the merchandise suggest, one of the hallmarks of NWT's contribution to the movement was its creative appropriation of the outlook, style, and signifiers of the California counterculture. An advertisement for the organization's first anniversary party, published in *The Toy* and the *Los Angeles Free Press*, provides a glimpse into the group's playful countercultural identity. Set against an image of *The Wedding Dance* by Dutch painter Pieter Brueghel the Elder, the ad spoofed one of the great tropes of modern advertising appeals—the promise of self-improvement through a consumer product—in making its pitch to prospective partygoers: "Feel useless? Stymied by an overabundance of worthy causes to support? Try a No War Toys party and put zing back into your life. Join the cause that's enjoyable. . . . Bring your favorite plaything."[34] If the sarcastic critique of consumer society and nod to the painting's festive liberated spirit (such dancing was forbidden in sixteenth-century Netherlands) reflected an antiestablishment stance, perhaps nothing better signaled NWT's ties to the city's alternative scene than the event's musical entertainment: the local experimental rock band the Doors, largely unknown to the nation at the time.[35]

Other NWT publicity efforts spoke directly to core counterculture values of authenticity, simplicity, and childlike innocence. Consider a 1967 poster created by Register and the photographer Michael Mouchette (see figure 2.1). Titled *No War Toys*, the black-and-white poster features Mouchette's photograph of two young white children, a girl and a boy, set against an empty white background.[36] The girl, who looks to be about six or seven years old, stands with her arm affectionately, and protectively, around the shoulder of the boy, who looks a couple of years younger and is several inches shorter; their intimate pose is one of siblings. Both children stare out and over the head of the viewer as if watching a passing airplane. While the slogan "No War Toys" appears in capital letters at the bottom of the poster, the boy's accessories convey that message clearly on their own: in place of the toy pistol that would normally fill the leather play holster around his waist is a bouquet of wildflowers.

If the image represents the NWT wish of a childhood without toy guns, it also draws imaginatively from the hippie counterculture's symbolic repository—above all its embrace of the Romantic ideal of the child as natural, pure, and innocent.[37] The poster not only gestures toward a future of empty holsters; it also seems to call for a return to Edenic innocence and

NO WAR TOYS

2.1.
No War Toys. Poster by
photographer Michael
Mouchette, 1967.
Author's collection.

authentic natural living. The substitution of nature's flowers for the guns of
civilization is just one example. Another is that the children not only lack
shoes and socks but, in the back-to-the-land spirit of the era, also seem perfectly comfortable without these conveniences of modern life. Meanwhile,
in a nod to the bohemian call for androgyny as one of the many ways to
liberate the self from restrictive gender norms, the boy's bangs partly cover
his eyes, mirroring the hairstyle of his older sister. Thus, through a picture
of what we might call natural play, Register and Mouchette fastened NWT
to the utopian image of "flower children" at the very moment that term was
coming to symbolize the idealism, experimentation, and discomfort with
consumerism of one influential segment of the youth demographic. Thanks to
Register and Mouchette's decision to sell reproductions of the poster through
a national distributor, that image circulated widely, probably even more so

than *The Toy*.[38] It is easy to imagine a poster like this on the walls of college dorm rooms, and not only because students at several University of California campuses had formed NWT chapters at the time of the poster's distribution.

This depiction of childhood disarmed was a notable departure by NWT from the imagery of the WILPF and WSP campaign literature, where respectably attired white middle-class children were without their guns but still played with commercial toys. Moreover, Register's shifting views on what counted as a war toy would put him outside the rhetorical frameworks established by WSP and WILPF. As those groups' campaigns took off in 1964, some leading activists suggested that not all toy guns were war toys and could be well left alone by the movement. The editors of the *Peace Education Newsletter*, for example, questioned whether "the time-honored games of cops and robbers or Cowboys and Indians" needed to come under fire; from this perspective, make-believe battles with World War II–era guns were unsettling, but realistically armed dramas of settler violence against Indigenous people were justified as innocent play.[39] Elise Boulding, who chaired the National Childhood Education Committee during the nationwide launch of Operation War Toys, expressed a bit more ambivalence around the issue. "How do you draw the line between permissible and nonpermissible toys in this context? It is not easy," she wrote in the *Saturday Review*. "At what point does the red-kerchiefed cowboy become a heavily holstered menace? Is a water pistol a gun?" Yet ultimately, Boulding concluded that the only toy weapons that unequivocally "should be boycotted" were "*toy versions of equipment in current or past use by the armed forces*."[40]

Initially, Register seemed to agree. The Vietnam War was the spark that ignited Register's toy activism, and his organization's name reflected that. So did NWT's original focus on conventional military playthings as the primary targets of protest. Yet by the end of 1966, the idea of ridding the nation of war toys alone seemed naive to him, given the great diversity of toys made expressly for pretend killing. In Register's shifting analysis, military toys were not the only kinds of commercial playthings that left children "psychologically impaired."[41] The movement, he insisted, needed to acknowledge and publicize it. In late 1966, Register formalized his revised perspective on the psychic dangers of toys by changing his organization's name from No War Toys to No Death Toys. If the new counterculture of the 1960s "defined itself by what it stood against, that is, as a culture of life against a culture of death," the name change gave powerful form to that conviction.[42] "NO DEATH TOYS moves toward the philosophical and psychological and away from the political implication of NO WAR TOYS," stated Register in a November 1966 publicity flyer.[43] The decision, he explained, was occasioned by several factors. One was a series of new developments "in psychiatric research." Accordingly, Stanford psychologist Albert Bandura, whose recent widely publicized experiments had suggested that watching violence could increase aggressive behavior, received mention, as did the prominent Columbia University psychiatrist Fredric Wertham, who had just published a new book on violence in children's popular culture. But it was also a marked shift "in the composition of the toy market," the flyer stated, particularly with respect to toy weapons, that had precipitated the name change, and it was that new commercial reality to which Register gave the most sustained attention in his statement.

As Register rightly observed, by the middle of the decade popular James Bond films like *From Russia with Love* (1963) and *Goldfinger* (1964) and TV series like *The Man from U.N.C.L.E.* (1964–68) had sparked a national fad for espionage-themed toys. More than simply a batch of new stylized guns with silencers, popular brands like Mattel's Agent Zero M and Topper Toys' Secret Sam included a range of covert weapons along with secret agent outfits and intelligence-gathering devices. The Agent Zero M line, for example, included both a rifle disguised as a radio and a pistol disguised as a camera. The Secret Sam line's special contribution to the genre was the Pipe Shooter, the instructions for which were to "just squeeze with your teeth and shoot."[44]

The 1966 name-change announcement also spelled out Register's view on the trend's psychological implications for the developing self, which in his mind were even more frightening than that of war toys. "The advent of the spy toy has changed NO WAR TOYS' perspective as to what the most extreme examples of death toys actually are," he wrote. "Up to that time, war toys seemed the most dramatic example: machine guns, atomic missiles.... But spy toys add a new dimension to death; they introduce an element of respectable deceptiveness that makes it even virtuous to lie and cheat and kill without warning and with weapons illegal in the eyes of both national and international law: concealed and silenced weapon, gas, germs—you name it."[45] Moreover, Register said, the danger went beyond these invitations to play make-believe mass murder with every weapon imaginable; spy toys, he argued, "teach not to trust anyone, even your brother, your best friend or wife; they may be on the other side; be paranoid, turn them in—in the interest of the state. You will be rewarded with adventure and enhanced opportunities for loveless sex."[46] If Register's leap from the imaginary play of children to the problems of paranoia and loveless sex might seem abstruse at first read, the basic sentiment was fairly consistent with his larger quest for social and moral renewal through play. To Register, the acts of subterfuge that these toys glorified was anathema to the child's formation of a healthy, creative, vital personality; the artifice of espionage, he believed, made authentic human relationships—in many respects the crux of the countercultural ideal, encapsulated in the "Make Love Not War" slogan—an impossibility.

The group's new name did not last long. As Register explained in a single-page, poster-style issue of *The Toy* in 1967 (the group was too strapped for cash to publish an entire newspaper), "Our brief change of name did not work out—back to the original No War Toys. Many felt that 'No Death Toys' was philosophically more in tune with the concerns of the movement, including its founder, but . . . [it] proved too hard and closed minds instead of opening them. Flip, flop."[47] And yet, if the name change was disappointingly short-lived in Register's mind, it was nonetheless a powerful illustration of his growing conviction—shared by many in the peace movement in the late sixties—that the disturbing violence of the era went well beyond the Vietnam War, and the language of protest needed to shift accordingly.

But perhaps the NWT initiative that best dramatized the differences—though hardly disagreements—between the middle-class consumer-based protest of the women's peace movement and Register's embrace of a more radical and utopian cultural ethos was its community sand castle project. Starting in August 1965, Register began a five-year run of monthly open-invitation community events at Venice Beach where locals were invited to build giant sand castles in a collective act of creative play and defiance against commercialized representations of violence. "HELP BUILD THE WORLD'S LARGEST SAND CASTLE. VENICE BEACH @ BROOK ST. BRING SHOVELS, BUCKETS, PICNIC LUNCH AND FRIENDS. NO WAR TOYS" read the first of many announcements Register put in the left-wing *Los Angeles Free Press* during the second half of the 1960s.[48] And they came. Two hundred people of all ages attended the inaugural event, with many hundreds more joining in over the next several years of NWT beach parties.[49] What originated as a one-time event became a local ritual, with its own traditions. Upon completing these towering structures (reportedly up to twenty feet high and two hundred feet in circumference), and digging out the huge moats (one report described one fourteen feet wide), builders would climb to the summit and plant the NWT flag, emblazoned with the group's smiley-face logo and name (see figure 2.2).[50] By marking these symbols of nature and impermanence as the material manifestation of the NWT spirit, one might say the sand castles became the ultimate creative playthings.

The historian Howard Brick has observed that "much of the counterculture's ideology evoked an old tradition of romantic anticapitalism, wherein

2.2. The inaugural No War Toys sand castle party made the front page of the *Los Angeles Free Press* on August 13, 1965. Image from the Independent Voices Collection (Reveal Digital / JSTOR), https://www.jstor.org/site/reveal-digital/independent-voices/.

the forces of life strove against the mortifying effects of money and machinery and yearned for fulfillment in uncommodified human intimacy."[51] Through the appeal to cooperatively construct sand castles, Richard Register not only brought the counterculture ethos to the anti–war toy movement but also redefined opposition to war toys as just one part of a larger struggle to reclaim humanity, creativity, and play from the toy manufacturers and others in the capitalist bureaucracy, whom he painted as forces of death rather than life. Fittingly, one 1967 invitation poster for the sand castle parties urged anyone unsympathetic to NWT values to just stay home: "People too dignified to help us children build or play are not encouraged to attend, as we are concerned with creative play."[52] The giant sand castles, with their call for spiritual renewal through communal creative play, would be Register's contribution to the unique theater of protest that defined the mobilization against the Vietnam War, from the Bread and Puppet Theater led by Peter Schumann to the early New Games movement initiated by Stewart Brand.[53]

By the end of the 1960s, Register's highly imaginative and unconventional cultural activism had earned him the title of "the ultimate pacifist" from the *Los Angeles Free Press*.[54] Meanwhile, new chapters of NWT sprouted outside the LA area and California's activist campuses, including in Miami, New York, Fresno, Santa Fe, Detroit, and Honolulu.[55] The huge appeal of his festive conception of public protest and spectacle also could be seen in the third annual demonstration at the Toy Fair in March 1966, where members of the New York NWT chapter and PRITI were joined by members of Los Angeles NWT, who had flown out for the occasion.[56] In a photograph that appeared in the *New York Times* and *Daily News* the following day, millions of Americans saw the picketers carrying the massive Bread-and-Puppet-style NWT smiley-face rag puppet down Fifth Avenue.[57] Although Register was not present, his playful vision of politics had come to the Toy Fair.

At some point in the late sixties, PRITI began using a striking new poster to publicize its cause. Featuring a disquieting photo of a crying baby doll, along with a lengthy statement, written in a rambling style straight out of the era's New Journalism, on why playing with toy guns is "not funny anymore," the poster repurposed the most famous of hippie slogans in a final, bold-typed plea: "Make love not war toys" (see figure 2.3).[58] While Register did not play a part in the poster's development—it was probably produced by PRITI leader Victoria Reiss's husband, Harold, who ran the New York advertising firm Friend-Reiss and often helped with the group's visual materials—it is difficult to imagine it coming to fruition were it not for his outsized influence. For it

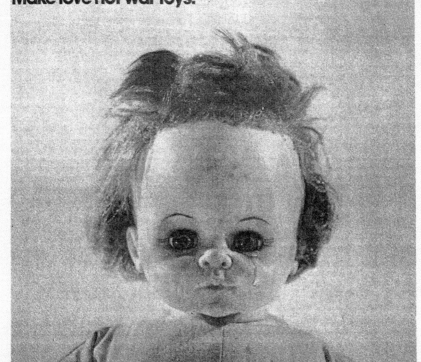

2.3. Poster produced by Parents for Responsibility in the Toy Industry (PRITI), circa late 1960s. Courtesy of Richard Reiss.

was Register, more than anyone else, who brought the counterculture to the toy movement, and the toy movement to the counterculture.

○

To rewind to a time before sand castles were politicized, it was only a few weeks after the inaugural Toy Fair protest of March 1964 that toy-industry leaders first responded to their critics. One of the first to speak publicly was Denton Harris, publisher of *Toy & Hobby World*, who dedicated his entire column in the magazine's April 1964 issue to the anti–war toy demonstration. In the piece, titled "Who Could Be against Toys?," Harris pushed back against activists' claims to know something more than toymakers about child development, defending toy guns as "part of the healthy, normal way of growing up."[59] But he didn't stop there. As Harris contended, it was actually the protesters, not the toy business, who represented the true threat to the kids. "Taking the delight of playing war . . . away from a youngster is like taking away childhood," he stated. Harris's suggestion that a dozen picketers outside the Toy Fair threatened American childhood with extinction might sound overdramatic. Yet if the results of the national uproar over crime and horror comics just a few years earlier were any indication of where controversies over children's culture might go—local ordinances prohibiting sales, comic-book burnings, Senate committee hearings—it becomes easier to understand why Harris resolved to not merely address the controversy but also try to stamp it out. Deflecting the specific criticism of the particular toys in question, he painted himself as a defender of childhood itself.

Indeed, the growing public clamor against war toys, along with the expanding domain of controversial playthings encompassed in newly popular terms like *toys of violence*—Register's short-lived *death toys* did not gain any traction—was bound to make toymakers nervous. At the broadest level, the campaigns posed an unprecedented threat to the industry's credibility as purveyors of wholesome children's entertainment. More immediately, however, it was terrible for the booming war-toy business. In the years prior to the controversy, few toy categories could have been named for more reliable profits. Hailed by *Playthings* as the "star sellers of toydom," gun and holster sets had become a "staple" of the 1960s; one trade observer went so far as to refer to them as the "bread or coffee in a toy store."[60] According to a 1962 article, "guns comprise the largest selling single category of toys for boys, accounting for 5 percent of total retail dollar sales, or upwards of 100,000,000 annually."[61] Moreover, the growth of the category—officially called "toy guns and sets" by the industry—in the previous decade had been phenomenal; retail dollars spent on toy guns more than tripled from 1956 to 1960.[62] With the alleged record-breaking sales of recent years, including one million of Topper's Johnny Seven O.M.A. guns in 1964 alone, there appeared to be little stopping the continued growth of this lucrative category. This was clear: consumers were spending more dollars on toys than ever before, with a disproportionate share going toward war toys. And young children were as often the beneficiaries of these purchases as older ones; according to a national consumer study conducted for the toy trade in 1964–65, children under five received 43 percent of the toy guns purchased.[63] If the protesters and the producers could agree on one thing, it was that there were more war toys in the United States than ever before.

Facing the largest consumer backlash in the trade's history, industry boosters like Harris, joined by the TMA trade association, spent a lot of energy in the mid-sixties trying to mute the criticism, discredit the movement, and protect the trade's public image from further harm. One frequently voiced rationale for making war toys was that toymakers, far from having any choice in the matter, merely gave consumers the products they wanted. *Playthings* magazine was typical in this fashion, with its editor invoking "the long-established fact that no one's going to produce goods for an imaginary market."[64] Others balked at the notion that the toy industry was at all responsible for what parents placed in their children's hands. "No one forces you to buy them," wrote one toy consultant, directly addressing parents in an unusual letter to the editor published in *Toy & Hobby World*. "If you are not strong enough to resist a child's nagging and a powerful sales pitch, don't blame the gun, blame the hand that puts the gun in the child's life: YOU."[65]

Industry officials also tried to downplay the campaigns' claims about the unprecedented scale of the industry's war-toy inventory. At a December 1965 press conference, the TMA cited a recent consumer research study that found that war toys accounted for 5 percent of the total toy dollars spent by the public; this was hardly evidence, said TMA officers, that military items were dominating the marketplace.[66] Still others invoked the theory of catharsis to make the case that toy guns were not just harmless but also healthy. A 1964 *Playthings* article titled "Ready-Made Talk on Toys"—talking points about toys and child development geared toward retailers and sales clerks—included this ready-made response to consumers who raised questions about the value of toy guns: "Let us remember that children, by nature, *have* aggressive tendencies. Far better to let them get rid of these aggressions in play with their toy guns than nurture them until they rid themselves of them in more dangerous ways."[67]

As for the manufacturers with the deepest investments in the war-toy market, most ignored the Toy Fair demonstrations and consumer campaigns altogether, choosing instead to keep the assembly lines running and distribution channels open in the belief—or maybe just the hope—that the controversy would soon pass. Topper Toys, for instance, pushed full speed ahead. Having watched its Johnny Seven O.M.A. outsell every toy gun on the market (and nearly every other toy of any kind, for that matter), in 1965 Topper introduced the new Johnny Eagle Rifle and bet heavily on a repeat of Johnny Seven's success when it bought $5 million worth of commercials for the fall children's television lineup.[68]

The efforts of trade leaders and boosters to downplay or deflect the controversy reflected a shared sense that the anti–war toy outcry threatened not only the companies that made war toys but also the public image of the industry writ large. And yet, for a tiny minority of manufacturers whose fortunes were not dependent on war toys, the protests looked less like a business crisis than a business opportunity. A year after Harris charged the anti–war toy movement with endangering childhood, he and the toy business not only had to contend with a growing controversy and shifting consumer mood around one of the trade's most lucrative toy genres; they also now faced an unexpected mutiny from within their own ranks. As it turned out, the campaigns against war toys would receive an unexpected boost from the toy business itself when several companies, seeing in the anti–war toy movement the makings of a new antiwar niche market, appeared to join their cause.

○

In March 1965, as the industry flocked to the Toy Fair and encountered showrooms filled with war toys, the men and women of the trade opened the latest issue of *Playthings* magazine to find an unusual message in the advertising pages, courtesy of one of the oldest, most respected companies in the business. "Lionel Levels with the Trade" was the headline, and, as the ad copy explained, the Lionel Toy Corporation—the leading manufacturer of electric trains since its founding in 1900—was no longer willing to stay silent about the industry's promotion of toys of violence; indeed, it was time for what the company called "the Lionel Crusade." The crux of that crusade, stated Lionel in this opening salvo, was an upcoming national advertising campaign aimed at parents, complete with a new company slogan: "Sane Toys for Healthy Kids."[69]

Anyone opening up the new Lionel trade catalog that spring—toy-shop owners, wholesalers, buyers for department stores, parents and kids—would have found the same principled message in the opening pages, where company president Francis R. O'Leary announced his firm's new direction: "A message for parents: Lionel has never tried to cash in on passing fads. Instead we make toys that children can play with and learn with year after year.... Our toys don't go 'bang-bang, screech-screech, or rat-a-tat-tat.' ... They are, first of all, toys to have fun with. But beyond that they are toys that have value and integrity. And if they help your child understand just a little more about what those words mean ... well, that isn't bad either."[70] Wagering $250,000 that parents fed up with the industry's ongoing appeals to war, violence, and horror represented a significant segment of its consumer base, Lionel hired the Madison Avenue firm Nadler and Larimer, Inc. to produce a series of full-page ads that ran in national magazines in the summer and fall of 1965. To complement the magazine appeals, the company's marketing team bought sixty-second radio spots on CBS Radio Network, with celebrity host Arthur Godfrey telling millions of listeners that Lionel was going "sane."[71]

The underlying promise of the new campaign was this: *someone* in the toy business had to speak out against the industry's exploitation of children's violent fantasies and indifference to children's psychological health, and only Lionel had the integrity to do it. As one of the new ads, which began appearing in magazines like the *New Yorker* in fall 1965, put it plainly: "Have you had your fill of trauma toys? Then make things sane again with lots of Lionels. They're good for thrills, but only the healthy kind."[72] Above the copy was a photo of a Lionel electric train racing around a circular track, along with the following headline of reassurance: "This toy doesn't kill, bite, scream, explode, conquer, destroy, or turn into a vampire" (see figure 2.4).[73] Another ad in the series was startlingly candid about what the industry's weapons producers were teaching children. "No boy ever held up a store with one of these," ran the headline in large print, above a junior-size microscope from Lionel's line of science toys. "Or," continued the copy at the bottom of the page, "learned to make war with a Lionel train. If you're ready to call it quits with violent toys, bring home a Lionel."[74]

Meanwhile, the company ran a parallel campaign in the trade press through early 1966 but with distinctive ads made exclusively for industry eyes. In one of the ads, Lionel's new slogan, "Sane Toys for Healthy Kids," was written in large graffiti-style letters across a brick wall, with no toys in sight.[75] Unusual by industry standards, in this case it made sense. What mattered was not the product but the message; everyone in the trade already knew what the company's trains looked like. Another ad created expressly for the trade was even more minimalist in its design, with the statement "Nice Toys Don't Kill"

This toy doesn't kill, bite, scream, explode, conquer, destroy, or turn into a vampire.

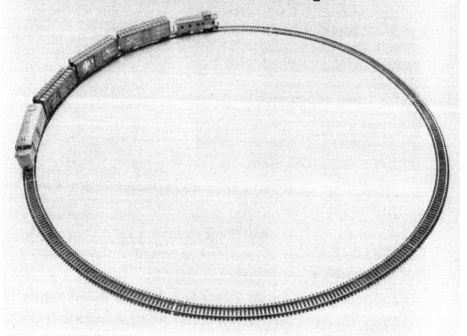

It just toots around in a happy circle.

Have you had your fill of trauma toys? Then make things sane again with lots of Lionels. They're good for thrills, too, but only the healthy kind. Trains, racing cars, space craft — all kinds of lab sets, toys made to last longer than a week or two. In fact, every Lionel toy carries a Warranty. See them all together in our new catalogue. Free at toy dealers, or write Lionel Toy Corp., Hillside, N.J. And peace.

LIONEL

sane toys for healthy kids

2.4. Lionel Corporation promoted its "Sane Toys for Healthy Kids" campaign (1965–66) in national magazine ads like this one. Magazine clipping from Women Strike for Peace Records. Courtesy of the Swarthmore College Peace Collection, Swarthmore, PA.

typed out in bold capital letters across an otherwise empty white background (see figure 2.5). At the bottom, the copy elaborated on what Lionel meant by nice when it came to playthings, speaking directly to industry toy buyers and dealers: "Nice toys are good sane fun and you sell them for that and you don't feel guilty making a profit on them."[76] If retailers and wholesalers had yet to feel pangs of guilt for selling what, following Lionel's sane/violent binary, one might have called "toys that kill," Lionel was insinuating that they ought to.

The Sane Toys campaign was a product of its time, reflecting some of the period's most significant commercial and cultural trends. For one, Lionel was not the only US company making sane toys, of course; most businesses did not sell "violent toys" at all. The added value of the campaign—to use the language of marketing—lay chiefly in the suggestion that Lionel alone did so intentionally rather than incidentally. The ads emphasized a philosophy of toymaking as opposed to the particular virtues of any toy; solidarity with what Lionel believed were the shared concerns of a significant segment of its consumers—that in this historical moment, developing a child's character had to take precedence over satisfying the child's desires—became a marketable good in its own right. The selling of corporate social consciousness as a desirable commodity reflected a savvy recognition on the part of Lionel and the advertising executives at Nadler and Larimer of what the political scientist David Vogel has called the "market for virtue."[77] In 1965, this sort of appeal to values over products was a fairly recent phenomenon, reflecting the changes in practices that historians have called the "creative revolution" in advertising. One of the key strategic innovations of Madison Avenue in the 1960s was advertisers' new attention to psychographics—that is, markers of group affiliation such as cultural identity, political values, and lifestyle choices—as a means of organizing newly specialized consumer niches. As the historian Lizabeth Cohen sums it up, this "revolution in segment marketing" shifted the subject of the advertising appeal "from product to user."[78] By recognizing the promotional possibilities of what Lionel called "a timely selling idea"—in this case, to play on parental anxieties about violence in the world—the Sane Toys campaign signaled the creative revolution's arrival in the toy market.[79]

The strategy was a resounding success, at least according to Lionel. "Do you believe a lady would sit down and write a letter saying how *grateful* she is for the new advertising campaign?" asked the company in a March 1966 *Playthings* ad, just one of the typically self-congratulatory messages that ran in the trade press on the anniversary of the campaign's launch. "We can show you the letter. And hundreds of others congratulating us."[80] Nor was Lionel's boasting empty rhetoric. Not only could it show off the letters; it also could

NICE TOYS DON'T KILL

Nice toys are good sane fun and you sell them for that and you don't feel guilty making a profit on them. Nice toys carry a Warranty and if they break they can be fixed. Nice toys sell out at Christmas and never create unnecessary inventories. Nice toys come from Lionel and Lionel wants nice guys to sell them. Call your local Lionel distributor or representative and ask about the New Lionel Program for Profits.

*see our ads in The New Yorker, Sports Illustrated, New York Times Magazine, Boy's Life, Parents' Magazine, and listen to Arthur Godfrey, CBS Radio

sane toys for healthy kids

2.5. This ad was one of several that the Lionel Corporation ran in the toy trade press in 1965 and 1966, informing toy buyers and industry competitors of its new opposition to violence-themed toys. Advertisement from *Playthings,* August 1965. Courtesy of Department of Science and Wellness, Free Library of Philadelphia, Philadelphia, PA.

point to the financial benefits of "going sane": the year of the Sane Toys pro-motion was the first since 1960 in which the company closed its books with a net profit.[81] "There is nothing so powerful as an idea whose time has come," the company announced in one of the graffiti-style ads that appeared in *Play-things* and *Toy & Hobby World*. "As a Lionel dealer in 1966, you will share the profits."[82]

In some respects, the promotion of users' values over the products' value was not wholly out of character for a company like Lionel. Since its founding in 1900, Lionel was known for catering not only to children's desires but also to parental ones, most famously in its appeals to fathers to make its train sets a tool for father–son bonding within the idealized nuclear family. By the mid-1950s, as rising consumer spending on discretionary goods combined with the ascent of the child-centered family as a national ideology, Lionel had leveraged the family-friendly image to become one of the top three grossing toy producers in the United States.[83] What distinguished the 1965 campaign was advertisers' keen sense for capitalizing on the particular cultural and po-litical anxieties of the moment rather than an unchanging idealized image of middle-class family life. The strategic use of the modifier "sane" to describe Lionel's products, and its implicit suggestion that other brands were the op-posite, brilliantly tapped into a favorite metaphor of liberals and leftists in the late 1950s and 1960s to describe the state of US politics and society—what the historian Charles DeBenedetti called the "motif of madness."[84] During the peace movement's recent campaigns for a nuclear weapons test ban, activists painted US leadership in the Cold War as irrational to the point of insanity, pointing to reckless decisions like the 1962 Cuban missile crisis that had put the world on the brink of a nuclear annihilation. Meanwhile, the organization that brought the nuclear test-ban campaign into the politi-cal mainstream in the late 1950s expressed the call for sanity in its very name: founded in 1957 as the National Committee for a Sane Nuclear Policy, it quickly became known as SANE. It is not hard to imagine the Lionel adver-tising team anticipating that consumers sympathetic to the cause of disarma-ment might make these connections, consciously or otherwise, and feel that, finally, there was a toy company that shared their view.

And yet perhaps the real genius of Lionel's new advertising appeal was its ability to cater simultaneously to the company's broader middle-class base, a much more politically diverse group. One of the important ways it achieved this was by signaling Lionel's concern for children's mental well-being through the signifying language of "healthy kids." The early 1960s were a time when midcentury changes to the discourse of child development began to solidify.

As the media scholar Henry Jenkins has observed, "The threat of childhood diseases and the problems of hygiene which dominated pre-war accounts [of proper child-rearing] gave way to a new focus on psychological health and social development. The parent's attention to mental health was as important as its focus on the infant's bodily development."[85] Indeed, by this time the healthy personality was widely recognized by postwar psychologists to be the principal goal of good child-rearing.[86] These psychological concepts gained wide currency in the middle-class culture, as evident in the popular success of child psychoanalyst Selma Fraiberg's *The Magic Years* (1958), the first parenting guide emphasizing child mental health.[87] One of the Lionel trade ads seemed to speak directly to the new concern with psychic development, reassuring consumers that in addition to not maiming or exploding, Lionel toys would not "scream, bite, conquer, or make bad dreams"—as did the unhealthy "trauma toys" (as Lionel called them) hustled by so many of its competitors.[88]

Lionel was hardly the first toymaker to use the authority of psychology to sell toys. The ever-expanding market that catered to affluent parents and progressive educators, led by the firms favored by WILPF and WSP, had been employing that strategy for decades. However, at a moment when the Lionel Toy Corporation had suffered four years without profits and faced unprecedented competition in the train business from more diversified corporate firms less committed to its standards—Marx Toys, for example, had launched a line of plastic electric trains in the late 1950s at half the price of Lionel's—the appeal to healthy kids and its placement in the highbrow *New Yorker* rather than mass-circulation magazines suggests an effort to distinguish the brand and to cash in on the new attention to psychologically minded toy buying among the college-educated classes.[89] Lionel's decision not to advertise on television, as it had in the past, suggests a similar attempt to rebrand itself as a company that catered to parents first. By the mid-1960s, TV ads had become standard for businesses hoping to achieve national sales, Lionel included. The best-selling toys were always TV toys. As the toy market grew larger and more competitive during these years, manufacturers chasing the comfortable classes such as Creative Playthings and Playskool strategically flagged their lack of a TV presence as a sign of commitment to selling mothers on their toys rather than (as many perceived it) manipulating children. Lionel executives seemed to be betting there was room for one more in that elite group.

Yet there was an unstated irony to Lionel's expression of solidarity that anyone following the company closely, especially young consumers, would probably have picked up on. Until the new promotional campaign, Lionel had actually been manufacturing war toys for nearly a decade. In the 1950s, as the toy industry establishment began to absorb the new Cold War imagery of US military power, Lionel had happily joined them. In 1958, for example, the company's catalog introduced the Marine Battlefront Special 4-Car Train Set, "all new and ready for you to place into combat!"[90] By 1963, the catalog listed nine different missile-bearing cars that children could link up to their traditional engines, coal cars, and oil freighters.[91] Furthermore, while Lionel officials criticized the "hard-sell television pitch men" pushing "boom-boom toys" on an innocent public in 1965, the company was as guilty as any of them; in fact, it had been using television ads to promote its military toys ever since the industry first turned to TV in the mid-1950s.[92] One 1962 commercial, for instance, featured a young boy cranking open the roof of Lionel's Turbo Missile Firing Car to reveal the tiny plastic missiles, which he then catapulted across the room at a group of train cars outfitted with aerial balloon practice targets.[93] This was hardly avoiding the hard sell on boom-boom toys. Nor was that ad exceptional. Just a couple of years prior to the Sane Toys campaign, the company's trade ads placed special emphasis on weapon-equipped freight cars like the Super "O" U.S. Army and the Missile Firing Car. Indeed, Lionel's investment in military equipment was so significant that the first page of a 1961 Lionel catalog insert in *Playthings* featured a photo of the company's president happily tinkering with one of the missile cars as he sat at his corporate desk.[94]

So why did Lionel decide to call it quits on violent toys? According to advertising director Eric Schlubach, his company wanted "to say something constructive," though he admitted at the time that it was not the only factor. "Let's face it," he told a reporter, "we're out for ourselves."[95] Ultimately, it appears that crude business calculations were less important to activists than what companies did. And Lionel had undoubtedly done the campaigns a great service: the company had not only broadcast the critique of war toys to a wider and more mainstream audience than the movement could have hoped to reach; it had also shined a spotlight on the relative silence of its competitors on the war-toy issue.

The company's call for Sane Toys quickly won applause from movement leaders and brought the Lionel brand a high regard that had previously eluded the toy industry establishment. In fact, the same WSP newsletter that one year earlier had painted Lionel as an enemy of healthy play—"even the boy's favorite toy train now comes equipped with missiles," an activist had lamented—now lauded Lionel for its stand and encouraged parents to show their appreciation of the gesture via letters of support and the concerted purchase of Lionel products.[96] Members of WILPF joined in too. In Syracuse, New York, the local WILPF branch celebrated the Lionel ads in their latest flyers, signaling to membership that change was possible and that their efforts were having an impact.[97] Meanwhile, Philadelphia WILPF's Evelyn Prybutok wrote directly to Lionel with a request to send toys for display in her group's outreach initiatives and toy fairs.[98] In this, she followed the advice of Elise Boulding, who a year earlier had recommended the pursuit of such reciprocity with the point that "this is advertising for them."[99] Germantown WILPF even borrowed Lionel's "Nice Toys Don't Kill" slogan for the title of its 1965 panel discussion.[100]

If Lionel had linked itself to the anti–war toy campaigns for its own purposes, the campaigns put Lionel's rebranding to work on their behalf. "We've had a number of requests from marchers and others for endorsements," said Lionel's Schlubach, "but we're not about to endorse them."[101] While it is true that the company made no official endorsements, Schlubach's claim at the time that "we're not active participants in the antiwar toy campaign" was a bit misleading. For as one journalist reported, Lionel had in fact sent a package filled with thousands of glossy reproductions of the new ads to the Anti-War Toy Committee of San Francisco Women for Peace.[102] Protesters had identified themselves as a new consumer niche, and Lionel was happy to cater to their desires.

Lionel would not be the only one to mobilize peace-movement images and ideals to sell its products. At the end of 1965, the LEGO Corporation, a company known for its miniature interlocking building bricks made of plastic in primary colors, followed Lionel into the controversy with a carefully orchestrated national magazine campaign proclaiming its own commitment to the anti–war toy cause. Created for LEGO by Grey Advertising, Inc., the new print ad showed a boy happily at play with the company's signature bricks, with the word *PEACE* in supersized type at the top of the image. Adopting language remarkably similar to Lionel's appeal to sanity, the copy assured parents that "there is, in this nervous world, one toy that does not shoot or go boom or bang or rat-tat-tat-tat. Its name is Lego. It makes things."[103]

The LEGO campaign was probably less surprising to anti–war toy critics than Lionel's; LEGO bricks, introduced into the US market just five years earlier (its distributor was Samsonite), were one of the newest additions to the middle-class progressive parent's canon of creative toys—hence the ad's exclusive appearance in magazines such as the *New Yorker*, *New York Times Magazine*, and *Parents* magazine. In fact, the previous year, LEGO had been included in a list of WILPF-approved companies in a holiday toy flyer. Of course, the new appeal to "peace" quickly brought LEGO more accolades, with WSP's *National Peace Education Bulletin* reprinting the ad copy and hailing the company as one of several "very outstanding toy manufacturers."[104] Here was another example of the reciprocal endorsement that, for activists, represented not a compromise or co-optation by the corporate toy industry so much as a necessary step toward cultural change in a consumer society.

There was one other national manufacturer that entered the new market for virtue at this time, and from a different angle. Amsco Industries was known primarily for its realistic operational household toys and contributions to the girls' market. Like LEGO, it did not have a single investment in war toys. But that did not keep Amsco from organizing an "Invent-a-Peace-Toy" contest to coincide with the 1966 Toy Fair. "The most important theme of this century is peace," announced the company in a colorful brochure, and "we think it has been neglected by the makers of toys."[105] To fill that perceived gap, Amsco was offering a $1,000 prize for "the best idea for a peace toy" and included a blank entry form in the brochure where entrants could sketch or describe their original peace-toy concept. The winning entry, the brochure stated, would be chosen by "a distinguished panel of judges." For Amsco, that meant a group of antiwar celebrities, including Steve Allen (the original *Tonight Show* host), the children's author Shel Silverstein, and Paul Stookey of the folk music trio Peter, Paul, and Mary, known the world over for their recent recording of Bob Dylan's antiwar song "Blowin' in the Wind."

Curiously, Amsco's contest was not open to the general public, or even the industry as a whole. Rather, as the company explained in the brochure, the contest was exclusively for Toy Fair buyers—representatives from retail chains, independent toy stores, and wholesalers who were there to place orders—with the drop-off spot for all entries in Amsco's Toy Center showroom. "We think that toy buyers, as the most knowledgeable people in the business, should have a chance to contribute their ideas," affirmed Amsco. Here was a new approach to marketing the antiwar sensibility. To be sure, Lionel had appealed directly to buyers in the pages of the trade press, but it did so by making the case that they should purchase Lionel products (and "share the profits") because consumers no longer wanted violence-themed toys—not because of what toy buyers thought about such toys. By contrast, Amsco's message to toy buyers was more akin to Lionel's and LEGO's messages to consumers; it was about promoting itself as a company with values—in this case, antiwar values—as well as a company that cared about buyers' values too.

As we have seen, anti-war toy activists were not out to discredit the toy industry but rather they believed the industry provided a useful and even critical service for their and others' children. They were not anti-consumption critics (with the exception of Richard Register at times) but customers telling the toymakers what they wanted to see (or not see) on the shelves. Purchasing power, they believed, not just protest, could be harnessed as a countervailing force against the business of war toys. As the efforts of Lionel, LEGO, and Amsco illustrate, some of the industry's leading companies recognized that they stood to benefit.

"The battle over military toys . . . has taken a new turn," the *New York Times* stated in an article on the Amsco contest.[106] But perhaps the most unexpected element of that new turn went unnoticed: joining Stookey and others on the jury was Michael Spielman, editor of *Toys and Novelties* and one of the most influential voices in the trade. Like the growing number of politicians in the Democratic establishment who broke ranks that same year to oppose the US war in Vietnam, Spielman decided it was time for him to speak out. In April 1966, in the editorial column with which he opened each monthly issue, Spielman delivered an unprecedented call to conscience. "Profit is of course, the businessmen's legitimate major concern—but it must not be his only concern," he began, but he quickly adopted a more philosophical approach:

> What, after all, do toys really stand for? Diversion and entertainment for the child, to be sure, but much more importantly they indicate what skills we, society, think he should develop, what activities of life he should be concerned with, what vocations, or attitudes or heroes he should glamorize. No one, I think, would give a child a game based on activities of the Ku Klux Klan, for example, although this is certainly a very real part of life; or how about a miniature Nazi concentration camp complete with crematoriums for turning tiny figures of Jews into soap . . .
>
> It is my personal opinion that there are toy items currently being produced which transgress just as far, but it is neither my intention, nor any of my business, to get into a discussion here of which items are good and which are bad. It *is* my intention to suggest to toy manufacturers and retailers, individually and collectively, that what is required is that much deeper and much more searching consideration be given to the values inherent in the toys they produce and sell.[107]

Here was not only the first of many future acknowledgments by the trade of one of the most fundamental assumptions of the peace movement: that toys had "inherent" values. It was also the most provocative internal attack on the industry yet and, importantly, from an individual, not just an ad campaign. By comparing war toys to hypothetical lynch-mob figures and crematorium sets, was Spielman not painting the US Armed Forces as equally destructive and deserving of censure as Nazis and the KKK?

A few months earlier, the TMA's president had confidently stated that "the public doesn't feel the way these crusaders feel about [war toys]."[108] Not only did industry reports and marketing trends in 1966 suggest that this characterization was wrong, but many in the toy business itself were coming to recognize that the "war toy craze," as one contemporary observer called the recent sales boom, might be coming to an end. Consider the result of a May 1966 survey of wholesalers by *Toys and Novelties*, which found that "while military items were nominated for popularity by 20% of those surveyed last year, this year only 5% classified the grouping as a hot category."[109] Trade advertising for war toys was also dropping significantly, another indication of industry uncertainty. By the 1966 Christmas season, ads for war toys in *Toys and Novelties* plummeted from roughly 15 percent of all toy ads in 1964 to just 5 percent.[110] Additionally, the nation's largest retailer, Sears, was listing war toys at markedly lower rates in its famous Christmas catalog; in fact, the proportion of war-toy ads to ads as a whole dwindled by roughly 300 percent in just a couple of years.[111] Scattered reports at the end of 1966 indicate that retail sales were down too. Some Washington, DC, stores saw a decline as high as 50 percent.[112] Another report, from Oregon, said that war-toy sales across that state had decreased by 65 to 75 percent.[113] Regional differences notwithstanding, one business observer noted that in most states the decline varied from 10 to 30 percent.[114] Monthly trend reports from retailers and wholesalers across the nation, published in *Toys and Novelties* and *Playthings*, support these observations.

Although relatively limited in its sampling, a survey of Detroit-area parents conducted in 1964 and again in 1967 testified to the category's weakening popularity: in three years, disapproval of war toys among the parents increased by 20 percent.[115] The same survey found that the percentage of these parents who reported not to have recently purchased war toys doubled between 1964 and 1967, from 15 percent to 32 percent.[116] Sales of Hasbro's G.I. Joe doll, one of the top five sellers in 1964, underwent a particularly devastating decline. From the end of 1965 to the end of 1967, gross sales of the doll, ranked among the best-selling toys in the country in 1964 and 1965, dropped by half, from $16 million to $8 million.[117]

Toymakers responded to these changes in a variety of ways, some quite dramatic. Remco, for example, halted production of its popular TV-advertised Monkey Division Line of guns and grenades mid-decade, on account of what its cofounder called "severe market decline."[118] Less severely, other companies cleverly tried to make the links between their guns and any past or contemporary conflict more oblique. *Toy & Hobby World* reported on toymakers who "took great pains to create a switch on military toys," remerchandising them as "devices in counter-espionage."[119] The trend in spy-themed toys that began a year earlier owed much to the popularity of the James Bond films and new television series. But a lot of the spy gear, observed the same report, was merely "military or western types in new form and against new backdrops of character and activity."[120] Similarly, some manufacturers merely gave their Army-green guns a new coat of paint—preferably red, blue, or yellow. As one manufacturer candidly told a reporter: "We are trying to get away from olive drab. Just because it's war doesn't mean it has to be dreary."[121]

In 1966 and 1967, as this flurry of pessimistic reports appeared not only in the trade press but also in national business media such as *Business Week* and the *New York Times*, industry cheerleaders and companies alike felt the need to reassure prospective buyers that there was nothing to worry about.[122] Consider *Toys and Novelties*' report on consumer trends among "sophisticated," "permissive" parents, by which they meant parents of the liberal, well-educated, Spock-reading classes: "The so-called hard-headed, sophisticated East, it turns out, is populated by permissive parents and super-permissive grandparents, some of whom may object to certain war toys in principle, but all of whom can be swayed from resolve by a barrage of 'pleases' and 'I just gotta have its.'"[123] Continued sales depended on selling wholesalers and retailers on the idea that the war-toy category, contrary to all the news, was not about to fold. In one unusual trade ad that appeared in *Playthings* and *Toys and Novelties*, Daisy suggested to buyers that they not worry about the criticism coming from experts or parents; the real experts, and the consumers that counted, were the kids (see figure 2.6). Beneath the header, which stated that "our experts have some hot ideas," was a photograph of eight young white boys, aged nine or ten, dressed in coats and ties at a large conference table, as if at a marketing meeting at the Daisy corporate office. The boy leading the meeting stands at the far end of the table next to an easel, directing his young colleagues' attention to a large diagram of a rifle. The table, meanwhile, is strewn with toys, mainly Daisy guns and military vehicles; the only nonwar toys, a cement truck and a dump truck, seem out of place. "When it comes to toys that sell, it pays to sound out the kids," the ad stated in the text below the image. "So we've held high-level conferences in backyards and playrooms, finding out what the 'experts' want."[124] Without mentioning the anti–war toy campaigns by name, the ad implicitly challenged activists' claims to know what was good for children or to speak on their behalf. Indeed, the

Our experts have some hot ideas

When it comes to toys that sell, it pays to sound out the kids. So we've held high-level conferences in backyards and playrooms, finding out what the "experts" want. Now we can let you in on the results: a '66 line with the "like real" features kids can't resist—and the honest value parents *buy*. See "the toys the kids want" at Daisy Toy Headquarters—Arcade. Suite 114—200 Fifth Avenue, New York City.

 Daisy QUALITY TOYS THAT LAST

Manufacturing Company
Rogers, Arkansas 72756 (In Canada: Preston, Ontario)

2.6. Daisy Manufacturing Company reaffirmed its commitment to making toy guns and other war toys when some toy-industry leaders began speaking out against them. Advertisement from *Playthings*, April 1966. Courtesy of Department of Science and Wellness, Free Library of Philadelphia, Philadelphia, PA.

ad suggested, it was Daisy's toy designers, not the critics, who truly listened to children.

Among the leaders of the toy-arms business that refused to surrender their guns, and in some cases appeared to step up their promotions, Mattel was more aggressive than most in doing so.[125] At a moment when the toy industry came under consumer fire like never before, in 1967 the company brazenly introduced an all-new toy machine gun to replace its previously best-selling Crackfire Rifle of 1966. What distinguished the M-16 Marauder machine gun was its repeating sound mechanism, making it, as one Mattel ad extolled, "the most authentic *sounding* rifle" and "most authentic *looking* rifle ever!"[126] What is more, while military-type toys were not selling well at retailers nationwide, and even sales of cowboy pistols appeared to decline in some regions, Mattel promoted the M-16 Marauder in spot ads on network TV. Despite diminishing consumer enthusiasm for war toys overall, it quickly became one of the most popular toys on the market.[127] The year of the Marauder was also the year in which several major companies first began making military replicas modeled specifically on the current US war machinery in Vietnam.[128] Mattel and a few others clearly believed that the war-toy critics represented a consumer minority; why else would they pour money into creating new guns when their existing ones were doing just fine?

At the end of 1967, as the WILPF and WSP continued their initiatives, as NWT built sand castles, as Michael Spielman joined Frank Caplan as a kind of conscientious objector within the business, and as a California state assemblyman proposed a bill requiring a label on all military toys reading "Toy depicting violence or war; may be harmful to children" (it did not pass), many American children were still playing with war toys.[129] At the same time, it seems that many of the same kids who in previous years would have been, were not; not only were the items harder to find, but many parents were no longer as willing to finance their children's desires when the list for Santa included a plastic M-16. By the end of 1967, the toys of war were not selling and, as demonstrated by the massive antiwar rally at the Pentagon and new polls showing a majority of Americans against the Vietnam War, neither was the real thing.[130]

In early 1968, *Toy & Hobby World* sent questionnaires to two hundred citizens chosen at random from the phone book, asking them "What is your stand on 'war toys'?" Respondents could choose from four options: For, Against, Undecided, and Other. There was also a blank space for comments. While the poll hardly met the basic requirements of modern public opinion polls, and it made no effort to target toy consumers in particular, the findings—released in May—suggested a cultural shift underway. While 43 percent of the respondents were "for" war toys, a plurality of 47 percent said they were "against" them.[131] The nation, it seemed, was as divided over war toys as it was over the war. But no one in the toy business, or the peace movement, for that matter, could have anticipated what happened next.

○

On June 6, 1968, California senator Robert F. Kennedy, running for president on a liberal antiwar platform, was shot and killed on the night of his own state's presidential primary. It was almost exactly two months to the day after an even more outspoken antiwar figure, Rev. Dr. Martin Luther King Jr., was assassinated in Memphis. For the organized peace-and-justice movement, as for all Americans who wished for change, Kennedy's sudden death only compounded the feelings of disillusionment and despair that the murder of King had set off in April. Paralleling federal action to regulate firearms the very next day, WILPF peace educators ramped up their public demonstrations and called for like-minded groups across the country to draw a connection between toy guns and the real ones that were used to kill King and Kennedy, not to mention all soldiers and civilians in Vietnam. A new batch of printed flyers created by PRITI that fall did exactly that, featuring headshots of King and the Kennedy brothers (see figure 2.7).[132] "THINK before you buy a toy of violence!" the header implored readers. "Do we really want our children to grow up thinking that violence is an accepted way of life? The answer is a resounding 'No!'"[133]

For the first time, children not only appeared at marches alongside parents but also became activists themselves, surrendering their toy weapons in large numbers. A week after Robert Kennedy's death, for example, a *New York Times* headline announced, "1,000 Pupils in Queens Scrap Toys of Violence."[134] More than one thousand kids had ceremonially tossed their own toy weapons into a garbage truck to be smashed into pieces. On the same day, halfway across the nation, students at the progressive University of Chicago Lab School also brought their make-believe firearms to school for destruction, filling up cardboard boxes with pretend shotguns and pistols (see figure 2.8).[135] Similar events took place at schools and in church groups across the country, as young people sickened by gun violence at home and abroad used their power as toy consumers to make a statement.[136] In some cases, surrendering their toy firearms could even bring a reward. The Amity Federal Savings and Loan in Chicago announced it would give ten cents for every toy gun a child tossed into a specially designated garbage can inside the

THINK

BEFORE YOU BUY

A TOY OF VIOLENCE!

AN APPEAL TO SHOPPERS: This Christmas more and more stores have stopped selling toy guns and war toys. Americans, at last, have been looking at themselves and asking why so much violence in our country . . . Martin Luther King, Jr. and Robert Kennedy assassinated within two months of each other, following just a few years after the shooting of President John F. Kennedy.

Do we really want our children to grow up thinking that violence is an accepted way of life? The answer is a resounding "NO!" That is why Sears Roebuck eliminated toy weapons and war toys from their Christmas catalog this year. So did Bloomingdale's, Macy's, Gimbels, A and S, Altman's, Sterns' and other great stores across the country.

Support this effort. Tell these stores how glad you are they don't sell toy guns. Where you do find stores selling toy guns, ask them, *"With so much violence, don't you think it would be wise not to sell toys that teach violence?"*

We don't say that playing with toy guns makes children grow up to be criminals, but by giving toy guns to our children we indicate approval of pretend killing. **IS THIS CHILD'S PLAY?** For those who argue that for years every little boy has played with guns, we answer that at this point we must counter-act the violence that surrounds our children by giving them toys which will provide a healthy outlet for aggression and tension. For example: darts, horseshoes, archery, skates, balls, bikes, boxing gloves.

Here are toys to help him express himself: paints, clay, crafts, blocks, construction kits. These are toys that help him to act out the grown-up world: trains, trucks, cars, planes, carpentry sets, dolls, housekeeping toys, science kits, microscopes, space adventure.

In this season of hope and love, join us in our concern for children.

For further information, write:
Parents For Responsibility In The Toy Industry
Room 411, 799 Broadway — New York, N.Y. 10003

2.7. Flyer by Parents for Responsibility in the Toy Industry (PRITI), November 1968. From Women's International League for Peace and Freedom Records. Courtesy of the Swarthmore College Peace Collection, Swarthmore, PA.

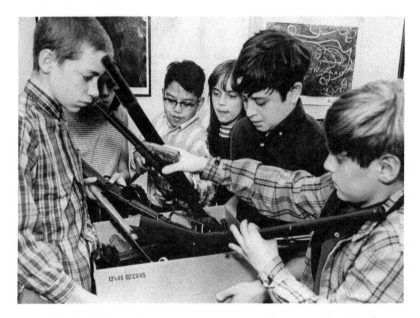

2.8. In the days following the June 6, 1968, assassination of US senator (and presidential hopeful) Robert F. Kennedy, children across the nation—including the sixth graders in this photograph, taken at the Chicago Lab School—handed in their toy guns at school-sponsored and other community events. Press photograph by Jack Lenahan for the *Chicago Sun-Times*, dated June 14, 1968. Author's collection.

bank, while in the nearby suburb of Rolling Meadows, the Roarin' West Fest carnival advertised two free rides for each toy gun the organizers received.[137]

Meanwhile, popular women's magazines took up more urgent opposition to war toys than ever before. Whereas in previous years some of them had published opinion pieces expressing that view by psychiatrists like Fredric Wertham and liberal authors like Eve Merriam, now the opposition had more of an official, mainstream air to it, coming from the magazine itself. The editors of *McCall's* published a piece called "What Women Can Do to End Violence in America," in which it called for "a determined boycott against toys that foster and glorify killing" among its top five priorities.[138] Another magazine, *Family Circle*, published a feature in the October issue addressing the question "What Can You Do to Stop Violence?" The piece included an interview with Dr. John Spiegel, director of the Lemberg Center for the Study of Violence at Brandeis University, who shared with millions of the magazine's readers—a demographic that was far from left-leaning—his professional opinion that through war toys a "child becomes habituated to an instrument of destruction."[139] As expected, also joining the expanding chorus of public critics was Benjamin Spock, who used his column in *Redbook* to reiterate some of the concerns about toy weapons and other violence-themed children's media that he had first shared with readers four years earlier.[140]

By July, toy disarmament had spread to national retailers, with Sears, Roebuck, Montgomery Ward, and other major chains removing toy guns from shelves and catalogs.[141] As the media reported throughout the months that followed, many toy manufacturers followed suit, swiftly pulling realistic toy weapons from their own advertisements in the trade press, television, and national magazines. That the climate of the US toy industry had dramatically changed was revealed in a July editorial in *Playthings*, which up until that point had been a vocal defender of war toys and their producers. As the editor explained the situation:

> No matter what you as a toyman or we as toy magazine publishers may think about the validity of the notion, an increasing number of people are coming around to the idea that toy guns instruct children in the ways of violence and ought not to be made and sold. . . . We've been running into many people who are in this frame of mind concerning real guns and make-believe guns. They're average citizens; for the greatest part, they aren't even pacifists, in the sense that most of us employ that term. . . . No one has a positive answer, but we at *Playthings*, in common with many toymen, are no longer so certain as heretofore that the anti-toy-gun arguments are completely specious.[142]

Of all the major producers of toy firearms, only Daisy refused to allow the public uproar to determine its business plans. It continued to advertise its signature products, and even went so far as to take out a full-page ad in the September issue of *Playthings* to express its view that "toy guns need not take a beating."[143] Unfortunately for Daisy, the only encouragement their plea received came from outside the industry, in the form of a letter to the editor of *Playthings* from the National Rifle Association.[144] Peace activists were not alone in seeing a strike against toy guns as a strike against real ones.

The events of 1968 would see the creation of a several-year-long national initiative, spearheaded by the US Congress, to study what observers across the political spectrum began calling America's "culture of violence" during these years—a culture they suddenly saw everywhere they looked, from network TV to Hollywood.[145] If talk of toys was conspicuously absent from those congressional panels and official reports—Richard Register had actually flown to Washington, DC, in hopes of testifying at the 1968 National Commission on the Causes and Prevention of Violence hearings, only to be denied entry—the best explanation is that unlike the TV and movie industries, the toy business had strategically avoided the possibility of new regulation by simply purging itself.[146] This is not to say the unprecedented burst of toy protest in 1968, and the unofficial moratorium that followed, led to the permanent abolition of war toys. But one of the things these events did was to prompt an unprecedented reckoning over toy guns and their meaning among psychologists, educators, and others concerned with children, and not just on the radical or liberal left. A new cultural ambivalence around war toys set in after 1968 that US society has yet to shake. For many Americans, realistic toy guns never looked the same.

If we take the 1968 *Toy & Hobby World* poll as a rough picture of America's divided public opinion on war toys in early 1968—before the murders of King and Kennedy, before sixteen thousand US soldiers had died in Vietnam over the course of that year alone, and before the wave of demonstrations and mass outcry in the media—one can reasonably speculate that by the end of that turbulent year, the needle had moved considerably further toward disapproval. Another way to measure that discomfort with and disinterest in commercialized war play, of course, is by looking at how the toy establishment interpreted the consumer mood. It is probably no surprise that when the controversy began to cool down a little in the early 1970s, some of the big companies like Mattel and Marx would gradually smuggle their toy firearms back into the catalogs. Yet few chose to style them along military lines, sticking largely to the tried-and-true western six-shooters and shotguns for which, as we have seen, even some of the activists could make exceptions. What is more, it appears that not a single manufacturer tried to sell them again on television commercials, this after a toy machine gun—Mattel's 1955 Burp Gun—had essentially launched the new TV-toy era just fifteen years earlier. When *Forbes* magazine asked the TMA's public relations director about how war toys were faring in 1971, his reply was "You can hardly give them away right now."[147] Even a representative from Mattel had to admit that the war-toy era that his company had dominated had ended. "War toys are a loser," he told a reporter.[148] The toy industry, however, reluctantly and largely through pressure, had come to acknowledge the movement's main point, what Michael Spielman of *Toys and Novelties* had told his readers back in 1966: that toymakers did not just produce goods; they also produced values.

o

Elise Boulding, the WILPF peace educator and sociologist who would go on to serve as WILPF's national president as well as create two of the first peace studies programs on American campuses (at the University of Colorado and Dartmouth College), was always ambitious and hopeful about what was possible in terms of societal change, in the toy aisle and beyond. A letter she wrote to Walt Disney in 1965 is one small yet meaningful example of that, and speaks to her enduring belief in both the power of toys and the special responsibilities of America's entrepreneurs of childhood. Boulding may not have known the creator of Mickey Mouse and Disneyland, but she thought that he could, and might even want to, be of help in not just eliminating war toys but countering them with what she called "peace toys."[149] What the toy marketplace desperately needed, Boulding wrote to Disney, were "Peace Corps equivalents" of soldier dolls as well as other "adventure roles . . . that relate to building a new and better society."[150] A few months before her letter to Disney, Boulding had outlined this same vision in a memo to her WILPF colleagues, imagining a line of toys that "can be used by the child to play-act roles in the larger society around him; the family, the community, the country, the world," and could compete with "the ever-popular jungle warfare kit and endless sets of toy soldiers."[151]

If Disney ever responded, Boulding did not share it with the campaign. Five years later, however, amid a very different national consumer mood around war toys, another prominent (if less storied) manufacturer of children's culture introduced an "adventure role" doll that was remarkably in line with what Boulding had in mind. The irony was that, back in 1965, this same manufacturer had been at the top of the WSP and WILPF lists of toy-industry "munitions makers."

That company was Hasbro, founded in 1923 as Hassenfeld Brothers, and famous long before the war-toy craze as the creator of the popular Mr. Potato Head line (1952). But the runaway success, in the mid-sixties, of its G.I. Joe brand—which included not only soldier dolls but a military-themed line of realistic toy guns and apparel, all of which were marketed on national TV— propelled it into the industry's top tier alongside names like Mattel and Ideal.

That relatively new position, built as it was on a pre–Vietnam War public appetite for military toys that was rapidly decreasing, might explain why Hasbro's leadership took the post-assassinations mood more seriously than most. Indeed, the massive sales drop of its flagship G.I. Joe toys at the end of the decade made for an uncomfortable reality that the company knew it had to address, not just through a public relations campaign but through products.[152] Stephen Hassenfeld, Hasbro's executive vice president, stopped short of crediting the anti–war toy movement for that drop in a late 1968 interview, instead attributing it to "the Viet Nam war and the violence in the cities"— probably a reference to the mass Black uprisings that followed King's murder, rebellions quelled by federal troops and the National Guard.[153] But whatever the explanation for why consumers had turned against its most famous toy, Hasbro expressed its sense of urgency with action in the realm it knew best— making toys. Within months of Hassenfeld's statement, the transformation of the G.I. Joe doll—ultimately, a two-year process—was underway.

Buyers at the 1969 Toy Fair were the first to see the changes to the brand. Many of them were probably relieved that Hasbro was still offering a modified version of the gun-toting, twelve-inch G.I. Joe in its trade catalog. But the theaters of World War II were no longer the brand's primary setting. Nor was battle the backstory for the other action figures in the line. Marketed under a new name, the Adventures of G.I. Joe, the line now featured not members of the Armed Forces, in full combat gear, but members of a motley crew of explorer types, mostly unarmed, such as the Land Adventurer, an archaeologist out to unearth mummies, and the Underwater Adventurer, who was fighting octopi instead of Nazis.[154] "Failing War Toy Succeeds as Peaceful Adventurer," announced the *New York Times*, as early sales indicated that the switch had paid off.

But Hasbro did not stop there, moving closer to Boulding's vision the following year. By the time of the 1970 Toy Fair, G.I. Joe can be said to have undergone a full body—and backstory—makeover. The heroic ideal of the antifascist World War II American soldier, of Dwight D. Eisenhower and even John F. Kennedy, was being left behind with the sixties. In 1970, Joe had officially received his discharge papers from all four divisions of the Armed Forces and had joined the Adventure Team—a thoroughly depoliticized, demilitarized, and disarmed group of figures that expanded on the previous year's partial reinvention of the line. The impact of the peace movement, antiwar as well as anti–war toy, was made visible, in miniature, through Joe's new occupations (astronaut, sea diver, etc.), new personal style (which included a counterculture-inspired beard), and new accessories (such as a pendant motif that resembled nothing so much as a peace sign, and which replaced the original doll's military-issued dog tag).[155] The new Adventure Team line would bring Hasbro its highest Joe sales ever in 1973, showing the company, and the industry, that, as the movement (and Boulding herself) claimed, peace could be profitable. The triumphalist vision of America that G.I. Joe had once embodied was beginning to unravel, in the toy business as in the culture at large.[156]

The assassination of John F. Kennedy had ignited an urgent national movement against war toys; the murder of his younger brother Robert had, in a way, helped bring it to a close. Two years before the movement began, Elise Boulding had written a prescient letter to the *Saturday Review* on the subject, invoking the promise of the Kennedy administration. "When the arms race and the toy race become synonymous," she asked, "what does this mean for a country whose President has just offered world leadership in a peace race?"[157] A decade later, the Kennedy who got the United States into Vietnam, as well as the Kennedy who promised to finally get the United States out, were dead, along, it seemed, with the hopes for peace and internationalism that they carried for the women of WSP and WILPF and so many other Americans. The arms race did not end, and some might argue that the peace race never started, but the toy race, thanks to activists like Boulding and Richard Register, and even some toy companies, was over. If the underlying goal of the movement was not to simply rid the world of war toys but to change how their society thought and talked about them—and more generally, about the values we communicate to our children through the things we give them—they could claim to have accomplished it. That profound change in the cultural conversation around war, toys, and childhood would prove to be a lasting one, a shift in attitudes that the return of toy guns in future decades—in the late 1970s, in the mid-1980s—could not reverse.

3 Integrating the Doll Shelves

In the wake of the King and Kennedy assassinations, with the anti–war toy movement more popular than ever, the chances of finding a pretend machine gun at the toy store in the days before Christmas 1968 were slim to none. Remarkably, however, the chances of spotting a Black doll on those same shelves had never been better. Recognizing this new and unexpected commercial reality, *Ebony* magazine ran a feature story in the December issue on the unusually large assortment of Black-oriented toys and games in the holiday marketplace. Heralding a new era for the nation's several million Black children, the article proclaimed that, at long last, "Christmas does not have to be white."[1] *Ebony's* announcement was prescient. That year would mark the start of a new and more hopeful chapter in what had heretofore been a painful history of demeaning representations and unjust exclusions of African Americans by the nearly all-white producers of mass-market toys, with the late 1960s and early 1970s proving to be watershed years in the industry's production of (ostensibly) nonstereotyped Black dolls. For it was during this moment that the concept of "ethnically correct" design—a term that referred to efforts to represent the associated physical features of nonwhite racial or ethnic groups rather than just changing the cream-colored complexion of the conventional white doll with European features—first entered the mainstream toy industry.

A collision of new historical factors—economic, political, and intellectual—underwrote these profound alterations to the color and character of representational toys. Recognizing a new level of Black purchasing power during the 1960s, increasingly conscious of (and in some instances sympathetic to) the civil rights movement's demands for inclusion in consumer culture, and surprisingly attentive to the concerns of midcentury social psychologists about the formation of a healthy racial identity, virtually every company in the business of dolls made a point of integrating its previously white doll lines. By the decade's end, however, some of these manufacturers also began to grasp that African Americans wanted more than just an equal (or at least fairly proportionate) number of Black dolls on the shelves; they also wanted changes in how Black people were represented—dolls that were, by design, recognizably and respectfully Black. A handful of toymakers took these appeals seriously, developing elaborate plans to court Black consumers with new race-conscious designs and marketing appeals. Yet the task of producing ethnically correct Black dolls without falling into old stereotypes was not without its challenges. During a period when civil rights groups successfully rattled (and reformed) the television, film, and advertising industries with sustained campaigns for more, and better, Black representation, the American toy industry managed to elude their attention almost entirely. But, as we shall see, the dilemmas of racial representation would beset even the most racially conscious among them.

o

The modern mass-market toy industry that arose in the first decades of the twentieth century was built in part on the sale of anti-Blackness. Indeed, toys and games populated with stock racist caricatures from blackface minstrelsy and vaudeville were commercially ubiquitous, manufactured by the leading companies and available for purchase in national department store consumer catalogs. In this sense, the toy business of that time can be credited with transferring the minstrel show's anti-Black imaginary into the play of white children. And in doing so, in actively profiting from these demeaning representations, toymakers were perfectly in step with the rest of the white-owned commercial culture, where the same racist stereotypes dominated packaging and advertisements for food, soap, cosmetics, and other everyday consumer goods.[2]

Yet as toy companies catered to the casual anti-Black racism of white middle-class families, while seeing no financial motive in making representational toys that might appeal to Black ones (much less other racial minorities), Black entrepreneurs and civil rights advocates did not stand by and wait for the mainstream toy trade to change. In the first decades of the twentieth century, as white industry leaders formed the TMA, a small number of

Black-owned businesses specializing in Black dolls sprung up to meet rising demand for such toys and new purchasing power to buy them. Two of the most successful were the Nashville-based National Negro Doll Company, launched in 1908 by Richard Henry Boyd, a minister, civic leader, and businessman who had been born enslaved; and Berry & Ross, Inc., founded in 1918 by Evelyn Berry and Victoria Ross in Harlem and later affiliated with Pan-Africanist leader Marcus Garvey's United Negro Improvement Association (UNIA).[3] Successfully promoting their dolls to Black consumers in Black-oriented newspapers, Garveyite publications, and the *Crisis* magazine of the National Association for the Advancement of Colored People (NAACP) during the 1910s and 1920s, these companies tapped into an expanding Black middle class of urban professionals with a desire to purchase Black toys for their children.[4] And yet this first era of Black-owned Black doll businesses proved to be short lived, with both manufacturers closing their doors by 1930. That Black-owned firms appeared to have been cut off from the national manufacturing, distribution, and marketing networks organized by the white-led TMA during the first half of the century was no doubt a key factor in this independent Black doll sector's demise.

It was only after World War II that major white-owned toy companies gradually began to integrate Black dolls into their established lines of white dolls. Indeed, across the industry, doll integration was as reluctant as it was tokenized, having less to do with the onset of a more militant national mobilization for African American civil rights (starting with the wartime Double Victory campaigns) than with announcements by ad industry publications like *Tide* of the "enormous new opportunities" presented by growing Black purchasing power.[5] A few efforts stand out. In 1947, the new Terri Lee Corporation introduced one of the first nationally marketed nonstereotyped Black dolls, the Patty-Jo doll, based on the comic-strip character drawn by the pioneering Black cartoonist Jackie Ormes.[6] Two years later, the Sun Rubber Company aimed to capitalize on these trends when it introduced a Black doll named Amosandra, named after the daughter born to Amos and Ruby from the popular radio show *Amos 'n' Andy*, a show notorious for its racial stereotyping.[7] A third effort at producing a Black doll for the commercial mainstream, the Sara Lee doll, was not tied to a commercial character but did have the unmatched brand recognition of the Ideal Toy Corporation, not to mention the sales reach of the Sears, Roebuck catalog, behind it. Introduced in 1951, the Sara Lee doll was also distinguished by its activist history. The original concept for Sara Lee had come to Ideal's president David Rosenstein not from his toy development staff but from Sara Lee Creech, a white civil rights activist who believed Black children ought to see a doll at stores that resembled them—and to that end gathered some of the era's most prominent intellectuals and advocates for racial equality, including Zora Neale Hurston, Ralph Bunche, and Eleanor Roosevelt, to support her project.[8]

Yet by the time the Supreme Court unanimously ruled in *Brown v. Board of Education* (1954) that racial segregation was unconstitutional—a landmark decision that was as much about segregation's negative impact on Black children's personality development as it was concerned with the quality of their education—none of the three dolls was on the shelves or in catalogs. Patty-Jo and Sara Lee were each pulled within two years of their introduction, and Amosandra not long after that.[9] Marketing executives may have been right about the unprecedented Black purchasing power that awaited American corporations, but the mass purchase of novelty brand-name Black dolls like Patti-Jo, priced much higher than conventional toys at discount and variety chain stores, was not yet a priority for Black consumers or, for that matter, white ones. It was only in the early 1960s—as the southern desegregation campaigns gained momentum through the sit-ins and Freedom Rides, as the violent white backlash intensified (and was televised), and as the grievances of a century of racial subordination since the end of chattel slavery finally found a sympathetic ear in the Kennedy White House—that a critical mass of the industry's established dollmakers could point to at least a few Black dolls in their lines.

The change in the retail outlook on this front was dramatic, appearing to happen overnight. The case of Sears, Roebuck's annual Christmas catalog, commonly known as the Wish Book (but not officially called that until 1968), is instructive. In December 1961, a child searching with anticipation through the Wish Book for a Black doll would have found only one; a year later, however, she would have the option of choosing from among sixteen different dolls.[10] When *Toys and Novelties* published its annual directory issue in 1963, there were thirty-eight different companies listed as purveyors of "Negro dolls," which along with "Colored dolls" was industry parlance for humanlike figures meant to look Black.[11] A few months later, the industry publication *Playthings* commented on "a noticeable profusion of... Negro dolls" at the 1964 Toy Fair.[12] At a moment when children's book publishers were facing criticism for what one critic dubbed the "All-White World of Children's Books," not to mention an organized lobby in the Council on Interracial Books for Children (formed in 1965), the US toy industry was somehow managing to elude the ire of civil rights groups, despite the snail pace of its integration efforts.[13]

Among the small group of mass-market toy and doll manufacturers that had come to dominate the business through the savvy use of TV advertising, Mattel, founded in 1945 by Ruth and Elliot Handler and Harold Matson, proved to be a kind of leader when it came to both committing to Black dolls across the company's various lines and telling buyers and consumers about it. In 1962, Mattel introduced the Colored Chatty Cathy talking doll—a brown-tinted version of the popular white Chatty Cathy, released in 1960; darker complexioned versions of other popular white dolls in the line, such as Colored Chatty Baby, soon followed.[14] What was not unique, however, but rather wholly consistent with industry practice, was Mattel's failure to see the ways it helped preserve the historically unequal racial status of Black dolls, even as it pioneered their integration into the commercial mainstream. For while the company always identified the brown-tinted facsimiles of its existing white dolls by race—for example, Colored Chatty Cathy—at no point did Mattel begin assigning race to the original cream-colored dolls; there never was a White Chatty Cathy. Thus, Blackness was racialized, and whiteness was not, as if people of European descent represented the human norm and everyone else represented something other than that, therefore requiring designation. Or, to put it differently, white dolls had the (white) privilege of being just dolls.

That *Playthings* featured Colored Chatty Cathy in a short item about what Mattel had in its pipeline for the next Toy Fair was another indication of its significance; up until that point, for all the Black dolls that the industry apparently did produce, a reader of the industry's three trade publications—or, for that matter, any of the mass-circulation women's and parenting magazines where brand-name toys were marketed—would not have seen a Black doll advertised in years. It was one thing for manufacturers to integrate Black dolls into their existing lines, another to feature them in ads as part of their available inventory. In the early 1960s, most of the industry's leading companies were still not ready to do that—at least not publicly.

As the sixties went on, this gradual move toward inclusion continued—this, despite the absence of outside pressure to produce more Black dolls from groups like the Congress of Racial Equality, which launched extensive campaigns protesting stereotyped images in network TV, Hollywood, and Madison Avenue. By 1967, for instance, 25 percent of the total number of dolls listed in the Sears Christmas catalog were now Black.[15] But it was 1968 that seems to have been the turning point in the industry's previously idiosyncratic commitment to Black representation, however uncoordinated it may have been. *Toys and Novelties* editor Michael Spielman was one of the first to comment, remarking after a visit to the Toy Fair showrooms in March 1968 that "it was heartening to find that a number of toy manufacturers now realize that the flesh color of their dolls ... need not always be white."[16] Significantly, this realization led some of Mattel's competitor brands, such as Ideal and Amsco, to at last follow their rival in producing Black versions of their most commercially popular white character dolls like Baby Giggles (Ideal) and Baby Heather (Amsco), while promotional photographs in *Playthings* granted them a visual presence.[17] Reports from the following year's Toy Fair announcing the "growing crop of black dolls" signaled that the industry-wide shift that Spielman celebrated in 1968 was more than a passing fad.[18] In the opinion of *Toy & Hobby World*, the "increasing number of 'black dolls' ... portend a new, potentially lucrative sales pattern for the toy industry that is first being explored."[19] "Negro dolls," observed another reporter, "are almost a standard in most companies' lines."[20]

Industry explorations into the Black consumer market during these years also included doll figures outside the familiar genre of baby dolls. Again, Mattel was at the forefront. Starting in 1967, the company began adding Black characters to its best-selling World of Barbie collection. The initial attempt followed the old formula: 1967's Colored Francie, like Colored Chatty Cathy, was but a brown-colored replica of the white Francie doll, who in Mattel's elaborate World of Barbie narrative was Barbie's cousin.[21] The next year, however, Mattel shelved Francie—and until the creation of Black Barbie in 1980, the old "Colored doll" formula itself—and introduced Talking Christie. Christie was not just white Barbie's first Black friend but the first Black doll in the fashion-doll category to be given her own name.[22] In 1969, Mattel doubled its inventory of Black fashion dolls when it released the Julia doll, which was based on African American actress Diahann Carroll's character, a nurse, from the popular NBC-TV sitcom *Julia* (1968–71).[23] Other companies also began adding doll likenesses of Black celebrities to their collections that year and, unlike in the past, took steps to inform their buyers and competitors. As *Playthings* reported, the Juro Novelty Company, known for its toy replicas of famous white ventriloquist dolls like Charlie McCarthy, now offered a replica of the Lester doll used by the famous Black ventriloquist Willie Tyler.[24]

To be sure, the production of a particular toy has never guaranteed its popularity, much less its distribution; it was imperative that national retailers stock and advertise them. The evidence suggests some of the largest ones did. For example, the inventory of Black dolls in the Sears Wish Book jumped by 50 percent from 1968 to 1969.[25] Equally significant were changes to Sears' promotional practices in its catalogs. The first was a marked change in the visual character of the company's promotional appeals. For much of the decade, most of the pictured dolls were white, even when the same company had a Black doll available; only the item listings at the bottom of the page, or in some cases a line of small-print text next to the featured white doll, revealed to consumers that the same doll was also available in a Black version. Starting in 1968, however, the catalog began to feature more images of the Black dolls; on some pages, every white doll had a Black counterpart.[26] In addition, Sears dropped the customary practice of exclusively assigning a racial modifier to the Black version of the doll in the item listings at the bottom of the page.[27]

Sales reports in the late 1960s appeared to affirm the toy industry's decision to make Black dolls a business priority as a financially savvy one. For one manufacturer, sales of Black dolls grew 35 percent from 1967 to 1969.[28] Another company saw a 20 percent increase between 1968 and 1969.[29] Others touted their move into Black doll sales as a financial success.[30] Major commercial retailers seemed to benefit too. In 1968, J.C. Penney and Sears department stores in San Francisco sold their entire stock of Black dolls a mere week into the Christmas shopping season; of course, whether that was due to consumer enthusiasm or a limited inventory to start is hard to know.[31] Similar enthusiasm was reported across the Midwest region at the end of 1969, where sales of Black dolls "were especially strong," according to *Toys and Novelties*.[32] Moreover, commercial success appears to have broadened promotions beyond niche markets. In 1968, for example, Remco Industries limited ads for its Black dolls to the pages and airwaves of Black-audience media.[33] The following year, however, this leading television advertiser decided to invest $5 million in expanding its customer base for those dolls by featuring Black and white dolls in all its network TV spot ads, in what may have been the first racially mixed doll ads in toy history.[34]

By the time the 1960s were over, reported one newspaper, "every toy manufacturer" carried "at least one black doll in its line."[35] No wonder *Ebony* magazine announced a "new 'integration' in the toy business."[36] Nor was the apparent political significance of the Black doll trend lost on white middle-class national media, where commentators were quick to frame it as a sign of social change akin to other recent civil rights victories. A 1969 *New York Times* headline, with its allusion to the sit-ins at Woolworth's lunch counters that helped ignite a decade of protest, is illustrative: "Integration Is Gaining on Doll Counters, Too." Given the white toy industry's long history of racial exclusion and, prior to that, outright denigration, these changes were striking. After all, as recently as the 1950s, even the types of Black dolls that one might expect to be a hit—either because they represented a famous Black pop culture character, like Amosandra and Patti-Jo, or, as in the case of Ideal's

Sara Lee, the doll was promoted by Eleanor Roosevelt in her nationally syndicated column—did not attract enough interest among middle-class white consumers to justify their continued production to their manufacturers. Roughly two decades later, however, changes in the commercial, cultural, and political meanings of race in America were commingling in ways that made the production and promotion of brand-name Black dolls a profitable new industry niche.

○

Among the several new factors that underwrote the Black doll boom of the late 1960s was industry recognition of African Americans as a significant consumer class with disposable income to spend on cultural goods like toys. "Throughout the 1950s," writes the historian Jason Chambers, "a variety of sources conclusively demonstrated that blacks were rapidly improving their capacity to purchase consumer goods."[37] By the 1960s, these conclusions were reaching the toy business. Starting in 1963, the trade press began heralding a new era of Black consumer spending that toy manufacturers ignored at their own detriment, and continued to do so for the rest of the decade. *Toy & Hobby World* exhorted industry professionals to take greater notice of the "Negro Market—Rich, Complex, Neglected."[38] *Playthings* expressed similar enthusiasm in proclaiming a profitable new sales arena in the "Vast, 'Untapped' Nonwhite Market."[39] The volume and variety of Black dolls for sale by the end of the sixties make it clear that the industry was indeed becoming fully "aware of the potential buying power of the Negro market," as another trade article put it.[40]

Other changes to African Americans' relationship to consumer culture also shaped the toy industry's new interest in their purchasing power. The national mobilization of the civil rights movement in the early 1960s, resulting in the landmark 1964 Civil Rights Act and 1965 Voting Rights Act, was paralleled by unprecedented campaigns to challenge racial discrimination and stereotyping in commercial popular culture, advertising, and mass media. The Congress of Racial Equality, the NAACP, and the National Urban League were among the most prominent organizations that ratcheted up their longstanding campaigns against the absence (or merely tokenized presence) of African Americans in white-produced cultural images. This activism had a long history in the Black freedom struggle, but the use of consumerism as a civil rights strategy acquired new urgency and new opportunity in postwar society. As the historian Lizabeth Cohen has shown, participation in mass consumption was coming to define Americanness in new ways during the

1940s and 1950s; the American Dream was commodified in goods as never before.[41] In this context, many African Americans, and not only professional activists, sought recognition by and access to mainstream consumer culture in their quest for full equality.[42]

But increasingly, many Black consumers wanted more than mere inclusion in national advertising appeals for existing goods; they also wanted a marketplace of cultural goods made specifically for them, symbolic products they could use to express Black identity and pride.[43] The key catalyst for this shift was a new era of Black consciousness, the product of recent developments in African American as well as African politics. In the US context, those developments included the outsized influence of the Black liberation leader Malcolm X, whose emphasis on Black self-respect and self-determination helped inspire the emerging Black Power movement before his assassination in February 1965, as well as the late 1960s flowering of the Black Arts movement with its call for Black self-definition through literature, drama, music, and the visual arts.[44] Meanwhile, anticolonial independence struggles across Africa and the Caribbean in the 1950s and 1960s, along with the Negritude movement and popular works of liberation theory like Martinican psychoanalyst Frantz Fanon's *Wretched of the Earth* (1961), revitalized Pan-Africanist ideologies of Black uplift and unity while emphasizing, often in psychological terms, the importance of cultural self-definition to political self-determination.[45]

But if the global phenomenon of Black consciousness became increasingly politicized in late 1960s America, it was also becoming newly commercialized, explains the historian Robert E. Weems, as manufacturers rebranded everything from haircare products to soft drinks with the imagery and rhetoric of Black pride, aiming to cater to Black interests.[46] For Black families shopping for young children, of course, among the most desirable Black-oriented cultural goods were Black representational toys such as dolls. As *Ebony* explained, while a playroom full of developmentally appropriate toys was recommended by child-rearing experts for all kids, the stakes were not just different but higher when those kids were Black: "Leading educators agree that play is as important to a child as work is to an adult. It helps him develop early concepts about himself, his family, and other people. So it is only natural for a black parent to be concerned about what kind of play material his child has access to. Do the toys contribute to his physical, emotional, intellectual, spiritual and social growth, or do they stunt his development by implying that only white is beautiful and legitimate in portrayals of human beings?"[47]

That such concerns could be good for companies that prioritized Black-oriented toys was not lost on industry observers. As early as 1966, a columnist for *Toys and Novelties* was alerting readers to the fact that burgeoning Black consciousness could be a driving force for the toy business. "The negro is taking pride in being a negro," he wrote, and this pride was "finding expression in the marketplace."[48] Perhaps the more surprising element here was the extent to which white toy executives from some of the largest companies expressed their awareness of, and at times even sympathy for, these specific concerns. As one industry spokesperson understood it, Black dolls offered parents of Black children "a subtle but effective way of saying, 'There is no need to copy white features.... We know black is beautiful.'"[49] Herb Holland, vice president for marketing at Mattel, appeared to wholeheartedly agree. In his view, "every Negro girl who plays with Julia," the doll based on Diahann Carroll, "has a model with whom she can identify. Now she can be sure that she doesn't have to be blonde and blue-eyed to qualify as the all-American girl."[50] The president of Vogue Dolls, meanwhile, offered an assessment of Black parental motivations that tied the Black freedom struggle directly to consumer purchases. "Because of the civil rights movement," he told a reporter, Black people "have developed a pride in themselves and their race and prefer to have their children identify with their own race."[51] The new crop of Black dolls, then, was not just profitable according to toymakers but satisfied both the symbolic needs of Black parents and the psychological needs of Black children. Black dolls, it turned out, were apparently good for everyone.

Given the toy trade's long history of ignoring African American children, and relatively sudden move to capitalize on Black pride, it may be unsurprising to find the influential observers at *Ebony* raising doubts about the authenticity of industry concerns. "Helping Negro children develop a sense of identity and racial pride is a fringe concern to businessmen," stated the magazine.[52] Remco's white board chairman Saul Robbins, who founded the company with his cousin Isaac Heller in 1949 and made it one of the most recognizable and successful toy brands of the 1960s, agreed with that assessment. In a 1968 interview, Robbins resisted the narrative that his company's new line of TV-advertised Black dolls might be part of, as he put it, a "sociological program."[53] "What we want the trade and public to realize is that we didn't come out with these dolls as some kind of gesture," Robbins explained. "There's no tokenism in our decision.... We're not looking for thanks but for business. We're trying to fill what we believe is an unfulfilled market demand. If we're right in our assumptions, these ... Negro dolls will turn a profit, which is why we're in business."[54]

o

Whether manufacturers' articulation of Black parents' priorities reflected genuine concern or a new race-conscious business savvy, their remarkable fluency in these psychological concepts says a lot about the popularization of the midcentury social science of prejudice, and in particular what was known as the "damage thesis": the theory that racial segregation and subordination damaged Black children's psyches, severely weakening their capacity to develop what psychologists of the time called the healthy personality, in which a positive racial self-image was a core element.[55] While the "image of the African American damaged by oppression" dated back to the late nineteenth century, explains the historian Daryl Michael Scott, it "reached its apogee" in the 1950s as prominent liberal researchers in psychology and sociology focused their attention as never before on the emotional impact of living in a white-dominated, segregated society.[56] "By 1948," notes the historian Ellen Herman, "a survey of hundreds of social psychologists, sociologists, and anthropologists found that their professional experience and scientific research had convinced almost all of them that legal segregation had detrimental psychological consequences for blacks and whites alike."[57] And those detrimental consequences were widely understood to be not just bad for the social and emotional health of individuals but bad for the health of democracy itself.

As a new consensus emerged among liberal intellectuals and civil rights organizations that preventing this alleged early psychological damage to Black children, and reversing the effects where damage had been done, should be a major focus of the Black freedom movement, dolls had a conspicuous role in forging it. No one deserves more credit for that role than the Black social psychologists (and married couple) Dr. Kenneth B. Clark and Mamie Clark. During the 1940s, the Clarks performed a series of clinical studies, famously known as the "doll tests," that were to indelibly shape public understanding of racial identity formation in the US context. The objective of the tests was to understand Black children's development of racial self-concept by assessing their attitudes about Blackness and whiteness; the dolls were projective instruments, not the subject of the studies.

Using one white doll and one Black doll, both produced by the toy manufacturer Effanbee and identical except for their color, the tests' administrators asked their study groups of Black children to say which doll was the nice doll, which was the ugly one, and which was the one that most resembled them. The majority chose the white dolls as nice and the Black dolls as ugly; meanwhile, many children stated that the white dolls resembled them. In the Clarks' interpretation, these results reaffirmed the conclusion that they and other psychologists had drawn from earlier studies of racial self-understanding (including their own): that Black children internalized the racial hierarchies around them from an early age, and therefore grew up feeling inferior to whites. Thus, they argued, the Jim Crow system of segregation and inequality, with its daily indignities of second-class citizenship and exclusion, wounded and irreparably impaired Black children's personalities, leading to self-hatred.[58]

If a 1947 article in *Ebony* helped introduce the doll tests into Black popular consciousness, the NAACP brought the Clarks' work into the consciousness of the nation's highest court.[59] In the early 1950s, writes Herman, the Clarks' combined research on Black children's self-image encouraged "fresh strategies among civil rights advocates. Having reiterated that racial distinctions were morally and politically unjustifiable for decades, to little effect, activists turned to emphasizing how racism destroyed the developing personality of the black child."[60] The doll tests ended up as part of the NAACP's legal strategy to dismantle racial segregation in schools, culminating in its successful representation of the plaintiffs in the landmark 1954 Supreme Court case *Brown v. Board of Education of Topeka, Kansas*. Indeed, the most important validation of the Clarks' work came in *Brown*, when Chief Justice Earl Warren, drawing on NAACP documents, cited the Clarks' research (though not the doll tests specifically) in the famous footnote 11 of the court's ruling opinion.[61] Following the prevailing assumptions of the era's damage psychology, Justice Warren made segregation's perceived harm to the "hearts and minds" of Black children—the phrase used in the ruling—the cornerstone of his argument that the half-century-old legal doctrine of separate but equal was unconstitutional.

Thanks to Kenneth Clark's popular writings, such as his books *Prejudice and Your Child* (1955) and *Dark Ghetto* (1965), the basics of damage psychology and the story of the doll tests were broadcast well beyond academic journals and legal briefs. For many racial liberals of the time, the doll tests, with their uncomplicated message and evocation of sympathy for their child subjects, would become a particularly vivid and accessible illustration— even proof—of the debilitating psychic effects of a racist society on racial minorities. Throughout the period, Clark reiterated the original thesis. As he wrote in *Dark Ghetto*, "By the age of seven most Negro children have accepted the reality that they are, after all, dark-skinned. But the stigma remains; they have been forced to recognize themselves as inferior. Few if any Negroes ever fully lose that sense of shame and self-hatred."[62] And yet a number of established Black and white psychologists who replicated the doll studies in the 1950s and 1960s found that many Black children never felt those feelings in the first place (or not to the extent Clark believed); in these newer studies, published in professional journals, a positive racial self-image was fairly widespread among the children in the test groups.[63] Curiously, these conflicting research studies had little impact outside the field, while the original tests continued to be cited as uncontested, objective evidence of African Americans' internalized racism. Such was the appeal, it seems, of the era's psychology-driven racial liberalism, with its conviction that the transformation (and repair) of injured hearts and minds could adequately address systemic anti-Black racism and historical injustice.

Nor were prominent experts and public intellectuals like Clark the only ones to popularize the image of the damaged and ashamed Black child who, as a manifestation of internalized racism, prefers white dolls to Black ones. Hollywood had a role in it too. In fact, one of the most acclaimed films of the 1950s, German director Douglas Sirk's Academy Award–winning film *Imitation of Life* (1959), features just such a child as one of its main characters. Young Sarah Jane is Black, but on account of her light complexion she easily passes as white and prefers to do so. She is embarrassed by her darker-complexioned, identifiably Black mother. When Sarah Jane's new friend Suzie, who is white, hands her a Black doll to play with, Sarah Jane reaches for Suzie's white doll instead (see figure 3.1). As a quarrel breaks out between the two girls—Suzie is not so quick to give up her favorite doll—Sarah Jane's mother comes into the bedroom to see what's going on. "I don't want the Black one," says Sarah Jane angrily as her mother puts the Black doll back into her hands. As her mother leads her from Suzie's bedroom through the kitchen, Sarah Jane discreetly drops the doll. The camera tilts down from Sarah Jane and lingers on the doll abandoned on the tiled kitchen floor. The bedroom door closes and the scene fades out.[64]

By the 1960s, then, the core features of damage psychology had become a recognizable and accessible framework for analyzing dolls' role in reproducing and communicating ideas about race—a kind of common sense about racial identification and, even more specifically, the impact of white racism on children of color. Consider an editorial letter, presumably written by a non-Black reader, that appeared in the *Los Angeles Times* in 1967: "Last week, we were in the toy department of a large national chain store, looking at the dolls, when a Negro couple bought a white one. They had no choice. There were no brown or black dolls. When we checked the Christmas catalog put out by this chain, we found 23 pages displaying dolls of all textures and many talents—but all white. How many little [Black] girls will face another Christmas with only white dolls?"[65]

3.1. Sarah Jane (*right*) rejects the Black doll offered by her new friend Susie (*left*). From the film *Imitation of Life* (dir. Douglas Sirk, 1959).

○

It was concerns about Black children's particular experiences and particular needs that inspired Dr. James P. Comer of the Yale University Child Study Center and Dr. Alvin F. Poussaint of Harvard University to write *Black Childcare: How to Bring Up a Healthy Black Child in America*, published in 1975. Over the course of the previous decade, the two noted psychiatrists were among the only Black childhood experts to cross over into the gated white media world of child-rearing advice. If both Comer and Poussaint had initially earned their reputations through clinical research, they quickly gained national prominence in the late 1960s and early 1970s by speaking frankly to lay audiences about the social issues that white experts overwhelmingly avoided; a series of articles they wrote for *Redbook* magazine on how to raise children in a racist society was the first of its kind. Even with their elite institutional affiliations and authority in the field, however, mainstream media had a hard time placing them in a parenting industry where the experts had always been white and white middle-class children the assumed (yet unspoken) subjects.

While *Time* gave Comer and Poussaint's first book a positive review, the use of the term *Black Dr. Spocks* in the article's title seems at once complimentary and belittling—as if the larger significance of their work lay not in their new racially conscious, research-based advice but merely in the fact that they were Black.[66] After all, when Dr. Benjamin Spock, who was white, finally began to address racism and the specific experiences of nonwhite children in later editions of *Baby and Child Care*, no one called him the "White Dr. Comer" or "White Dr. Poussaint." But they certainly could have, given these two experts' distinctive contributions to child development and the psychology of race.

The first mainstream advice book to treat Black child-rearing as its own distinct field, *Black Childcare* put forward a simple premise: that Black children's psychic needs were different from white children's. The era's outspoken celebration of racial pride colored the book's advice from the start. "This book," wrote Comer and Poussaint in the introduction, "is for all people who are involved in the important job of helping black children develop in a healthy way . . . beautiful and black."[67] Reflecting that orientation, one of the first questions the experts explored was how parents might most effectively "promote racial pride in [their] infants"; as they told parents, "Race is a subject you should discuss with your child in an easy and natural way."[68] Yet it took more than a conversation to develop a positive racial identity. Dolls, as communicators of parental values, could aid that process. "Providing your infant with black dolls . . . as well as white ones helps to make black, brown, and white normal—like the real world," they advised.[69] If an exclusively white doll collection taught children that Black Americans were not equal members of society, the existence of Black dolls conveyed their rightful place. Of course, the belief that Black dolls were positive reinforcements of racial identification had an earlier history in the cultural nationalism of the Garveyite movement and the New Negro ideology of uplift. Now, in a new era of Black pride rhetoric and imagery in mainstream culture, these ideas would come with the authority of Black scientific experts, repackaged in the recognizable frameworks of social psychology. In that sense, when *Ebony*'s 1968 article stated that Black dolls "are of major importance to parents sensitive to positive black consciousness," it would have hardly been news to African American readers. What was less predictable—especially given manufacturers' comments about racial self-image, and despite the widespread sentiment that, to quote one toymaker, Black dolls' "primary appeal is to the child in the Negro community"—was the extent to which Black dolls were increasingly understood to be of major importance to those concerned with the psychological needs of white children.[70]

Among them was an interracial group of Christian activists in the Southern California Synod of the liberal United Presbyterian Church (UP-CUSA), who in the late sixties made Black dolls part of their new program for anti-racist education. In April 1968, the same month Martin Luther King Jr. was assassinated, Hughston R. Payton and Lynne Reade of the Synod's Committee on Religion and Race and Committee on Christian Education published a booklet titled *You, the Church, and Race: A Study/Action Guide on White Racism*, one piece of a greater "Social Awareness Project" underway, and targeted to a white audience.[71] As its title suggests, project leaders were interested in not only informing white Americans about racism; they also wanted to encourage white readers to take concrete action to combat racism in their communities. In addition to making suggestions for what the guide called group-based "social change projects," under the heading "IN YOUR PERSONAL LIFE" the authors also listed a series of "actions you may take to promote better racial understanding in an individual way." Anticipating Comer and Poussaint, between their suggestions to purchase a subscription to *Ebony* and read Kenneth B. Clark's *Prejudice and Your Child* was a call to buy a Black doll: "If you have young children or grandchildren, supplement their interracial experiences by giving them a black baby doll to love." Showing their awareness of the commercial obstacles to finding one, they added, "You may have to ask a store to order a black doll for you if you live in a segregated area."[72] In May of the same year, UPCUSA activists decided that individual orders of Black dolls, while benefiting the child whose parents made the request, did little to change the larger problem: retailers that didn't buy Black dolls or, when they did have them in stock, did not actively display them as they did their white dolls. These practices not only curbed Black doll sales but also gave the false impression that manufacturers did not produce them, which, of course, was no longer the case. So, in Los Angeles and New York City, and probably other cities as well, participants in UPCUSA anti-racism initiatives went beyond just advocating consumption by organizing drives to get retailers in white neighborhoods to prominently display Black dolls in store windows.[73] After all, if white families were going to buy these toys, making a purchase that added human diversity to their child's playthings and helped demonstrate the viability of the Black doll market to an uncertain industry, they needed to know their local stores carried them.

The UPCUSA's Black doll initiative was just one manifestation of the enduring significance of another hallmark of the midcentury psychological approach to racial problems: contact theory. As the historian Christopher W. Schmidt explains, contact theory was based on "the idea that increased interaction between diverse groups would lead to improved inter-group relations. . . . Contact theory assumed that prejudice was produced by ignorance and that the best remedy was exposure and education."[74] In short, Black people's perceived psychological deficit could be fixed by contact with white people, while white racial tolerance could be fostered through contact with Black people. Thus, the notion of the damaged Black psyche had a coun-terpart, in which white supremacy damaged white psyches too.

These ideas had important roots in the intercultural movement of the interwar years, in which progressive activists from all racial backgrounds in the overlapping arenas of social work, education, and child guidance came together, as the historian Jonna Perillo has put it, "to heal the damaged black psyche while improving the psychological health of white America."[75] Thanks to a spate of popular psychologically oriented analyses of US racism, beginning with Swedish economist Gunnar Myrdal's *An American Dilemma* (1944), by the 1960s the idea that, for US race relations to improve, even white children needed psychological rehabilitation had become an accepted feature of anti-racist advocacy.[76] So it was not surprising when at the 1960 White House Conference on Children, the National Urban League's Lester B. Granger lamented society's failure "to understand the irreparable damage inflicted by racial segregation not only upon the personalities of colored young people . . . but also upon the children of those very ones who have established the aggressive pattern, who fight to retain racial discrimination."[77]

A decade later, child-rearing experts were now publicizing the importance of Black dolls to healthy white childhoods in mainstream media. Comer and Poussaint led the way in a 1972 column in *Redbook* magazine titled "What White Parents Should Know about Children and Prejudice." Speaking di-rectly to white parents, they argued that white children needed Black dolls as much as Black children did. "Providing your [white] child with Black and white dolls helps them understand at the very earliest age that ours is a multiethnic society."[78] And dolls did more than reflect America's racial demographics and build Black children's self-esteem; they also helped white parents "raise children to be free from bias."[79] Without a racially diverse toy box, white children's de-velopment of tolerance—a requisite of the healthy personality—might be at risk. Limited evidence of white toy buying during these years suggests many white parents were heeding Comer and Poussaint's advice. As early as 1969, *Playthings* reported that in Los Angeles, "one big store claimed [that sales of] Negro dolls have rocketed, and [the store] isn't located in a predominantly Negro community."[80] Meanwhile, according to *Toys and Novelties*, "many buy-ers [in Midwest cities] said they were selling almost as well in predominantly white areas as in predominantly black areas."[81] Few manufacturers published demographic data on consumer buying, yet according to one company that produced and distributed Black dolls to a national market, white consumers accounted for 80 percent of sales between 1968 and 1973.[82]

In an interview, Remco's Saul Robbins suggested that some white parents did purchase Black dolls to "teach tolerance," as Comer and Poussaint advised.[83] Of course, the efficacy of interracial contact—at least, according to contact theory—depended on more than just having white children interact with representations of Black children. And yet the belief that dolls could do some part of this important cultural work at all is significant. Among other things, it reflected the growing conviction among racial progressives that the consumer culture itself was not one of the problems—as it had been for earlier generations of consumer critics, including Martin Luther King Jr.—so much as the relative omission of Black representations from it. With the right dolls on the shelves, the expanding commercial culture of childhood promised new ways to build the interracialists' vision of social harmony, one purchase at a time.[84]

And so, for different reasons and with apparently little coordination, the nation's white-owned doll companies came to recognize that the combination of Black purchasing power, Black pride, and the advancing momentum of the Black freedom movement demanded major changes in the industry's representational practices. "Anybody who's in dolls has to be thinking about Negro dolls, if he's awake," quipped Lionel Weintraub, president of Ideal Toys, in 1969.[85] But the question of how even the most awake were supposed to successfully—and respectfully—translate the era's Black freedom yearnings into material form was not easily resolved.

The most formidable and politically fraught challenge of the new Black doll era was the need to construct Black features without falling into the terrain of racial stereotype and essentialism. One of the most successful companies of the 1960s thought its staff could solve that challenge and make it profitable. As Black Americans demanded not only political and economic equality but also an end to stereotypical media characterization, the executive leadership at Remco Industries saw a potential market for a line of Black dolls with facial features that distinguished them from the company's existing white dolls. The term Remco would use to describe such a Black doll, which soon became part of industry vocabulary for all dolls of color designed along racially distinctive lines, was "ethnically correct."[86]

The industrial process by which a doll was made to "look" Black was fairly standardized in the mass-market toy industry of the 1950s and 1960s. "Although nonwhite dolls have been on the market for some time," noted one reporter in 1968, "these have been no different from their white counterparts except for their tinted plastic resins used to achieve desired skin tone."[87] Indeed, the nation's largest doll manufacturers gave virtually no attention to unique, recognizable, or even stereotypical signifiers of Blackness.[88] As *Ebony* sharply described the customary practice, "'colored' dolls were exactly that: dolls cast in the same mold as the company's white dolls, but with a brown tint added."[89] This practice is why Mattel's new brown-tinted Chatty Cathy simply got the name Colored Chatty Cathy, and why *Playthings* described Amsco's new brown-tinted Baby Heather Doll as a "colored version" of the white one.[90]

Now, the concept of a uniquely designed commercial Black doll, one that aimed to signify Blackness beyond altering color, was not entirely new. In fact, producing a Black doll that, in the social science–inflected parlance of an earlier era, appeared "anthropologically true" was the original impetus behind Sara Lee Creech's creation of the Sara Lee doll for Ideal Toys, back in 1951; Creech had even enlisted Sheila Burlingame, a white artist known for her representations of people of color, to design the mold.[91] As mentioned previously, that doll had a disappointingly short commercial life span, though it is unclear whether its racially unique design was a factor. Now, fifteen years later, Remco threw down the gauntlet, hoping to succeed where its competitor Ideal had not: designing, manufacturing, and marketing a specialized Black doll that would not only appeal to Black children and their parents but also achieve financial viability in the American mass market.

○

In 1966, a toy industry consultant insisted to readers of *Toy & Hobby World* that "the Negro, no less than the whites, must be able to 'identify' if he is to be influenced to buy. . . . He has racial pride, more than ever before, and he is not content to be an *imitation* white."[92] Remco's new line of four Black dolls, which the company began to develop that year, pursued the implications of this interpretation of Black consumer desire to the letter. First, Remco's executive leadership recognized that while Black Americans wanted the inclusion of Black images in commercial popular culture, they also wanted racial authenticity in these representations. As Remco's Saul Robbins put it in an interview about the new doll line, "the key to the success of just about any toy item is the degree of its realism."[93] With that in mind, Remco set out to code realistic Blackness and challenge the imitative tradition of "colored versions" with what it announced as "the first truly authentic colored dolls."[94]

The company's initial steps toward that objective reflected an unusually thoughtful consideration for each stage of the doll development process, an acknowledgment that creating these dolls would have to be different from past efforts. The first and most significant was the hiring of the African American artist Annuel McBurrows to design the new doll line and oversee the process.[95] It was an unusual move for a large company with in-house product designers: McBurrows was an industry outsider, in his late twenties, who had been exhibiting his own portraits of Black youth in New York City galleries when he spotted Remco's job posting in the *New York Times* and recognized his unique qualifications.[96] So did Remco. Yet given the timing of the company's entry into this largely uncharted territory of doll design, with the Black Arts Movement's calls for Black cultural self-definition reverberating across American life, the decision to hire not only a Black artist but one who specialized in depicting young Black subjects seems particularly shrewd and even forward-thinking for the era. Remco also went ahead and created a separate division within its existing manufacturing outfit to produce the new Black dolls—an industry first—and gave McBurrows the job of supervisor.[97] While the move reflected Remco's serious financial investment in the project, not to mention its faith in McBurrows, the separation of production by race was an unfortunate irony.

So what did "truly authentic colored dolls" mean for McBurrows and Remco? It meant, for instance, that Tippy Tumbles, one of the four uniquely designed Black dolls introduced in 1968, was distinguished not only by her brown color (she had the same rooted, straight synthetic hair and chin-length style of the white Tippy Tumbles); she also had what *Ebony*, in an article on the new line, described as "typically Negroid features"—a slightly broader nose, higher cheekbones, and fuller lips than the company's white doll of the same name (see figure 3.2).[98] Not since Ideal Toy Company's 1951 Sara Lee had a Black-audience publication praised a Black doll for its positive representation. In the pages of *Playthings*, McBurrows explained his approach to authenticity: "The faces are representative of the way I 'see' Negro children. They're an expression of my own feeling."[99]

It does not seem unreasonable that some white toymakers, including the ones committed to racial equality and Black children's healthy development, might have bristled at Remco's notion of a distinctive Black doll. The 1960s were, after all, an era when mainstream demands for racial integration favored "color-blind" conceptions of equal access and opportunity. "Authentic" Black dolls may have appealed to some Black consumers, but their standardized and essentialized "Negroid" features also ran the risk of reproducing the old racial stereotypes. For Remco, it appears to have been a calculated risk. That the company recognized the potential for racial controversy over such design choices is suggested by its extensive efforts to court African American

3.2. Remco Industries' Tippy Tumbles doll (1968) was one of four new "ethnically correct" Black dolls designed by Annuel McBurrows. Press photograph, December 23, 1968. Author's collection.

consumers through a novel marketing strategy, one that stressed not only the dolls' realism but also the company's sympathy for Black children in light of their exclusion from American culture.

A full-page advertisement that ran in *Ebony* in October 1968 is illustrative. Claiming to have produced "the first truly authentic, realistic group of dolls for your child. And it's about time," Remco not only celebrated its dolls as racially groundbreaking; it also acknowledged the industry's (and its own) shamefully late inclusion of African Americans in its representations of US society.[100] Moreover, in explaining to consumers that its new line had been produced "in answer to a crying need"—the ad's header, in large type—Remco mobilized what literary scholar James Kincaid has identified as one of the most evocative iterations of childhood innocence: the figure of the unhappy child. As Kincaid writes, "an unhappy child was and is unnatural, an indictment of somebody: parent, institution, nation."[101] While ostensibly meant to signal the company's sympathy for Black children deprived of dolls that looked like them (and maybe even to critique the competitors whose lack of Black dolls had made those children cry), it is not hard to see how the ad worked rhetorically on another level as an indictment of the nation itself. This was especially resonant given the centrality of Black children (and adult concerns about their well-being) to the civil rights movement over the previous decade: the *Brown v. Board* decision's emphasis on damage to children's "hearts and minds," the outcry over the 1955 lynching of fourteen-year-old Emmett Till, the violent 1957 backlash to the Little Rock Nine at Central High School, the Birmingham Children's Crusade against Bull Connor's militarized police forces in 1963, and the white terrorist bombing that killed four young Black girls at the Sixteenth Street Baptist Church later that same year.[102] Where Remco arguably erred in its depiction of vulnerable, tearful Black children was the extent to which the recent civil rights surge was defined not by tears but rather by the emotional courage, determination, and often joyful struggle of Black youth, who were often singing, not crying, as they filled up the jails in Birmingham. This is not to deny or minimize the genuine fear and pain exacted on these young people by police dogs, fire hoses, and police batons but rather to say that by emphasizing tears, Remco adopted the prevailing imagery of the damage theory. In this narrative, Remco's dolls were tools to help repair a broken child.

If Remco's ad contended that Black girls deserved dolls that resembled them, it stopped short of suggesting that they should only play with toys representing Black people. "If your daughter wants to play with a little blond-haired, blue-eyed doll, that's fine," Remco told parents, but "we think she deserves a choice. Why shouldn't she have a little brown-eyed image of herself for her very own?"[103] With many intellectuals and critics apt to interpret such affection for a white doll as a symbol of internalization of white cultural ideals, as a sign of what psychologists called racial self-hatred, Remco's statement that a Black child ought to make her own toy choices seems not only somewhat unexpected but even a bit radical for the moment. For it suggested that Black children deserved a right long afforded exclusively to white children: to be viewed as an innocent child, to have a choice in one's playthings and autonomy in one's play.[104]

It is perhaps little surprise that the toymakers at Remco, entering the realm of Black media to make a race-based consumer appeal, took other conspicuous steps to publicly shore up the company's credentials. As if anticipating criticism from those who, in the context of late 1960s battles over cultural representation, may well have viewed the white-owned firm as lacking in authority to define Black images, Remco featured a headshot of Annuel McBurrows not only in its print ads but also on the doll box itself.[105] The use of McBurrows in this way suggests the company's desire to legitimate its efforts toward authenticity, indicating to consumers that this potentially controversial representation of Black difference by a white corporate outsider had been sanctioned by a racial insider. In other words, McBurrows conferred on Remco the cultural authority necessary to produce Black dolls in good faith with Black consumers. Of course, the picture of McBurrows also showed consumers that Remco's commitment to racial equality could be seen in its staffing too, including in design and supervisory positions.

When Remco's promotional campaign for the Black doll line came to the pages of *Playthings* in 1969, the company suggested it had a unique understanding of the Black doll consumer and, more specifically, had developed her trust. Backhandedly criticizing its rivals' tendency to signify racial difference solely through color, the 1969 advertisement, once again picturing McBurrows, assured prospective toy buyers, "We've learned that Negroes don't take kindly to imitations. We don't blame them. A white doll painted black is just that" (see figure 3.3).[106] Through its advertising rhetoric and visual strategies, Remco created a standard of authenticity for Black dolls that no established business had ever created for white dolls. Seizing on the increasingly militant language of civil rights demands, the company urged retail buyers not to "settle for less in black dolls."[107] In this analysis, the more authentic the portrayal of Blackness, the more the dolls represented to Black consumers a symbolic refusal to "settle" for racial inequality in all forms, political as well as cultural. As the ad affirmed, such efforts had worked for Remco: "Look to

We're spending 5½ million dollars on color TV this year.

We've learned that Negroes don't take kindly to imitations. We don't blame them. A white doll painted black is just that. That's why Remco is so successful. Annuel McBurrows, who designed our line of authentic replicas of Negro babies, was deluged with fan mail. And we're mighty proud of our dolls, too.

Our dolls were publicized last fall on Johnny Carson. The Merv Griffin Show. Huntley-Brinkley. Everywhere. And our ad in Ebony scored highest read of all the ads in the October issue according to the Starch Readership Report. Ebony gave us added publicity in a 5-page editorial devoted to our "step forward" with Negro dolls. It was a great season.

It will be bigger this year. With 5½ million to help us tell our story to even more people. There'll be a Remco black doll on every Remco Doll commercial we run. *Every* commercial. No other doll manufacturer is doing this.

So don't settle for less in black dolls. Look to Remco. Like millions of Negroes. And put your doll business in the black. In more ways than one.

Remco Industries
200 Fifth Avenue
New York, N.Y. 10010
(212) AL 5-2500

REMCO

Designer Annuel McBurrows

1/ Brown-Eye Tumbling Tomboy 2/ Brown-Eye Baby Know-It-All 3/ Brown-Eye Tippy Tumbles 4/ Brown-Eye Baby Grow-A-Tooth 5/ Brown-Eye Bunny Baby 6/ Brown-Eye Tina 7/ Brown-Eye Billy 8/ Li'l Winking Winny

© 1969 Remco Industries, Inc., Cape May St., Harrison, N.J.

3.3. Remco tells readers of *Playthings* not to "settle for less in black dolls." Advertisement from *Playthings*, June 1969. Courtesy of Department of Science and Wellness, Free Library of Philadelphia, Philadelphia, PA.

Remco. Like millions of Negroes. And put your doll business in the Black. In more ways than one."[108] Nor was McBurrows's appealing design the only reason the new Black dolls were, according to the ad, uniquely capable of having that outsized impact on sales. The other reason was that, unlike its competitors, Remco would be racially integrating its national television promotions: "There'll be a Remco black doll on every Remco Doll commercial we run. *Every* commercial. No other doll manufacturer is doing this."[109]

All the while, Saul Robbins and others in Remco's management continued to deny any political motivation or sympathies in their pioneering development of Black toys, attributing the move to market considerations.[110] Yet their advertising's expressed concern for African American children and obvious support for the cause of Black equality indicated that while Robbins and his company could deny ideological intent, they could not escape ideology. Whatever the motivations, Remco had identified a new approach to the Black doll market, an approach that recognized the desire of African Americans to be represented respectfully in commercial culture and to express their cultural identities through consumer goods. Through a complex interaction with consumers and the political currents of the moment, Remco helped construct the racially conscious Black consumer public—and more precisely, the racially conscious Black parent consumer—as a vital market niche for the toy business.

Thus, Remco not only catalyzed a new era of Black-typed dolls; it also created another new "market for virtue" within the toy business, as the marketers of Lionel Toy Corporation had done a few years earlier in response to the anti–war toy campaigns. If Remco sold a unique kind of Black doll, in its 1968 ad it also branded itself as an ally in the Black struggle for equality. The issue of racial representation—how Black people appeared as dolls—was obviously important to manufacturers because the commercial appeal of the doll partly depended on it. But it was not the only priority; equally important was the need to establish what one might call white racial virtue: how a white-owned company in the business of Black representation appeared to Black consumers, in terms of its politics rather than its products. Projecting its heightened racial consciousness appears to have been an effective marketing appeal for Remco. The year 1968 proved to be a record one for the company as sales swelled by 37 percent, generating a net profit increase of more than 87 percent.[111] In 1969, buoyed by this success and the positive response to Tippy Tumbles and the other new Black dolls, the company expanded the ethnically correct line to eight different Black dolls, each of them designed by McBurrows and newly marketed as part of the so-called Brown Eye line in catalogs and on boxes.[112] While Remco may have adopted the term *Brown Eye* for the Black dolls to help toy dealers distinguish between the Black and white versions of the various named dolls when placing their orders, in doing so the company arguably took a step backward into the industry's less racially progressive past. By leaving the white versions without a racial designation—for example, the company advertised the brown-complexioned Polly Puff as Brown-Eye Polly Puff, but the cream-colored, blue-eyed one was simply Polly Puff—it had in a sense reproduced the old hierarchy where white dolls were just dolls and the Black ones "colored versions" of them.[113]

Remco's virtuous vision of ethnically correct Black doll manufacturing pointed to new possibilities for racial signification in toys. It also promised a new set of strategies for brand differentiation in a field growing crowded. Media coverage of Remco's ethnically correct line, which included *Ebony*, the *Wall Street Journal*, and countless regional newspapers (thanks to a syndicated article from the Newspaper Enterprise Association), along with Remco's pointed critique of its own industry in the trade press, appeared to have an immediate impact on competitors. Already by 1969, other major manufacturers were replacing their brown-tinted white dolls with specially sculpted Black dolls. Horsman's "expanded line of Black dolls" for the 1969 Toy Fair, for instance, was marked by "new styling, including ethnically correct physical features," according to an item in the trade press.[114] Likewise, a 1970 report on the Black doll trend in *Today's Health* magazine noted a "move in the direction of authenticity."[115]

Yet executing authenticity, it turned out, was not a simple matter. The move toward ethnically correct design required extra care, but even the most careful attempts to make that move were fraught with tension from the start, threatening to fall into the "wrong" side of the history of racial representation. After all, it was not that long ago—certainly in the lifetime of many toy-industry professionals—when most commercially available toys representing Black people were little more than racist artifacts that played on demeaning anti-Black stereotypes. No major business wanted to offend potential consumers with its attempts to portray authentic Black features, and there was no industry playbook to reference for a business hoping to be on the right side. Remco's extensive narrative of its doll production suggests it recognized as much: that even a well-intentioned effort toward "positive" racialization of a Black doll required a lot of preparation, development, and explanation, not to mention new staff, to avoid the commercially exploitative practices of the past.

o

By the early 1970s, the toymakers at Fisher-Price appeared to know all this as they set out to produce a Black doll as part of the company's first-ever line of dolls. Introduced to the marketplace in 1974, the Fisher-Price Dolls, as the line was called, included six different "little girl" dolls with plush bodies, hard molded plastic heads, and rooted hair.[116] Each of the dolls had its own name and what the company described as "a personality all its own"; that is, each had an individually designed face, distinctive hair, and unique clothing.[117] For the five of the six dolls who were racially white, the design process proceeded rather unremarkably. Yet the development of the one nonwhite doll in the group, a Black doll that the company named Elizabeth, would prove to be more complicated.

Founded in 1930, Fisher-Price had pioneered the mainstream middle-class market for infant and early childhood playthings, often known as preschool toys. It did this in two ways: by invoking child development theory as the cornerstone of its toymaking philosophy; and by emphasizing its extensive toy research and development process, which included testing in its in-house laboratory in East Aurora, New York. More than most national toy manufacturers of the time, then, Fisher-Price prided itself on a level of quality, supposed cognitive benefits, and, in industry parlance, the production of "play value"—the capacity of a toy to keep a child's interest and invite a range of uses.[118] With the development of the Elizabeth doll, the Fisher-Price tradition of research-driven commercial success was put to the test in a whole new way. The decision to include a Black doll in the proposed new line was shaped by the ongoing reverberations of the 1960s Black liberation struggle. The cultural changes unleashed by the civil rights, Black Arts, and Black Power movements had altered not only popular representations of Black people but also commercial understandings of what one might call the responsibilities of representation where images of Black Americans were concerned. While Black dolls were widely understood by the early 1970s as good business because there was now a profitable market for them, by the time Fisher-Price came to the doll category it was not only profitability that made Black representations a business imperative but also a new moral commitment to Black inclusion.

Karen Donner joined the company's doll department as a staff designer in 1973 and immediately began working on the new line with a small team of three, none of them Black, led by veteran doll designer Annette Shelley. As Donner recalled, at that time "you couldn't do a line of dolls and not have a Black doll. That would be horrible. Totally insensitive."[119] As for other dolls of color, however, they were not even a consideration—at Fisher-Price or elsewhere in the industry. Yet as we saw with Remco, signifying race in a Black doll in an era when brown tinting was understood as insufficient or worse was easier said than done. Fisher-Price dollmakers could no longer not make a Black doll, but having never made one before, they were less assured than usual in planning for production.

Consider the issue of head molds. For the white dolls, so long as the faces were pale and freckled, and the hair long and straight enough to be combed into multiple styles, there were probably few white consumers apt to raise questions about the dolls' ethnic or racial accuracy. By contrast, the racialized design of Black dolls carried different cultural and political weight. As *Ebony* suggested in its enthusiastic reporting on the Remco line, many parents of Black children wanted more than just the old white dolls painted brown. To be sure, these parents, like everyone else, wanted a soft doll that a child would want to hold and snuggle. But in a newly race-conscious doll market where coded "Black" features were no longer indistinguishable from company to company, the specifications of those features—especially skin color, facial structure, and hairstyle, which included texture—mattered.

Elizabeth's Blackness, unlike the other dolls' whiteness, would be new and uncertain terrain for Fisher-Price. People of color had long been a rarity in Fisher-Price's other representational toy lines. Starting in the mid-1960s, the popular Play Family line of miniature human figures and plastic social environments, such as a hospital, school, airport, and merry-go-round, began scattering token Black figures—light-brown-colored versions of the white ones—in some of the sets. But the original Play Family set, which included a conventional nuclear family along with grandmother and grandfather figures, was still only available in white versions.[120] No wonder special steps were taken at all phases of Elizabeth's development. First, the company hired an outside consulting firm to conduct focus-group tests exclusively for Elizabeth, with the hope of better understanding the combination of features that produced an attractive Black doll in the eyes of the people they presumed would be the doll's main consumers: Black mothers of young Black children. Focus-group tests are just one type of market research and, in some respects, the most in-depth and reliable. What distinguishes them from other market research is that they are qualitative. Administrators of the groups bring together people from a particular consumer demographic or a broad mix and then initiate conversations about their product interests and desires.

Two key findings emerged from the Elizabeth focus-group tests, all of which—there was more than one, and probably several—took place in midwestern cities, which were viewed by marketers as good barometers of popular tastes. First, the Black women who participated not only wanted the dolls to be brown in color but also made it very clear that a head mold that did not have recognizably Black facial features that distinguished it from the white dolls—in short, that was not ethnically correct—would be insulting. Second, their preference was for a doll with sufficiently long and straight rooted hair that could be combed and fashioned by a child into the greatest variety of styles.[121] The focus testing was soon followed by a second round of market research, albeit of a different kind. This time, instead of directed interviews with Black mothers, Fisher-Price marketers visited shopping malls (likely in the same midwestern cities). To put this in context, it was not unusual for a company like Fisher-Price to employ more than one type of market-research tool; it was this kind of multipronged strategy for getting to know its potential consumers that helped the company's sales swell six-fold since the mid-1960s.[122]

Setting up tables with a selection of different Elizabeth doll models—no actual head molds would be made until every element of design was finalized—they surveyed hundreds of women shoppers who walked by about which Black doll heads, hair, and color were most appealing, along with questions about pricing. It is unclear how many prototypes were used, but one of the main features that differentiated them, recalled Donner, was the texture and style of each model's rooted nylon hair. One was very short, curly, and matted, with a coarse texture; another was long and tied into pigtails, and had the conventionally thin Saran-hair texture of most mass-market doll hair. Upon its return from the malls, the marketing team presented some curious and, somewhat confusingly for the people who had to make the doll, discrepant discoveries. As Donner remembered the findings, the women who were surveyed at the mall—it was not clear if all or most of them were Black—had tended to prefer the Elizabeth model with the very short, curly hairstyle when asked to make a choice.[123]

Since the early 1960s, growing numbers of Black women had been making hair an important and often controversial signifier of Black female political identity—a means to challenge white-defined beauty norms and show their solidarity, often couched in the terms of African sisterhood, with the worldwide movement for Black liberation.[124] By the time Fisher-Price came to the doll business, natural styles like the Afro might still contain those meanings for many women, but they also had become mainstream commercial styles, embraced by the fashion and advertising industries with little reference to their Black consciousness and Black feminist roots.[125] Women's magazines of the time—from those that until recently featured only white women, such as *Harper's Bazaar*, to a Black-oriented glossy like *Ebony*—indicate a clear preference for natural over other styles that some perceived (negatively) as more conventionally "white." As Donner recalled, these perceptions were very much on the minds of her supervisors as they interpreted the discrepancy between the two sets of market-research data regarding Elizabeth's hair. "That was probably a tough decision for them," Donner said.[126] For while they wanted, as with all Fisher-Price products, to create the doll with the most play value—which was what mattered most to the Black mothers in the focus groups—they also wanted to reflect the most mainstream (and according to the women at the mall, preferred) hairstyle for Black girls, especially given the political meanings that many of these women assigned to it. Ultimately, the decision was made to move forward with a short-haired Elizabeth.

At last, the doll department went to work. Six head molds were sculpted and cast. Six distinct hair components were developed and rooted into the mold. Six different outfits were sewn. Audrey was given red hair and freckles. Mary had blond pigtails and a button nose. Baby Ann appeared to be pouting. Jenny wore shoulder-length hair and bangs and Natalie a bonneted bob. Beyond these distinguishing features, these five were all racially coded to look white. The color of their plastic heads was a creamy pinkish-white hue. Their straight hair, although differently styled and differently colored, also invoked European ancestry. Elizabeth, by contrast, was undeniably marked as Black, and not only by the tinting that made her vinyl skin brown. Her head mold, for example, is at first glance quite similar to that of Baby Ann—the only white doll in the group that actually has a realistically simulated nose with nostrils and not just a small nub to represent a nose.[127] Yet close comparison of the two dolls demonstrates that the Fisher-Price team followed the focus groups' guidance on the issue of ethnically correct facial features. For instance, adopting what had become the most common stereotypical markers of African American appearance in the doll industry, Elizabeth's nose was slightly broader than Baby Ann's; her lips were fuller in their rosebud shape; and her cheekbones were more defined. But perhaps the most visible and material difference that set her apart from the others was her hair. Unlike the other dolls, Elizabeth's rooted hair was not long and stringy but thick and matted. If the other dolls' hair ranged from shoulder length (Jenny) to just below the ears (Baby Ann), Elizabeth's was not more than an inch above the scalp all around, probably shorter in length than any white doll's hairstyle had ever been. The Fisher-Price design team had closely followed their directives from marketing (see figure 3.4).[128]

3.4. Elizabeth doll (1974), Fisher-Price Toys. Author's collection.

The disproportionate level of energy expended on behalf of Elizabeth was apparently not matched by consumer desire. After the Fisher-Price Dolls line had been on the market for some time, Donner learned that while Jenny and the other four white dolls had sold well, Elizabeth had not.[129] The reasons for this are hard to pin down with any precision. Of course, the apparent lack of consumer interest may have had little to do with the doll itself. One possible structural explanation is that the market simply had no room for another Black doll of Elizabeth's size and target consumer. Recall that all the major doll manufacturers had at least one Black doll by this time, and most large retailers carried them. Moreover, this expanded assortment of Black dolls had for several years included Black versions of the industry's best-selling TV-advertised toys, such as Kenner's Baby Alive and Mattel's Tender Love collections. Fisher-Price designers had actively sought to manufacture a Black doll that would not traffic in racial stereotypes and would have broad appeal to little girls and their parents. Yet it appears the Fisher-Price staff behind the new line's promotion could not avoid racialized thinking either. Indeed, some of the materials that Fisher-Price issued to trade publications and retailers are populated with Black stereotypes and presumptions about racial difference and preferences that the designers had hoped to avert.

Consider, for example, the pages of the 1974 catalog that featured the new dolls. At the top of one page are six individual wallet-size pictures, each of a child playing with a different doll. While the white dolls are being cuddled exclusively by white girls, Elizabeth is in the hands of a young African American girl.[130] For industry toy buyers viewing the catalog, the message was clear: the Elizabeth doll was the line's product for Black children, while the other dolls were catered to the white majority. These images did not dictate inventory, of course; but given that retailers take important cues from the manufacturer's merchandising materials, one can imagine how such a message might shape the market. If a store had a limited Black clientele, a retailer might choose not to buy many, or any, Elizabeth dolls. Since white consumers purchased many Black dolls during these years, Fisher-Price's race-typed merchandising of the dolls may have worked against Elizabeth's commercial success. In this case, Fisher-Price toymakers had not done their research, instead making (incorrect) assumptions about who would and wouldn't want a Black doll. Moreover, these same images were reproduced on the back of the doll boxes, conveying a clear sense of what Fisher-Price, known as a company attentive to healthy child development, defined as racially normative play.[131] For parents of white children shopping for a Black doll, or open to buying one if their child asked for it, Fisher-Price's messaging about who should play with which doll may have stopped them or made them question its appropriateness.

Race-based distinctions that worked to mark Elizabeth as different from the rest of the group were also evident in promotions that ran in the trade press. The differentiated marketing of the individual dolls in *Playthings* provides a case in point. When the Elizabeth doll appeared in a *Playthings* photo item, her racial identity was the defining feature of the promotion. "Black is Beautiful," proclaimed the heading, while the doll was named "Elizabeth the Soul Sister" in an attempt to exploit Black pride's commercial appeal.[132] Two months later, when the white Natalie doll appeared in *Playthings* in a similar style of ad, the copy next to the image simply gave her name, with no discussion of her perceived ethnic heritage or racial consciousness.[133] By marking Elizabeth as Black through the slogans and stereotypes of "soul" and leaving Natalie racially unmarked, Fisher-Price effectively placed the Black and white dolls into separate categories. As such, it replicated the industry's old division of dolls in which the white doll retained freedom from racial categorization, defined as simply a "doll," while the Black doll was defined as the racial imitation. Thus, Fisher-Price marketers were unable to escape, and arguably gave credence to, the powerful racial myth that Elizabeth was supposed to help break down, a myth that naturalized whiteness and painted Blackness as "other."

It is impossible to know whether these instances of Elizabeth's racialization contributed to the doll's lower sales compared to the other dolls. It may even be that the use of Black consciousness slogans like "Black is beautiful" and "soul sister" actually *helped* sell more dolls to store buyers and consumers than if Fisher-Price had avoided these special marketing frames. Yet inside the company, recalled Donner, dollmakers had a different explanation for Elizabeth's relative unpopularity: her hair.[134] According to this theory, the natural style that the company believed to be both the more Black-conscious and more mainstream aesthetic—supported by the mall research and popular among Black women but, according to the focus group participants, less fun to play with—had led the design team to produce an undesirable doll in the eyes of the very Black mothers and children for whom it was created. When it came to a child's play with hairstyling, Elizabeth's hair was fairly limited compared to the others' hair, a limitation that designers acknowledged at the time. In reality, of course, women and men with tight curls have always styled it in numerous ways. But in doll form, Elizabeth's version of Black hair texture and style resisted restyling, combing, or picking. While her hair might have resembled the hair of many Black girls, it also might have diminished the doll's appeal to children, Black or otherwise. Taking steps to include a consumer group whose voices had long been ignored, Fisher-Price had reached out to Black mothers to learn what they wanted for their children and what they thought those children would most enjoy. Yet, in the end, company leaders overrode these women's expertise and experience as Black parents—and, at one time, as Black girls—to impose what they believed was a better, more racially sensitive vision. The Fisher-Price Dolls were not created equal.

o

In the late 1960s and early 1970s, white toy-industry professionals finally began asking themselves, and in rare cases Black consumers, how Black Americans wanted to be depicted in dolls. Whether Black parents and children found their answers satisfying is hard to interpret, but the evidence suggests rather mixed success. While Remco's ethnically correct initiative represented a step forward in Black representation, the story of Elizabeth reveals the obstacles to progress, which were not technical so much as historical: white Americans' ongoing resistance to Black people actually having a say in the making of the popular culture, including self-representation. Together, these stories of Black dolls speak to the different ways the toy industry and toy activists mediated children's relationship to racial change in the 1960s and 1970s, and the new issues that manufacturers had to address once they had acknowledged that the nation was not as white as they had long pretended. According to a 1975 industry study, a remarkable 93 percent of a sample of five thousand stores across the country carried Black dolls.[135] According to another report, "the black doll share of the total doll market had jumped at least 15 percent over a nine-year period"—from 1 percent in 1968 to an estimated 15–20 percent in 1977.[136] It is worth recalling that less than ten years earlier, shoppers on a search for Black dolls at a major department store in Los Angeles, one of the nation's largest cities and by that time a disproportionately Black city, had come up empty-handed.

There was no neat correspondence between toy integration and societal integration; the same period in which Remco and Fisher-Price entered the Black doll business was a period of massive and often violent white resistance to federally backed efforts to integrate public schools in cities across the country, not to mention a wave of new court rulings that threatened to reverse recent civil rights victories. But the lasting historical significance of the Black doll trend, while incomplete, uneven, and at times troubling, lies elsewhere. The widespread integration of Black dolls into manufacturers' product lines, retail catalogs, and store aisles brought the logic of the *Brown v. Board of Education* ruling to the realm of children's consumer culture, inseparable in postwar society from the white middle-class definition of the child. Indeed, the new realm of Black dolls, with a range of features, outfits, and characters, gave Black children new opportunities for equal play in a society that affirmed access to developmentally appropriate toys as part of a good, healthy childhood. The industry's long-overdue inclusion of Black dolls recognized Black children as potential customers and acknowledged them, for the first time, as human beings, deserving of equal representation in an industry that made images of young people its business. In this sense the racial integration of the American doll industry can be said to have affirmed Black children's legitimate place not just in the world of toys but also in the world of childhood itself.

Black Power in Toyland

In the early spring of 1968, around the time that Remco introduced its new Black dolls at the Toy Fair, Elliot Handler, cofounder and president of Mattel Toys, Remco's chief rival, convened an auspicious meeting at his company's Los Angeles headquarters. Joining him that day were a small group of other Mattel leaders, including Arthur Spear, executive vice president for operations, as well as two special guests with no ties to the company whatsoever. The Mattel executives were white; the guests, veteran civil rights activists Lou Smith and Robert Hall, were Black. Since the fall of 1965, Smith and Hall had been running Operation Bootstrap, Inc. (OB), a job-training and community-based economic development organization they had founded in the aftermath of the Watts Rebellion, which had erupted in August of that year in the predominantly Black neighborhoods of South Los Angeles. Neither Smith nor Hall had any experience in the toy business. Yet Handler was not looking to hire experienced toymakers. What he and his executive management team wanted to know was whether Smith and Hall were interested in learning the trade, not so the activists might contribute to Mattel's financial success but so Mattel might contribute to theirs.

In the plan that Handler and Spear laid out, proposed at the first meeting and hammered out with OB leaders at a second meeting soon after, Mattel would finance and help launch a new toy-manufacturing operation in South LA, entirely owned and operated by OB as its latest (and largest) community development venture.[1] Making toys, they all believed, could well be OB's ticket to long-term economic development in South LA, creating new jobs, expanding industrial training opportunities, and bringing in revenue for its educational and community programming. Under the charismatic leadership and entrepreneurial savvy of Smith, Hall, and the rest of the OB group (as well as several new hires with industry experience, including at Mattel), the new company, called Shindana Toys, would become much more than that. Following the political inclinations of its parent organization, which had strong ties to LA's Black Power and Black Arts movements, Shindana chose to specialize in Black-oriented toys for a long-ignored African American children's market. With an unprecedented loading of intention at all phases of the commercial process, Smith and Hall would transform the commercial field of Black dolls in ways no one in the toy establishment, including Mattel, could have ever imagined.

It was a propitious moment for a firm committed to Black-oriented products. As we have seen, the late 1960s marked a new era in the toy trade for the production, consumption, and, perhaps most significant, commercial visibility of Black dolls. Like Remco, Shindana's vision of racial identity for its products intersected with and drew on recent developments in the ongoing Black struggle for equality. But this moment also marked a pivotal change in the freedom movement that eluded Remco, when prominent figures and organizations began to shift the movement's chief focus away from integration and voting rights—the Civil Rights Act of 1964 and the Voting Rights Act of 1965 had ostensibly won those long-sought-after protections—to the localized community development strategies of Black Power. As the historian Waldo Martin Jr. has pointed out, the freedom struggle of the 1960s not only transformed the law; it also transformed the popular culture by catapulting the socially charged cultural products and idioms of Black liberation into the American mainstream.[2] Led by Black activists turned toymakers, Shindana took inspiration and iconography from the era's Black cultural movements with an expressively unapologetic vision of "authentic" Black image making. In doing so, it was arguably the only toy producer of the time to participate in, and not merely appropriate, the period's particular celebration of Blackness.[3]

African American race reformers had long looked to Black dolls as special resources for promoting racial pride and identity. Just as several Black-owned firms sprouted to satisfy this need in the early twentieth century, a new generation of Black activist entrepreneurs would revive this tradition to meet the needs and aspirations of the time. In 1968, that explosive year of political assassinations and Black rebellions in America's cities, Remco's Saul Robbins distanced himself from any type of "sociological program" for Black children when the press celebrated his company's Black dolls. Shindana Toys joined the industry later the same year, but with an entirely different view. Turning Black Power into toys, and toys into Black Power, the women and men celebrated by *Sepia* magazine as the "Black Toymakers of Watts" would rewrite the industry's rules of racial representation.[4]

○

Shindana's origin story is one of social, economic, and cultural rebirth. In August 1965, the city became a textbook case for what came to be known as the urban crisis. On August 11, the arrest of a Black motorist in the predominantly Black district of Watts ignited a weeklong mass uprising of Black residents that spread across several neighborhoods of South LA. To many of the area's residents, the event would be known as the "Los Angeles Revolt." To outsiders and the mainstream white media, it was the "Watts Riot." Both were correct. By any definition, the explosive events in Watts wreaked havoc on area communities: thirty-four dead, hundreds injured, and nearly $200 million of destruction in what was already the most densely populated, and poorest, section of the city. The unemployment rate in Watts topped 34 percent; in Avalon, a neighborhood several miles to the north, the incidence of poverty was even higher.[5] It was there, in the fall of 1965, that two African American movement activists planted the first seeds of the grassroots community development program that would one day build Shindana Toys.

The August 1965 uprising "spawned almost a decade of radical Black activity" in the city, writes the historian Daniel Widener, and Lou Smith and Robert Hall were among the contributors to this flowering of social and political activism.[6] Smith had first come to LA in 1965 as the new western regional director for the Congress of Racial Equality (CORE), bringing with him an organizing (and organizational) history that linked the northern and southern freedom struggles. Several years earlier, after serving in the military, Smith had found himself unemployed in Philadelphia when a friend invited him to a CORE-sponsored event. The interaction with the civil rights movement placed him on a new trajectory. He became active in the Philadelphia struggle, where he met the movement activist (and his future wife) Marva Amis, and in summer 1964 he was dispatched to the Freedom Summer voter registration project in Meriden, Mississippi, as the replacement for Michael Schwerner, one of three civil rights workers who were brutally murdered by white supremacists earlier that summer.[7]

After a stint with CORE's Harlem office in 1965, Smith was sent to Los Angeles to coordinate CORE in the west. It did not take long for him to meet Robert Hall. At the time, Hall was chairman of the Non-Violent Action

Committee (N-VAC), a direct-action offshoot of LA CORE that had recently begun calling for more militant protest against racial discrimination in the city, starting with long-ignored areas of housing and education.[8] Ironically, Watts erupted in rebellion amid the most sweeping federal efforts to combat urban poverty since the New Deal, and only days after President Lyndon B. Johnson signed the 1965 Voting Rights Act. The details of these efforts are important. In 1964, President Johnson had created the Economic Opportunity Administration (EOA) as the central vehicle for waging the "unconditional War on Poverty" that was the capstone of his Great Society program. One of the EOA's chief aims was to empower local residents of economically distressed communities by giving them the tools and resources to fight the problems unique to their neighborhoods. To that end, local organizers could apply for EOA funding through the creation of community action agencies whose goal was "maximum feasible participation" (in the program's terms) at the grass-roots level. According to this thinking, the economic and social distress of America's inner cities would be reversed through local action assisted and supervised by federal officials rather than implemented as a top-down measure.[9]

The mid-1960s were also a moment of volatility and uncertainty for the civil rights movement. Many younger Black activists involved in the militant sit-in and Freedom Ride campaigns, whether affiliated with CORE or the Student Non-Violent Coordination Committee (SNCC), began to question the reformist logic of prominent organizations like Martin Luther King Jr.'s Southern Christian Leadership Conference. As they saw it, the achievement of the movement's chief "civil rights" goals in the passage of antidiscrimination and voter protection bills, although undeniably important, did not address the bigger problem of systemic institutional racism, the invisible structures of racial discrimination that sustained and often compounded the disadvantages of Black Americans even as Jim Crow was declared unconstitutional.[10]

It was during this moment that CORE's national leadership under chairman James Farmer called for a strategic redirection of the movement, in terms of both organizing and geography. Farmer wanted to divert the struggle from the southern-based efforts for voting rights and federal legislation, where most of the national groups' attention had been focused during the previous decade. The new plan was to empower Black communities in the urban north through local development and self-determination projects. The centerpiece of these projects was the development of "community centers" that, in the words of one contemporary observer, could offer "a program of service to develop community roots" while fostering "indigenous organizations with the ability to help themselves economically and politically."[11]

Lou Smith's placement in California represented phase 1 of this reorientation. As western regional director, Smith was charged with the crucial task of developing the new community center concept. LA's Black communities were concentrated in the southern part of the city and struggled with unemployment that topped Depression-era levels. This was not the result of recent economic downturns, however, but decades of racist public policy that had channeled the allocation of resources (jobs, housing, transportation, and so on) away from Black neighborhoods and into white suburbs, thereby entrenching segregation and inequality by race.[12] For CORE's national office, LA would serve as a test case for the new community development idea.

Smith and Hall shared younger activists' growing skepticism about the government's capacity to combat the entwined problems of racism and poverty in LA and the nation. In their view, the explosion of violence and looting during the Watts Rebellion was a glaring testament to the fact that the War on Poverty had come too late to their city.[13] If predominantly Black neighborhoods like Avalon and Watts were going to win that war, then more government was not the answer. Following in a long tradition of Black leaders who called for self-initiative and Black-owned business ventures as the best routes to advancement rather than organized demands on the state, Smith and Hall believed that residents of these communities needed to wage the war on their own terms; they needed to pull *themselves* out of poverty conditions, not individually but together. The organization they formed would be the vanguard of an emerging national movement focused on community control and economic self-determination that its proponents began calling Black Power.[14]

○

In November 1965, Smith and Hall gave wings to their vision for grassroots antipoverty activism when they decided to form a nonprofit community development corporation, or CDC, in Avalon. Choosing a name that left no questions about their belief in self-reliance as the key to Black advancement, they called the organization Operation Bootstrap, Inc.[15] Smith later described OB's agenda to a reporter in terms that affirmed the organization's emphasis on capitalist enterprise: "We have to produce Black Power, time to get off the talking game and do it."[16] Inspired by the Reverend Leon Sullivan's self-help jobs program in Smith's former hometown of Philadelphia, OB located Black Power less in Black control of political resources and more in economic and psychological empowerment.[17] Reflecting this mission, Smith and Hall aimed for OB to serve as a jobs training program on two levels. First, it would offer classes in both administrative and industrial skills. Second, in an effort to complement vocational education with real-world opportunities, OB organizers would oversee the creation of local business ventures that served as both training sites and revenue generators for future OB programs.[18]

Observers might have noted that OB's emphasis on rehabilitation through jobs and training appeared to reflect the basic formula of the War on Poverty's community action programs. However, in keeping with their self-help philosophy, the organization boldly rejected the use of federal resources to accomplish that goal. "WE DO NOT SOLICIT GOVERNMENT FUNDING," declared an early OB statement.[19] Lou Smith explained the organization's thinking in a fundraising letter to supporters, stating that "the administration of a community project *must* rest within the community itself in order for it to succeed."[20] Yet outside assistance was not entirely off-limits. Operation Bootstrap's local development ideology reflected what political scientist Michael Dawson calls "community nationalism" in that it licensed the participation of private-sector institutions in realizing the organization's goals—through gifts, loans, or volunteerism—so long as those outside groups waived any rights to an official voice in the use of funds or the direction of OB programs.[21] Elenore Child, OB's director of training, elaborated on the organization's uncompromising position about outside influence in an interview with the Black-interest public television program *Black Journal*:

> We don't accept any government funds: that's local, state or federal, or any large foundation funds. And the reason for this is that, we wanted it to be, exactly as I called it, a self-help organization. We know by looking at what happens to other projects and other organizations that when you get that large chunk of government funds or foundation funds then you run into all kind of hang-ups. You got people coming in and telling you how to do, what to do, when to do it, where to do it, and why they think you should be doing it.[22]

This commitment to self-determination reflected OB's larger aspirations for Black community control in South LA. Whenever Lou Smith had the media's ear during his years as OB's president, chief fundraiser, and spokesperson, he would expound upon his group's long-term community goal: the development of what he called Freedom City, a semiautonomous, nongovernmental Black enclave in South LA, sustained by Black-owned businesses and centered on an alternative educational system running from preschool up to a University of Watts.[23] In addition to such appeals to Black economic nationalism, which echoed earlier calls by Black American leaders, going back to Booker T. Washington and W. E. B. Du Bois, for the creation of self-sustaining Black community economies, OB's founding ideology also reflected the burgeoning Afrocentric cultural nationalism of the era, in which Africa and its diverse peoples became a potent source of group identity and spiritual renewal for many Black Americans.[24] As the political scientist Melanye Price has noted, Black cultural nationalists believed that "Blacks had to shed white-centered perspectives about what the Black community could achieve and embrace new narratives of Blackness."[25] Since OB leaders actively embraced these narratives from the start, including Afrocentrism's sometimes racially essentialist conception of universal African values, they were able to harness them to their agenda of group identity building and community development. "We [at OB] moved into the realm of cultural development to develop a new cultural lifestyle, bringing on African culture and cultural dignity [to] develop a whole new way of being, a new morality," said Elenore Child. "We had a lifestyle in the past. Everyone worked for the enhancement of the tribe."[26]

One of the ways OB incorporated this Afrocentric vision was through its adult education program, which included classes in Black history and the East African language Swahili.[27] The project of Black empowerment took other forms too. Inspired by the teachings of Malcolm X, Lou Smith believed it was crucial for his organization to support Black people's development of a positive self-image in a white supremacist society. As he told an interviewer, "Malcolm used to always tell us, 'Man, stop being Negro and start being black. The only chance we have for survival is really to go into a black acceptance.'"[28] To that end, OB hosted weekly consciousness-raising groups, led by volunteer psychiatrists, for community members.[29] To Smith, self-love and professional success went hand in hand. "Job training is mostly changing attitudes," he said, "knocking out that bag that we're only half as good as whites."[30]

Smith once told a reporter that "our whole thing is education," and nothing underscored this sentiment better than OB's official motto.[31] During the Watts Rebellion, a notorious chant by some participants was "Burn, baby, burn." Rather than ignore the chant, and the intense frustration and anger it coalesced during the uprising, Smith and Hall nodded to its significance while remaking it into a slogan of self-growth: "Learn, baby, learn." Through a program combining commercial enterprise, vocational training, and Black-oriented education and uplift, Lou Smith, Robert Hall, and their OB colleagues forged a new model for community-based economic development and antipoverty work, anchored by the ideology of self-help and Black pride.

The presence of OB in the Avalon community was enthusiastically welcomed. From the fall of 1965 through the end of 1967, neighborhood residents, local churches, and volunteers from throughout the city found both time and money to give to the fledgling organization. No offers were rejected; even the ultra-right-wing John Birch Society dispatched volunteers to help paint OB's new office space, no doubt out of admiration for the group's rejection of federal assistance and emphasis on self-reliance.[32] Lou Smith also met with some success in convincing large corporations to join OB's local war on poverty. The Singer Sewing Corporation and IBM were among the big businesses that donated industrial equipment; the sewing and punch-key machines they sent, respectively, were immediately put to use in OB training classes. The financial gifts OB received were enough to supply the start-up capital for several business outfits, some of which capitalized on LA's status as the West Coast epicenter of both the Black Arts and Afrocentric movements.[33] The new ventures included an autobody shop, a Black-oriented publishing business, and a clothing operation specializing in African textiles and fashion that soon had two stores, one in the neighborhood and one downtown.[34]

By early 1968, OB appeared to be well on the road to Freedom City. Starting with no money and a band of dedicated community workers, this small community agency in the poorest section of LA had launched nine businesses in total, was employing and training dozens of local men and women, and had waiting lists for its course offerings.[35] The mainstream press, from the *Los Angeles Times* to *Business Week*, celebrated the organization and proclaimed a new grassroots model for fighting poverty. Moreover, politicians from both the left and the right found something to praise: in a remarkable sign of OB's unique blend of radical and conservative politics, the list of high-profile visitors to the group's headquarters included both Sargent Shriver, the liberal director of the War on Poverty, and Ronald Reagan, then Republican gubernatorial candidate.[36]

But publicity and praise could not themselves cover the costs of running OB's many training and social programs. Small donations and small-business subsidiaries failed to accumulate the necessary capital to cover basic operating costs; both Smith and Hall were now working full time but as unpaid volunteers.[37] Faced with the challenges of community development without state assistance, Smith went scouting for major manufacturing corporations that might be interested in helping OB produce its business-centered vision of Black Power on a larger scale—the sort of commercial operation that could provide advanced industrial training, employ larger numbers, and improve OB's deteriorating financial situation in ways that a fender shop could not.[38] Smith wrote that "1968 is the year in which Operation Bootstrap must get enough businesses started to support itself financially."[39]

Several miles west of OB headquarters was the city of Hawthorne, long a so-called sundown town that barred Black residents not only from owning homes but also from being within city limits after dark.[40] It was here, in a city that once prided itself on white supremacy, where Mattel Toys had its corporate headquarters. In 1967, officials with the Johnson administration had approached Mattel executives about participating in the new Test Program in Job Development.[41] This initiative, part of the Model Cities program of Johnson's War on Poverty, aimed to partner corporations with urban communities of color whose residents would receive extensive training, with the ultimate goal of employment by the firm.[42] By the late 1960s, Mattel had become America's largest and most recognized toy brand. In less than two decades, it had done more than any of its competitors to shape the billion-dollar business of toys: first, by pioneering the use of televised advertising to market toys directly to children during the 1950s; and second, by creating the Barbie doll, the first commercially successful female toy character to invite girls to fantasize about inhabiting the teenage culture of consumption rather than the world of domesticity.

In many respects, the federal government's suggestion that Mattel might share its expertise and material resources with a local economically distressed community had great appeal to company cofounders Ruth and Elliot Handler. The two had become leaders in corporate philanthropy and had earned praise from the National Urban League for their efforts to hire Black employees.[43] At the time, Mattel vice president Arthur Spear said that the company's leadership "felt it should be taking some responsibility in the community."[44] But Mattel wanted to develop such a community partnership on its own terms, without federal supervision. In fact, company president Elliot Handler had a radically different plan for using Mattel resources to help a local community. As he imagined the partnership, Mattel would train a group of local residents in toy design, manufacturing, and sales, just as the federal government had proposed. But the company would not hire them; instead, industrial training would take place in the context of an independent toy business owned and operated by the community itself—entirely separate from Mattel.[45] Spear and another colleague, Clifford Jacobs, vice president of marketing planning, had personal contacts in the city's activist circles, and through them learned of OB's goals and needs.[46] That OB had also rejected overtures from the Johnson administration, favoring the ideology of self-help, immediately appealed to Mattel leaders. As Spear explained, "We liked their positions: that Mattel wasn't doing them any favor and that they didn't want any government subsidy."[47]

In the early spring of 1968, Mattel leaders invited Smith and Hall to their offices in Hawthorne for a series of meetings and explained what they were prepared to offer OB in the way of technical and managerial assistance.[48] The conditions for the arrangement, the joint development of a new toy-manufacturing subsidiary, could hardly have been better suited to OB's immediate economic goals, not to mention its political ideals. Mattel had no problem meeting OB's strict standards for private-sector collaboration. The company offered $200,000 in cash for industrial equipment, the lease of a factory, and start-up capital, with no strings attached; it also promised to help orchestrate an additional $100,000 in loans through Chase Capital Corporation's new minority enterprise program and the Bank of Finance, a prominent Black-owned bank in the city.[49] Surprisingly, Mattel expressed no interest in maintaining a controlling voice in the new manufacturing outfit's management, or an official voice of any sort. According to the plan, Lou Smith and Robert Hall would assume the positions of company president and general manager, respectively, and in that capacity exercise full control over hiring. Mattel would assist that and other processes through informal channels only.

Lastly, and perhaps most remarkably, Mattel's leaders promised to provide OB leadership with on-site training and advice from top management and design staff, including veteran manufacturing manager Dolfe Lee, for the company's first two years, at no cost. Moreover, said Mattel, should any major problems arise in later years, Smith and Hall should not hesitate to call.[50] When the company got to the point where it started producing, Mattel directed members of its sales team to help sell those first dolls to local toy stores. Howard Neal, a Mattel sales representative for toy retailers citywide, was encouraged to spend whatever time in his day was necessary to make sure the new products were on the shelves.[51] Like the other subsidiary businesses of the nonprofit OB, all sales of the new company's products would be used to build the company as well as future community programs.[52] The creator of the Barbie doll expressed no interest whatsoever in profiting from the collaboration. As Spear put it, "Mattel is a $300-million company. What's $200,000 to us?"[53] White corporate America's surplus capital was to help fund the production of Black economic power in LA.

Not unexpectedly, some activists in the diverse Black Power movement were uneasy about OB's acceptance of corporate money, seeing it as a dangerous form of accommodation to white power. But Lou Smith believed that other activists would be wise to follow the same path and find their own Mattel. In his "Open Letter to Black Power Organizations," he spelled out his rationale: "The answer I have come up with is that we must use the system's weapon against it. It is a must that we establish our own economic base from which to finance our struggle.... The time has arrived when Black Power organizations ... must broaden their base to include people who have ideas along economic lines. Our initial ventures should be things directly related to the Black revolution.... All the profits from these ventures should be used to finance the work of the organization as well as creating jobs for our ghetto-trapped brother."[54] According to this notion of community-based capitalism, nonprofit subsidiaries represented alternative marketplace mechanisms that modified capitalism by infusing the market with an ethical position similar to the communalism advocated by Elenore Child. "We want to show that entrepreneurship doesn't have to be a greedy, gimme kinda thing," Smith told *Black Enterprise*. "Operation Bootstrap doesn't have any shareholders. We use ... profits for the benefit of our employees and the community."[55]

Particularly intriguing is Smith's proposal that in order to advance the social and economic goals of Black Power in capitalist America, producers should develop a more unified vision of Black capitalism that acknowledged Black consumption as part of any successful struggle. In this view, the commercial production of Black Power involved not only Black ownership of the means of production and reliance on the creativity and labor of the local Black community; it also required the manufacturing of symbolic goods consistent with the ideals of the Black freedom struggle. Linking Black-specialty products to their economic program was not an entirely new idea to OB; its clothing boutiques, run by Black fashion designers and selling imported African fabrics, gave consumers ways to express political solidarity through purchases as well as sartorial style. Yet with the vast resources and unique manufacturing opportunity that came with the Mattel partnership, making "things directly related to the revolution" took on new proportions.

According to Smith, it was at the original meeting of OB and Mattel executives where Elliot Handler floated the idea that OB's new toy division might draw on the talents of the Black women and men of South LA to create a line of Black dolls specifically for the growing Black consumer market.[56] While Handler's proposal seemed to presume that Black Americans would want to make Black-oriented toys only, or that they would be particularly good at it, there is no evidence that the group's leaders were turned off. To be sure, Smith knew that the new company needed to be profitable; trying to tap into an unfulfilled market demand for Black-oriented children's culture was surely a good bet. Yet even outside of Mattel's suggestions, Black dolls had special appeal to Smith and his organization. From his perspective, most commercially available Black dolls failed to help Black children construct the very positive Black self-image that had been a crucial OB goal since its founding.[57] "I'd always had a fantasy about manufacturing black dolls," Smith later said.[58] It would have been hard to find a product line more in sync with Smith's interest in producing goods "directly related to the revolution," not to mention the financial and administrative backing of the most successful toy company in the world.

The official OB toy company was officially launched on October 11, 1968, with a ceremony at its new factory site, located several miles south of OB offices in the area then known as South Central. Leaders of OB and Mattel were in attendance, as was Los Angeles mayor Sam Yorty.[59] The potent symbolism of a phoenix rising up from the ashes was probably not lost on the attendees, given the devastating impact of the uprising in South LA just three years earlier. Nor would they have missed the cultural nationalist ethos that undergirded the whole enterprise, showcased in the name that OB leaders chose for the fledgling company: Shindana, a Swahili word for *competitor*.[60] By the end of the month, using toy materials from Mattel suppliers, Shindana Toys, Division of Operation Bootstrap, Inc., was already manufacturing its first doll, called Baby Nancy, at a stunning rate of one thousand per week. In a rare celebration of an industry competitor, Mattel officials hailed the new factory's productivity.[61] What Mattel could not know was that productivity would be the least of the ways Shindana would raise industry standards for doll production in the months and years ahead.

○

It did not take very long for Shindana's unusual story to find its way into the national media spotlight, within the industry and far beyond it. *Toys and Novelties* and *Playthings* both reported on Shindana's creation in the final months of 1968, and even *Newsweek* magazine mentioned the company in a piece on the Black-oriented holiday market.[62] Baby Nancy's debut at the 1969 Toy Fair, which Mattel helped facilitate by sharing one of its well-visited Toy Center showrooms, only raised Shindana's profile.[63] *Toy & Hobby World* immediately hailed the company's contribution to the Black doll genre, while Shindana itself added to the publicity by placing a full-color, glossy two-page advertisement in *Playthings*, likely financed by Mattel and created by its longtime advertising agency.[64] Soon thereafter, feature stories with photos of the toy factory and staff appeared in major Black-audience media, including *Black Enterprise*, *Sepia*, and *Ebony*, and, as mentioned previously, *Black*

Journal did a ten-minute segment inside the Shindana factory that aired on public television stations across the nation in October—ideal timing for the upcoming Christmas sales season.

Encouraged by industry recognition and buoyed by Mattel's capital investment, commercial success came shockingly fast. By the new year, all twelve thousand Baby Nancy dolls were sold.[65] In 1969, the company added two new baby dolls, Dreamy Dee Bee and Baby Janie, with the latter doll manufactured exclusively for Sears, Roebuck.[66] With the addition of several new vinyl baby dolls, rag dolls, fashion dolls, and celebrity action figures in the early 1970s, there was no disputing Shindana's claim to have "the most complete line of Black dolls" in America.[67] And thanks to the swift establishment of regional sales offices in New York, Chicago, and Prairie View, Texas, that line could be found in stores nationwide, including mass retailers like the toy superstore Toys "R" Us and department store chains like Macy's and Korvette, as well as in popular consumer catalogs such as the one from Sears.[68]

The combination of Mattel's resources and the explosion of Black interest in the cultural consumption of racial pride in the late 1960s and early 1970s meant that OB had a shot at bringing its larger Black uplift project to a national consumer audience, even as it continued to nurture the production of Black business power in South LA. Furthermore, the team was united by a desire to economically empower local Black men and women by helping them develop and obtain marketable skills in a major commercial trade. Initially, Robert Hall hired and trained more than twenty local workers to run the factory line operation and brought in another smaller, elite group, including former Mattel employees such as Bob Penny, to direct the company's research, design, and public relations departments. Some of the new team members brought experience in industrial trades, including the toy business, but most were new to industrial production. Fulfilling OB's goal of community participation, the majority of the newly hired workers were residents of South Central or adjacent neighborhoods, and all were Black except for a small number of Mexican American and Puerto Rican employees who joined the factory staff.[69] Other organizers from within the OB organization joined Smith and Hall in taking on executive managerial roles within the new company, among them Herman Thompson, who became director of marketing and later company president.

The psychology of prejudice and the concept of the damaged Black psyche, central to OB's multipronged approach to individual and community rehabilitation, were also now incorporated into its marketing appeals for Shindana. Smith, Hall, and others made it plain in media interviews and other venues that they shared the perspective of most movement activists, child experts, and Black parents that the absence of positive Black images in mainstream commercial culture had damaging psychological effects on the personality development of the young girls who were the market's target audience. Invoking the doll tests of Kenneth and Mamie Clark to support their arguments, Smith, Thompson, and other company leaders asserted that white dolls led many Black children to internalize feelings of racial inferiority.[70] In an advertisement that ran in Black newspapers, Shindana broadcast this view. "Even today, white dolls outsell Black dolls in the Black community," the ad stated. "And that's not healthy. First, children must learn to love themselves and what they are or real love may never find a place in their lives."[71] While the ad acknowledged that the company's dolls were not "going to change a person overnight," it portrayed them as "a start." "Black dolls mean something to Black kids," it continued. "Call it identification or pride or whatever. But they relate to them. And that's what we think is important."[72]

In saying so, Shindana placed itself in a long tradition of mostly African American dollmakers and activists who understood and marketed Black dolls as agents of racial uplift. At the same time, Shindana had a very particular vision of what racial uplift through Black dolls required. To Lou Smith and others, not every Black doll on the toy shelves had the power to function in this way. This was because, as they saw it, not all Black dolls were equally Black. It was a premise that would drive the development of a Black doll design process unlike any other.

That process began with the company's belief that, because the facial features of most commercially available Black dolls were originally sculpted to look Caucasian, they were not actually Black dolls but rather, to quote Smith, white dolls "dipped in chocolate."[73] Smith was right to note that most Black dolls were essentially facsimiles of a company's white ones, tinted brown with little or no attempt to signify racial difference. To him, it symbolized the everyday ways that white society naturalized white standards of beauty and white bodies as the ideal human form. "Until now, it's always been a white Christmas," Smith told *Newsweek* magazine. "They have always left us out. After all, can you imagine Black kids trying to identify with blond blue-eyed dolls?"[74] Smith did not see brown-tinted dolls with the same head molds as their white counterparts as much of an improvement over the tan-colored, blond, blue-eyed ones. For example, Baby Nancy certainly was, by all industry standards, a Black doll. And yet, while Shindana argued that "Black dolls mean something to Black kids," it was clear from the start that company leaders did not see all Black dolls as being either equally Black or equally meaningful.[75]

For Lou Smith and his staff, the industry's conventional practices represented an affront to Black self-representation in popular culture. An authentic Black doll, by contrast, would reflect what Smith called "the ethnic characteristics of Black people."[76] And this was the only kind Smith cared to make; as far back as the initial discussions with Elliot Handler about the prospect of manufacturing Black dolls, Smith had made clear his desire that they not be "colored versions of white dolls."[77] Another Shindana manager, Robert Bobo, explained what that meant: "Our concept is to create a doll with *our* features—features we are known for having . . . like heavy lips, short noses. Our cheek bones are different."[78]

The process by which Shindana created Baby Nancy illustrates well the extensive production apparatus and loading of cultural intention that its contribution to ethnically correct design required. To start, Shindana held a competition across three local high schools for the best portrait of a Black female toddler.[79] The company's design team then combined the best entries with its own sketches of a local six-year-old African American girl into a final drawing to be used in sculpting the mold.[80] One OB organizer with a hand in the Shindana project told *Toys and Novelties* what marked Nancy as authentically Black: "Baby Nancy is a Black doll. She is not a white doll with Black skin. She is not a Black doll with Negroid features that is unpleasing to look at. She is an authentically beautiful Black doll."[81]

This was not just an in-house perspective. According to observers outside the factory and the OB community, Baby Nancy was, in the words of *Black Enterprise* magazine, "not only Black but *Black*."[82] Baby Nancy's lips were described as "soulfully thick," and her nose was "broad and stubby," unlike the "thin lips and aquiline noses" of other Black dolls. Moreover, the writer commented, "even the bone structure was *together*."[83] Even *Playthings* noted the difference, drawing on scientific conventions of racial classification when it described Nancy as "a Negroid-feature number."[84] Within months of Baby Nancy's appearance on the market, there seemed to be a consensus that the doll was indeed the "Black belle of the toy world," as Shindana had described her in a rare two-page, full-color announcement in the trade press.[85]

Yet achieving Shindana's strict standards for authentic Black features could be challenging in the toy industry of the late 1960s. For example, during its start-up phase Shindana required the help of outside toymakers for certain stages of production. One job the company outsourced to another firm was that of creating molds from the prototypes sculpted by its own technician,

James Toatley. When that firm botched an order, Toatley, who was Black, refused to see it as simply an honest mistake. As he explained the situation to a *Black Journal* reporter, "When we sent the doll out, they lost the end of the nose. They cut the lips down, they made them too ... too Caucasian, for us.... What I'm going to do is, I'm going to fix it up, send it back to him, tell him to give me back the thing that I sent him originally.... We've got to stay on these guys. They'll change it. They make it white every time."[86] Mattel's contacts in the industry and technical support were crucial to Shindana's early success; as Lou Smith told a group of activists in 1970 about Mattel, "Their muscle got us through doors we couldn't touch before."[87] But that muscle only went so far. Bumping up against industry practices that reflected long-standing racist perceptions of normative physical appearance, Shindana was on its own.

Toatley's refusal to accept the "white" alterations to his prototype spoke powerfully to the ways Shindana toymakers carried on OB's commitments to core principles of Black Power, self-definition and self-determination among them, despite pushback from the white-dominated toy business. Everyone on staff took steps within their own phase of production to make those commitments central to the company brand, from designing each doll's unique features and particular complexion to developing merchandising materials that narrated Black experiences and identities that felt authentic, not in the abstract sense of authentic versus fake but rather as meaningfully real and relevant to the people creating them.

In the same Shindana print advertisement discussed previously, the company's advertising team pointed toward where that authenticity originated: in the authentic Black experience of the toymakers themselves. What fundamentally distinguished Shindana's dolls from the rest was that, as the ad's tagline put it, using African American vernacular terms that portrayed Black people as family and appealed to racial solidarity, they were "Brother and sister dolls made by brothers and sisters."[88] At the bottom of the ad, below an image of the entire doll line, the company fleshed out this understanding of the intimate relationship between Black identity and the production of authentic Black toys. "We make good Black dolls," the ad asserted, "because we know what being Black is all about."[89] According to this formulation, an elusively defined yet deeply embodied sense of Black experience, or Blackness, was critical to the dolls' meaning. Shindana affirmed that belief when it stated that its dolls "don't just look Black. They *are* Black."[90]

Within a year of the Shindana factory's opening, employees were affectionately referring to the dolls as "soul babies," employing a term that, in the context of Black Power, writes the ethnomusicologist Portia K. Maultsby, "became a signifier of 'Blackness.'"[91] And it is not hard to see why. Shindana staff began their self-conscious process of encoding Blackness by drawing broadly and creatively on the era's visual idioms of soul, a set of styles, stances, and sounds that were not only racially charged but also deeply gendered.[92] Baby Nancy's hair is a case in point. When the company first produced the doll in late 1968, it gave the doll a conventional head of rooted black synthetic doll hair: long, fine, and straight, and styled into pigtails. Yet the choice of pigtails was less a calculated design decision than a practical one; rushing to produce the doll for the Christmas selling season, the factory team had little time to consider how it might signify African American hair in line with Shindana's emerging vision of ethnically correct dollmaking, and thus did its best with materials provided by Mattel.[93]

By early 1969, however, the company's design team had made a conscious choice to offer two different versions of Nancy. As they knew well, a growing number of Black women in the late 1960s, including at the Shindana offices and factory, were wearing their hair natural for reasons ranging from the personal to the political. If that usually meant a coarse Afro, in toy terms crimped hair presented a significant challenge to Shindana; in fact it was something the doll industry had never been tasked with before. But Shindana toymakers did not shirk the challenge. To make Nancy's hair resemble this popular style and offer an alternative to what some parents and children might perceive as the relaxed or treated look of most Black dolls' hair (sometimes characterized, as previously mentioned, as a "white" style), the company imported a special oven from Italy and slid the synthetic hair under the heat to achieve the matted texture.[94] After the oven treatment, with its ironic resemblance to the hot irons used to straighten thick hair, the factory line workers would use a hair comb to fluff out the "natural" and give it a more realistic appearance.[95] Consumers could now choose between the original Nancy doll, now called Pretty Pigtails, or the more politically potent Shorty Curls Nancy, which employees nicknamed Natural Nancy (see figure 4.1).[96]

Curiously, America was not ready for Natural Nancy in 1969; Shindana sold four times as many Pretty Pigtails dolls.[97] It would be difficult to ascertain why consumers chose this version of Nancy. Perhaps girls, or their parents, wanted a doll whose hair was longer and easier to comb into a variety of styles; alternatively, the white consumers who bought the doll may have viewed a natural style as an unwarranted overemphasis on racial difference. But the preference for pigtails did not last very long. By the end of 1970, Natural Nancy was outselling Pretty Pigtails Nancy, a development that Lou

4.1. Shorty Curls Baby Nancy doll (1969, in box) and Pretty Pigtails Baby Nancy doll (1968, standing), Shindana Toys, Division of Operation Bootstrap, Inc. Author's collection.

Smith attributed to "all the Black stars in the movies and on TV with their naturals."[98] Natural Nancy's sales suggested a new generation of girls were successfully receiving the movement's message that Black was beautiful; Shindana merchandisers helped that messaging along by stamping the slogan directly on the doll boxes.[99]

Shindana also deployed and highlighted other politically charged signifiers of Blackness that broke new ground in the girls' Black doll market. For instance, in another nod to the cultural nationalism of OB, many of the dolls that followed Nancy were given Swahili names.[100] But no doll took Afrocentric symbolism as far as the Malaika doll, introduced in 1970.[101] Standing fifteen inches tall and made of vinyl, the Malaika doll was billed as "a *realistic* Black fashion figure" and sported a "rooted, Natural hairdo"; each of the three different versions came dressed in a different set of "Afro-print clothing" that evoked the very dashikis and other African-inspired women's clothing sold by OB's fashion shop subsidiary.[102] In a curious twist, Mattel, the company's erstwhile patron, soon adopted this very fashion style for the Black dolls of its World of Barbie collection, as did many other toy manufacturers, with none of them mentioning the obvious inspiration.[103] The notable difference was that while the Black dolls made by companies like Mattel and Hasbro could be slipped out of what the former called "Afro style clothes" and changed into any number of different European skirts or jumpers, Malaika had no alternative wardrobe beyond her South-LA-by-way-of-Africa outfits—produced by a local business run by Black women, a fact Shindana printed on the box—as if to say that only African styles befit this "authentic BLACK fashionmate."[104] For all their efforts, Mattel's and Hasbro's Black dolls were not much more than an updated, trendier "colored version." The idea that Black female identity was rooted in African heritage was also signified in the doll's packaging material. According to the catalog, Malaika was "created in African fantasy," and the backdrop image in the box's interior illustrated that fantasy with a huge bright-orange sun floating above the savannah, an iconic scene of African grasslands that American children in the 1970s would have recognized from *National Geographic* magazines (see figure 4.2).[105]

By stating on the very front of the box that Malaika meant "angel" in Swahili; dressing the different versions of the doll in vibrant textile designs that reflected a range of West and East African styles and motifs, from Yoruba-inflected dashikis to Kenyan deras; and giving the dolls accessories like the kufi hat (which across many African cultures was exclusively worn by men), Shindana presented Africa not as a single essentialized place or generic heritage but as an imagined repository of history and symbols, an inspiring cultural geography to draw on for the practices and meanings of African American identity in the Black diaspora. Combining evocative imagery with a fluidly African narrative of Blackness, Shindana encouraged young Black girls, their target consumers, to see themselves in a greater history and global community of beautiful Black women.[106]

That community, of course, included apartheid South Africa, a potent reminder for many African Americans of the persistence of white colonial oppression on the continent and a political rallying point as they fought for their own liberation from the American system of Jim Crow. But South Africa was also the birthplace and, until her exile, homeland of the singer and activist Miriam Makeba, perhaps the most recognized and beloved Black female celebrity outside the United States. I bring up Makeba for two reasons: in

4.2. Malaika doll (1970), Shindana Toys, Division of Operation Bootstrap, Inc. Author's collection.

the late 1960s, as the historian Tanisha Ford has shown, there was probably no international Black artist whose politically inflected soul style weighed as heavily on the African American cultural imagination; and one of the most popular songs she recorded and performed at her concerts, including in a 1965 duet with the Black Jamaican singer and activist Harry Belafonte, was a love song called "Malaika" (also known as "You Are My Angel").[107] While we do not know if the Shindana employees were thinking of Makeba when they chose the Malaika doll's name and outfitted her in and of the African continent, it is hard not to see this singular doll as a loose analogue, or even tribute, to the woman known to her fans as "Mama Africa."

While Nancy and Malaika dolls suggested that Blackness could be performed visually and materially through symbolic fashion choices and style, elsewhere Shindana argued that Blackness was verbally constituted as well. In 1970, it brought what it considered to be linguistic indicators of authentic Black life to the doll industry in the form of a doll named Tamu, its first pull-string talking doll.[108] Like Natural Nancy, the Tamu doll, meaning *sweet* in Swahili, had coarse rooted hair that *Black Enterprise* described as "a natural as tall as Kathleen Cleaver's," a leader of the Oakland Black Panther Party for Self-Defense, and was outfitted in a floral-print dashiki-style tunic that fit loosely on its cloth body.[109] Likewise, the vinyl head was sculpted with the stylized broad nose and emphatically rounded and full lips that featured prominently in all Shindana dolls.[110]

What distinguished Tamu from the rest of the Shindana line at that point was its capacity to speak. Like other talking baby dolls of the era, Tamu's hidden voice box contained eighteen different programmed phrases.[111] But as a writer from *Sepia* magazine observed with some surprise after pulling the cord several times, a few of Tamu's sayings were "as different from conventional dolls' talk as her appearance is."[112] What the writer meant was that the doll spoke jive, an African American vernacular with roots in jazz culture, with unconventional phrases—like the imperative "Cool it, baby," and the query "Can you dig it?"—in its otherwise conventional repertoire of expressions like "I love you" and "I'm hungry."[113]

Tamu's capacity to speak from within the historically constructed, in-house language culture of Black communities suggested new frontiers for radical playthings. It also represented for the first time a doll that literally spoke to the everyday reality of African American life for many; indeed, Tamu added a new verbal dimension to Shindana's list of what being Black was all about. The doll also can be said to have indirectly suggested that the Black identity of its direct competitors, like the Black version of Mattel's Drowsy, was inauthentic; after all, with Tamu having entered the marketplace, those dolls *only* spoke the standard English associated with the privileged white middle class.[114] Lou Smith regularly told interviewers that Shindana equally aimed to reach white children with its dolls, in the belief that white kids who played with Black dolls "will have less chance of growing up with racist attitudes."[115] Yet Tamu's expression "I'm proud like you" appears to be a notable exception to that claim. For given the specific racial connotation of this affirmation in 1970, Shindana was basically assuming that a child playing with Talking Tamu, as the catalog called her, would be Black.

All these efforts to construct a positive racial self-image for young Black girls resonated with an emerging critique by Black feminist writers and intellectuals that portrayed dominant white cultural standards as pernicious threats to the formation of a healthy Black female identity. In fact, the year of Tamu's introduction also saw the publication of *The Black Woman*, a ground-breaking anthology edited by the Black writer Toni Cade. Consider Cade's own contribution to the volume, which powerfully articulated a key strand of Black feminism in calling for a revolution in Black female self-understanding. As she wrote: "The revolution begins with the self, in the self.... The individual, the basic revolutionary unit, must be purged of poison and lies that assault the ego ... [for] we have been programmed to depend on white models, or white interpretations of non-white models."[116]

It would be hard to find a more apt cultural metaphor for Cade's critique than Shindana's concept of the authentic Black doll. As a challenge to the "chocolate dipped" facsimiles of the industry's white dolls, Shindana dolls communicated the message that young Black girls should refuse the white models as well as the white *interpretations* of nonwhite models of womanhood promoted in mainstream consumer culture. Through dolls like Nancy, Malaika, and Tamu, Shindana toymakers creatively sculpted, manufactured, and styled the visual idioms of the era's new Black aesthetic into the vinyl and cloth materials of children's play. They even supplied Tamu with a means for coding Blackness in sonic dimensions. The appearances of these dolls in toy stores across the country, with their varied brown complexions and uniquely styled naturals, and listed by Shindana as "Black" dolls rather than "Negro" or "Colored" ones, were some of the earliest moments that the message "Black is beautiful" found a place in mainstream American children's culture.[117]

Yet Shindana fleshed out its particular understanding of "what it means to be Black" in other elements of commercial toys, nowhere more than in the elaborate backstories and merchandising materials that the design and production staff wrote into three of its new lines in the 1970s: Li'l Souls, Wanda Career Girl, and Slade Super Agent. Through these toys, the company constructed new Black-centered narratives of family, race, class, and gender that challenged not just the toy industry's ugly history of Black cultural representations but American popular culture's as well. Indeed, we might usefully understand Shindana as the Norman Lear of its own industry, doing for toys what producer Lear's pioneering Black TV sitcoms of the 1970s did for a virtually all-white world of American TV. That Shindana would, in the mid-1970s, become the first and only firm to license and sell character dolls of the Black stars of those programs, including comic actors Jimmy Walker and Redd Foxx, could hardly have been a more fitting role for it to fulfill.

o

The history of cloth dolls is woven deeply into the history of African American childhoods. Scraps from torn clothing and other used materials from cloth to buttons were often the only items available for the toys that Black children enjoyed during the horrific centuries of enslavement. These practices of homemade toy production, in which dolls were designed, embroidered, and sewn by African American women, continued well after Emancipation, less so because of the prohibitive cost of manufactured dolls than because most commercially available dolls representing Black people were based on racist archetypes such as the pickaninny, mammy, and other minstrel characters.[118] With the introduction of the Li'l Souls Family line in 1971, Shindana offered its own unique contribution to this tradition of African American–made rag dolls while taking it in radical new directions.

In its original iteration, the Li'l Souls were rag dolls of varying sizes representing four Black child characters: Wilky, Sis, Natra, and Coochy. They sported yarn Afro hairstyles; had simple, cheery faces; and wore colorful, removable cloth outfits covered in popular slogans such as "Peace," "Right On," and "Learn, Baby, Learn," the OB motto.[119] But a child received more than just the doll upon the purchase of Wilky or Sis, for inside every box of the original dolls was *The Li'l Souls Story Coloring Book* (see figure 4.3). In the book's twelve-page illustrated story, two African American siblings named Wilky and Sis move from Alabama to join their city-dwelling grandmother, who "lived in a housing project."[120] The night they arrive, Sis paints two popular expressions of Black consciousness, "Say It Loud" and "I'm Proud," on her blank sweatshirt.[121] The next day, Sis meets the other children who live there, "Black ones and white ones and some she had never seen before."[122] Wondering "if they would like her," Sis remembers her old friends in Alabama, who, as the page's illustration suggests, were Black.[123] Would she find a place of belonging among these kids, most of whom were not Black?

As Sis wonders how she will fare in this new, racially diverse neighborhood—an indication that she is there not for a short visit but for a longer stay—she is suddenly interrupted by Grandma, who calls over Coochy and Natra from the swings to meet Sis and Wilky.[124] While the story doesn't identify their familial relation, their shared ties to Grandma suggest that Coochy and Natra may be cousins of the new arrivals. All we know for sure, however, is that Shindana's toymakers wanted consumers to see the four children through the framework of kin, for why else choose Li'l Souls Family for the name of the dolls? Establishing their exact relationship, it seems, is less important than the fact of their intimate connection to an elder matriarch. In a striking counternarrative to the white middle-class nuclear ideal that continued to

4.3. Sis doll (in box) and Wilky doll, with *Li'l Souls Story Coloring Book* (1971), from the Li'l Souls collection, Shindana Toys, Division of Operation Bootstrap, Inc. Author's collection.

populate toys, television, and Hollywood, family in the world of the Li'l Souls was less about biology than relationships of care.

This was not an uncontroversial view at the dawn of the 1970s, especially where Black families were concerned, as American society continued to reproduce a racist and sexist discourse on the structures of Black family life that began in 1965 with the publication of a government study titled *The Negro Family: The Case for National Action*, popularly known as the Moynihan Report. In an effort to explain and propose solutions for the disproportionate rates of poverty and unemployment in Black communities, the report focused not on disproportionate economic discrimination and the long history of racist policies but on the incidence of woman-headed households and what the report characterized generally as "the deterioration of the Negro family."[125] Civil rights groups were not the only ones to challenge the report's negative stereotyping of Black families as deviant and the insidious charge that Black people, not a white supremacist government, were responsible for economic inequity. A group of progressive sociologists soon joined them, not through protest but by conducting new ethnographic studies that explored contemporary Black families on their own terms, with respect and dignity. Collectively, they established that many urban Black families not only benefited from the assistance of relatives and unofficial kin for economic reasons but also valued a larger kinship network for child-rearing than the one offered by the conventional middle-class model.

One of the most influential of these studies was *All Our Kin: Strategies for Survival in a Black Community* (1974), written by white sociologist Carol B. Stack.[126] As Stack concluded, urban Black families often had "shared community expectations of rights and duties toward children," expectations that offered "a commanding contrast to the characterization of the Black family life as 'broken' and 'disorganized.'"[127] In other words, there was nothing pathological about family structures where, to take the example represented in the Li'l Souls storybook, children "may be transferred back and forth, 'borrowed' or 'loaned'" among kin, depending on family circumstances that were subject to change, often due to forces beyond parental control.[128] Whereas most sociologists of the time saw such practices as an explanation of poverty and its persistence, Stack argued that the families from the community she studied had practical as well as cultural reasons for their choices. "Shared parental responsibilities are not only an obligation," Stack wrote. "They constitute a highly cherished right."[129]

Given these political and academic contexts in which the so-called Black family was discussed during the late 1960s and early 1970s, there are a number of ways one can interpret the Li'l Souls Family dolls and their coloring book. To be sure, learning about two Black children being sent off to their grandmother in another part of the country, without mention of a mother or father, might have appeared to some parents and children as a story of abandonment. For those who had already accepted the popular stereotypes of Black life courtesy of the Moynihan Report, the story would have confirmed their beliefs. At the same time, we can surmise that for many Black children (and perhaps many other children of color, not to mention recent immigrants of all backgrounds), the notion that grandmothers and other elder kin could serve as primary caretakers of children, in addition to mothers and fathers, would not have been unfamiliar or strange at all.

Shindana employees did not need *All Our Kin* to tell them that the organization of Black cultural life was inherently valid and valuable, even in cases when it diverged from the white normative model of a married straight couple with two children in a single-family home, with father as provider and mother as caretaker.[130] Through the narrative of Sis and Wilky, Shindana both anticipated and dramatized what Stack (and others) later called the "adaptive strategies, resourcefulness, and resilience of urban families."[131] In the fictional world of the Li'l Souls Family, as in the real world of many Black families, Grandma could be more than an elderly relative who visited (or was visited) on holidays, as was the practice of the suburban white middle-class families on network TV; she could also be a trusted guardian, an important role model, and an agent of socialization into cherished values, including a positive Black identity. Furthermore, the geographical markers used in the Li'l Souls storybook placed Sis and Wilky in an important cultural narrative of migration that defined the African American experience in the mid-twentieth century: the Second Great Migration, when more than three million Black men, women, and children between the 1940s and 1970 fled the racist violence, segregation, and lack of economic opportunity in the South for what they hoped would be a better life in the cities of the North, Midwest, or West.[132] Through the narrative of Sis and Wilky, these migration journeys found a place for the first time in American toy culture.

Finally, Shindana's Li'l Souls portrayed Black departures from idealized conceptions of family structure as not only normal but also, in ways that undermined the popular pathologizing of Black families, as healthy, happy, and good for children. When the non-Black kids on the playground, a boy named Tony and a girl named Ricky, ask Sis to explain the slogans on her sweatshirt, including "I'm Proud," she appears to happily oblige.[133] Although the reader does not see Grandma in the book's last illustration, one gets the sense that she is watching through the window. For as the racially diverse group of children all run off to play together, it is Grandma, proud of her grandchildren's strong Black identity, who proclaims in the final line of the story, "Right on—Sis—Right on—Wilky—Right on!"[134]

○

In 1972, just one year after the debut of the Li'l Souls, Shindana indirectly addressed where Sis and Wilky's mother might have been while challenging negative representations of Black womanhood with its first entry to the fashion-doll genre: the nine-inch Wanda Career Girl doll. With its brown

4.4. Wanda Stewardess doll (1972), from the Wanda Career Girl collection, Shindana Toys, Division of Operation Bootstrap, Inc. Author's collection.

complexion, natural hairstyle, and Black-coded facial features, Wanda bore a striking resemblance to Mattel's own recent Black fashion dolls, Talking Christie (1968) and Julia (1969).[135] But Wanda was different. In her first incarnation, the doll came in three versions, each of them dressed in one of three career-oriented outfits: Wanda Nurse, Wanda Ballet Dancer, or Wanda Stewardess (see figure 4.4). Along with accessories specific to the career, the box contained "a special brochure featuring three real live career girls in action"—that is, a small booklet with an in-depth, first-person discussion of three different occupations.[136] The booklet also included photographs of real Black women who held one of the jobs, along with short notes addressing the reader in their voice. "Hello, my name is Dorothy and I'm a nurse just like Wanda," began one of them. "I work with very sick people in what is called the intensive unit at a community hospital."[137]

Moreover, while Wanda's twist waist and movable arms and legs defined her as a fashion doll by industry standards, Shindana viewed the doll as an alternative to the sort of girls' toys exemplified by Mattel's Barbie collection. This distinction had less to do with the dolls' vinyl bodies than with their manufacturer-given identities. Though Shindana never made a talking version of the Wanda doll, she most definitely would not have declared, as Mattel's Talking Christie did, "Let's go shopping with Barbie."[138] In fact, the company made this perfectly clear in *Shariki Ana*, OB's newsletter: "'Wanda' is not a fashion doll; she is a career doll."[139] This is because the Wanda Project involved more than just the dolls. Inspired by Wanda's career orientation and the character's real-life "friends," young girls began writing to the company during the doll's first Christmas selling season in 1972. In response to the high volume of mail, and perhaps noting a key element of Mattel's successful marketing strategy for Barbie, Shindana created the Wanda Career Club. Within its first five months, its membership reached one hundred girls; in a matter of two years, more than five thousand had joined.[140] Charged with the task of corresponding with each club member as the "real" Wanda, which she apparently did, was Jeep Ransaw, an OB volunteer who, when she was not at her regular day job as a secretary, attended night school in hopes of one day becoming a lawyer. Given her own career aspirations, it is perhaps no surprise that Ransaw, who was Black, went far beyond a form letter in her correspondence. "When the child indicates her interest in a specific career," stated an article about the club in *Shariki Ana*, "Jeep (Wanda) does extensive research regarding schooling and background required, as well as the scope of that particular field or industry. She then sends the child the report" (see figure 4.5).[141] As the club's membership grew, Ransaw began sending members a monthly newsletter that discussed different professions and the educational requisites for entering them.[142]

Through Wanda, Black womanhood was defined not only by the company's charged Black aesthetic, as the doll's features reflected Shindana's style of racial coding, but also by the ethic of Black economic empowerment and professional self-reliance at the core of OB's program. As with the Li'l Souls dolls, Wanda also seemed a deliberate response to the 1965 Moynihan Report by taking the hard work and accomplishments of Black working women—depicted by the report as the cause of poverty in urban Black communities, based on the argument that women's labor market participation weakened Black men's identity—and recoding them for a new audience.[143] In this way, Shindana gave form to the reality of Black women's experience as both workers and citizens, while affirming the importance of economic

4.5. Jeep Ransaw, Shindana Toys volunteer and head of the Wanda Career Club, reads and responds to letters from Career Club members about their professional aspirations. Publicity photograph by Long Photography, Inc., circa 1974, from a press kit prepared by Harshe-Rotman & Druck. Courtesy of Kirk Hallahan.

self-determination and self-actualization through career fulfillment to a new generation of Black girls. As Lou Smith described his larger agenda of female empowerment, "instead of just giving [Wanda] a beautiful wardrobe, we use the Black doll as a career woman to introduce career opportunities," especially, he argued, to girls who might not have access to that information.[144]

Wanda Career Girl reached toy stores during a moment of growing discussion among intellectuals and observers about the special economic and psychological challenges facing young Black women. As mentioned before, the Moynihan Report powerfully shaped that discourse, in which Black women were blamed for poverty as well as the disproportionately high rates of Black male unemployment. In 1971, the Black sociologist Joyce Ladner challenged the racist and misogynistic premises of the Moynihan Report while reorienting long-standing social scientific assumptions about Black female youth when she published her groundbreaking book, *Tomorrow's Tomorrow: The Black Woman*. Based on Ladner's lengthy interviews with dozens of Black adolescent girls in an urban St. Louis public housing development, the book documented and analyzed "what approaching womanhood meant to poor Black girls in the city."[145] Ladner found that while the young women she interviewed faced the combined obstacles of poverty, racism, and sexism, with few opportunities to rise above them, their views, experiences, and dreams hardly reflected prevailing conceptions of Black female deviance and limited aspirations. Still, she concluded, the social forces that worked against these young Black women's success were formidable. Whatever the actual demographic that purchased the lion's share of Wanda dolls, it was Black girls like those in *Tomorrow's Tomorrow*—girls who "will enter womanhood in an era when the demands for commitment to the fight for survival will be more necessary than at any other time in history"—to whom the Wanda Project spoke through its play scripts of Black female achievement and encouragement by successful Black women.[146]

To be sure, the three occupational paths presented by the original Wanda line of 1972—nurse, flight attendant, and ballerina—could easily be understood as narrowing rather than widening young Black girls' career aspirations. The professional ballet, for one, was unlikely for most girls on account of both access and the significant financial investments required by the family. But it was especially unlikely for Black girls in an elite, white-dominated ballet field still guided by European standards of ideal body type and appearance. Meanwhile, the two more common and salaried professions (and for flight attendants, recently unionized) in large ways confined young female ambitions to socially defined "feminine" careers that prioritized helping and service-oriented labor over traditionally "masculine" skills like leadership and creative problem-solving. Shindana did not offer Wanda Doctor or Wanda Attorney, let alone Wanda CEO, or, in a year when Black congresswoman Shirley Chisholm mounted a campaign for the White House, Wanda President.

And yet, situating Wanda in the fashion-doll market of the time illuminates the extent to which she pushed against boundaries of gender and race. In the early 1970s, even with the limited (and limiting) career pamphlets and outfits available for Wanda Career Girl, the contrast between Wanda's explicit career orientation and the main interests of the top-selling fashion doll, Mattel's new Malibu Barbie, was stark. Malibu Barbie, which was also the top-selling toy of any kind in 1972, crystallized the transformation of the Barbie character from a young woman of diverse interests in the early 1960s, including a career path, to a young teen whose main interests were surfing, dating, driving sports cars, and enjoying the relaxed life of a middle-class extended childhood.[147] Living outside—or, in light of the after-work outfits that every Wanda doll came with, on the margins—of a vast world of conspicuous consumption inhabited by the leading fashion-doll characters of the era, Shindana's Wanda offered a striking alternative to Barbie and her friends (Christie included) that in important respects affirmed the burgeoning Black feminism of the time.

By the mid-1970s, most major companies manufactured Black female fashion dolls with flexible bodies and accessories, including Hasbro, Topper, and Kenner. Yet none of these popular TV-advertised character figures gave a hint of career interests, which likely explains why in 1978 Shindana resolved to drop Wanda's career theme altogether, transforming Wanda Career Girl into the fashion-conscious, night-clubbing Disco Wanda. The decision to remake Wanda as a disco queen was probably the result of market considerations. After all, "Shindana" did mean *competitor*. At the same time, celebrating the relative freedom of disco's underground culture for Black women and the lead contributions of Black women musicians to the music that provided its beat and anthems—Disco Wanda as an analogue to Gloria Gaynor ("I Will Survive") or Anita Ward ("Ring My Bell")—was very much in keeping with Shindana's approach to culturally relevant Black toys.[148]

Wanda may have switched professions from Career Girl to cover girl by the decade's end, but whatever the reasons, the combined forces of the dolls and the Career Club encouraged countless young Black girls to fantasize about their futures and see people who looked like them making those futures a reality. When Shindana urged them to "become what you wish as Wanda Career Girl," they saw in the Wanda booklet that such dreams did come true.[149]

○

Most of the dolls Shindana produced in its first years were gendered female and aimed at the girls' market. In the early 1970s, however, the company began to pursue the boys' market with a series of talking cloth dolls based on the likenesses of the most famous Black male celebrities of the era, including the TV-show host Flip Wilson and actors Redd Foxx, Jimmy Walker, and the young star Rodney Allen Rippy.[150] *The Flip Wilson Show* (1970–74) had earned Wilson the designation of "TV's First Black Superstar" by *Time Magazine* in 1972. Foxx's *Sanford and Son* (1972–77) and Walker's *Good Times* (1974–79) had each made it to the top of the Nielsen ratings by depicting some of the first three-dimensional Black characters and their families experiencing both joy and struggle. It is hard to know with any certainty which of Shindana's toys were most successful, but the wide popular appeal of these Black celebrities was likely to make these novelty dolls some of Shindana's best sellers. One can also imagine that they reassured the Shindana marketing team that the company's unique Black brand could successfully enter the boys' toy market too.

But the Jimmy Walker doll could hardly have prepared the toy industry for Shindana's first fictionalized Black doll catered to boys, which it introduced in 1976. A sort of male counterpart to the Wanda Career Girl albeit with a less conventional career, the new ten-inch-tall, Black-featured plastic action figure was not a jokester but the furthest thing from it: a serious crime-fighting detective with the code name Slade.[151] Slade Super Agent, as the company officially called him, was not exactly a career doll in the Wanda mode. Created more in the spirit of the superhero than the career man, he would offer an image of heroic Black masculinity unlike any that the white-owned corporate toy industry had dreamed up for the action-figure genre during the previous decade (see figure 4.6).[152]

There were already several Black male action figures on the market by the time Shindana introduced Slade. That list included Hasbro's Black member of the G.I. Adventure Team, a revamped version of the original Black G.I. Joe from 1965; Mego Corporation's Black version of its adventure hero named Action Jackson, which was also available as a white figure with the same name; Mattel's Big Jack, a Black muscleman who served as one of the sidekicks to the white character Big Jim in the Big Jim line; and Kenner's Bob Scout, an African American Boy Scout companion for the white Steve Scout. In his coloring and head mold, Slade was not all that different from these competitors. In fact, they all had the now customary ethnically correct Black features: brown-tinted skin, a broad nose, and short natural hair (usually painted on).

What distinguished Slade was his story. In contrast to other Black action figures, Slade led a life that was grounded in the racial, political, and national realities of midcentury America and Black urban life. In other words, Slade was historically constituted, a reflection (and celebration) of a specific moment in Black Americans' ongoing struggle for self-definition, self-determination, and cultural representation, and a rejection of some of the most demeaning stereotypes of Black men then circulating in American culture.

There are several ways of thinking about Slade Super Agent as a product of the social and cultural climate of 1970s America. The most obvious reference point (and inspiration) for Slade, a private detective working in an urban

4.6. Slade Super Agent (1976), Shindana Toys, Division of Operation Bootstrap, Inc. Author's collection.

landscape reminiscent of Harlem or Chicago (as seen on the back of the box), was the Black action-hero archetype mythologized in the crime films of the so-called Blaxploitation era of the early to mid-1970s. The Blaxploitation category, an umbrella term for a genre that also included horrors, comedies, and westerns, had curried controversy from the start, when civil rights groups charged the films with sensationalizing contemporary Black urban life in ways that perpetuated the worst stereotypes of Black (and especially Black male) criminality, violence, and hypersexuality. Other critics and scholars, then and since, have pointed to these films, especially those directed and written by Black filmmakers like *Shaft* (1971, directed by Gordon Parks Sr.) and *Super Fly* (1972, directed by Gordon Parks Jr.), as important popular expressions of Black Power's call to affirm Black agency, culture, and identity, all while giving Black audiences what they had long been denied from Hollywood: Black heroes, not just sidekicks, with all the same physical skill, style, and glamour of the James Bonds and Steve McQueens of white-centered action movies.[153]

Dressed in a brown patent-leather jumpsuit, with additional items available for purchase such as bulletproof vest, stack of ransom money, and climbing rope, Slade had a stylized outfit and persona that certainly placed him of the genre. But it is the head mold, with its distinctive sideburns, mustache, and features, that links him to one iconic film in particular: *Shaft* (1971), notable for being the genre's most commercially successful film and for its Academy Award–winning soundtrack composed by Isaac Hayes. Slade's resemblance to Richard Roundtree, the actor who played the title character—the fearlessly independent Harlem private detective John Shaft—is hard to deny. Add to all this the fact that Slade's leather coat and turtleneck are basically the same color and style as Shaft's, and one might be forgiven for thinking that Slade was not an original character but Shindana's latest licensed celebrity doll. Given the company's past success in producing likenesses of America's best-known Black actors, which by the mid-1970s now included an official Marla Gibbs doll (dressed as her unforgettable character Florence from *The Jeffersons*), it would not be at all surprising if Shindana had tried to sign on Richard Roundtree but failed to do so. As Slade's design makes clear, Shindana's sculptors effectively went along and made the Roundtree doll anyway, producing the toy industry's one and only answer to a movie genre that, like Shindana, challenged cultural representations of Blackness in lasting ways.

And yet, as his backstory reveals, there is more to Slade than a ten-inch likeness of Richard Roundtree / John Shaft. Indeed, his trajectory diverged from that of the typical Blaxploitation hero in important ways, reflecting Shindana's core values. Consider the résumé of sorts that appeared on the back of the toy box. "Education: Neighborhood, War, College," it states, and from those experiences, "he learned it all!"[154] But while the company affirmed the authentic educational value of Slade's segregated childhood neighborhood, explicitly stating that "he grew up in the ghetto," the bigger takeaway is that Slade is not just street smart but book smart too.[155] For it was in college where he "learned to live through education."[156] As the extensive narration on the box recounts, "being strong in math, computer electronics & business, he searched for a job to make use of all his talents, his thirst for thrill and adventure, his hunger for more excitement & knowledge."[157] He ultimately found it, explains the Shindana catalog, "as a tough secret agent out to stop corruption and crimes by using the most sophisticated techniques."[158] The ghetto had valuable lessons to teach, said Shindana, but so did the world beyond it.

In noir films and novels as well as superhero comics, a community needs an independent crimefighter in part because law enforcement professionals, from street cops to district attorneys, are not doing their jobs; in many cases, it goes beyond that, to situations where law enforcement is the source of (or complicit in) corruption and crime. This was a major theme in Black action movies of the 1970s, *Shaft* included. But it was also part of the reality of being Black in a Black neighborhood, where policing by white officers was not only corrupt but marked by casual racist violence and constant harassment. Police brutality was the impetus for the Black Oakland activists Huey P. Newton and Bobby Seale to create the Black Panther Party for Self-Defense in 1966, and for the more than three dozen additional chapters that soon after formed across the country (including one in LA). Nor could Black Americans count on federal law enforcement to serve and protect them, as FBI agents involved with the Counterintelligence Program (COINTELPRO) in the 1960s and early 1970s carried out countless acts of sabotage of Black-led organizations and even assassinations of Black leaders such as Fred Hampton.[159] Fighting crime without violence, for he had no weapon, Slade represented a powerful alternative to the FBI's definition of what a secret agent does.

Slade's character also spoke reflexively to the Shindana story itself. As a Black American who "grew up in the ghetto," sought an education to satisfy a "hunger for excitement and knowledge," and in his own way pursued the Black Power movement's emphasis on community protection and improvement, Slade exemplified OB's founding convictions: first, that the challenges of the so-called urban crisis could be met only by Black people who knew and understood the people they aimed to serve; and second, that education ("Learn, Baby, Learn") was the path to both individual success and the success of Black America.[160] Harder to interpret along these lines is Slade's recent wartime service, implicitly in Vietnam, especially in light of OB's antifederal outlook and the general tendency of Black movement leaders to frame the US presence in Vietnam as a racist war that Black soldiers should have no part in fighting. It may be that, with the Vietnam War over, Shindana hoped to tap into (or revitalize) earlier histories of Black military service, especially during World War II, in which Black soldiers had invoked their sacrifice for the nation to make claims to equal citizenship and mobilize movements for civil rights. It also may be that Shindana marketers recognized that patriotism—this was the bicentennial year, after all—sells. But it also could be that what at first blush seems like an implicit appeal to the value of serving one's country was less about politics than about painting a realistic portrait of the experience of being a Black man in the Vietnam era. Military service may have consumed Slade's life for a period, as it had for hundreds of thousands of Black men during these years, including James Edwards, Shindana's head designer around the time of Slade's creation.[161] Yet, given Slade's curious lack of weapons for a crimefighting hero, it seems reasonable to imagine that the experience of fighting in Vietnam had made him a pacifist, as it did for many other veterans of his generation.[162]

Lastly, Slade busted stereotypes as well as criminals and corrupt officials. His life story and achievements undermined a series of racist social-scientific conceptions about Black men, popularized in recent years by the Moynihan Report and numerous magazine articles and books, which painted them as by turns hostile, aggressive, emasculated, and damaged.[163] Slade did not conform to any of these psychological diagnoses; he was neither psychotic nor filled with uncontrolled rage, nor was he incapable of obtaining higher education, holding down a job, or contributing to society. Instead, with his impressive résumé and community-oriented commitments, Slade represented a forceful counterattack on these pernicious images, the first in toy history. Through Slade, Shindana communicated the message that national service, college, advanced technological knowledge, and making a career out of one's concern for justice—however unlicensed Slade's trade—were realistic and laudable aspirations for Black boys, including those growing up in marginalized, segregated neighborhoods like his own.

Ultimately, Slade was not a superhero in the conventional sense. He did not fly, and, although the illustration on the box does show his body repelling bullets, there is no mention anywhere else of this or other superhuman strengths or senses. But he did have special powers of sorts, all flowing from his lifelong commitment to the OB ethic of "Learn, Baby, Learn." Grounded in his historical moment like no other Black action figure of his time, Slade suggested that leaping over racial and gendered barriers in a single bound was not just the stuff of fantasy.

○

Shindana threw down the gauntlet on the cover of its 1970 trade catalog: "New Malaika, Dee-Bee, and Nancy are statements. Statements of fact about how one part of the Black community competes in an integrated society. There's room. We do it with dignity, pride and without losing our identity."[164] And yet this open celebration of the company's distinctively Black cultural sensibility did not preclude its designers from representing people who didn't share that experience. In fact, while Lou Smith aspired to make Shindana the world's largest producer of Black dolls, he aimed for its lines to be multiracial rather than exclusively Black. Early on, the company had partly fulfilled that goal by making a place in the line for white versions of both Baby Nancy and Baby Zuri, an infant doll introduced in 1972, in what were probably the first (and maybe only) white dolls in toy history that appear to have been created from a head mold designed to represent Black features: what Smith might well have called a Black doll dipped in white chocolate.

In 1976, however, Shindana completed its multiracial vision of doll play with the introduction of the Little Friends collection, a group of large vinyl dolls (18 inches tall) representing not only white and Black children but also, for the first time in toy-industry history, Hispanic and Asian children (see figure 4.7).[165] Following customary practice at Shindana, each of these new dolls of color had an individually designed head mold that reflected the company's best attempt to respectfully represent the racialized physical features stereotypically associated with people of those ancestries.[166] On the side of every Little Friends box was a message to the adult who bought the product, one that expressed Smith and others' embrace of the contact theory of prejudice—that is, that interaction with racial groups other than one's own can reduce prejudicial attitudes—and their hope that racially unique dolls could have a similar effect on a young child. "Dear Customer," it stated, "Little Friends opens a whole new world for them. A realm of friendship. With Little Friends they become more aware of the people around them. They can learn to appreciate the differences in people."[167] Echoing the rationale behind the interracial encounter groups that met regularly at the OB offices in the late 1960s, Shindana believed the Little Friends collection could offer fun play but also a lesson in the beauty of human diversity.

As the scholar Ann duCille has argued, manufacturers' claims that their dolls have "authentically African American . . . features may bring us dangerously close to the scientific racism of the nineteenth and early twentieth centuries."[168] The presence of this danger in Shindana's appeal to authentic Black features (or Asian or Hispanic ones) is hard to overlook. Racial essentialism was a part of Shindana's politically charged brand of cultural representation from the start, as it mobilized racial distinctions to sell goods—distinctions that, in slightly different form, had historically been used to depict African American people and culture as subhuman and laughable. In this sense, the company's essentialist constructions of "what being Black is all about," or what an "authentic" Black nose looks like, show that in some respects it

4.7. Hispanic Girl, Asian Girl, and Asian Boy dolls (1976), from the Little Friends collection, Shindana Toys, Division of Operation Bootstrap, Inc. Author's collection.

could not resolve the dilemmas of racial representation that beset Remco and Fisher-Price.

And yet, at the same time, as Waldo Martin Jr. points out, "strategic essentialism has been crucial to both Black identity construction and the ongoing Black freedom struggle."[169] It is through this framework, in which Shindana toymakers came to highlight selected physical and cultural markers of Blackness as a way to expose and counter the dominance of whiteness as the unmarked ideal human form, that Shindana's distinctive practices of Black dollmaking are best understood. In other words, the dolls that Shindana made in its South Central factory were not products of racialist science, nor were they just commercially savvy attempts to exploit what the historian Robert E.

Weems, describing corporate advertising appeals of the time that "extolled Black culture and customs," calls the "soul market."[170] Shindana translated an underrepresented and often-disparaged narrative of Black culture and identity into objects of Black beauty, joy, and pride for children, crystallizing a specific historical moment and cultural mood of the late 1960s and early 1970s. In Shindana, the aspirations of Freedom Summer, the Watts Rebellion, and Black Power converged.

By the mid-1970s, the company was expanding the possibilities of racial representation in the doll industry and transforming the racial composition of the toy business itself. In 1974, Shindana made industry history when it leased a permanent showroom in Room 534 of the Toy Building, the long-standing seat of industry power and the nucleus of the annual Toy Fair. As *Playthings* and *Toys* both duly reported, it was "the first permanent display of Black dolls and games in the building," and, though neither mentioned it, probably the first permanent space leased to a Black-owned company.[171] It had been a significant step to rent an exhibit space in the Toy Center just for Toy Fair week; to be able to afford a showroom that toy dealers could visit year-round, and inside the historic Toy Building no less, was an accomplishment not lost on company leaders. "This show room signifies just how far we've come since the beginning," said Shindana's Herman Thompson at the time.[172] Taking full advantage of the opportunities created by the new space's location, the company began to use it as headquarters for its expanding mid-Atlantic and Northeast sales force.

Meanwhile, Shindana's enhanced industry standing brought with it a growing need to diversify its products. One of the ways the company fulfilled that need was through the purchase, also in 1974, of the Detroit-based Soular Products, which had been manufacturing (and under Shindana's ownership, continued to manufacture) a series of Black-oriented board games such as the Afro-American History Mystery Game and the Jackson Five Action Game.[173] The following year, Shindana would bring in sales of $2 million, making 1975 its first profitable year.[174] Such revenue was sufficient to finance the creation of the Honeycomb Child Development Center, a major step toward the development of Smith's Freedom City. Equally major was that by that time, more than one hundred residents, nearly all of them Black, were obtaining valuable technical and managerial training through paid employment at the Shindana plant on Sixty-First Street and Central Avenue.[175] Nor were these economic and community goals the only ones the company achieved by mid-decade. Interestingly enough, this toy company catering to Black consumers unexpectedly owed its initial success to white ones, who bought up more than half the dolls in the company's first five years; by 1975, however, Black consumers were accounting for 80 percent of purchases, thereby fulfilling one of Smith and Hall's original objectives.[176]

Even as Shindana leaders took their project onto the national and international stages—for instance, the mid-1970s brought new distribution points in several African nations—they took steps to maintain and communicate its deep connection to the local community from whence it came.[177] Nowhere did the company so poignantly convey that message than on the cover of its 1972 catalog, which featured not the customary product photos but a full-page image of the Watts Towers—a massive steel-cable and mortar sculpture (its tallest spire reaches 100 feet) created by Italian American artist Simon Rodia that had long been a source of community pride in South LA (see figure 4.8).[178] Likewise, ever since the first boxes of Baby Nancy dolls were sent off with a little sticker on the front that stated, "This toy was completely designed and made by a black-owned company," Shindana toy boxes never stopped notifying consumers of the community development project that both created the products and benefited from their sale.[179] "Shindana, Swahili for 'Competitor,' is owned, managed, and staffed by Black people," read one of these messages (the company modified them over the years). "As part of Operation Bootstrap, we share the slogan 'Learn, Baby, Learn.' Our goal is to develop the jobs and skills necessary to build a successful Black business which will become a permanent part of the community."[180] Of course, these particular reminders of the products' provenance and animating spirit did not last long past the point of purchase, as a child ultimately threw the packaging away. But if one looks just beneath the hairline on the back of every doll's neck, one finds that Shindana's identity as a local nonprofit community organization was written into more than just the merchandising materials. The hairline imprint is not just "© Shindana Toys" but "© Shindana Toys, Div. of Operation Bootstrap, Inc." True, these were Shindana dolls, but in every dimension, they were Operation Bootstrap dolls too.

o

Shindana used the title of its 1970 sales catalog to celebrate its unusual story, calling it *Dolls Made by a Dream*. Yet, for all its early success, it became increasingly clear by the second half of the 1970s that the company inspired by that dream was becoming unsustainable. As a business that had invested its fortunes in a single and relatively new niche market, Shindana gradually found it could not compete successfully with the handful of corporate toy giants that, using their national distribution networks and vast advertising

SHINDANA TOYS 1972
™ A DIVISION OF OPERATION BOOTSTRAP INC.

THE MANUFACTURER OF THE WORLD'S MOST COMPLETE LINE OF BLACK DOLLS.

From the ashes of Watts came a dream . . .
new Li'l Souls, Baby Zuri, Jo Jo, and
Wanda are a testament to the fact that
one segment of the Black Community
competes in an integrated society.
There's room . . . and we do it with
dignity and pride, and without
losing our identity.

4.8. An image of the artist Simon Rodia's Watts Towers, located in South Los Angeles, graces the cover of the 1972 Shindana Toys catalog. Author's collection.

budgets, most of it spent on TV promotions, came to dominate the US toy business on a new scale.[181] By the mid-1970s, they all produced Black versions of their most popular TV-advertised white dolls. If most of these dolls' features still tended toward what Shindana designer James Toatley described as generically white, some of the established companies followed the Shindana template for racial coding with fairly good accuracy, at least in the way of facial features; not one of them was ever able to replicate the much-celebrated distinctive texture of Tamu's and Malaika's natural hair. For many consumers of Black dolls, those racial distinctions may have been good enough; after all, the big brands were less expensive than Shindana dolls, benefiting from the economies of scale that large firms could exploit. This combination of factors made Shindana's uphill ascent in the mass-market doll business an even tougher climb. The company's founding faith that "there's room" for what it had to offer was becoming less and less realistic.

Compounding these business challenges in the latter half of the decade was the loss of Lou Smith, the charismatic cofounder and longtime leader of the diverse OB operation, when Smith and his son tragically died in a car accident in December 1975. (Cofounder Robert Hall had left Shindana in 1970 to join the nearby Watts Labor Community Action Committee, and died of a heart attack three years later.)[182] As the sociologist William Russell Ellis Jr. has written about the seismic impact of Smith's death, "All the troubles that he held at bay with the shield of his leadership soon emerged to disrupt the Dream."[183] At the time, Shindana still owed $1.2 million to banks and investors.[184] Neither a $150,000 loan from Equitable Life Insurance's responsible investments corporation that year nor a Federal Economic Development Administration loan in 1980—a symbolic blow in that it violated OB's founding principles—was sufficient to keep alive Shindana and its parent organization.[185] After trying to survive during its final years by outsourcing production to East Asia, a move that at its core seemed to undermine the company's original commitment to local jobs, Shindana Toys closed its doors in 1983, soon to be followed by OB.[186] Ironically, the company's final year of existence was also the one during which its specialized doll design was seen by millions of people on the big screen. In one of the top-grossing films of 1982, Steven Spielberg's *E.T. the Extra Terrestrial*, the child actor Drew Barrymore's character carries a well-loved doll everywhere she goes. Close inspection reveals it to be none other than one of Shindana's Li'l Soul dolls.

Smith, Hall, and their OB colleagues had come to the toy business somewhat inadvertently. Yet by adapting the financial and technical assistance of Mattel to their own community needs and particular vision of Black identity, they quickly seized on the possibilities of children's culture as a politically meaningful as well as marketable vehicle for OB's larger agenda. Like an earlier group of African American cultural producers in Chicago who successfully navigated their own white-dominated, discriminatory business world, the toymakers of Shindana "sought their own definitions of labor, just profit, and culture industry."[187] In doing so, they joined a long tradition of Black "activist entrepreneurs," to use the historian Joshua Clark Davis's term, who made dolls their business.[188] What was different this time was that Shindana made Black dolls the industry's business too.

Equal Play

Nicki Montaperto was living in the New Jersey suburb of Roselle, just outside New York City, when she helped put toys on the feminist agenda. It was the early 1970s, and Montaperto, a journalist by training, was working as a stay-at-home mother with five children in her care. She was also increasingly active in her local chapter of the National Organization for Women—Union County NOW. The projects she worked on speak to the awesome range of feminist organizing and action during this period, from helping establish the first shelter in her area for victims of domestic abuse to leading a successful fight to open up local youth athletic leagues to girls. One of her roles within the chapter was to chair its Image of Women Task Force, charged with combating negative representations of women across American culture. It is within that context that we can best understand her turn to toys.[1]

If the women's liberation movement popularized the now-famous slogan that the personal is political, Montaperto's emergent toy activism is a case in point. As she grew more politically involved with NOW, her own children's struggles with sexist stereotypes were thrown into high relief. Nowhere was this more apparent than in their interactions with American toy culture. At the toy store, her young daughter's love of trucks and trains was constantly thwarted by packaging images and promotional rhetoric that made it perfectly clear to even a toddler that those items were meant for boys. Montaperto also had four sons. One of them, like his sister, was also discouraged from certain realms of play, though less by the toy industry than the dominant boys' peer culture. While he loved to sew and play with sewing equipment, his male friends made fun of him for enjoying what society perceived as—and told them was—women's work. Buoyed by his mother's unwavering support for his toy preferences, he didn't stop sewing. But he always made sure not to do so when his male friends were around.

Montaperto grew frustrated seeing her children have to hide their true selves or feel they were abnormal or deviant because their interests didn't correspond to society's expectations for their gender. She came to see that the traditional line dividing her parenting and her public activism obscured the interconnectedness of private life and the political world. The same sexist imagery she was fighting outside her home had already seeped into it, affecting her kids in ways she believed were psychologically harmful. Curious to know whether the familiar sexist stereotypes that she encountered in her years of visiting the toy aisles were specific to the truck ads or widespread, Montaperto visited local toy stores with a different objective than usual: research, not shopping. Altogether she cataloged hundreds of items, tallying which toys were catering to which gender and taking notes on the advertising rhetoric. Her research simply confirmed what she already knew. It wasn't just the packages for the truck toys on her daughter's Christmas wish list that trafficked in sexism; it was virtually everything.

Around the same time, she and some fellow NOW members learned of an upcoming convention of toy manufacturers in Washington, DC. As Montaperto recalled fondly, she left her five kids at home with her husband and took a rare weekend trip, four hours south, to demonstrate outside the convention building with her fellow activists and register their opposition to what they saw as sexist toys. Yet she also wanted to broadcast the message beyond the manufacturers. Drawing on her skills as a journalist, she wrote an article on how sexist attitudes and images dominated children's toys and sent it off to leading national magazines. One enthusiastic response came from an editor at *Ladies' Home Journal*. The good news, the editor told Montaperto, was that she felt the piece was important and needed to be published. But there was also bad news: much to the editor's own disappointment, her magazine could not be the one to do it. There were major toy companies among *Ladies' Home Journal* regular advertisers, she explained; the idea of running a piece critical of the industry as a whole was too big of a risk for the magazine to take. Fortunately, another magazine less beholden to such commercial pressures decided to print it. In November 1972, Montaperto's article appeared in the popular magazine *Mothers' Manual*, an offshoot of *Parents* magazine aimed at new and expectant mothers and a standard in OB-GYN office waiting rooms.

Montaperto did not know at the time that she was at the vanguard of a movement to transform the ways Americans thought and talked about toys and the ways the industry manufactured and marketed them. In fact, she was unaware that NOW had named her as the coordinator of its National Toy Campaign a few months after the article was published. Learning about that from me in an interview, a half century later, Montaperto was surprised. But it did not change how she thought about the work itself, at the time or since. To Montaperto, carving out a space in those years to take on the toy culture was not an aberration or distraction from her other feminist work, something less deserving of her time and energy. The little things figured in her vision of a broader feminist awakening and struggle as much as what we normally consider the big things. And she was not alone.

During the early 1970s, an influential network of predominantly white feminist activists, educators, and journalists began calling out the toy trade for the blatant sexism, family stereotypes, and normative whiteness of its products, packaging, and promotions. Combining the feminist media movement's attack on the construction of gender difference with the consumer movement's call for corporate social responsibility, they took on the industry and brought their concerns to the public. They conducted consumer research, organized publicity campaigns, threatened product boycotts, and put pressure on national chains and local retailers. They picketed outside major department stores during the Christmas shopping season and joined the anti–war toy protesters outside the annual Toy Fair. They launched local initiatives with the backing of NOW, and they founded a new consumer advocacy group called the Public Action Coalition on Toys (PACT). Through the movement's new national media, led by *Ms.* magazine, they shared their dissatisfaction with the toy market and promoted a new feminist consumer ethic to mothers, hoping to force marketplace change by guiding consumer choice. One feminist educator even decided to take up the mantle of toymaker herself. In all these cases, the feminist activists who took on American toy culture positioned themselves not just as critics but as cultural educators in the broadest sense. They did not want to tear down the toy industry and popular understandings of toys but to remake them in accordance with the era's broader liberal humanist ethos: a feminist vision of equality and opportunity, to be sure, but also human liberation from the restrictive and oppressive norms of gender, sex, race, class, and family.

Letty Cottin Pogrebin, cofounder of *Ms.* and the leading voice for racially inclusive, nonsexist children's culture during this era, harbored no illusions that children's toys were *the* solution to eliminating sexism in American life. "A toy is not a magic talisman," wrote Pogrebin in 1973, in the first of several toy columns she published in *Ms.* during that decade. "It can't dispel the spirit of sexism in a society that is obsessed with notions of 'manliness' and 'femininity.'"[2] But for Pogrebin and a growing number of other movement activists, the right toys could help dismantle sexist gender ideologies by revising some of postwar American children's earliest object lessons about what it means to be human. "After all," she stated, "healthy children spend over 10,000 hours at play before they enter first grade. Toys and games make a vital contribution to a growing character, personality, and temperament." For that reason, it was time "to take toy buying seriously" and make it a feminist issue.[3] Over the next several years, that is exactly what she and others did, and with a surprising amount of assistance from the toy industry itself.

○

It turned out that Nicki Montaperto was not the only one doing fieldwork at her local toy store on behalf of the women's movement. In 1972 and 1973, NOW members from several chapters were making similar visits to department stores and toy supermarkets in their areas. Assuming the role of consumer researchers, they, too, surveyed the toy landscape and cataloged what they found. They tallied the numbers of toys aimed exclusively at either boys or girls. They took notes on the language and visual construction of these appeals, paying attention to product design, packaging, and other promotional materials. They examined and analyzed thousands of toys as material culture, objects of interest not for their *play value*, as the industry would have it, but for the *values* they were perceived to communicate to their young consumers.[4]

What the toy surveys made unmistakably clear was that the gap between visions of womanhood inside Toyland and the reality of women's lives outside it was vast in the early 1970s. While the women's movement erupted as a nationwide force and won a number of legislative victories and Supreme Court rulings, the women of the industry's imagination were still bound to the home, where normative femininity was best cultivated through cosmetics. In the toy business's patriarchal vision of the labor force, girls lacked the ambition and skills to pursue most jobs outside the home. When they did leave the house, certain themes recurred. Girls could never be doctors, only nurses. Girls could dream of being phone operators or secretaries but not electrical engineers or architects. In the rare instances when girls were featured on the packages for science-, technology-, and engineering-themed toys, more often than not they were observing boys at play, not participating. In one study of eight hundred toys at a large chain toy superstore, education- and science-themed toys depicted boys sixteen times more often than they did girls. Another survey observed a similar pattern, finding three of four toy chemistry sets pitched exclusively to boys.

Second, while marketers tended to promote basic wooden block sets as appropriate for both sexes, the more sophisticated engineering toys, such as Erector sets, were deemed boys-only. Even operating any large machinery, automobiles included, was apparently out of the question for women: one survey found that 98 percent of illustrated packages for car, truck, and train toys exclusively featured boys at play. Such data certainly validated feminist complaints that the toy business offered boys a broader and more varied spectrum of skills to develop and themes to fantasize with. Indeed, across the various categories, toys in general seemed to be made with boys in mind: a survey of all genres of preschool-age toys at one major toy chain revealed that the toys of early childhood were being marketed to boys at the rate of two to one. This was not just an unequal distribution of roles; it was an unequal distribution of fun.

While feminist surveys focused on the mass marketplace, other areas of the business trafficked in these same sexist tropes. "It's never too soon to start the ironing," ran a typical item in *Playthings*, this time to drum up enthusiasm for Tico's Little Miss Housekeeper Play Iron, one of countless items selling an idealized female domesticity at the 1972 Toy Fair.[5] Like toy companies and retailers, trade magazines also reinforced the ideology of natural gender differences by habitually grouping toys into "girls' toys" and "boys' toys" in their annual Toy Fair lists and guides to age-appropriate toys. Toy vacuums, irons, and dolls were always on the girls' list, while trucks, construction sets, and doctor kits were invariably on the other.[6]

Prescriptions for this traditional conception of the women's sphere were equally commonplace among national retailers. Well into the 1970s, the Sears catalog unabashedly peddled what Betty Friedan famously criticized as "the feminine mystique"—the cultural belief that a woman's nature required her to make homemaking her principal duty and to find personal fulfillment in that role. In Sears' marketing division, household labor was the natural domain of little girls, the use of cleaning technology their greatest pleasure. "Little Girls love to help Mommy iron," read one item, below which a young girl was beaming before her child-size toy ironing board. In the 1970 catalog, a similarly ecstatic young girl waits by the stove for the arrival of a boy with groceries. "Delight your little homemaker with a dream kitchen of our finest steel appliances," urged Sears.[7] If the question of who should fill the role of homemaker/nurturer was unclear to any parents prior to entering the toy store, it was clear where the toy business stood. Baby dolls and toy vacuum cleaners were pitched to girls, and virtually any toys representing professions that required higher education and training—engineer, scientist, doctor, police officer—for boys.

For the feminists conducting the toy studies, many of them, like Montaperto, mothers of young children, the industry's sexist vision of human potential was not merely unnerving or in bad taste; it was a social problem deserving the movement's critical attention and resources. Why, they wondered, was the industry selling sexist stereotypes and male privilege at the very moment that women as a class were winning an array of legal and political victories and undergoing dramatic changes in their work status? What could they as women, mothers, consumers, and activists do about it?

By the time activists began publicizing their survey results and articulating an explicitly feminist perspective on toys in the national media, a loosely coordinated all-female network of educators, journalists, and activists had begun to coalesce around the twin goals of combating sexist toys and paving the way for what one organization aptly called "equal play." Over the next several years, they would take their criticisms directly to industry leaders while establishing nonstereotyped toy fare as a cornerstone of progressive parenting.

○

Some of the earliest writing of the new women's movement included references to toys. Three years before her book *Sexual Politics* (1970) propelled her into the national spotlight, Kate Millett underlined toys' place in a culture that taught girls to place motherhood over career ambitions. "By the time a girl is ready for medical school, she doesn't want to go any more," she wrote in an early NOW pamphlet titled *Token Learning*. "She never really had a choice. She's been conditioned to her role ever since she got the doll to play with."[8] In 1970, the Boston Women's Health Collective echoed Millett in *Our Bodies, Ourselves*, soon to become the bible of a grassroots women's health movement. "It seems pretty clear to us as women that from the moment we're born, we're treated differently from little boys," wrote the authors. The gender norms for play, and the messages they contained about girls' future role in society, were part of that differential and unequal treatment. "Our toys are different. Dolls instead of chemistry sets."[9]

Such comments reflected one of the hallmarks of the new feminism's social scientific framework: the belief in the fundamental significance of role socialization in the reproduction of a sexist society.[10] Led by a new generation of feminist-oriented researchers such as psychologists Nancy Chodorow and Eleanor Maccoby and sociologist Jesse Bernard, the 1970s would be "the heyday of feminist enthusiasm for sex-role theory."[11] As the historian Kirsten Swinthe describes this period of upheaval in these social scientific fields, "feminist psychologists tore down biological accounts of female development" while their "peers [in sociology] critiqued dominant models of male and female roles and demonstrated socialization's importance in shaping social roles. By the middle of the 1970s, a generation of feminist scholars had undercut once-hegemonic beliefs about women's psyche and roles."[12] What was significant too was how quickly these theories found a place in mainstream feminist discourse, where readers eagerly embraced a growing body of research that confirmed what was intuitive to many who grew up female in the United States.

One of the researchers whose work quickly found its way into popular feminist discourse was Nancy Chodorow. In the chapter she contributed to *Woman in Sexist Society*, a seminal 1971 anthology of feminist writings edited by Vivian Gornick and Barbara K. Moran, Chodorow conducted a review of recent studies of children's leisure and career preferences (including toys); what she saw was "the clear cultural evaluation of masculine pursuits and characteristics as superior, an evaluation that is probably made more evident to the girl as she grows up and learns more about the world around her."[13] "The tragedy of woman's socialization," she concluded, "is that [her basic sexual] identity is clearly devalued in the society in which she lives."[14] Meanwhile, the sex-role socialization of boys had elements of tragedy too, Chodorow wrote. Based on recent studies showing that from kindergarten age onward, "boys are much less likely to claim a preference for anything feminine than girls to prefer masculine roles or objects," she concluded that while boys didn't internalize their own inferiority, they learned early on to reject anything culturally marked as feminine and conform to the macho norms of straight masculinity—what some feminists were now calling the masculine mystique.[15]

Such theories of learned inferiority and superiority were strikingly similar to the midcentury psychology of racial prejudice that shaped the late 1960s discussion of Black dolls, substituting gender for race. In the same way that experts saw Black children's personality as irrevocably damaged by the racist culture's message of inferiority, and white children's personalities injured by the prejudice they had learned, feminist psychologists and critics contended that a sexist society had a similarly devastating effect on young people's hearts and minds—girls as well as boys. In *Woman in Sexist Society*, Gornick and Moran argued that while feminists needed to remake "electoral politics" and "the politics of money, prestige, and real power," the "more subtle, and perhaps more final," arena of women's oppression as a class was the "politics of personality."[16] For the women's liberation movement, then, much like the Black freedom struggle, it wasn't only that the personal was political. The personality was political too.[17]

Drawing on these social scientific assumptions about the importance of early childhood in the gendering of human personality—along with a belief, buoyed by the influential social constructionist theories of anthropologists like Ruth Benedict and Margaret Mead, that the personality could be engineered through culture—the early 1970s marked a watershed moment in feminist educational and media activism around the problem of young children's socialization.[18] During this period, activists documented widespread sex stereotyping in children's elementary school readers and launched campaigns to demand replacements that gave boys and girls equal attention and respect.[19] The mass-market children's book industry found itself the subject of study by feminist scholars and activist groups, who in a series of widely publicized reports exposed the prevalence of stereotyped illustrations and storylines in mainstream picture books.[20] Others lobbied the producers of children's TV programs like *Sesame Street* to create less stereotypically passive roles for female characters.[21] And in some instances, such as the widely acclaimed 1972 multimedia project *Free to Be . . . You and Me*, feminist media activists went beyond cultural criticism and demands for more nonsexist representations in mainstream media to independently produce their own.[22] Thus, the turn to toys paralleled, overlapped with, and made its own special contributions to the feminist reevaluation of popular media and campaigns to effect cultural change at the level of childhood.

o

While NOW's Brooklyn chapter had launched a nonsexist child-rearing initiative that included toys in 1971, and members of NOW-NYC had joined Victoria Reiss's PRITI for a joint rally against sexist and violent-themed toys the same year, it was not until 1973 that toys officially found a place on NOW's national agenda. In late February of that year, probably to coincide with the Toy Fair, the organization issued a press release announcing its first National

Toy Campaign, with Nicki Montaperto, who had recently published her article on sex stereotyping in toys in *Mothers' Manual*, as coordinator.[23] When Montaperto shifted her attention to her other NOW initiatives, Allenna Leonard, a member of Howard County NOW (Maryland), took over the nascent national campaign. As chair of the new NOW Subcommittee on Toys, she would direct the organization's work on toys and nonsexist socialization for the rest of the decade.[24]

Although NOW became best known as a policy-oriented organization aimed at eliminating legal, political, and economic discrimination against women, its agenda from the very beginning included efforts to combat sexist stereotypes and conditioning in commercial mass media, from journalism to network television. In fact, NOW leaders in the New York national office formed the Task Force on the Image of Women in the Mass Media in 1967, just one year after the group's founding. In this light, NOW's attention to cultural conditioning through toys reflected long-standing concerns.[25] Perhaps less expected was the entry of the Women's Action Alliance into the toy-reform campaign during these years. The Alliance, as it was known, was founded in 1971 by movement activists Dorothy Pitman Hughes, Gloria Steinem, and Brenda Feigen Fasteau, with the aim of serving as an information clearinghouse and support organization for fledgling women's groups. In its first years, the Alliance's programming docket ran the gamut, from helping women find female medical professionals in their area, to lobbying for anti–sex discrimination legislation, to opening the first domestic violence shelters. As it turned out, toys would find a spot on the agenda too, as part of the Non-Sexist Child Development Project (NCDP), one of the organization's first in-house initiatives.

The NCDP grew directly from grassroots voices, following the Alliance's commitment to supporting under-resourced women organizers and listening to their concerns. After receiving an "outpouring of mail from women all over the country who were stating that their pre-school age children were already being forced into rigidly defined sex roles," Alliance staff realized that despite recent victories for the cause of gender equity in education—Title IX of the 1972 Education Amendments prohibited sex discrimination in all federally funded school activities—"virtually no one was designing a program for the first-level of education, the pre-school child."[26] With that in mind, the Alliance posted a job listing on university employment boards around the country, in search of an educator capable of developing an early childhood curriculum "free of sex stereotyping and that works to decondition parents, teachers and children."[27] While sex-role socialization would be the driving concern at first, it quickly became clear that any effective program would have to recognize the intersecting lines of gender socialization with those of race, class, family, and culture.[28]

In 1972, Barbara Sprung, a teacher (at the progressive Calhoun School in Manhattan) and NOW member who was completing her master's degree at Bank Street College of Education, spotted the job listing on a Bank Street bulletin board and applied.[29] She was soon invited to come in to the Alliance offices, where she was interviewed by Letty Cottin Pogrebin, the feminist writer and activist who had helped found *Ms.* magazine and the National Women's Political Caucus the previous year. Few people were as intimately involved (officially and otherwise) in the birth and early years of so many influential women's rights projects as Pogrebin was, the Alliance among them. But it was also particularly fitting for Pogrebin to be Sprung's interviewer for the NCDP position, as 1972 was the year when Pogrebin took up the cause of feminist child-rearing on the national level—publishing an important article, "Down with Sexist Upbringing," in *Ms.* magazine's first issue in the spring, and serving as an editorial consultant to the influential children's album and book *Free to Be . . . You and Me*, released in the fall.[30]

The Alliance and *Ms.* magazine also shared more than just leaders like Pogrebin and Gloria Steinem; both organizations had offices in the same Manhattan building. As Sprung recalled, on the day of her interview at the Alliance, Pogrebin only had to take the elevator down one floor from her *Ms.* office. Ultimately, Sprung got the job offer and accepted it, becoming the NCDP's founding director. Over the next several years, she would develop the NCDP into a nationally recognized program for teachers and educators, working to eliminate stereotyping in the early childhood classroom and, with her own specialized toys, create the tools for fostering what the Alliance called "equal play."[31]

Feminist organizing around toys also led to the formation of a new activist organization. At the 1973 NOW national conference, Allenna Leonard was talking with Patricia Powers, an organizer with Ralph Nader's Citizen Action Group who was in the midst of a lobbying campaign for stricter federal toy-safety guidelines. If the two shared a good deal demographically—white, well-educated professionals with young children—they also quickly discovered a shared interest: moving society forward through its toys. As Leonard recalled, "A bunch of us were up in one of the rooms [at the NOW conference] saying, 'How do we pull this toy thing together? Let's have an organization and let's combine strengths here."[32] It did not take long for Powers to reach out to Victoria Reiss of PRITI, which had continued to stage its annual Toy

Fair demonstrations against war toys through the early 1970s.[33] Moreover, while the three of them had different motives, from "saving lives" to "changing values"—which is how Powers put it—they built on that diversity by pooling their knowledge, resources, and contacts and launching a big-tent toy-reform group.[34]

On the eve of the 1973 Toy Fair, at a hotel just blocks from the Toy Building, Reiss and the others, including Nicki Montaperto from NOW, held a press conference to announce the founding of the Public Action Coalition on Toys (PACT), the first incorporated consumer watchdog group dedicated exclusively to the toy industry and the education of parents about play (see figure 5.1). In an early sign of the industry's unwelcoming position, the new group's attempt to make its announcement *inside* the fair by securing a booth at the Statler Hilton Hotel—part of the extended Toy Fair complex in recent years—was thwarted by the TMA's president as being "inappropriate."[35] That one of PACT's stated goals was "to see that the toy manufacturers get a social conscience and begin putting little people before profits" may help explain the TMA's lack of enthusiasm for the group's appearance on the scene.[36] Powers, Reiss, and Leonard came out swinging. They also wanted to open their umbrella coalition to any citizen group hoping to "encourage the toy trade to take a more socially responsible position toward the children who buy and play with their products."[37] More than a dozen opted in as members, including the Women's Action Alliance, Action for Children's Television (ACT), and the Council on Interracial Books for Children. The organization also quickly assembled an advisory board of prominent experts that over the course of the decade included Benjamin Spock; noted child psychologist and parenting author Lee Salk; former New York City Commissioner of Consumer Affairs Elinor Guggenheimer; and even Bella Abzug, the fiery feminist congresswoman from New York.[38]

While PACT's call for better toy-safety regulations continued to be a talking point, the group's leaders increasingly turned their focus toward the social justice concerns of the women's, Black liberation, and antiwar movements of the time. In this they would play a critical role in broadening the definition of equal play, taking it beyond the most recognizable feminist concerns with sexism. "If we acknowledge that toys are of enormous importance to the growth and development of children, then we must also acknowledge that as adults we have a responsibility to make certain that the toys our children play with are good for them," PACT stated in *Guidelines for Choosing Toys for Children*, a widely distributed 1976 booklet covering all its member groups' concerns. "We must take an active stand against toys which warp,

5.1. The Public Action Coalition on Toys (PACT) announces its formation at a press conference in New York City on the eve of the 1973 Toy Fair. Seated at the table are (*from left*) Glenda Ernst, Nicki Montaperto, Victoria Reiss (*at the microphone*), Mr. Leonard (first name unknown), and an unidentified student activist looking on. Photograph by Dorothy Marder, February 26, 1973. Courtesy of Richard Reiss.

impede or hamper the growth and development of children because they are unsafe, violent, racist or sexist. It is up to us."[39] The coalition's understanding of toys that warp, impede, and hamper also included baby dolls that lacked visible genitalia, reflecting the influence of the women's health movement— which made knowing one's body a centerpiece of its holistic conception of sexual health—as well as encouragement by Benjamin Spock and others to end taboos on nudity in the home.[40] Barbara Sprung, who coauthored PACT's toy guide, expressed her concerns about the impact of anatomically inaccurate dolls on children's psychological growth this way: "It is unfortunate that most dolls are anatomically incomplete, that is, they have no sex organs. This undoubtedly gives children the impression that their sex organs are something to be secretive about. It is also certainly a source of confusion to them, since other parts of dolls' bodies are usually quite detailed (baby dolls have dimples, folds, navels, etc.)."[41] Why was it, quipped PACT cofounder and NOW toy coordinator Allenna Leonard, that "the boys' organs remain so sacrosanct that even a baby boy doll comes without them?"[42]

○

Sarcastic humor like Leonard's was just one of the various tactics feminists used to take on the industry and publicize their concerns to consumers. They staged public demonstrations and picket lines at the annual Toy Fair in New York and at numerous regional toy fairs in Atlanta, Dallas, and Los Angeles. They passed out flyers urging manufacturers to "End Toy Sexism" and "Catch up with the times and give us toys that reflect the consciousness of the seventies."[43] And they encouraged members of their organizations and readers of *Ms.* to join in boycotts of companies that relied on gender-typed appeals and cultural stereotypes. In the mid-1970s, that encompassed most of the industry. "Why not use consumer power to reform the Neanderthals?" asked Letty Cottin Pogrebin.[44] Activists answered her question in the affirmative by flooding corporate offices with letters that threatened to withhold their dollars until manufacturers committed to change. To assist them in that effort, lists of commercial offenders were circulated through NOW newsletters and flyers.[45] The publicity efforts won extensive media coverage in national newspapers, while NOW members marshaled the group's status as the leading voice of the women's movement to land interviews on TV and radio to discuss their concerns about toys and socialization.[46]

Along with raising the specter of boycotts, toy activists hoped to convince toymakers that feminism was not just ethical but profitable. Some suggested using the language of the marketplace to appeal to the trade. "Approach them on a business level," advised members of Howard County NOW.[47] After all, the principal goal of equal play was to convince toymakers to revise their promotional materials, not declare their sympathies for the women's movement. When Pogrebin and Steinem secured a meeting with officials at Lionel Toys in the company's New York City office, they pitched equal opportunity in economic terms: if Lionel would just advertise its famous trains to girls, the company would double its market overnight.[48]

While toy companies that seemed to revel in exploiting gender stereotypes were publicly written up and faced direct action from consumers, companies whose products met the feminists' standards for good toys were publicly celebrated. Detroit NOW, for instance, gave out awards to manufacturers for nonstereotyped images of men and women.[49] But it was PACT that raised the bar for this kind of normative signaling when in 1975 it began staging an annual awards gala, complete with a celebrity panel of judges, on the eve of the Toy Fair.[50] In addition to handing out certificates to manufacturers who produced what the coalition called "life-enhancing toys," PACT also hoped to encourage the industry by giving citations to companies that had recently taken positive steps toward meeting the group's criteria for good toys.

Unlike other feminist media initiatives targeting TV and radio, appeals for government regulation were never really on the table for the toy campaigns. The closest thing to demands for structural reform of the industry's operations was PACT's 1974 petition to the TMA to be granted official status as an advisory group to the trade. As the petition charged, the toy industry had "far too little contact with childhood specialists and consumer concerns."[51] In order to close that perceived gap, PACT proposed the establishment of "permanent *working* boards composed of consumers and experts mutually agreed upon by PACT and TMA."[52] The working boards would meet on a monthly basis to address consumer concerns. Feminists and their professional allies in toy reform would be effectively integrated into the industry itself.

The idea of the TMA retaining an advisory board of childhood specialists was not new; in fact, the trade group already had one. In 1948, the TMA had established the American Toy Institute as its official research division, with Grace Langdon, a veteran early childhood educator and administrator, in the role of child development adviser. In the 1930s and early 1940s, Langdon had served as national director for the nursery schools program of the New Deal's Works Progress Administration. She later received her PhD from Teacher's College, Columbia University; served on its faculty; and by the 1950s was a sought-after consultant, working with the American Red Cross, among other organizations, and writing several books.[53] As the American Toy Institute's spokesperson, Langdon authored its first consumer publication, an "educational leaflet" (as the institute called it) titled *How to Choose Toys* (1948).[54] Under her direction, during the 1950s the institute regularly published multipage, catalog-like promotional inserts in *Life* magazine featuring toys from Fisher-Price, Mattel, and other leading companies.[55] Highlighting the virtues of American-made toys (this was a trade association, after all) and stressing the crucial developmental importance of buying them year-round, the inserts promoted not only goods but also the institute's commitment to children's healthy development. As one 1953 insert announced, free copies of Langdon's leaflet were being made available by mail to parents, "to help you choose the toys that will best fit the interests and essential play needs of the children on your Christmas list."[56]

In the early 1960s, the TMA ended its direct oversight of the institute due to growing concerns that, according to one institutional history, "the Institute might be perceived as a marketing effort rather than a serious research and information resource."[57] It was that perception, a decade later, that led PACT to question the institute's legitimacy; as the group charged in a press release, the institute was "really not a functioning body [despite the fancy description given to it in the TMA booklet for members]."[58] There seems to have been some truth to that characterization. By the 1970s, the institute still retained a rotating group of prominent advisers, such as the pediatricians Milton Levine—the doctor with war toys in his office—and T. Berry Brazelton, a Harvard University professor and popular child-rearing author. Yet other than organizing occasional events for the trade, like a 1972 panel discussion that included Benjamin Spock and Margaret Mead, the institute of the early 1970s appeared to be taking a backseat role to the TMA's own expanding public relations and consumer education efforts.[59] Although TMA officers could (and did) disagree with PACT activists over the definition of a "functioning body," for Reiss and her coalition, at minimum it meant including the voices of consumers. A PACT pamphlet thus called for nothing less than a "revitalization of TMA's Toy Institute to be planned jointly by consumer and industry representatives."[60] It was the first and the last time toy activists proposed reforming the TMA by joining it.

While reformers aimed to establish their authority at the national level, their campaigns did not ignore the potential for change at the grassroots by putting pressure on retailers. Mothers who shared feminists' concern were thus called into action to monitor their local toy marketplace and put their purchasing power to work. The Alliance's Barbara Sprung suggested that "if the toy store stocks only the standard TV toys which usually have sexist (and frequently racist) packaging you might suggest to the store keeper that you would rather buy neutral toys in neutral packages for your child and for the presents you give."[61] Sprung also stressed that community organizing would have a much greater impact than individual action. "If you can have several other parents in the neighborhood mention the same thing, the storekeeper may get the message and begin to carry some alternative toys as well as the standards," she advised.[62] If retailers would simply "refuse to place orders" for stereotyped toys, as one group proposed, corporate manufacturers would be forced to listen.[63] Following in the footsteps of WSP and WILPF, activists imagined the power of the consumer to force change within the industry. What was different this time was the scale of both the grievance and the demand: with a few exceptions, like Daisy, most of the big toy companies during these years might benefit from sales of war toys but hardly depended on them for their survival; toy guns, after all, were just one of their lines. Gender stereotypes, by contrast, were everywhere. It is easy to take a gun off the shelves until the protest quiets down, or even for good. It is a whole other thing to redesign every package, advertisement, and often the toy itself to make one's products completely gender neutral.

○

The language that feminists employed in their criticism underscores the extent to which they saw toys as not just a personal issue but a political one; it also highlights the power and influence they assigned to toys as agents of socialization. The Alliance, for example, clearly saw the gender division of toys as an equal-opportunity matter, charging the toy industry with "denying children access" to images of equality.[64] Meanwhile, members of NOW-NYC denounced "sexual apartheid in the toy department"; "little girls are *not* second-class children," they declared.[65] As women's groups framed it, toy promotions' limited vision of womanhood violated one of the foundational tenets of liberal feminism: equality of opportunity. The 1966 NOW Statement of Purpose avowed that "NOW is dedicated to the proposition that women, first and foremost, are human beings, who, like all other people in our society, must have the chance to develop their fullest human potential."[66] Yet as activists contended, the toy industry failed to support that mission. Just as NOW and other women's groups had petitioned the Equal Employment Opportunity Commission in the late 1960s to strike down gender-specific "Help Wanted" ads for job listings, toy activists aimed to strike down what they saw as gender-specific ads for career aspirations. Breaking down barriers to women's employment was crucial, but so was cultivating a sense of the possible in girls. Access to nondiscriminatory toys quickly became a feminist talking point—and not just for girls. "If we want our children to be healthy and happy, we must instill in each child the virtues in both sex roles," Howard County NOW stated in a flyer promoting nonsexist toys: "Let everyone be skillful *and* sensitive, self-respecting *and* helpful, courageous *and* kind. Let's not stint our children."[67] Here was the principle of equal play, which became central to the feminist toy campaigns. For it was not just little girls whose capacity to "develop as *individuals*" was being compromised by sexist stereotypes in toys.[68] Boys also needed to be protected from the industry's narrow messages of human potential, said the critics, messages that not only limited possible futures of manhood but foreclosed on feminist visions of a nonsexist, egalitarian society to come. Asserting that, as one NOW flyer put it, "a Good

Toy is good for a girl or a boy, a Bad Toy isn't good for either," 1970s feminists added their own contribution to American understandings of what a good toy was and what it did.[69]

As feminists theorized the relationship of toys to healthy male development, their concerns reflected the new literature on sex-role socialization. The Alliance's Barbara Sprung argued that "boys' development is arrested on the emotional level. . . . They're not allowed to develop their nurturing or gentler emotions. They're not supposed to show fear or sadness. We're conditioning boys out of feeling a whole side of their humanity."[70] Toys were part of that cultural conditioning, and NOW-NYC had a similar take, asserting that "in spite of their greater range of choices, little boys are also conditioned for the masculine mystique. . . . [They] are denied toys which teach the qualities of nurturing and sensitivity to others."[71] Howard County NOW put it more bluntly: "Boys suffer, too."[72]

For these reasons, feminists contended, the industry needed to include boys in the domestic world of traditional girls' toys just as much as girls needed to be cast in historically male roles. And there was no more conventionally "feminine" toy as important to boys' nonsexist personality development as the baby doll. During the late 1960s and 1970s, one major point of agreement across the diverse women's movement was to convince men to shoulder an equitable share of child-rearing labor. As the radical feminist intellectual Shulamith Firestone stated in her 1970 book *The Dialectic of Sex: The Case for Feminist Revolution*, "the first demand for any alternate system" needed to include "the diffusion of the childbearing and childrearing role to the society as a whole, men as well as women."[73] Dolls, suggested feminists, could help do that cultural work. "If we're going to raise men interested in childcare, we have to break down the stereotyped roles," said Kathleen Reber, president of Brooklyn NOW. "And men who are able to do this must start when they're little. We must not put down their interest in dolls."[74] Sprung agreed: "There is nothing 'sissyish' about having a good, loving, nurturant father—it is an ideal we all like to experience," she said. "Yet doll play which increases understanding of this role has become associated in our minds with femininity and is therefore considered highly inappropriate for boys."[75] Refusing to offer boys a doll violated the feminist principles of equal-opportunity play. "Most of us have just never stopped to consider that boys have as much right and need to examine the role of fatherhood through doll play as girls have to examine the role of motherhood," stated Sprung in an early draft of a guide to nonsexist education.[76] Boys had a right to play with dolls.

Moreover, according to Sprung and other advocates of nonsexist socialization, dolls could help carry out Firestone's vision of an equitable division of labor within the realm of child-rearing. As Sprung surmised, it was the culture's disapproval of boys' doll play, part of a dominant ideal of masculinity that painted emotional awareness and care work as signs of weakness and failure, that helped explain men's inability to achieve the qualities of the new manhood that many straight feminists desired in a male partner. "It is truly ironic and sad that we condition our little boys away from doll play," she wrote, "and then are angry and resentful when as adults they seem unable to show affection, tenderness, and nurturant qualities as husbands and fathers."[77] These concerns "may seem [like] very serious issues to attach to the importance of doll play," Sprung stated elsewhere, "but I strongly believe there is a connection between the two."[78] Doll play could help produce a new and better male parent and partner.

As many feminists saw it, the industry had a crucial role to play in changing these entrenched cultural attitudes about appropriate boys' play. In a 1974 letter to the *New York Sunday News*, Felicia George of the Alliance argued that it is "hard for people to make a choice when no real choice exists, as is the case if manufacturers continue to produce dolls for 'boys only' and other dolls for 'girls only.' If dolls were made for *children*, then maybe parents would be more willing to buy dolls for their boys."[79] George's last point here speaks to a critical aspect of feminist toy activism, which was that insofar as feminists demanded significant change in the business of toys, they never opposed commercial toys per se. As they often pointed out, there was nothing intrinsically wrong with toy vacuum cleaners or miniature metal trucks; the problem arose when companies marketed either of these items exclusively to one gender. As Pogrebin put it, "Most toys are sexually anonymous. It's only the way we present them to the child that reflect stereotypes and causes them to be perpetuated."[80]

At the same time, some were skeptical that putting boys on the packages of every Chatty Cathy or Tippy Tumbles doll would be enough. As Kathleen Reber told a reporter, many parents were not ready to purchase them because "most women still believe that if their sons play with dolls, they won't be completely masculine."[81] What is more, she suggested, such concerns masked homophobic fears of having a gay son: "They're worried about homosexuality, about their sons being called sissies."[82] Such worries were widespread in postwar society, the result of a narrow definition of normative boy behavior that valued physical strength over care and compassion. During the 1940s and 1950s, writes the historian Julia Grant, many psychological experts characterized the "sissy, effeminate boy" as "a threat to the image of a strong, masculine, and virile America, untainted by feminine impulses and able to stand up to Nazis and Communists alike."[83] By the 1970s, the stigma attached to gender non-conforming boys persisted, to the point that even the three relatively sensitive Brady brothers on the popular network TV show *The Brady Bunch* (1969–74) received a hearty warning by their father to avoid the girls' world of doll play. As he announced to the whole Brady family, to the subsequent roar of the studio laugh track, "If my boy wanted to play in anybody's dollhouse, I'd take him to a psychiatrist."[84] According to some experts, Mr. Brady would have been right to send his boys for psychiatric guidance. Well into the decade, boys' preferences for traditionally feminine-typed toys like dolls were still used as a tool for diagnosing male gender pathology, a way to help psychiatrists distinguish between (to use their terms) "normal" and "feminoid" boys.[85]

If only Mrs. Brady had come across Benjamin Spock's monthly *Redbook* column just two seasons later, she might well have objected to her husband's cheery gender bullying. For in 1971, Spock made waves in feminist circles when he reversed his earlier position on dolls, just as he had done on war toys, telling millions of *Redbook* readers that dolls provided a boy with "a way of practicing his future role as a parent"—part of what he described to the *New York Times Magazine* as a "change of heart on traditional matters of sex and child rearing."[86] Like the change of heart on war toys, this one, too, would have to wait four years to get into the next revised edition of his best-selling book.

And yet, to return to the question of promotions, the mere appearance of girls and boys on a toy box or advertisement, much less the approval of Spock, who faced heaps of movement criticism for promoting child care as a woman's job since 1946, did not by itself define a toy as authentically feminist. There were other factors in judging feminist value in toys, and no institutional voice did more to articulate that critical standard than *Ms.* magazine.

o

According to the historian Amy Erdman Farrell, *Ms.* magazine, founded in 1971, "worked to be a mass media umbrella for feminism, positioning itself as the space in which women could share their experiences, their various opinions and strategies, across boundaries of race, ethnicity, class, age, and sexuality."[87] To that end, it also functioned as a kind of *Consumer Reports* for feminist women, and Pogrebin's annual toy column exemplified liberal feminists' embrace of the postwar consumerist ethos. In 1974, she proposed that toymakers "need to hire feminist consultants the way they hire marketing specialists."[88] Yet, in the absence of any employment offers from the industry, and the TMA's outright dismissal of PACT's proposed consumer advisory board, Pogrebin assumed the role of feminist consultant to both the trade and the public. Taking a sledgehammer to the toy industry with her scorching wit and tongue-in-cheek performance of the consumer advocate, she advised feminist-minded mothers on how to navigate a sexist and racist toy market. In doing so, she reinvested mothers' expected role as shoppers for children, disparaged by feminist critics as central to the feminine mystique, with new political meaning and possibility.

In her very first toy column in December 1973, titled "Toys for Free Children," Pogrebin spelled out her vision of equal play while naming the roadblocks that stood in its way. Echoing the NOW slogan that "a Good Toy is good for a girl or a boy," she made it clear that nowhere was sexism as rampant and accepted as it was in promotional materials such as ads and packaging. But Pogrebin also wanted to help readers spot sexist attitudes when they found expression in the toys themselves. "We want toys that don't insult, offend, or exclude one sex by inference or omission," she stated.[89] More elusive were the defining characteristics that made for what feminists had begun to call sexist toys, as Pogrebin made it her work over the next several years to educate readers on the less conspicuous ways traditional gender and sex norms, not to mention misogyny, showed up in the designs and narratives of commercial playthings. Consider the 1975 Fisher-Price Adventure Team line of small action figures, which came under Pogrebin's fire for symbolic employment discrimination. In some of the themed sets, she explained, Fisher-Price featured male and female figures in the same role; but in others, they didn't, and she was not going to let the company off easy for making a partial commitment to gender equity. "Avoid *Wilderness Patrol* and *Construction Workers*," Pogrebin advised, for "their all-male crews suggest that heavy work and danger are man's domain."[90] The same went for preschool-age puzzles, games, and other figure sets that depicted men in virtually all professional occupations. "Job bias is illegal in adult society," she quipped, "but it proliferates among so-called educational toys."[91]

Likewise, Pogrebin roundly critiqued the commercially segregated yet similarly gendered worlds of fashion dolls for girls and action figures for boys. Fashion dolls following the Barbie template "should be avoided," she opined, because they "encourage acquisitive values and feed the image of woman as ornament."[92] While Barbie had once been outfitted for dozens of professional careers—including that of astronaut in 1965, four years before a woman astronaut went into space—the endless stream of new fashion dolls that flooded the 1970s market, with the exception of Shindana's Wanda Career Girl, emphasized clothing, cosmetics, and consumption as a young woman's proper pursuits.[93] Many of the era's male-gendered action figures came under fire too, for the ways in which they narrowed the narratives of heroic manhood to expressions of physical strength, aggressiveness, and combat. As Pogrebin queried readers, "Do the macho lifestyles of these play figures serve as unspoken ideological accessories of the toy?"[94] And while gender bias and discrimination may have been Pogrebin's main concerns when it came to promoting equal play, they were not the only ones. According to her definition, a feminist toy was not just nonstereotyped in its representations and unisex in its advertising rhetoric and promotional imagery; it was also, as she put it, "nonracist," meaning free of racial stereotypes and advertised to children of all racial identities.[95]

As the first explicitly feminist parenting columnist in US history, Pogrebin launched a lasting intervention in the most influential arenas of American cultural debate over child-rearing: the pages of women's magazines. At a time when the feminist movement often found itself stereotyped as anti-family by the traditionalist Christian Right, Pogrebin revalorized motherhood as a key site for feminist action and self-definition. Toy buying, her columns suggested, could serve as an extension of feminist responsibility, a way to bring feminism into the home.[96] Over the course of the 1970s, Pogrebin not only developed a savage, surgical critique of how American toy culture reproduced normative gender and racial ideals but also put anti-sexist, anti-racist toy selection on the agenda of liberal-minded parents everywhere. As we will see, she and her colleagues in NOW, PACT, and the Alliance put it on the agenda of a few leading toymakers too.

Feminist Toys

In December 1973, Lionel Toys held a historic press conference in New York, not to unveil a new toy line but to announce a sweeping change to its advertising practices of nearly three-quarters of a century. Since the company's founding, Lionel had marketed its famous electric train sets exclusively to boys and fathers, mostly in the pages of boys' magazines. By the time Dr. Spock was writing his parenting column, they had become recognizable symbols of masculine play. Toy trains, Spock wrote in *Redbook*, were "a particularly exciting symbol of masculinity because they represent enormous power that is nevertheless under complete control, from a distance, as if by magic."[1] Yet girls also enjoyed the magic of trains, insisted the leaders of the feminist toy insurgency. As discussed in the previous chapter, Letty Cottin Pogrebin and Gloria Steinem were among a group of activists who met with Lionel executives to make this very point. Moreover, the activists had argued, the addition of girl consumers as targets of Lionel appeals had the potential to double profits. What good reason, then, did Lionel have not to open up its brand to girls?

At the December press conference, Lionel officials basically confessed that they did not have a reason. Therefore, they announced, they were taking concrete steps to make girls part of the marketing picture, starting with a new TV ad campaign targeting girls and their mothers.[2] Explaining the decision, they invoked the feminists' main arguments, saying it was a wise business move as well as "the proper thing," while crediting their feminist awakening not to the activists but to a seven-year-old girl who wrote Lionel a letter wondering why the company only seemed to care about boys.[3] Whether or not the feminists perceived it as a slight, they had succeeded in their goal of forcing visible change. Better still, a year into the feminist toy campaigns, a year after Montaperto and Pogrebin published their first articles and Reiss, Powers, and Leonard got together to form PACT, visible signs of change could be found across the industry, often in surprising places.

This final chapter examines how the toy industry responded to feminist calls for change through the production of new types of toys and newly imagined toy consumers. During the high point of feminist activism in the mid-1970s, most toymakers stayed silent on the question of girls' equality and nonsexist toys. Many likely did not want to be bothered. Some may have feared the kind of public controversy that embroiled manufacturers during the debate over war toys a decade earlier. Others may well have withheld what they perceived to be unpopular views. By contrast, the TMA, charged with guarding the industry's reputation, was not so risk averse. As was to be expected, TMA officials were quick to defend the industry from what they saw as unrealistic demands and unfair charges. "The great mass of the American people," contended TMA president Randolph Barton in 1974, "doesn't want their little boys to play with dolls, or their daughters to be carpenters."[4] It would be irresponsible of the toy business, he said, to remake industry practices according to the views of a "small, intellectual . . . minority."[5] Other prominent voices in the trade became defensive, saying that the industry was being unfairly blamed, even smeared, for simply giving consumers what they wanted. "This is not a big, bad, selfish, immoral, arrogant, profit crazy industry," wrote Denton Harris in *Toy & Hobby World* upon hearing the news of PACT's formation.[6] Indeed, the idea that the industry's public image was under siege as never before led the TMA to launch the biggest national public relations campaign in its history, hiring the well-known PR firm Harshe-Rotman & Druck to run it.[7]

All the while, however, a small but influential group of manufacturers followed Lionel's lead, understanding that the toy industry's successful navigation of this new era of toy activism depended on its ability to connect and communicate with a new generation of progressive-leaning consumers. One of the biggest challenges they faced, no doubt, was figuring out how to do so without abandoning (or appearing to abandon) their more socially conservative base. After all, this was the mid-1970s, an era marked by both landmark legislation and court rulings for women's rights and the birth of an organized antifeminist backlash.[8] The nation's split consciousness on the politics of gender hardly made selling toys any easier. But, of course, as we have seen in previous chapters, social conflict and political polarization had never stopped the toy industry before.

The industry's feminist-oriented responses during these years took a variety of forms, from expressing commitments to the cause and eliminating gender-typed advertising, to creating all-new "feminist" toys in the name of empowering young girls. In one case, as we will see, an influential toy manufacturer came to believe that the best way for it to incorporate feminist thinking into future designs was not just to listen to feminists but to collaborate directly with them. At one point, even the TMA appeared to open itself up to feminist concerns, inviting a prominent activist from NOW to speak at the group's annual convention.[9]

In 1965, Lionel had proclaimed, "Nice Toys Don't Kill," making common cause with the anti–war toy movement and inspiring other industry leaders to use their platforms to speak out against the war. Eight years later, the company was the first in the industry to express solidarity with the goals of women's liberation. It would not be alone.

○

In March 1974, three months into Lionel's new ad campaign, two new toys on display at the Toy Fair indicated that some in the industry establishment were willing to go further than remaking their ads, instead designing totally new products that spoke directly to core feminist values. What if the producers of fashion dolls, the most sexist of all categories according to the critics, would be better off profiting from feminism than fighting it? This was the question that two of the largest purveyors of TV toys, Kenner and Ideal, seemed to be asking as they independently set out to redefine the fashion doll with a feminist appeal for change.

The 1970s marked a new era for the fashion doll in American children's culture. This is not to say that Mattel's Barbie, introduced in 1959, did not continue its reign as the best-selling doll of its kind. Less than fifteen years after Mattel's creation of the Barbie doll, the company claimed that 90 percent of American girls between the ages of four and eleven owned a Barbie doll, with the average girl owning two.[10] "Barbie is an established fact," announced Mattel's director of product management in 1975, and there was little use in contending otherwise.[11] However, the success of the vast World of Barbie collection did more than just make Mattel a household name and the world's largest toy producer by the end of the 1960s. What we might call the Barbie effect also unleashed major cultural and commercial changes in the nature of girls' play. In 1959, baby dolls accounted for 80 percent of all dolls; by 1975, the proportion of baby dolls had dropped by half, to 38 percent, replaced by a growing assortment of articulated and poseable female-gendered doll figures with accessories for additional purchase.[12]

The new girls' dolls were divided into two basic types. The first was the fictional character doll—usually a teenager or young woman with a manufacturer-scripted identity and backstory. Inspired by Barbie's success, many of them closely resembled Barbie's design, image, and conventionally feminine personality—so much so that even brand-name figures with unique identities like Ideal's Crissy and Topper Toys' Dawn quickly came to be known by children as simply "Barbies."[13] The second type was the licensed celebrity doll, a genre consisting of jointed dress-up figures based on television and movie stars, the characters they played, and sports heroes. By the mid-1970s, these plastic likenesses of female personalities—most of them following the standard Barbie size—soon flooded the market, including dolls resembling actress Farrah Fawcett, pop singer Marie Osmond, and Jaime Sommers, who played the Bionic Woman on TV.[14]

In a 1973 remark about Dawn, the newest Barbie copycat from Topper Toys, an official from Topper openly acknowledged that the popularization of feminism had created a new cultural gap between mothers and daughters that the toy industry needed to mind strategically. "A girl five, six, seven doesn't know about Women's Lib. Now, if I was pitching [Dawn] to their mothers, there might be problems."[15] The following year, two manufacturers with major investments in the girls' market turned this argument on its head. Rather than trying to elude the critical attention of feminist mothers, they tried to mobilize it. One was Kenner Products. Founded in Cincinnati, Ohio, in 1947, by the seventies Kenner had emerged as one of the industry's top companies thanks to best-selling toys like the iconic Easy-Bake Oven and Baby Alive doll—an infant doll that could drink and wet as well as eat specially made food and expel simulated feces into a diaper. In 1974, Kenner made a dramatic departure from this invitation to the reality of parenthood by introducing Dusty, a fictionalized character of the fashion-figure genre backed by a national TV advertising campaign. Like Barbie and most of her copycats, Dusty was a white teenager with platinum hair and blue eyes that stood eleven and a half inches tall. But if she did not match Barbie's physical appearance entirely— Dusty had freckles, hair that fell just above the shoulders, and bangs, giving her a younger look—it was the doll's body design and character that indicated a major revision of the traditional fashion-doll template (see figure 6.1).[16]

Packaged and advertised exclusively with sports-related accessories and outfits for playing tennis and several other sports, including softball, volleyball,

6.1.
Dusty doll
(1974), Kenner
Products. Author's collection.

and golf, Dusty had leisure interests that reflected the growing conviction in American society that girls could be athletic and competitive, traits usually reserved for boys. Two years earlier, in 1972, Congress had passed the Education Amendments with the Title IX provision that prohibited sex discrimination in all educational programs receiving federal funds. One of the many immediate effects could be found in the public schools and higher education, where girls and young women could now join equally funded female sports teams. In 1973, Title IX's basic premise of gender equity received new credibility when female tennis champion Billie Jean King defeated male player Bobby Riggs in the highly publicized "Battle of the Sexes" at the Astrodome stadium in Houston, Texas.[17] Thus Dusty nodded to the shifting terrain of normative femininity in American society.

As a teenager, however, Dusty's analogue was not Billie Jean King so much as Phyllis Graber. In 1970, the teenager from Queens, New York, submitted a claim of sex discrimination to the New York City Commission for Human Rights for being closed out of the all-male tennis team at her high school. A year later, the city's Board of Education met Graber halfway, granting girls the right to compete in noncontact "male" sports such as tennis.[18] Other teenagers and young women across the country pursued similar petitions, and usually won; between 1970 and 1972 alone, before Title IX became federal law, the number of high school girls participating in team sports jumped from 300,000 to 800,000. By the end of the decade, that number had multiplied six-fold.[19] Given that Kenner promoted the tennis-playing Dusty as the flagship version of the doll, one might say she was quite literally the product of these young women's protests.

Obviously, Kenner hoped to capitalize on a new era of female participation in popular competitive school sports, but the company also sought to push the boundaries of the industry's feminine mystique by introducing a new doll category exclusively for Dusty. Merging the popular Barbie design aesthetic with the label reserved for male-gendered doll figures in the boys' market, Kenner proclaimed Dusty the first "fashion-action" doll in toy history. The designation was reflected not only in the fictional character's interests but also in her material qualities. As the scholar Regina Buccola notes, Dusty's waist was "rather thicker than the average Barbie," her chest "considerably smaller," her "feet flat, rather than molded to accommodate stiletto heels," and her knees bendable.[20] But the most significant modification of the Barbie mold was Kenner's trademarked "spring-loaded" action, a mechanism built into the right arm and waist that enabled the user to make Dusty swing a tennis racket or do any number of other things. It is little wonder, then, that Pogrebin's praise for Dusty as a major improvement on the Barbie brand was based on the fact that the doll "actually does something."[21]

Yet whatever shades of a feminist sensibility Dusty had going into the marketplace in 1974, by the following year Kenner had taken steps to undermine them. In 1975, Kenner designers and marketers together tried to adapt her merchandising appeal and materiality to what they perceived to be a girls' market that wanted more fashion than action. A comic-book advertisement, for example, highlighted Dusty's "trendsetter fashion" and sex appeal at the expense of her other pursuits; the character's competitive athleticism, depicted in small illustrations of Dusty playing sports beneath the lead image of the doll in a glamorous new jumper, seemed almost an afterthought. The revised Dusty's promotion of stereotyped ideals of women's (and girls') interests and cares was made clear in the heading: "She's a Knockout."[22]

Nor was Kenner's effort to rebrand Dusty along more conventionally feminine lines limited to advertising appeals. In fact, in 1976, Kenner offered consumers a chance to trade in their old Dusty for a modified "new-look" version of the doll. Yet the new Dusty followed even more closely the conventional fashion mold, sporting longer hair and, curiously, no freckles. Without any explanation, Kenner had even removed the doll's spring-loaded arms and torso, the features that gave material meaning to the second part of "fashion-action."[23] Without the action element, one would be forgiven for mistaking her for not just any Barbie, but the original. Meanwhile, the company continued to downplay Dusty's strength and talent as her main virtues in favor of her body and appearance: the "new-look" version was dressed in a swimsuit (not one of the sports in which she excelled), and, "to show off [her] fresh good looks," as the catalog put it, the doll now came packaged in a window box—where the consumer can see the actual product inside—as opposed to the old closed one.[24]

In 1975, the Metropolitan Detroit chapter of NOW joined Pogrebin in honoring Kenner's challenge to the reign of Barbie, citing Dusty's laudable character as a nonstereotyped female role that was "healthy, positive, and realistic."[25] A year later, the same group might well have wondered whether it had chosen the wrong recipient for the award. For while Kenner boldly announced with Dusty that playing hard on the tennis or volleyball court was not an activity reserved for boys, it increasingly indicated that being a "knockout"—an identity to be achieved through the development of fashion consciousness, the white beauty ideal, and one's body—was a more valuable activity. Without Dusty's trademark action feature, Kenner was urging girls to quite literally give up their athletic ambitions for beauty.

Kenner was not the only major manufacturer to identify a potential niche within the female character doll market for a vision of strong, active, athletic young womanhood. The same year, Ideal Toys introduced its latest addition to the genre, seven-inch-tall Derry Daring. "Today's little girl is no longer satisfied to do only what little girls have done," stated Kenner in the 1974 catalog. "Oh, she still loves cuddly dolls and little-girl games . . . but she also wants the kind of play action and adventure that used to be reserved for boys."[26] As Ideal proudly announced in *Playthings*, Derry Daring was the "first female action figure," a classificatory move that shattered the gendered division of articulated miniature dolls that Hasbro had constructed exactly a decade earlier.[27] It wasn't just talk either; the new Ideal catalog created a separate section for "Female Action Figure," just for Derry Daring.[28]

But what did it mean to be a female action figure? At first glance, outside the doll's size, it did not deviate far from the conventional white female ideal associated with Barbie. Derry Daring was racially coded as white, with rooted yellow Saran hair and painted blue eyes. Where Derry pushed the boundaries of conventional gender norms was less about how she looked than what she—the character—did. If she sounds a lot like Kenner's Dusty, the similarities ended there—for Derry's passion was not for athletic pursuits where young women traditionally competed but the kinds of extreme sports and other "daring" professions that were still male domains. Dusty could be purchased with a tennis racket or softball bat, but Derry—celebrated as "the action girl of today" in a full-page comic-book ad—could be purchased separately in one of five versions.[29]

The most popular and widely advertised Derry Daring was outfitted in a hot-pink jumpsuit with silver racing stripe and cape and came with a Trick Cycle in the box (see figure 6.2). Equipped with a special motorized mechanism and launching pad, the cycle could be wound up and sent zipping (with Derry holding on tightly) across the floor. "Derry's gyro-powered trick cycle is a snarly beast, but Derry tames it with ease," the catalog told readers. "Who said a girl can't handle a hot machine?"[30] Here was the toy industry's version of the 1970s New Woman, with a name signifying a cultural redefinition of womanhood as independent, strong, and capable of participating in professional fields long closed to women on account of sexist assumptions of what they couldn't do (e.g., understand and repair a motorcycle) or what would be too dangerous for them (e.g., ride one and do tricks). But this was not the only Derry Daring doll available for purchase. There was also Racing Adventure Derry, a modified version of the one with the Trick Cycle that wore a more colorful jumpsuit but also came with mechanic's accessories; Mountain Climber Derry, with ropes and harness; Western Derry, with full rodeo star regalia; and finally, Action News Reporter Derry, equipped with TV camera and tape recorder (and a helmet just in case).[31]

Derry Daring was "the toy industry's first real woman of today," contended Ideal, and while the character was a work of fiction, she appears to have been loosely based on a real woman.[32] Yes, Derry's principal persona as daredevil rider had a real-life analogue in Debbie Lawler, who in 1972 emerged as America's most famous stunt cyclist after Evel Knievel. As *People* magazine reported in 1974, Lawler "began jumping professionally as the female Evel Knievel two

6.2. Derry Daring doll with Trick Cycle (1974), Ideal Toy Company. Author's collection.

years ago, and has quickly caught on as a show- and heart-stopping sensation (in addition to beating Knievel's indoor jump record by clearing 16 trucks recently). 'The crowd expects to see a 300-pound tattooed lady with chains hanging down her back,' coos Debbie. 'They don't expect me.'"[33] Few probably expected to see her likeness in a doll either, though that would change after 1973, the year that Ideal's Evel Knievel action figure became the best-selling toy in America and the twenty-one-year-old Lawler won the "World Record for motorcycle distance jumping–female" from Motorsports International for flying seventy-six feet in the air over a line of cars.[34] Those two facts—the Knievel doll's success amid Lawler's rise to stardom—would lead not only Ideal but also one of its competitors to identify the lucrative market for a female stunt figure toy to join Knievel on retailers' shelves. Ideally, the toy could be produced with the blessing (and official licensing agreement) of Lawler herself.

But if Ideal Toys did make a bid to officially obtain Lawler's name for a Knievel counterpart figure, as most industry observers would have expected the company to do, either it was not enough money or it simply came too late. For Lawler had signed an agreement with Ideal's rival—Kenner Products. Kenner would introduce its Debbie Lawler Daredevil Jump Set at the 1974 Toy Fair, just days after Lawler broke Evel Knievel's own *Guinness Book* indoor world record.[35] Curiously, however, beyond a few newspaper advertisements and the Kenner catalog listing, there is little evidence of a major promotional campaign in 1974, certainly nothing close to what Kenner put together for Dusty. A year later, Kenner's Daredevil Jump Set—not really a doll so much as a nonjointed white-jump-suited figure attached to a stunt motorcycle— would be off the market. We can speculate on what ended the toy's short life, but the most plausible explanation lies in real-life events rather than commercial developments: a career-ending crash for Lawler in late March 1974, only weeks after the toy's Toy Fair debut.

Ideal had missed its opportunity to obtain the Lawler name for licensing purposes. But that did not stop the company from trying to cash in on her celebrity and symbolism. Absent the rights to use Lawler's name and image, Ideal toymakers created a young female daredevil doll who would be the next best thing to that. Of course, they had to tread carefully, keeping in mind that too close a resemblance to the real stuntwoman could land the company in legal trouble. But evoke the second-most-famous stunt cyclist in the world, they did. For instance, Derry Daring had all the main features of Lawler's often-described physical appearance behind the helmet, including her blue eye color, long blond hair, and petite frame. (Her seven-inch-tall body had nothing to do with her real-life physicality but followed the specifications of the Knievel doll so that Ideal could use the same vehicles and other accessories for both dolls.) Other choices by Ideal's design team suggest similar attempts to tie Derry to Debbie, from nods to Lawler's "feminine" fashion style, which was sometimes pink and flamboyant in the tassel-studded stuntperson style of the era, to choosing a similar-sounding first name. And of course, the doll's last name spelled out the Lawler personality so that even the youngest child could grasp the unusual kind of woman she was. Barbie had no last name; Derry was Daring.

Just as Dusty's "action" was built into the doll's form, Derry Daring was also designed to signify a more expansive conception of female potential. Most fashion dolls on the market were constructed of relatively stiff plastic that permitted little more than rudimentary movement of the head, arms, and legs. With her bendable knees and twist waist, Dusty was certainly an improvement on Barbie. But Derry Daring arguably took Dusty's flexible femininity even further, as her entire frame was made of a poseable rubberized plastic that, surrounding a wire skeleton, not only could be bent but also could hold its shape. The possibilities were endless, restricted only by a child's imagination. To give just one example of Derry's unique capacity to transgress the traditional lines of feminine behavior afforded by fashion dolls, a child could cross Derry's legs per female convention, but she could equally be seated in the stereotypically unfeminine cross-legged position.[36] In contrast, trying to manipulate a Barbie or even Dusty in this way would snap the figures into pieces. In this sense, Derry Daring seemed to symbolize nothing so much as pop singer Helen Reddy's declaration in her 1972 women's liberation anthem, "I Am Woman," that "you can bend but never break me."[37] Derry's grip was strong enough to allow her to do handstands on the handlebars of her trick cycle as it raced across the room.[38]

Ironically, while Derry Daring externalized certain bedrock feminist principles, her apparent inspiration was a harsh critic of the women's movement, albeit in part because she seemed to misunderstand it. "I'm no woman's libber," Lawler told an interviewer at the time. "I like men. Especially masculine men."[39] Given its clear aims of reaching feminist-identifying mothers and their daughters, Ideal wisely stayed clear of Lawler's seemingly conservative cultural politics in Derry Daring's commercial persona. Instead, Ideal became the only major toymaker during this period to explicitly invoke the women's liberation movement, describing Derry in the catalog as a "liberated daredevil."[40] Ideal officials reinforced the message with public statements in the toy press on the need for a liberated doll for girls. "Ideal has broken with the sexist tradition generally associated with doll play," announced the manager of the company's toy division to *Playthings*.[41]

At the same time, much like Kenner—and much like network television's representations of women during these years—Ideal's merchandising rhetoric reflected a notable ambivalence about how to represent the new female image of the 1970s in ways that would simultaneously appeal to feminists and yet still cater to mainstream tastes.[42] For example, as if to reassure skeptical buyers that Derry Daring's normative gender development was not at risk, the catalog pointed out that "despite the wonderful sense of adventure about her, there's never any doubt that Derry is all girl—a beautiful, posable, 7-inch doll with rooted blond hair that cascades to her waist."[43] The doll's listing in the Sears catalog was more suggestive in maintaining Derry's conformity to heteronormative femininity when it noted that the stunt cycle's "special gyro-mechanism keeps her running straight."[44] Such ambivalence over breaking with tradition would mark Ideal's intervention in the fashion-doll genre until the company canceled the line.

When NOW's Nicki Montaperto lamented that toymakers "give our daughters no worthy female figures to identify with or to emulate," back in December 1972, she probably did not imagine that this "serious sin of omission in the toy industry" (as she called it) would be addressed by the toy establishment anytime soon.[45] Whether or not the Dusty or the Derry doll met her standards for role models, it does seem that toymakers at both companies were listening and wanted to respond—either because they felt it was important ethically or politically, or because they saw a ripe opportunity to carve out a feminist niche market for mothers like Montaperto. The success of the dolls, of course, depended on whether they could create a doll that would at once resonate with *Ms.* readers and still appeal to their more conservative consumer base. As it turned out, that cultural and commercial tightrope walking would prove too difficult. By the time the 1977 catalogs rolled around in the springtime, both dolls were missing in action.

The most likely factor was the vicissitudes of the market. It seems plausible that Dusty and Derry Daring were merely victims of larger forces that also spelled the demise of countless other female character dolls of the time. When most manufacturers entered the fashion-doll field in the 1970s, in some cases with multiple contributions, the market became saturated. But to deny the role of America's confusing politics of gender in the popular reception of these dolls is to ignore an important, if elusive, factor propelling the business of gendered toys. Buccola suggests that Dusty's removal from the marketplace was not just due to existing mainstream tastes but was a product of the era's conservative backlash; the doll, she writes, was "too progressive on too many fronts at once."[46] Buccola's "too many fronts" refers not only to Dusty's athleticism and the doll's divergence from the Barbie template but also to what she sees as Dusty's unstated lesbian cultural politics—from the nod to the lesbian softball culture of the 1970s to Dusty's friendship with Skye, a Black female teenager companion doll that Kenner added to the line in 1975, Dusty's second year on the market.[47] Buccola's argument here is that these elements of queer gender and sexual expression, while unnamed, were discernable by the typical girl or her mother as different enough—or nonconforming enough—to weaken Dusty's appeal next to the array of heteronormative (and thus safer) characters in the market.

"The challenge for the great women athletes of this era," writes the historian James Pipkin, "continued to be overcoming the assumption that sports and femininity were incompatible."[48] In this light, the failure of Derry Daring and Dusty speaks to the prevalence of that assumption by the end of the 1970s. After all, *Ms.* subscribers and other like-minded parents would hardly have been able to keep these dolls on the shelves by themselves—if we can even presume that they would follow Pogrebin's celebration of these dolls as worthy of feminist dollars. The conservative mood of the mid-1970s may well have frustrated Ideal's and Kenner's parallel efforts to appeal to an imagined feminist consumer market. And yet perhaps Dusty and Derry Daring lived fairly short lives because in a newly diverse field of female character dolls, many of which now *did* things, they were actually not progressive enough.

There is little question that Ideal and Kenner at turns diluted, distorted, and even devalued certain feminist ideals and aspirations in their efforts to tap into the consumer desires of a growing women's movement cultural mainstream.[49] But acknowledging the levels of contradiction and confusion that tend to beset the task of gender representation does not prevent us from recognizing the feminist sensibilities and nonnormative female identities that these toys briefly carried into the lives of tens (or even hundreds) of thousands of young girls.

○

The other genre in which toymakers appeared to follow up on feminist complaints with new products was perhaps the loneliest in the doll business: baby dolls with genitalia. In 1976, three leading mass-market toy manufacturers simultaneously introduced baby boy dolls with a simulated penis and scrotum.[50] If their uneasiness with the decision was written all over the promotional material, such apprehension in this field of baby dolls had a historical explanation. In fact, the last effort to produce such a doll had produced a moral panic of national proportions. In 1967, Frank Caplan's attempt to import a so-called anatomically correct boy doll from France, and then sell it in his Creative Playthings shops and catalogs, set off a public outcry before it ever reached Caplan himself. As soon as the public got news of Caplan's decision—and it is unclear who told them—pressure groups formed in several states to keep the toy off the shelves. Channeling the anti-vice campaigns of the late nineteenth century, the Ohio-based Citizens' Committee to Protest Little Brother Doll, for example, contacted the US Customs Office in New York to report the trafficking of obscene material and launched a letter campaign that sought the ears of everyone from women's clubs and clergy to President Johnson.[51] "Toys are, should be, and must remain objects of play," the letter stated. "Sex organs are not." The Creative Playthings office received its share of complaint letters too, recalled Berte Benedict, who headed the company's public relations and marketing during the 1960s. As for the people who wrote them, Benedict quipped, "They must have gone to bed with their clothes on."⁵² Refusing to sell war toys while hocking apparent sex toys, Caplan was certainly not winning any consumers with traditional notions about American values.

Caving to the pressure, the federal government—including the Department of Commerce; the Department of Health, Education and Welfare; and the Food and Drug Administration—soon began its own inquiries into the purported pornographic toy trafficking of Creative Playthings, as did local city council members. Many laughed when they found out the identity of the object of investigation, reported Caplan, who went on to sell them in Creative Playthings stores and in the high-end toy shops and department stores that licensed his products. At the time, most of the child experts interviewed by reporters took a sympathetic view of Little Brother, testifying to the growing influence of sexual liberalism in the home, classroom, and popular culture. Three years after the controversy died down, some child experts still lamented the public opprobrium that met Little Brother's arrival. In 1970, even Dr. Muriel Brown, a former Children's Bureau psychologist and recent director of the American Toy Institute, suggested that the doll "could have been a valuable adjunct to sex education, and it's too bad that he wasn't popular."⁵³ When Letty Cottin Pogrebin went scouting for signs of such a doll around New York City in December 1975, she found only one toy store—the Tiffany's of toy retailers, the FAO Schwarz chain's flagship shop on Fifth Avenue—that sold a male baby doll with genitalia. Imported from Europe, it was probably a Little Brother doll. Yet seven years after Caplan's debacle, she reported, the venerable retail chain was still reluctant to place the doll in its catalog or display it (clothed or not) outside the box.⁵⁴

Three months later, Pogrebin would have had better luck. As if they had read her column and were convinced by her plea, a trio of leading doll manufacturers—Mattel, Ideal, and Horsman—all arrived at Toy Fair in the spring of 1976 with new anatomically correct baby boy dolls in their lines. This would not just be for the liberal upper classes but the masses. In a statement to the media that was unlikely to alleviate any anxiety about the rollout, Ted Erikson of the TMA was both realistic and ambivalent. "It's clearly going to be a controversial sort of thing," he said. "Whether it should be or not depends upon the point of view you bring to it."⁵⁵

Mattel seemed to see the potential in that controversy. The national ad campaign for the newest addition to the popular Baby Tender Love line, now called Baby Brother Tender Love to let consumers know what gender they were getting, did not play down the novelty of a doll with a penis but instead did the opposite. Indeed, nothing was kept under wraps in the company's bold, full-page print ad, which appeared in women's magazines nationwide with the headline "It's a Boy" and a picture of the doll, unclothed (see figure 6.3).[56] Mattel's merchandising department gave an even more emphatic wink to the newly added extremities, declaring on the boxes, "It's a Boy. A *real* boy."[57] While Mattel acknowledged that making such a doll was risky (and risqué) business, it took conscious steps to diminish the chance of public disapproval. According to Mattel officials, its decision to picture the doll without any clothing on the box was mainly a way to ensure that consumers knew what they were taking home. Explained Mattel's product manager for large dolls: "We feel the worst thing that could happen, would be for a consumer to take the doll home, and be offended when she found that it was an anatomically correct doll." Moreover, the company deliberately chose not to advertise on television because, as the official put it, "it wouldn't have been in good taste."[58]

Good taste mattered to Ideal Toys, which had an even more storied reputation to maintain. In 1903, the Ideal Novelty Toy Company was founded when Morris and Rose Michtom, the husband-and-wife owners of a Brooklyn stationery store, began selling a stuffed bear they named the Teddy Bear, after president and naturalist Theodore Roosevelt. Now, seven decades later, Ideal took a chance on a product that was bound to appear less huggable to many millions of parents. For Baby Brother Tender Love, Mattel had innovated by modification, molding a penis and scrotum on the existing (and sexless) Baby Tender Love doll. By contrast, Ideal Toys decided it would not just add genitalia to a doll line already in production but instead brand its anatomically correct toy with its own distinctive identity. The result was the Joey Stivic doll, named after the fictional newborn son of the characters Gloria and Michael "Meathead" Stivic from the top-rated network sitcom *All in the Family*. Centered on the trials and tribulations of Archie Bunker, an openly racist, homophobic, all-around bigoted blue-collar conservative who lives with his wife, Edith, in working-class Queens, the program was the first in a series of politically charged sitcoms created by Norman Lear in the 1970s. Whether the company simply hoped to capitalize on the name recognition or believed that by associating the doll with one of the youngest celebrities on national TV it might soften the shock factor—who would dare call US Customs on Archie and Edith Bunker's grandson?—is hard to know. With Ideal's entry in the anatomically correct market, the 1970s socially conscious TV comedies that the sociologist Todd Gitlin referred to

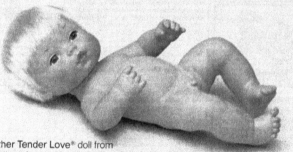

Baby Brother Tender Love® doll from Mattel. He's here for a very special purpose.

To be a bouncing brother to all the other dolls in your child's family.

Children are sure to love him, because he's just about as real as he can be.

He has that natural baby-soft Tender Love skin. Drinks from his own bottle. Wets when he's full. Slips in and out of a sporty blue-and-yellow outfit. And he's built exactly the way little boys come into this world.

We think he's wonderful. And parents from coast to coast seem to agree.

Welcome, baby brother!

Baby Brother TENDER LOVE

6.3. Mattel announces its new anatomically correct Baby Brother Tender Love doll (first introduced in 1976). Advertisement from *Good Housekeeping*, May 1977. Author's collection.

as "relevant" television can be said to have given birth to "relevant" toys.[59] Initially, Ideal planned to market the doll directly to children on TV. But the company quickly scrapped its plan after protests from consumers; instead, in an unprecedented move, Ideal marketed the Joey Stivic doll exclusively to parents on late-night television—after the kids had gone to sleep. "This is a conscious company policy," said Ideal's vice president of the doll division. "We feel that the parent should make the decision."[60]

The third company to enter this suddenly competitive field was Horsman Doll Company, one of the country's most respected and relatively high-end manufacturers. Yet unlike Mattel and Ideal, Horsman's contributions to the category reflected a commitment not only to realism but also to equal play. Alongside its new anatomically correct boy doll called Li'l David was a sister doll named Li'l Ruthie, the first national market female baby doll with simulated labia. One can only imagine what action the Citizens Committee to Protest Little Brother would have taken in response, had the coalition still been around. If Mattel and Ideal recognized their radical departure from industry norms and took preventive measures to avoid controversy, Horsman did too, placing an official-looking manufacturers' warning on the front of the box that made public the same fears of backlash that had informed internal conversations at Mattel and Ideal: "This doll has true-to-life features which differentiate little girls from little boys. For those who feel they do not want their children to be aware of this difference, we do not recommend this doll."[61] Nearly a decade after the Little Brother affair, and not without trepidation, America's toy manufacturers appeared to acknowledge that the parenting culture was changing, and with it, the definition of good toys.

o

At the same time that Nicki Montaperto and others in NOW were calling out the industry for what it was failing to produce, the Alliance's Barbara Sprung decided to go and make it herself. In 1972, Sprung entered into a remarkable collaboration with one of the toy industry's most venerable producers, Milton Bradley Company, developing a line of representational toys that would finally meet feminists' criteria for quality because this time they were designed by one. If Sprung and Milton Bradley appeared to be ideologically opposed on paper—the company was a frequently cited "sexist toy" offender in feminist literature—they found a way to forge a mutually beneficial partnership. The success of those products, however, would have to travel an alternative route to the world of children. As it turned out, the mass-retail marketplace of toy superstores like Toys "R" Us and national variety chains was neither the only path nor necessarily the best one for getting nonsexist, multiracial toys into the lives of the nation's youngest future citizens.

When Sprung became director of the Non-Sexist Child Development Project in 1972, the first thing she did was to survey the field of early childhood institutions in order to figure out where her attention should go. Like her fellow NOW members who were out visiting toy stores, she and a colleague visited two dozen child-care centers and preschools across New York. They interviewed parents, teachers, and administrators, and assumed the role of ethnographers, observing and documenting "the messages of limitation by sex that were being imparted by teachers and parents" and the play materials used by the children.[62] To their disappointment, such messages of limitation were multiple and ubiquitous across the different centers but especially conspicuous in the toys. Wherever there were depictions of people in puzzles, or cut-out figures, or board-based games, traditional gender and sex norms prevailed. She and her staff also observed a dearth of early childhood playthings featuring images of people of color, a reality that had less to do with educators' choices than availability. Despite the Black doll trend, outside the doll category, most manufacturers had done little or nothing to make their representational toys racially diverse. Even when they did, as with the case of Fisher-Price's Play Family Little People line, they were token figures. If a Black child wanted to depict her predominantly Black school, or even a racially integrated one, her parent would have to purchase a dozen Play People School sets to collect a dozen Black child figures, as each set only included one. The prospect of assembling a Black family, meanwhile, was impossible: as mentioned previously, the only Play People Family (which included grandparent figures) was a white one.[63]

Given the industry's failure to depict the diverse reality of American society in children's toys, Sprung soon came to the conclusion that "consciousness-raising with teachers and parents would not be enough. No lasting impact could be achieved without changing stereotyped materials."[64] Pressure on the industry could have an impact, but perhaps, thought Sprung, it was time to "design totally new toys."[65] Any such toys would require more than just nonstereotyped representations of women. Good toys, Sprung told a reporter, were "non-racist, non-classist, and non-sexist"; the Alliance's project was "interested not only in breaking down sexual stereotypes, but also racial stereotypes and family stereotypes."[66] At a time when many predominantly white feminist organizations were beginning to face not only accusations of racism but also criticism for their focus on straight, married, middle-class life, Sprung's commitment to representing a range of racial, class, and family experiences revealed a more inclusive vision of feminist culture.

In late 1972, Sprung reached out to major manufacturers that produced toys for the preschool category, including the Milton Bradley Company. Since its founding in 1860 by the white businessman and toy inventor of the same name, the company was best known for popular board games such as the Game of Life and Candyland.[67] Less known to the average consumer was that it also had one of the oldest and largest educational toy departments in the country, the Milton Bradley Educational Division, which marketed its expert-approved products directly to teachers and other childhood workers in special school supplies catalogs, teacher stores, and ads in professional journals. As Sprung recalled, there was no reason to start small; if she and the Alliance wanted to fundamentally reform the way toys represented the possible and permissible roles of women and men, it was necessary to tap industry leaders that could set trends throughout the business. "We need a line of professionally made equipment which will reflect our point of view," Sprung stated in a letter to Ron Weingartner, director of product development for Milton Bradley's Educational Division at the time. She continued:

We need lotto games redesigned to show pictures of a) working mothers, extended families, and fathers caring for their children; b) showing different types of work performed by men and women such as a female doctor or dentist and a male teacher or tailor; c) showing boys and girls in active sports—girls and boys playing baseball, swimming, bicycling, etc. We need puzzles of men and women in community jobs and boys and girls in active play. We need block accessories (wedgies) showing fathers and children and women police; grandmothers and grandfathers and community workers of both sexes.... If you would like to produce a line that will sell today's market, we can assist and assure its distribution.[68]

Around the same time, Sprung decided to follow the do-it-yourself philosophy that characterized so much 1970s feminist activity and make prototypes of the nonsexist toys herself; until she found a commercial producer, she would at least have something tangible to present to educators as models of what was possible.[69] With assistance from a woodshop teacher at the school where she taught part time, Sprung designed, carved, and painted two separate sets of wooden people figures (known as wedgies) that a child might use in imaginative play scenarios with blocks or other objects. Free from the commercial demands and concerns of the mass market manufacturer, she made no compromises with these first attempts at what the Alliance called "truly feminist products."[70] The first set embodied the theme of equal opportunity in the workforce. The figures depicted both male and female characters of different races in each of six different careers that had long been associated with (and professionally limited to) one gender: police officer, mail carrier, doctor, nurse, construction worker, and business executive (see figure 6.4). Sprung also gave material form to her expansive conception of family, creating a group of white and Black figures of all ages that could be mixed and matched by children into any number of configurations. In addition, reflecting her desire to project new images of masculinity, Sprung crafted other play materials to go along with the block accessories, including a prototype puzzle featuring a father playing with his child as well as lotto games (a picture-based version of bingo) with images of boys and girls doing the same activities. Here were toys that would affirm every child's life—and the people who inhabited it—as authentic and valuable.

6.4. Nonsexist toy prototypes, designed and created by Barbara Sprung, 1973. Courtesy of Barbara Sprung.

As it turned out, Sprung would not have to manufacture, market, and distribute her toys on her own. In early 1973, Ron Weingartner from Milton Bradley got back to her with good news, as did two of the other companies. For Sprung, the call from Weingartner expressing his interest in producing the block accessory figures had special significance. As she wrote in a grant proposal to help fund the NCDP, such figures would "for the first time in the educational equipment field represent the marvelous variety of human beings."[71] Here was her description of the Milton Bradley–made toys, telling in its holistic attention to representation: "People will be shown with various skin pigmentations within a race; various body types and modern hair styles and clothing will be apparent in both sexes. The materials will show Black, Caucasian, Latin and Asian people in work roles and in family roles. Every effort is being made to keep these materials free from stereotyping."[72]

When the national magazine *Saturday Review* published an article on the Alliance's NCDP in March 1973, letters flooded the Alliance office from Head Start directors, teachers, and other childhood professionals across the nation.[73] While the article gave only brief attention to the NCDP's play component, the toys received special interest. The librarian at Toys 'n Things, a children's resource center in Minneapolis, wrote the Alliance with a sense of urgency. She had "$20,000 in grants to buy toys and equipment for day care homes and day care centers in St. Paul," she explained, and was hoping to acquire "a catalog of the non-sexist toys you will be having produced, [and] order forms if production is that far along."[74] That a large metropolitan-area organization concerned exclusively with children's toys was ready to depart with all its funds for Sprung's toys is just one indication of how little was out there. Sprung also heard from chapters of national civil rights and social justice groups such as the Urban League and Anti-Defamation League. It was not just feminist organizations that recognized the value of socially conscious representational toys.

Ordinary parents also wrote to express their appreciation and to applaud. "Hurray for you!" exclaimed one woman who wrote to the Alliance. "I have two girls 4 and 5 ½ years of age and have always felt they should be brought up free of sex-stereotypes. I am so pleased to see somebody is finally doing something about sex-role conditioning.... My husband and I have always tried to buy nonsexist games. We also have many 'girls' toys and many 'boys' toys. I personally feel that stereo-type [*sic*] 'girls' toys are very limiting and after we had a few dolls, pots + pans, maybe a dust mop etc. there was very little else."[75] An elementary school teacher also wrote enthusiastically about the prospect of toys that promoted less gender-differentiated play, "I have read in

Sat. Review about the non-sexist curriculum guide & materials designed by Barbara Sprung," she said. "I will be teaching first graders in an Archie Bunker community & will greatly appreciate any information you can send me!"[76] For this particular teacher, teaching young children was political; while she unfairly stereotyped an entire community by blanketly assigning it the values associated with Bunker, the bigoted and notoriously sexist character on the TV sitcom *All in the Family*, what is most striking is her faith that nonsexist playthings could counter the conservative gender values that she assumed her students would be receiving at home.

"We are always glad to hear that our message about non-sexist toys is reaching people," Sprung stated in a letter to one educator. But if there was "little commercially available" when she wrote that letter in December 1973, the following year would be a different story.[77] The 1974 Milton Bradley Educational Division catalog listed two new sets of cardboard figures: Our Helpers Play People and My Family Play People. Available separately, they followed the same design: reinforced-cardboard paper-cut figures with plastic stands, with colorful, realistic illustrations of the people (including front and back views of their bodies). Conceptually, these Play People, as Milton Bradley called them, were virtually identical to Sprung's shop-class prototypes.

Just as Sprung had conceived it, all the occupational roles depicted in Our Helpers had both a male and a female gendered person in that job. And while there was regrettably no attempt to represent an Indigenous person, America's four largest racial groups—Black, white, Asian, and Latino—were represented (see figure 6.5). Making toy history, Our Helpers featured a diversity unlike anything the makers of occupation-themed figures had ever seen or attempted, including a Black female postal carrier, a Latino male and a white female construction worker, an Asian male nurse, and a white woman in a business suit (perhaps a lawyer or business executive). Our Helpers put children's occupational aspirations in new perspective, broadening traditional gender expectations that had made a girl's desire to attend medical school academically untenable, or a boy's interest in nursing socially unthinkable.

By contrast, the My Family set was less racially diverse than Our Helpers, an oversight that significantly limited its use for Sprung's original objective of representing the lives of all children. And yet, relative to what was currently available on the toy market, it was trailblazing for its time: a dozen Black and white Play People of all ages, from young children and teenagers to middle-aged adults and elders, to be configured by children in ways that reflected their personal reality (see figure 6.6). Complicating the mass media's idealized

6.5. Our Helpers Play People (1974), Milton Bradley Educational Division. Author's collection.

nuclear family, or the normative assumption that one's family had to live under one roof, My Family opened up all possibilities of family structure as equally authentic. Whatever the child's personal experience of family—single parents, married or cohabiting couples (same gender or not), siblings from different parents, aunts and uncles, cousins or friends, grandparents or other elders—that experience could, for the first time, be represented in toys (if only with Black and white Play People), while receiving the special validation that, for a child, only commercially made toys could offer. The new sets of Milton Bradley Play People not only reflected the reality of American life in the 1970s; they validated (many) children's worlds while giving them license to imagine what was possible for them in terms of the full human experience of gender, race, sexuality, and family. Here was Sprung's version of equal play.

Weingartner described Sprung as "almost the author of what we were putting in that package," and this was true in more ways than one.[78] While Sprung was glad Milton Bradley wanted to produce and distribute My Family and Our Helpers, she also wanted the opportunity to introduce the toys to the educators and parents who used them. On Sprung's request, the company

6.6. My Family Play People (1974), Milton Bradley Educational Division. Author's collection.

agreed to print a detailed preface, written and signed by Sprung, directly on the inside cover of the boxes. A description of the toy's origins and purpose, along with suggestions for how teachers might integrate the Play People into their curriculum, the preface laid out a feminist take on nonsexist socialization that would be read by thousands of teachers and parents over the coming years (and maybe longer since it was written into the box). As Weingartner recalled, Sprung's preface "gave an authenticity and expertise to the product."[79] That authenticity and expertise was mutually beneficial: Milton Bradley's new line won a stamp of approval by a leading expert, while the Alliance won a national platform for promoting its principles of equal play and distributing toys to help realize them. By partnering with the mainstream toy industry rather than going out on her own, Sprung neither had to produce them herself nor accept the limited market reach of a small independent toy manufacturer. With Milton Bradley selling truly feminist toys, she also managed to overcome what was perhaps the most difficult challenge: distributing them beyond the communities of the already converted to both more moderate and conservative communities around the US. In a remarkably short time span, Sprung had gone from a graduate student and part-time teacher to become a national authority on children's toys and stereotyping, not to mention the designer—or author, to use Weingartner's term—of the country's first explicitly multiracial, nonsexist representational toys. In 1975, Scholastic Press cemented Sprung's new status when it published her revised thesis as *Non-Sexist Education for Young Children: A Practical Guide* (1975), the first book for educators and parents about traditional sex-role conditioning and how to offset its negative effects.

In 1976, Alliance staff sought to assess the impact of the Milton Bradley sets. The questionnaires they distributed to a group of teachers and parents who had purchased the toys directly through the organization—the only other ways to find them were in teacher-equipment catalogs, and maybe in some specialty toy shops—offer a rare window into the reception of the new socially conscious toys of the era. The overall response was positive, and a handful of the teachers who returned the evaluations detailed their experiences in the "Comments" section at the bottom. One classroom of children was adamant about the boundaries of appropriate gender roles; the children enjoyed the toys, wrote their teacher, "but most of them were insistent that 'girls should be nurses—boys, doctors.'" At another school, in Queens, New York, home of the fictional Bunkers, the children expressed "shock at the idea of a male nurse." A preschool teacher likewise recounted that "most made shocked comments—a woman dentist! a woman fixing cars!—wow!" Whether or not the kids could get past their shock, what educators described suggests that the toys were doing the important cultural work that Sprung assigned them: disrupting children's received understandings about who should get to do which jobs, while prompting them to consider an alternative, however unusual the notion of a male nurse or female construction worker might have appeared to these four-year-old kids.

And yet some respondents, teachers as well as the children for whom they spoke, felt that the society these toys helped children envision was not as egalitarian as it could have been. For example, one teacher wondered whether Our Helpers had gone far enough in its efforts to interrupt normative ideas of gender and, more specifically, the idea that women's advancement depended on taking on masculine roles and presentation. "We are concerned that policewomen, etc. are expected to wear uniforms that are making them appear to look like men," she explained. "Isn't there a more non-sexist uniform—or shouldn't there be?"[80]

It was a valid question, and the kind that Sprung, as a practitioner of progressive education, would have wanted to be both asked and explored in the classroom setting. In some ways, My Family and Our Helpers raised as many questions about gender, race, family, and class as they answered. The diversity of individuals and conception of inclusion may not have met everyone's expectations or hopes for progressive playthings, but there is no question that their pluralistic vision of America represented a radical break from toy-industry traditions. As Shindana had said of its dolls, it was a start.

○

On February 18, 1975, as toy manufacturers and retail buyers descended on New York's Toy Center for the annual Toy Fair, representatives from a small group of toy companies attended a very different industry event twenty blocks uptown. There, at the Robert F. Kennedy Theater for Children, the Public Action Coalition on Toys staged its first star-studded awards banquet to publicly recognize companies that had met the group's criteria for socially responsible toymaking and to encourage others in the industry to follow suit.[81] Ten companies had been cited for a specific toy product, and PACT had invited them all to pick up their prize in person. Each received a Certificate of Commendation, signed by a PACT leader, acknowledging the company's "conscious effort to humanize children's play experience with a life-enhancing toy whose packaging invites the involvement of children of both sexes and all races."[82] The coalition also announced an additional group of special citations for what PACT praised as "constructive policies," including the decision by Quaker Oats, the corporate owner of Marx Toys, to halt the production of toy guns after half a century in the business—this, after concerted public protest by Victoria Reiss and Parents for Responsibility in the Toy Industry.[83]

"We wanted to create a ceremony that would recognize the good guys and the bad guys," recalled Letty Cottin Pogrebin, who as a member of PACT's advisory board came up with the awards idea and organized the annual event each year from 1975 to 1977.[84] She also took steps to drum up publicity, enlisting her Free to Be... You and Me collaborator, actor and activist Marlo Thomas, as well as Broadway stars Rita Moreno, Maureen Stapleton, and Raul Julia, to hand out the prizes. In a clever strategic move, Pogrebin put the onus on the manufacturers to nominate themselves for a Certificate of Commendation and the positive public attention it could bring. By inviting companies to apply for consideration if the companies themselves believed they had produced a worthy product, PACT not only created a strong incentive for toymakers to pursue its definition of good toys; it also shifted the power roles so that the toy companies—if they took the bait—had to actively pursue PACT rather than the other way around.

Not surprisingly, one of the good guys of 1975 was Milton Bradley, which received a certificate for the Our Helpers cardboard figures designed by Barbara Sprung. Nor was it the only winning toy with Sprung's imprint, as the educational toy company Instructo received a commendation for a nonsexist, multiracial family-themed flannel board that she had helped it develop.[85] Other winners included Bell Records for *Free to Be . . . You and Me*, as well as Fisher-Price for a set of character puppets from the award-winning *Sesame Street*. And yet, while many of the first PACT awardees were major companies with a national market reach, with the exception of boardgame maker Parker Bros. they were not leading purveyors of "TV toys"—the companies whose logos and slogans flashed across the commercials of children's television programming every weekday afternoon and Saturday morning, and which were responsible for the best-selling commercial toys each year.

The following February, when PACT held the ceremony for a second year, two things were different. First, while PACT again planned the event to coincide with the opening of the Toy Fair, this time the industry's erstwhile critics had managed to obtain approval to hold the festivities inside the Toy Fair complex itself.[86] Three years earlier, such a request for a Toy Fair booth—to announce the coalition's formation—had been denied by TMA officials. Now, the industry was not just accepting the reformers' existence; it was incorporating them into the most important event of the year. The second change was that the president of Mattel Toys, the largest and most influential toy business in America, was in attendance. As it turned out, his company not only applied for consideration by the esteemed PACT panel of judges; it won an award—for its Baby Brother Tender Love, which the group commended for being both anatomically realistic and commercially available in Black and white versions. That Mattel had submitted any product was itself significant, to the extent that in doing so it validated PACT's authority to judge value in toys. But perhaps even more remarkable is that Mattel's winning entry was none other than the exact toy that PACT had wished for the previous year. "If we had a baby boy doll who was anatomically realistic and who was produced in a white-skinned and ethnically accurate brown-skinned version," a PACT member told the *New York Times* in February 1975, "it would have been an instant winner."[87] Thanks to Mattel, they now had one, and it was.

Replacing pickets with prizes, as the *Times* put it, PACT activists had found a means to draw the industry into their orbit, to convince toymakers to engage on their terms. And it worked. Not only was this a surprising power reversal given the preceding years of industry pushback and rancor. Here was the largest toy company in the world asking PACT for its approval as the nation's toy experts, and perhaps even looking to the coalition for new selling ideas. And not only that. So assured was Mattel, it seems, of the commercial and cultural weight of PACT's approval that the company stamped the PACT logo and "Commended by PUBLIC ACTION COALITION ON TOYS" on the backs of the Baby Brother Tender Love boxes before distributing them to retailers.[88] It is hard to think of a better example of the industry finally taking toys seriously or, at least, taking seriously PACT's power to shape the public discussion and the ways Americans thought about toys.

Ultimately, the 1976 PACT awards were less a turning point than a crystallization of the transformations that had taken place in the relationship between the consumers and producers of toys, not to mention the design and marketing of the toys themselves, over the previous fifteen years. When PACT ceased giving out awards after 1977, it was in part because of its success. In the years before the all-volunteer group disbanded in 1983—a decision that seems to have had less to do with the organization itself than the fact that by decade's end Patricia Powers had moved to the Midwest to teach college, Allenna Leonard turned her attention to television reform, and Victoria Reiss was now back at work after being home with her sons—mainstream lifestyle magazines like *Glamour* and *Woman's Day*, authors of leading child psychology textbooks like Louise Bates Ames's *Child Care and Development*, and countless Head Start centers and public libraries were now reaching out to PACT for the group's perspectives and publications rather than the other way around.[89] The group also received an influx of grant funding, from expected nonprofits like the Ms. Foundation for Women as well as establishment philanthropies like the Rockefeller Foundation.[90]

By the time Ronald Reagan was elected to the White House in 1980 on a campaign promise to reverse the cultural transformations unleashed by the radical and liberal political mobilizations of the sixties and seventies—that is, the challenges to normative America that inspired a decade of struggle over toys—those cultural transformations had already been established in America's toy consciousness, thanks to Elise Boulding, Richard Register, Lou Smith, the founders of PACT, and many others. In fact, the years just prior to the dissolution of PACT in 1983, and the shutting of the Shindana factory that same year, were hardly a last gasp of toy activism. Many of the reformers featured in these pages continued their work, and in some cases found themselves reaching even broader audiences and even settling into mainstream institutions. For instance, Letty Cottin Pogrebin retired her "Toys for Free Children" magazine column, but her colorful consciousness-raising around nonsexist socialization now reached a new generation of parents in her well-publicized 1980 parenting guide, *Growing Up Free: Raising Your Child in the '80s*.[91] Meanwhile, Barbara Sprung continued to develop new products for the Milton Bradley Educational Division, including the first lotto game set in industry history to feature nontraditional family structures and people who used wheelchairs.[92]

There also were moments when the 1960s and 1970s imagination leaped out of the past to spark a brief round of toy protest, like when peace groups quickly organized to combat a revitalized war-toy business in the early 1980s, or when an activist network calling itself the Barbie Liberation Organization a decade later stealthily switched the voice boxes of Talking Barbies and Talking G.I. Joe dolls in toy stores across the country, a fun-loving act of guerrilla cultural protest that WSP toy activists would have appreciated.[93] Likewise, the founders of Shindana and the leaders of PACT, too, would have been encouraged to hear about the birth and early mainstream success of Olmec, Inc., a toy company founded by Black entrepreneur Yla Eason in 1985 that specialized in fantastical superheroes of color, including Black, Mexican, Asian, and Native American characters.[94] In the hundreds if not thousands of preschools and elementary schools that purchased Milton Bradley products, in the pages of the *New York Times* (which ran a feature story on Pogrebin's book), and in the action-figure section of toy superstore chains like Toys "R" Us, an earlier era's vision of radical play was not just alive and well but had found a home in the cultural mainstream.

Epilogue

On September 9, 1976, six months after Mattel started stamping PACT's seal of approval on its Baby Brother Tender Love boxes, the Los Angeles Bicentennial Committee convened in the city's Griffith Park. There, members dedicated a special time capsule, not to be opened for one hundred years, filled with objects representing what the committee described as "a sampling of Los Angeles lifestyle."[1] The complete list of contents in the capsule, itself an artifact of the time (a propellant tank used by the 1971 NASA Mariner program), is unknown to all but those who were in attendance; after all, the point is for our descendants not to know until they dig it up and open it. The following day, however, the *Los Angeles Times* revealed a handful of the items the committee had chosen, including a pet rock (a fad of the moment), a skateboard, and a dress worn by the singer and comedian Cher.

What the city's leading newspaper did not mention was that, as *Playthings* reported, two toys manufactured by Mattel had also been included.[2] One of them, a swimsuit-wearing white Malibu Barbie, was perhaps to be expected. More remarkable was the other Mattel doll that would be sharing the capsule with Barbie for the next century: a Black anatomically correct Baby Brother Tender Love.[3] Here was a doll that satisfied virtually all of PACT's demands for a progressive toy in a single product: nonviolent, a positive representation of a Black child, sexually realistic, and a rare baby doll representing an infant boy, with its unstated suggestion that a boy could love a doll too. While affirming the enduring cultural appeal of white Barbie, city officials had decided to give the mid-seventies' new definition of progressive playthings equal weight (see figure E.1). It is hard not to see the cultural equivalency of Barbie and Baby Brother in the capsule not merely as a draw between the toy industry and the

Mattel dolls to reappear at Tricentennial

LOS ANGELES — Barbie and Baby Brother Tender Love, two dolls from Mattel, achieved 100 years of immortality as they were sealed in a time capsule by the City of Los Angeles to emerge in 2076 when the nation celebrates its Tricentennial. The Los Angeles Bicentennial Committee prepared the capsule as a climax to the city's celebration of the nation's 200 birthday. Barbie was selected as one of the best-known toys of our time, and Baby Brother Tender Love doll was chosen because of the national publicity he received as the country's first mass-produced "anatomically correct" baby boy doll available in both black and white versions.

E.1. "Mattel Dolls to Reappear at Tricentennial." Photograph item from *Playthings*, December 1976, 34. Courtesy of Department of Science and Wellness, Free Library of Philadelphia, Philadelphia, PA.

activists but sealing a kind of victory for Reiss, Smith, and Sprung. One can be assured that, had the LA Bicentennial Committee made its choices from among Mattel's toy inventory just a decade earlier, the doll sitting next to Barbie in Griffith Park right now would not have been Black, anatomically correct, or male. Given Mattel's top sellers of that era, chances are that second toy would have been a gun, maybe even the Crackfire Rifle. When this time capsule is opened in 2076, Los Angeles residents will no doubt have many questions about what these two objects say about the American children's culture of an earlier time.

It only takes entering the toy section of a big-box store to see the extent to which we are still living in that time capsule. The toy industry's embrace of the sixties liberal humanist ethos—its once-radical calls for gender egalitarianism, racial equality, and disarmament in the broadest sense—has been at best uneven and notably ambivalent. And considering the enduring cultural divide between progressives and conservatives in American life, one can expect it will continue to be. Our toys *are* us. Yet the impact of the radical toy imagination of the time reached far beyond visible changes in design or branding, some of which endured and some of which are now relics of the age, curiosities from the Sears catalog that populate countless Pinterest pages and eBay and Etsy sites. Indeed, the most lasting changes are not relegated to the toy aisles alone, although it is there that one can find dolls of all complexions and racial groups, representations of women in all occupational roles, and few if any war toys at all. For what the collisions and collaborations of activists, toymakers, marketers, experts, and ordinary parents during this era also succeeded in doing was to reshape the interpretation of toys in American culture—the way we think and talk about what toys mean and what toys do. Ideas about toys that were once perceived to be, by turns, unconventional, out of step, or even utterly misguided by the American toy industry and the experts have become a part of our collective toy common sense.

These revised cultural understandings of toys and play help us explain the absence of realistic toy guns like the Daisy BB rifle from the Strong Museum of Play's National Toy Hall of Fame, even as Daisy's cultural significance goes uncontested; why the LEGO Corporation pulled online ads for police-themed toys in the days after George Floyd's murder by Minneapolis police in late May 2020; why Mattel keeps pouring its resources into new socially conscious lines like the Creatable World of gender-neutral dolls and Barbie-doll likenesses of trailblazing Black women like Rosa Parks and Ida B. Wells-Barnett; and why, when the Barack Obama administration convened a major conference on gender stereotyping in toys and children's culture in 2016, it invited toy companies to participate alongside the usual psychological experts and advocacy groups.[4] What the German Jewish writer Walter Benjamin poetically observed almost a century ago, that toys embody "a silent signifying dialogue between [the child] and their nation," was always understood by the makers and marketers of American toys.[5] What changed in the 1960s and 1970s was that diverse Americans, some with no previous connection to the industry and others with deep roots in it, determined that it was time for that dialogue to undergo radical change.

Abbreviations

NYT	*New York Times*
PACT Records	Public Action Coalition on Toys Collected Records (CDG-A), Swarthmore College Peace Collection, Swarthmore, PA
PT	*Playthings* magazine
SDOTCC	Stephen and Diane Olin Toy Catalog Collection, Brian Sutton-Smith Library and Archives of Play, The Strong, Rochester, NY
TCOF	Twentieth Century Organizational Files, Southern California Library for Social Studies and Research, Los Angeles, CA
THW	*Toy & Hobby World* magazine
TN	*Toys and Novelties* magazine
WAA Records	Women's Action Alliance Records, Sophia Smith Collection, Smith College, Northampton, MA
WILPF/US Records	Women's International League for Peace and Freedom Records (DG043), Part III: U.S. Section, Swarthmore College Peace Collection, Swarthmore, PA
WSP Records	Women Strike for Peace Records (DG115), Swarthmore College Peace Collection, Swarthmore, PA

Notes

Introduction

1. Victoria Reiss, phone interview by author, October 29, 2008; Richard Reiss, phone interview by author, February 9, 2022.

2. "Interview with Lou Smith."

3. Barbara Sprung, interviews by author, November 24, 2009, November 18, 2010, and March 25, 2022, all in New York, NY.

4. The story of American Jews in the making of the modern toy business, while beyond the scope of this study, deserves a book in itself. In fact, scholars have written about the role of Jews in virtually every major US culture industry except toys, with the notable exception of Gould, "Toys Make a Nation." On the role of Jews in other businesses of American popular culture, see, for example, Karp, "The Roots of Jewish Concentration"; Buhle, *From the Lower East Side to Hollywood*; Hoberman and Shandler, *Entertaining America*; and Gabler, *An Empire of Their Own*.

5. My thinking about the toy industry's relationship to social movements owes much to Sasha Torres's analysis of network television and the civil rights struggle in the 1960s. See Torres, *Black, White, and in Color*, 5–6.

6. Salesman quoted in Alben Krebs, "Military Toys Come under Fire," *St. Petersburg Times*, March 11, 1964, 4D.

7. On new toy production methods and materials, see Cross, *Kids' Stuff*, 153. On the impact of the discount stores, see Leonard Sloane, "Discount Stores Broaden Inroads," *NYT*, July 19, 1964, F4; and Tom Mum, "Are the Department Stores Losing Faith?," *PT*, July 1975, 31.

8. On how TV changed the trade, see Henry Orenstein, "How to Sell More TV Toys," *TN*, October 15, 1967, 29; and Stern and Schoenbaum, *Toyland*, 23. On how discount stores and TV affected distribution, see Schneider, *Children's Television*, 45–46. The fact that contemporary observers understood this combination of developments to have dramatically altered the business of toys in a very compressed time span can be seen in "All's Swell at Mattel," *Time*, October 26, 1962, 90.

9. Spigel, *Make Room for TV*, 111.

10. Chudacoff, *Children at Play*, 162. On the centrality of children to the postwar middle-class family ideal, see Mintz, *Huck's Raft*, chap. 14; Coontz, *The Way We Never Were*, chap. 2; and Mintz and Kellogg, *Domestic Revolutions*, chap. 9. On the Cold War's influence on American childhood, see Grieve, *Little Cold Warriors*. For an innovative study of children's experiences during the 1960s, see Rhodes, *Growing Up in a Land Called Honalee*.

11. Henry, *Culture against Man*, 75. The toy business was not the only culture industry to reap the benefits of the new obsession with children's emotional health and happiness. The links between postwar childhood and the commercial marketplace are discussed in Mintz, "The Changing Face of Children's Culture."

12. Herbert Brock, "The Beginning of a New Toy Era—Year-Around Sales," *PT*, August 1961, 118.

13. Rupp, "The Survival of American Feminism," 37.

14. On the growing preoccupation among postwar social scientists with the relationship of child-rearing to culture change, see Sammond, *Babes in Tomorrowland*, chap. 4.

15. See Cahan, "Toward a Socially Relevant Science," 28–30; and Beatty, *Preschool Education in America*, 192–94. On the importance of developmental psychology to the Children's Television Workshop, which created *Sesame Street*, see Morrow, *Sesame Street and the Reform of Children's Television*, chap. 2.

16. One might say the cognitive revolution fed and spread the existing middle-class preoccupation with toys that were said to enrich the child's mind. See Ogata, "Creative Playthings"; and Almqvist, "Educational Toys, Creative Toys."

17. Benjamin Spock, "Creative Use of Toys," *Ladies' Home Journal*, December 1961, 36–37; Benjamin Spock, "What Toys Mean to Children," *Redbook*, December 1963, 46–47, 121–22, 124; Benjamin Spock, "Playing with Toy Guns," *Redbook*, November 1964, 24–32.

18. Hartley and Goldenson, *The Complete Book of Children's Play*, 5. On the emergence of a popular preoccupation with developmentally appropriate, educative play in the midcentury decades, see Seiter, *Sold Separately*, 66–74; Ogata, "Creative Playthings"; and Almqvist, "Educational Toys, Creative Toys."

19. "Toys and the Education 'Explosion,'" *PT*, June 1964, 48. In fact, this was the second editorial to focus on the new psychologically savvy, well-educated consumer in the past year. See "What the Public Thinks of Us," *PT*, November 1963, 40.

20. A. C. Gilbert Jr., "Toys as Part of the Booming Leisure-Time Industry," *PT*, December 1962, 120.

21. In thinking about children's media, what it is and what it does, I found Heather Hendershot's exploration of children's television to be essential reading. See Hendershot, *Saturday Morning Censors*.

22. See Mickenberg, "The Pedagogy of the Popular Front."

23. On the Council on Interracial Books for Children, see Mickenberg, *Learning from the Left*, epilogue. On *Free to Be . . . You and Me*, see Paris, "Happily Ever After," 524–26; and Lovett and Rotskoff, *When We Were Free to Be*. Another key contribution to this era's liberal children's media programming was *Sesame Street*, first broadcast on

public television in 1969. See Kamp, *Sunny Days*; Ostrofsky, "Taking *Sesame* to the Streets"; and Morrow, *Sesame Street and the Reform of Children's Television*.

24. For other studies that explore the role of business in the social and cultural revolts of the 1960s and 1970s, see Frank, *The Conquest of Cool*; Weems, *Desegregating the Dollar*; J. Davis, *From Head Shops to Whole Foods*; and Hogan, *The Feminist Bookstore Movement*. On the revitalized progressive movements of the 1960s and 1970s, see Rossinow, *Visions of Progress*; Schulman, *The Seventies*; Isserman and Kazin, *America Divided*; Hečlo, "The Sixties' False Dawn"; and Farber, *The Sixties*.

25. Studies in cultural anthropology that have influenced my thinking include Appadurai, *The Social Life of Things*; Douglas and Isherwood, *The World of Goods*; and Geertz, *The Interpretation of Cultures*. For starting points into the cultural history of toys, see Halliday, *Buy Black*; Brandow-Faller, *Childhood by Design*; Lange, *The Design of Childhood*; Ogata, *Designing the Creative Child*; Bernstein, *Racial Innocence*; Chudacoff, *Children at Play*; Thomas, "Sara Lee"; Jacobson, *Raising Consumers*; Cross, *Cute and the Cool*; Cross, *Kids' Stuff*; Forman-Brunell, *Made to Play House*; Best, "Too Much Fun"; Attfield, "Barbie and Action Man"; Rand, *Barbie's Queer Accessories*; Kline, *Out of the Garden*; Mergen, "Made, Bought, and Stolen"; Mergen, *Play and Playthings*; and McClintock and McClintock, *Toys in America*. Other studies of toys and play that influenced my thinking include Henricks, "The Nature of Play"; Pugh, "Selling Compromise"; Nelson-Rowe, "Ritual, Magic, and Educational Toys"; Seiter, "Toys Are Us"; Sutton-Smith, *Toys as Culture*; Barthes, *Mythologies*, 53–55; and Benjamin, "The Cultural History of Toys." For illuminating studies of other types of children's material culture in the twentieth-century United States, see, for example, Capshaw, *Civil Rights Childhood*; Mickenberg, *Learning from the Left*; and Cook, *The Commodification of Childhood*.

26. Douglas and Isherwood, *The World of Goods*, 57.

27. Hartman, *A War for the Soul of America*, 5.

28. Hartman, *A War for the Soul of America*, 5.

Chapter One. Parenting for Peace

1. *Exhibitors 1946*, 1, directory booklet published by the Toy Center, author's collection.

2. *Exhibitors 1946*, 3. Gary Cross writes that more than three-quarters of the nation's toy companies were leasing a space by the 1960s. See Cross, *Kids' Stuff*, 152.

3. Michael Specter, "Not All Fun and Games at 5th Ave. Toy Center," *NYT*, April 26, 1981, S8, 8.

4. Leonard Sloane, "Visions of Christmas Sales Captivate Toy Buyers," *NYT*, March 10, 1964, 51; "Toy Fair to Open Here Tomorrow," *NYT*, March 8, 1964, F22.

5. "Mothers Picket against Violent Toys," *THW*, April 6, 1964, 1, 3.

6. "Mothers Picket against Violent Toys," 1.

7. Sloane, "Visions of Christmas Sales."

8. My information on WSP's role in the event is from Margaret Kannenstine, phone interview by author, August 25, 2021. Curiously, none of the newspapers and magazines

that covered the event mentioned the protesters' affiliation with WSP or other civic groups.

9. See Mickenberg, "The Pedagogy of the Popular Front."

10. Spock, *The Commonsense Book of Baby and Child Care*, 265.

11. The term *peace-and-justice* comes from the historian Amy Schneidhorst, as a way to call attention to activists' understanding of their movement as one concerned with nuclear disarmament as well as peace work in the broadest sense, including social causes such as civil rights and educational equity. See Schneidhorst, *Building a Just and Secure World*. On Black women's participation in WILPF, especially in pressing the organization to recognize the links between militarism and racism, see Blackwell, *No Peace without Freedom*. On the long history of American women's peace-and-justice activism, see Alonso, *Peace as a Women's Issue*. For a different treatment of the 1960s anti–war toy campaigns that draws on some of the same source material as this chapter, see Rhodes, *The Vietnam War in American Childhood*, chap. 3.

12. On the construction of this postwar ideology of domesticity, see May, *Homeward Bound*; and Plant, *Mom*.

13. On the WCTU campaign, see Stephenson, "Women Leaders in the Peace/Anti-war Movements," 283. For a useful starting point on the peace-education movement of the early twentieth century, see Zeiger, "The Schoolhouse vs. the Armory."

14. On the WILPF initiative, see the "Disarm the Nursery" manifesto written by members of the Palo Alto branch of WILPF and published in the *Friends' Intelligencer*, December 30, 1922, clipping, Subject File: Children and War & Peace, Folder: 1894–1929, WILPF/US Records. On WILPF and war toys during the interwar years, see Goossen, "Disarming the Toy Store and Reloading the Shopping Cart." On Canadian anti–war toy activism in the post–World War II decades, led by the organization Voice of Women, see Hutchinson, "Fighting the War at Home."

15. The characterization "sporadic and localized" comes from a 1960 report on WILPF anti–war toy activities during the previous decade. See Marie Lyons, "'Study' and Evaluative Report to White House Conference on Children and Youth 1960" (draft, typescript), 3, National Committee on Childhood and Education, Series A4, Part 1, Box 2, Folder 5, WILPF/US Records.

16. Women's International League for Peace and Freedom, *Junior Disarmament* (pamphlet, n.d.), Series A4, Box 2, Folder 5, WILPF/US Records.

17. Katherine L. Camp, "WILPF against War Toys," official WILPF statement, March 1969, Series A5, Box 14, Folder 21, WILPF/US Records.

18. Mary Ellen Fretts to Mrs. Olmstead, October 8, 1963, Series A4, Part 1, Box 2, Folder 7, WILPF/US Records.

19. Bess Lane memo to Branch Chairmen and Childhood Education Chairmen, November 1963, 1, 2, Series A4, Part 1, Box 2, Folder 7, WILPF/US Records.

20. Rita Morgan to Dagmar Wilson, December 2, 1963, Series A4, Box 1, Folder 13, WSP Records.

21. Rose Della-Monica to Women Strike for Peace, printed in *Memo*, February 28, 1964, 4, WSP Records.

22. Elise Boulding, "Toys, Tots, and Terrors," Letters to the Editor, *Saturday Review*, December 2, 1961, 35.

23. "Jersey Parent Unit Begins a Campaign over Warlike Toys," *NYT*, December 12, 1963, 41. One toy buyer at the time told Carol Andreas, a sociologist who studied the war-toy controversy, that "military men from Washington" visited Toy Fair to promote the war-toy category. See Andreas, "War Toys and the Peace Movement," 89.

24. William Honan, "Toys and Boys and Christmas," *New Republic*, December 1963, 7. See, for example, Remco's Polaris submarine ad, *PT*, September 1962, 150. On the military defense buildup during these years, see J. Patterson, *Grand Expectations*, 419–21.

25. Quoted in Honan, "Toys and Boys and Christmas," 7.

26. "Mattel Line Offers Dolls, Hobbies, Games and Guns," *PT*, April 1963, 124, 144. See also "What's NEW in THE WORLD," *THW*, August 19, 1963, 30; and Sears Christmas Book, 1963, 171.

27. Mattel ad, *PT*, January 1963, 198.

28. Transogram ad, *THW*, July 1, 1963, 9.

29. "Johnny Seven O.M.A.," *PT*, November 16, 1964.

30. "Deluxe Reading," *THW*, September 7, 1964, 46.

31. World War II nostalgia swept the nation during the early 1960s. One reason was the 1960 election of John F. Kennedy, a decorated and fabled war hero, to the presidency. On World War II in the popular imagination, see Engelhardt, *The End of Victory Culture*, 69–89.

32. "Review of Trends and New Toys at the 60th Annual Toy Fair," *PT*, April 1963, 71.

33. Newcombe, "From Old Frontier to New Frontier," 289. See also "Western Goods Overdue for a Comeback in '65," *PT*, December 1964, 46.

34. Newcombe, "From Old Frontier to New Frontier," 289.

35. "New Guns," *THW*, January 1962, 10. See also the Nichols ad, *PT*, June 1963, 21. On the history of Daisy Manufacturing Company, see Kerstens, *Plymouth's Air Rifle Industry*.

36. *Marx Toys 1962 Toy Line* (New York: Lou Marx, 1962); *Marx Toys 1963 Toy Line* (New York: Lou Marx, 1963); *Marx Toys 1964 Toy Line* (New York: Lou Marx, 1964). Thanks to Francis Turner for sharing his collection for my research. For more on Turner's collections, see Marx Toy Connection, http://www.marxtoyconnection.com.

37. On the fanfare surrounding the introduction of G.I. Joe, see "Bright New Lines Spark Slow 'Unofficial' Toy Fair," *THW*, March 16, 1964, 1, 21; and "'Top Secret' Line Unveiled at Toy Fair," *THW*, May 4, 1964, 17–18.

38. For an example of this live-action style, see Marx's commercial for the Gung Ho Commando set, in "Commercials 17: Toy Guns," Internet Archive, Community Video collection, posted by "NoseSilo," https://archive.org/details/Commercials17ToyGuns.

39. *Marx Toys 1964 Toy Line.*

40. Mattel ad, *PT*, April 1964, 29.

41. "At the Toy Fair," *THW*, March 1962, 10; Iskin ad, *PT*, July 1963, 30.

42. Iskin ad, *PT*, July 1963, 30.

43. "Nichols '63 Sales Up Nearly 50%; Firm Adds 3 New Guns to Line," *PT*, March 1964, 405.

44. Remco ad, *THW*, February 17, 1964, 25.

45. See "Two-Thirds of Surveyed Toymen Report Sales and Profit Gains," *PT*, March 1965, 290.

46. Mary Ellen Fretts to Mrs. Olmstead, October 8, 1963, Series A4, Part 1, Box 2, Folder 7, WILPF/US Records. See also Frances Eliot to WILPF, quoted in Bess Lane memo to Branch Chairmen and Childhood Education Chairmen, November 1963, 1, Series A4, Part 1, Box 2, Folder 7, WILPF/US Records.

47. Boulding, "Toys, Tots, and Terrors," 35.

48. "Educational Toys to Gain in '64," *THW*, April 6, 1964, 11, 32.

49. On the women's peace movement and the Second Red Scare, see Alonso, "Mayhem and Moderation."

50. Swerdlow, "Ladies' Day at the Capitol," 494.

51. Swerdlow, "Ladies' Day at the Capitol," 494.

52. DeBenedetti, *An American Ordeal*, 27–78; Swerdlow, *Women Strike for Peace*, 42–44.

53. Lyons, *People of This Generation*, 22. Charles DeBenedetti referred to the more moderate fraction of the movement, many of whom entered through the antinuclear campaign, as "peace liberals." See DeBenedetti, *An American Ordeal*, 18.

54. Swerdlow, *Women Strike for Peace*, 2.

55. On the organization's strategic use of maternalist rhetoric, see Estepa, "Taking the White Gloves Off."

56. See Naomi Marcus's correspondence with the publicity director of an unnamed department store, published in Bess Lane memo to Branch Chairmen and Childhood Education Chairmen, February 1964, 1, Series A4, Part 1, Box 2, Folder 7, WILPF/US Records.

57. Rose Della-Monica, letter printed in *Memo*, February 28, 1964, 4, WSP Records.

58. Rita Morgan to Dagmar Wilson, December 2, 1963.

59. Mrs. Tamora Furnish, Letters section, *Suburban Life* (Chicago), December 12, 1963, reproduced in "LETTERS TO THE EDITORS" (flyer, n.d.), produced by the Chicago West Suburban branch of WILPF, Series A4, Part 1, Box 2, Folder 7, WILPF/US Records.

60. Kennedy, "Address to the UN General Assembly."

61. Swerdlow, *Women Strike for Peace*, 89.

62. Quoted in Swerdlow, *Women Strike for Peace*, 95–96.

63. San Francisco Women for Peace, "Ask . . . What You Can Do for Your Country" (flyer, n.d.), Series A4, Box 1, Folder 13, WSP Records.

64. Sherry, "Death, Mourning, and Memorial Culture," 165.

65. Sarah Ramberg memo to Branch Chairmen and Childhood Education Chairmen, April 1964, Series A4, Part 1, Box 2, Folder 7, WILPF/US Records. I discovered scores of news articles covering the event through the invaluable digital database Newspapers.com.

66. See Lofland, *Polite Protesters*, 7–8. On the peace movement's militant wing, see Mollin, *Radical Pacifism in Modern America*.

67. Barbara Ulmer to WSP, printed in *Memo*, March 1, 1964, 2, WSP Records. Prior to her involvement with WSP, Ulmer had chaired Northern California WIL-PF's Childhood Education Committee. Barbara Ulmer, phone interview by author, August 26, 2009.

68. New York War Toy Committee, "Is Killing Child's Play?" (flyer, n.d.), Series A4, Box 1, Folder 13, WSP Records. On consumer boycotts in the United States, see Glickman, *Buying Power*. On the history of consumerist strategies and tactics, see Hilton, "Consumer Movements."

69. *Memo*, January 1967, 14, WSP Records.

70. Dolores Alexander, "Women Pickets Lower Boom on Toys for Killing" (n.d., newspaper clipping), reprinted in WSP's *National Peace Education Bulletin*, December 1965, 11, Box 5, Folder 9, WSP Records; Leonard Sloane, "Makers of Military Toys Are Picketed by Mothers," *NYT*, March 8, 1966, 49, 57.

71. There is some discrepancy as to the founding of PRITI. According to my interview with Reiss, she and a small group of New York City–based WILPF and WSP activists decided to form the group at a Mother's Day rally against the Vietnam War in Washington Square Park. In the interview, as well as in an article she wrote for WSP's newsletter, *Memo*, Reiss dated the founding to 1966. Yet Reiss is actually named as PRITI's chair in a WILPF internal memo from October 1965. While I was unable to find any evidence of the Mother's Day rally she mentioned, I suspect that it took place in 1965. What matters here is less the precise date than the fact that the group grew directly out of its members' antiwar activism. Victoria Reiss, phone interview by author, October 29, 2008; Victoria Reiss, "War Is No Game," *Memo* (Commemorative Issue), April 1973, 10–13, WSP Records; Libby Frank memo, Series A4, Part 1, Box 2, Folder: Childhood Education Committee 1965–66, WILPF/US Records.

72. Dove Award advertisement in *The Toy*, no. 5 (Winter 1966–67): 8, author's collection. On the formation of PRITI, see Reiss, "War Is No Game," 10.

73. Libby Frank, Chairmen of Childhood Education Committees, January 1967, Series A4, Part 1, Box 2, Folder 12, WILPF/US Records.

74. Frances Eliot to WILPF, quoted in Bess Lane memo to Branch Chairmen and Childhood Education Chairmen, November 1963, 1, Series A4, Part 1, Box 2, Folder: Committee on Childhood Education 1963–64, WILPF/US Records.

75. *Memo*, September 1964, 5, WSP Records.

76. *Memo*, February 1966, 14, WSP Records; *Memo*, December 1964, 9, WSP Records.

77. Sarah Ramberg memo to Branch Chairmen and Childhood Education Chairmen, April 1964, Series A4, Part 1, Box 2, Folder 7, WILPF/US Records.

78. Malvina Reynolds, "Playing War," *Memo*, February 1965, 9, WSP Records. Reynolds wrote the song in 1964. See the mention in *Memo*, August 1964, 10, WSP Records.

79. On Reynolds's activist past, see Kelsen, "The Life and Times of Malvina Reynolds."

80. Tom Paxton, a fellow contributor to the folk revival newsletter *Broadside*, also used song to paint the toy industry's appeals to boys' warrior fantasies as the equivalent of childhood basic training. "Dedicated to the toy manufacturers of the world who are arming our youth so effectively," wrote Paxton in the liner notes to his 1965 song

"Buy a Gun for Your Son," from *Ain't That News* (Elektra Records, 1965), LP. That the song appeared on an album that included a tribute to the three civil rights activists murdered in Mississippi in 1964, as well as a protest song against the Vietnam War, is another indication of the seriousness with which left-wing observers viewed the war-toy trend at this time.

81. *Memo*, August 24, 1964, WSP Records.

82. Ramberg memo to Branch Chairmen and Childhood Education Chairmen, April 1964.

83. Bess Lane memo to Branch Chairmen and Childhood Education Chairmen, November 1963, 1, Series A4, Part 1, Box 2, Folder 7, WILPF/US Records.

84. *"Let's Train Them for Peace": A Study and Action Kit on Toys of Violence*, Prepared for the Childhood Education Committee of Women's International League for Peace and Freedom by the So. Suburban–Minneapolis Branch, January 1967, 2, Series A5, Box 14, Folder 21, WILPF/US Records.

85. Mickenberg, *Learning from the Left*, 33. On the discourse of progressive parenting, see Mickenberg, "The Pedagogy of the Popular Front."

86. On the fifties anti-comics crusade, see Gilbert, *Cycle of Outrage*, chap. 6. Controversies over children's culture have a long history in the United States. See West, *Children, Culture, and Controversy*.

87. Lane memo to Branch Chairmen and Childhood Education Chairmen, November 1963, 1.

88. Barbara Ulmer, letter printed in *Memo*, March 1, 1964, 2, WSP Records; Ulmer interview.

89. *"Let's Train Them for Peace,"* 2.

90. *Toys in Wartime*, 2, 16–17.

91. Cross, *Kids' Stuff*, 161.

92. Mattel TV commercial, "Thunder Burp Machine Gun," YouTube video, posted by "tvdays," March 17, 2009, https://www.youtube.com/watch?v=d554SF5ua2Y; Ideal ad, *PT*, October 1958, 87.

93. On Levine, see "Pediatric Party," *New Yorker*, March 31, 1975, 24.

94. Reiss interview.

95. Sarah Ramberg, "Should We Give Our Children War Toys?," *Friends Journal*, November 15, 1966, 563. Activist Victoria Reiss made the very same point in an interview with me, emphasizing that the problem was the gun as symbol.

96. Barbara Ulmer correspondence, printed in *Memo*, March 1, 1964, 2.

97. New York War Toy Committee, "Is Killing Child's Play?"

98. See Strickland and Ambrose, "The Baby Boom," 538.

99. Spock quoted in Graebner, "The Unstable World of Dr. Benjamin Spock," 620.

100. Spock, *The Commonsense Book of Baby and Child Care*, 270.

101. Spock, *Dr. Spock Talks with Mothers*, 134.

102. Spock, *Dr. Spock Talks with Mothers*, 143.

103. Spock was listed as a Sponsor on the organization's official stationery. See, for example, Libby Frank to Evelyn Prybutok, November 16, 1965, Series A4, Part 1, Box 1, Folder 9, WILPF/US Records.

104. Graebner, "The Unstable World of Dr. Benjamin Spock." See also Grant, *Raising Baby by the Book*, 218–27; and Fass, *The End of American Childhood*, 183–90.

105. Graebner, "The Unstable World of Dr. Benjamin Spock."

106. Spock and Morgan, *Spock on Spock*, 173–83.

107. Grant, *Raising Baby by the Book*, 220.

108. Helen Rand Miller to Dr. Benjamin Spock, April 15, 1964, Series B2, Box 2, Folder 13, WSP Records.

109. Rand Miller to Spock, April 15, 1964.

110. Dr. Benjamin Spock to Helen Rand Miller, April 23, 1964, Series B2, Folder 13, WSP Records. Noting that "I'm just a contributor, not an editor," Spock also expressed his regret that he could not help Miller publish her article in *Redbook*.

111. Spock to Rand Miller, April 23, 1964.

112. Benjamin Spock, "Playing with Toy Guns," *Redbook*, November 1964, 24.

113. Spock, "Playing with Toy Guns," 28.

114. Spock, "Playing with Toy Guns," 26.

115. Spock, "Playing with Toy Guns," 28.

116. Spock, "Playing with Toy Guns," 30.

117. Spock, "Playing with Toy Guns," 30.

118. On the origins of the democratic, nonauthoritarian family ideal in child-rearing discourse of the 1930s and 1940s, see Grant, *Raising Baby by the Book*, 182–85. On the ways Spock's thinking on the subject was indebted to the "culture and personality school" of anthropologists led by Ruth Benedict, see Graebner, "The Unstable World of Dr. Benjamin Spock."

119. Spock, "Playing with Toy Guns," 30.

120. Zuckerman, "Dr. Spock." See also Petigny, *The Permissive Society*, 40.

121. Spock quoted in Zuckerman, "Dr. Spock," 199; see also Spock, "Playing with Toy Guns," 32.

122. Spock, "Playing with Toy Guns," 32.

123. Toy Committee to Manager of the Toy Department at Sears, Roebuck and Company, April 29, 1964, Series B2, Box 2, Folder 13, WSP Records.

124. See *Memo*, May 1964, WSP Records.

125. See Evelyn Prybutok to Dr. Benjamin Spock, November 1, 1965, Series A4, Part 1, Box 2, Folder 9, WILPF/US Records; and Spock's reply in the form of a statement, Dr. Benjamin Spock, "Violence and War Toys," November 5, 1965, Series A4, Part 1, Box 2, Folder 9, WILPF/US Records. See also Libby Frank's memo to Chairmen of Childhood Education Committees, October 1967, Series A4, Part 1, Box 2, Folder 12, WILPF/US Records. By 1965, Spock was even sharing his distaste for war toys in his political speeches, such as the one he delivered to tens of thousands at the SANE-sponsored Emergency Rally Against the War in Vietnam, held at Madison Square Garden in New York City on June 8, 1965. The speech was later published in the pacifist Quaker magazine *Fellowship*. See Benjamin Spock, "Why Do We Betray Peace and Justice?," *Fellowship*, November 1965, 10.

126. New York War Toy Committee, "Is Killing Child's Play?"

127. The cover of *Memo* in February 1968 illustrates the extent to which WSP linked Spock's antiwar politics to his job as child-care adviser. "Dr. Spock didn't raise our boys to be soldiers," stated the caption beneath three photographs of Spock. *Memo*, February 1968, WSP Records.

128. The most prominent among them was psychiatrist Fredric Wertham, author of the best-selling book *Seduction of the Innocent* (1954) and a leading critic of comics in the fifties. As Wertham wrote in *A Sign for Cain* (1966), "If children are not destruction-minded, the toy business is doing its best to make them so" (70). See also Wertham, "Is TV Hardening Us to the War in Vietnam?," *NYT*, December 4, 1966, SX, 23.

129. Toy Committee to Manager of the Toy Department at Sears, Roebuck and Company, April 29, 1964.

130. Polster quoted in Jack Smyth, "Toy Makers, Women's Group Battle over Effect of War Toys on Children," *Philadelphia Sunday Bulletin*, November 28, 1965, L3.

131. On Froebel, see Beatty, *Preschool Education in America*, chap. 3. On Pratt, see Beatty, *Preschool Education in America*, 137–42. See also Ogata, "Creative Playthings," 130–32. The notion of purposeful play was famously articulated by the English philosopher and physician John Locke in his 1692 essay "Some Thoughts Concerning the Education of Children." See Cross, *Kids' Stuff*, 129; and Chudacoff, *Children at Play*, 26–27.

132. Cross, *Kids' Stuff*, 143.

133. See Ogata, *Designing the Creative Child*.

134. Ogata, "Creative Playthings"; Ogata, *Designing the Creative Child*, chap. 2.

135. Benjamin Spock, "What Toys Mean to Children," *Redbook*, December 1963, 121.

136. Sutton-Smith, "The Role of Play in Cognitive Development," 367–68.

137. *"Let's Train Them for Peace,"* 1.

138. "Play Is the Child's Key to Tomorrow!" (WILPF National Office flyer, November 1964), Series A4, Part 1, Box 2, Folder 7, WILPF/US Records.

139. Philadelphia WSP pamphlet (n.d.), Series A4, Box 1, Folder 13, WSP Records.

140. The sociologist Annette Lareau, writing about a later generation of upper-middle-class families, has aptly called this intensive parenting style "concerted cultivation." See Lareau, *Unequal Childhoods*, 2.

141. Ogata, "Creative Playthings," 148.

142. On the company's history through the 1960s, when it was sold to CBS, see Ogata, "Creative Playthings," 147–56.

143. "Creativity for Sale," *TN*, March 1968, 346.

144. Quoted in *Memo*, March 1966, 11, WSP Records.

145. Reiss, "War Is No Game," 10.

146. "Play Is the Child's Key to Tomorrow!"

147. *"Let's Train Them for Peace,"* 2.

148. Smyth, "Toy Makers, Women's Group Battle," L3.

149. "Play Is the Child's Key to Tomorrow!"

150. "Creativity for Sale," 347.

151. "Creativity for Sale," 347.

152. "Creativity for Sale," 348.

153. The relationship is a case study in the sociologist Pierre Bourdieu's theory of "cultural-capital-intensive" toy businesses. As Bourdieu wrote, such firms "benefit not only from the intensified competition for educational qualifications and the general rise in educational investments, but also from the unsolicited advertising given to products which suit their taste by those who present their own life-style as an example to others and elevate the inclinations of their own ethos into a universal ethic." Bourdieu, *Distinction*, 224.

154. DeBenedetti, *An American Ordeal*, 76.

155. Pugh, *Longing and Belonging*, xi.

Chapter Two. No War Toys

1. "From the Toy Editor," *National Peace Education Bulletin* 2, no. 2 (December 1965): 2.

2. For some examples, see Ellen W. Buzbee, "Who Bombed Santa's Workshop," *New York Times Magazine*, December 12, 1965, SM87, 98; Dave Felton, "Super-Sleuth of North Pole Plots Bang-Up Yule Caper," *Los Angeles Times*, December 13, 1965, B1; Eve Merriam, "We're Teaching Our Children That Violence Is Fun," *Ladies' Home Journal*, October 1964, 44; William H. Honan, "War Games for Kids This Christmas," *New Republic*, December 19, 1964, 9; and John G. Fuller, "Trade Winds," *Saturday Review*, December 25, 1965, 7.

3. Lichty, *Grin and Bear It* comic, *Philadelphia Evening Bulletin*, November 3, 1965, G88, reproduced in *The Toy*, no. 4 (Spring 1966): 12, author's collection.

4. Al Capp, *Li'l Abner* comic, December 25, 1965, reproduced in *The Toy*, no. 4 (Spring 1966): 12. It appears Capp had been taking note of the war-toy trend for a while. A year earlier, during one of his regular appearances on the NBC-TV *Tonight Show*, Capp joked, "It's now hard to tell a toy store from an arsenal." Al Capp quoted in *Variety*, December 9, 1964, tear sheet, Subject File Box: Children and War & Peace, Folder: Children and War and Peace, 1950–69, WILPF/US Records.

5. Libby Frank, Report to WILPF Annual Meeting, June 10–13, 1966, Series A4, Box 2, WILPF/US Records.

6. Brick, *Age of Contradiction*, 114. See also Braunstein and Doyle, "Introduction."

7. McBride, "Death City Radicals." See also Farber, "The Counterculture and the Antiwar Movement."

8. Rossinow, "'The Revolution Is about Our Lives.'"

9. Richard Register, interview by author, Oakland, CA, September 5, 2008.

10. Register interview.

11. Register interview.

12. *Minneapolis Tribune* columnist Irv Letofsky carried out his own investigation of the alleged Soviet ban in 1965 and found that "a wide variety of such weapons are made by state factories and sold in state shops." Irv Letofsky, "Some War Toys Go Boom, but Others Go Bust," *Minneapolis Tribune*, December 17, 1965. The origins of this rumor are hard to pinpoint, but it seems Benjamin Spock may have had a hand in circulating it. A pamphlet produced in the early 1960s for the National Committee for a Sane

Nuclear Policy—which I discovered in the records of Women Strike for Peace—includes the following quotation, attributed to Spock: "I would like American parents to know this one little fact: in the Soviet Union it has always been forbidden to make war toys for children." National Committee for a Sane Nuclear Policy, "Dr. Spock on War and Peace" (pamphlet, n.d.), Series A4, Box 2, Folder 14, WSP Records. Another likely contributor to the story's wide circulation was a December 1963 column by William H. Honan in the *New Republic*, in which he makes the same claim. William H. Honan, "Toys and Boys and Christmas," *New Republic*, December 21, 1963, 8.

13. Register interview.

14. Janet Rapoport, "Arms Race in the Playroom," *Sanity* (Toronto), November 1, 1965, 3. The quote comes from "No War Toys Concept" (pamphlet, n.d., ca. 1967–68), Subject File: Children and War & Peace, Folder 1950–69, WILPF/US Records.

15. The group's first publicity document appears to be a listing in the classified section of the *Los Angeles Free Press* (called the "unclassified" section, following the paper's satirical sensibility). "War Toys Are Dangerous," *Los Angeles Free Press*, May 21, 1965, 7. The reference to the group's office as the No War Toy Coffeehouse comes from Claude Hayward, "'No War Toys' Sand Castle Built on Venice Beach," *Los Angeles Free Press*, August 13, 1965, 1.

16. Register interview.

17. "No War Toys Concept."

18. "No War Toys Concept."

19. "Statement of Purpose," *The Toy*, no. 4 (Spring 1966): 1, author's collection.

20. Register interview. The idea for the exchange originated with NWT member and artist William Brun. See "No War Toys Progress Reports," *The Toy*, no. 4 (Spring 1966): 4.

21. "Who Are the Supporters of No War Toys?," *The Toy* (Winter 1965–66): 5, author's collection; "Erich Fromm Joins, Paul G. Hoffman Supports No War Toys," *The Toy*, no. 4 (Spring 1966): 1.

22. Cohen-Cole, "The Creative American," 238.

23. My summary description of the book's key ideas is drawn from Cohen-Cole, "The Creative American"; and Turner, *The Democratic Surround*, 170–75.

24. The biographical information in this paragraph comes from Richards, "Frank Barron and the Study of Creativity"; "This Week's Citation Classic," *Current Contents*, no. 14 (April 7, 1986): 18; and Erica Goode, "F.X. Barron, Who Studied Science of Creativity, Is Dead," *NYT*, October 13, 2002.

25. "This Week's Citation Classic."

26. Register interview.

27. Anthony Ripley, "'Peace' Toymaker Urges Creativity," *NYT*, December 22, 1968, 40.

28. "No War Toys Concept."

29. "No War Toys Concept."

30. Ripley, "'Peace' Toymaker Urges Creativity."

31. Rhodes, *The Vietnam War in American Childhood*, 72.

32. Frank X. Barron, "Vitality or Violence," 3, reprinted in the NWT pamphlet "No War Toys Concept." Historian Joanne Meyerowitz has rightly noted that the work of

midcentury personality theorists "could—and would—be used, in different ways and to different ends" by 1960s advocates of liberal social change but does not mention peace activists among them. Register's work with Barron suggests we should add it to the list. See Meyerowitz, "'How Common Culture Shapes the Separate Lives,'" 1084.

33. Rhodes, *The Vietnam War in American Childhood*, 69.

34. Ad for No War Toys anniversary party, *The Toy*, no. 4 (Spring 1966); see also the ad in the *Los Angeles Free Press*, April 22, 1966.

35. Ad for No War Toys anniversary party. While the Doors never addressed war toys in their music, war toys figured as a new antiwar motif in the work of other musical groups of the countercultural revolt. In 1966, the rock band Napoleon released a single titled "No War Toys," the story of a young boy whose childhood immersion in war toys (thanks to his permissive parents) renders him unable to "see good from bad." A year later, Frank Zappa's experimental rock group the Mothers of Invention described the war and horror toy displays at stores in a song titled "Uncle Bernie's Farm." See Napoleon, "No War Toys," comp. Brian Ross and Maurie Bercov (A.P.I. Records, 1966); and The Mothers of Invention, "Uncle Bernie's Farm," comp. Frank Zappa, *Absolutely Free* (Verve Records, 1967).

36. Michael Mouchette, *No War Toys*, 1967 poster for No War Toys, author's collection. Information about the poster's creation is from Michael Mouchette, phone interview by author, August 16, 2016.

37. On the construction of the Romantic vision of childhood in late eighteenth- and nineteenth-century Western art and culture, see Higonnet, *Pictures of Innocence*, 15–71.

38. Mouchette interview.

39. "Peace Education Newsletter," *Memo*, August 1964, 3, WSP Records.

40. Elise Boulding, "Toys, Tots, and Terrors," Letters to the Editor, *Saturday Review*, December 2, 1961, 35.

41. "NO WAR TOYS Becomes NO DEATH TOYS, Announcement of Change of Name and Plans for Christmas Season, 1966" (flyer, November 23, 1966), copy in author's collection, courtesy Richard Register.

42. Brick, *Age of Contradiction*, 116.

43. "NO WAR TOYS Becomes NO DEATH TOYS." Register later elaborated on the name change in his group's newsletter. "No War Toys Becomes No Death Toys," *The Toy*, no. 5 (Winter 1966–67): 1, author's collection.

44. On the spy trend, see Ted Erikson, "Retailers and Jobbers Summarize 1965 Sales, Profits, and Trends," *PT*, March 1966, 278; and the "Toys on the Move" columns in the September, October, November, and December issues of *Playthings*. See TV commercial for the Zero M Sonic Blaster in "Commercials 17: Toy Guns," Internet Archive, Community Video collection, posted by "NoseSilo," https://archive.org/details/Commercials17ToyGuns. For the Pipe Shooter, see the 1966 Topper commercial, posted by "TV Toy Memories," YouTube, November 29, 2011, https://www.youtube.com/watch?v=5DkYTRYB6tU.

45. "NO WAR TOYS Becomes NO DEATH TOYS."

46. "NO WAR TOYS Becomes NO DEATH TOYS."

47. *The Toy*, no. 5½ (Spring 1967), author's collection.

48. NWT announcement, *Los Angeles Free Press*, August 6, 1965, 7.

49. Hayward, "'No War Toys' Sand Castle Built on Venice Beach," 1. The events appear to have only grown more popular over the years. According to the *Los Angeles Times*, the August 8, 1966, sand castle party had an estimated three hundred attendees. See "Peaceful Castle," photo caption, *Los Angeles Times*, August 8, 1966, 3.

50. See the photographs in *Los Angeles Times*, July 27, 1967, WS3; "'No War Toys' Tots Build a Substitute," *Evening Vanguard* (Venice, CA), July 6, 1966, 1; *The Free Venice Beachhead*, no. 8 (June 1969): 1.

51. Brick, *Age of Contradiction*, 117.

52. *The Toy*, no. 5½ (Spring 1967).

53. On Bread and Puppet, see Harding and Rosenthal, *Restaging the Sixties*, 353–58. On the antiwar origins of the New Games movement and Brand's role, see Kirk, "The Whole Earth Catalog."

54. Ripley, "'Peace' Toymaker Urges Creativity."

55. "Directory," *The Toy*, no. 5 (Winter 1966–67): 1.

56. "Action in N.Y.," *The Toy*, no. 4 (Spring 1966): 1, 4.

57. "Action in N.Y."

58. *Make Love Not War Toys* (poster, n.d., ca. late 1960s), produced by Parents for Responsibility in the Toy Industry, courtesy of Richard Reiss.

59. Denton Harris, "Who Could Be against Toys?," THW, April 6, 1964, 2.

60. "How to Stock, Display, Promote and Sell Western Guns and Toys," PT, June 1960, 55; "A Full-Service Toy Store with a Supermarket-Style," PT, November 1961, 24.

61. Dorothy Barclay, "Behind All the Bang-Bang," *New York Times Magazine*, July 22, 1962, 164.

62. Anderson, *Guns in American Life*, 68–69.

63. A. J. Wood Research Corporation and Toy Manufacturers of the U.S.A., *Toy Buying in the United States*, A-26.

64. "'We Shot It Out with Sticks,'" PT, April 1966, 68.

65. "On 'Violence' Toys," Letters Page, THW, July 6, 1964, 2.

66. "Toy Makers Say Only 5% of Playthings Are Guns," NYT, December 14, 1965, 63. See also "'We Shot It Out with Sticks.'"

67. "Ready-Made Talk on Toys," PT, June 1964, 62.

68. Topper Johnny Eagle ad, PT, August 1965, 35–36.

69. Lionel ad, "Lionel levels with the trade," PT, March 1965, 173.

70. Lionel Toy Corporation, *Lionel Toys for 1965*, 3, Railroad, Business, and Labor Collections, Thomas J. Dodd Research Center, University of Connecticut at Storrs.

71. "Toy Drive Is Aimed at Parents," NYT, July 8, 1965, 37; "Lionel's 'Sane Toys' Theme Reflected in Science Kit Push," PT, June 1965, 113.

72. Lionel ad, "This toy doesn't kill, bite, scream, explode, conquer, destroy, or turn into a vampire," magazine tear sheet, Series A4, Box 1, Folder: War Toy Committee, WSP Records. The ad appeared, among other places, in the *New Yorker*, October 23, 1965, 25.

73. Lionel ad, "This toy doesn't kill." The reference to vampires reflected a recent industry fad featuring ghouls, monsters, and other macabre themes, inspired by a spate of new popular monster-centric TV shows like *The Addams Family* (1964–66). See Philip Shabecoff, "Advertising: Monster Market Creeping Up," *NYT*, August 30, 1964.

74. Lionel ad, "No boy ever held up a store with one of these," magazine tear sheet, Series A4, Box 1, Folder: War Toy Committee, WSP Records. On the new science toys, see "Lionel Says It Had Profit in '60; Concern Unveils Series of Science Toys," *NYT*, March 13, 1961, 5.

75. Lionel ad, "Sane toys for healthy kids," *PT*, March 1966, 171, and *THW*, March 1966, 261.

76. Lionel ad, "Nice toys don't kill," *PT*, August 1965, 34. In 1966, the American Institute for Graphic Arts selected a different version of "Nice Toys Don't Kill," this one targeting consumers, for its Fifty Advertisements of the Year list. See "Nice Toys Don't Kill," AIGA Design Archives, http://designarchives.aiga.org/#/entries/lionel/_ /detail/relevance/asc/11/7/14270/nice-toys-dont-kill/1.

77. Vogel, *The Market for Virtue*.

78. Cohen, *A Consumers' Republic*, 299, 307. Market segmentation replaced the old "mass marketing" strategy that appealed to the average consumer. On the development of this new approach, which began in the late 1950s, see Cohen, *A Consumers' Republic*, chap. 6. On the creative revolution and the marketing of dissent in the 1960s, see Frank, *The Conquest of Cool*. On the evolution of lifestyle marketing during these decades, see Binkley, *Getting Loose*.

79. Lionel ad, "Sane toys for healthy kids."

80. Lionel ad, "Dear dear Lionel," *PT*, September 1965, 61.

81. "Lionel Shows Profit for '65 Operations after 4 Bad Years," *TN*, April 16, 1966, 55.

82. Lionel ad, "Sane toys for healthy kids."

83. "The Little King," *Time*, December 12, 1955, 93.

84. DeBenedetti, *An American Ordeal*, 69–71.

85. Jenkins, "The Sensuous Child," 216.

86. See Hulbert, *Raising America*, chap. 7.

87. Fraiberg, *The Magic Years*, 271. Fraiberg's book received the Book of the Year Award from the Child Study Association and went on to sell more than 1.5 million copies by the end of the 1960s. See C. Brown, "Selma Fraiberg."

88. Lionel ad, "Nice toys don't kill."

89. On the competition from Marx, see "The Little King," 92–94.

90. Lionel Corporation, *Lionel*, 1958 catalog, 5, Internet Archive, Building Technology Heritage Library, https://archive.org/stream/Lionel027SuperoHo /LionelCca146943#page/n3/mode/2up. The company changed its name from Lionel Corporation to Lionel Toy Corporation in 1965. See Doyle, *Standard Catalog of Lionel Trains*, 8.

91. Honan, "Toys and Boys and Christmas," 7.

92. Lewis S. Sanders quoted in "Toy Drive Is Aimed at Parents," *NYT*, July 8, 1965, 37.

93. See Lionel TV commercial, "LIONEL TRAINS TV AD (1960s) LIONEL Trains Turbo Missile Car, Aerial Target Car & Recon Copter Car," YouTube video, posted by "Our Nostalgic Memories," January 20, 2020, https://www.youtube.com/watch?v=wpYHEIQcss0.

94. Lionel ad insert, *PT*, March 1961, 117. Lionel forgot to remove the listing for one of its military cars when it created the 1965 spring catalog on the "sane toys" theme; only after a journalist pointed it out did a company representative publicly acknowledge the oversight. See Letofsky, "Some War Toys Go Boom, but Others Go Bust," reprinted in *"Let's Train Them for Peace": A Study and Action Kit on Toys of Violence*, prepared for the Childhood Education Committee of Women's International League for Peace and Freedom by the So. Suburban–Minneapolis Branch, January 1967, 2, Series A5, Box 14, Folder 21, WILPF/US Records.

95. Eric Schlubach quoted in Letofsky, "Some War Toys Go Boom, but Others Go Bust."

96. *Memo*, August 1964, 3, WSP Records.

97. See Syracuse branch flyer, Series A4, Part 1, Box 2, Folder 9, WILPF/US Records.

98. Evelyn Prybutok to Lionel, October 27, 1965, Series A4, Part 1, Box 2, Folder 9, WILPF/US Records.

99. Elise Boulding memo to Branch Chm. and Chm. Childhood Education Committee, September/October 1964, 2, Series A4, Part 1, Box 2, Folder 7, WILPF/US Records.

100. Jack Smyth, "Toy Makers, Women's Group Battle over Effect of War Toys on Children," *Philadelphia Sunday Bulletin*, November 28, 1965, L3.

101. Schlubach quoted in Letofsky, "Some War Toys Go Boom, but Others Go Bust."

102. Schlubach quoted in Letofsky, "Some War Toys Go Boom, but Others Go Bust."

103. The LEGO ad appeared, among other places, in the *Los Angeles Times*, November 28, 1965; *New York Times Magazine*, December 5, 1965; and the *New Yorker*, December 11, 1965. See Seiter, *Sold Separately*, 71–72. On LEGO, see Fanning, "Building Kids."

104. *National Peace Education Bulletin* 2, no. 2 (December 1965): 2, 12, Box 5, Folder 9, WSP Records.

105. Amsco brochure, "Toy Buyers: Invent a Peace Toy and Win $1,000," Series A4, Box 2, Folder: Childhood Education Committee 1965: television program on war toys, WILPF/US Records. See also "'Peace Toy' Contest Announced by Amsco," *TN*, March 1, 1966, 389; and "Peace-Toy Contest Offers $1,000 Prize," *NYT*, March 13, 1966, F11.

106. "Peace-Toy Contest Offers $1,000 Prize," F11.

107. Michael Spielman, "A Matter of Values and Good Taste," *TN*, April 1, 1966, 41. In his column a month earlier, Spielman had rather dismissively referred to the antiwar toy picketers outside the Toy Fair, now in their third consecutive year, as "mother hens marching up and down" the sidewalk. What exactly changed his mind about their point of view between March and April is hard to know. See Michael Spielman, "A Fable for Toy Fair," *TN*, March 1, 1966, 297.

108. "Toy Makers Say Only 5% of Playthings Are Guns."

109. "Annual T&N Survey Seeks Trends from Wholesalers," TN, May 15, 1966, 42.

110. Andreas, "War Toys and the Peace Movement," 85–86.

111. Regan, "War Toys, War Movies, and the Militarization of the United States," 53.

112. "War Toy Sales Down This Year; Some in Industry Blame Drop on Vietnam," *The Gazette and Daily* (York, PA), December 22, 1966, clipping, Series A4, Box 2, WSP Records.

113. "War Toy Sales Down This Year."

114. "War Toy Sales Down This Year."

115. Andreas, "War Toys and the Peace Movement," 97.

116. Andreas, "War Toys and the Peace Movement," 97–98.

117. Leonard Sloane, "Sales of War Toys Decline," NYT, December 10, 1967, B209.

118. Saul Robbins quoted in "Battle to Ban War Toys Gains after Assassination," *Santa Barbara News Press*, October 4, 1968, clipping, courtesy of Richard Register, copy in author's collection.

119. "Military Toys Sell despite Protests," THW, February 6, 1967, 4. On the growing spy trend, see the "Toys on the Move" column in *Playthings* during the final months of 1965.

120. Erikson, "Retailers and Jobbers Summarize 1965 Sales, Profits, and Trends," 278.

121. "Toy Industry Faces Fickle Buying Public," *Los Angeles Times*, August 28, 1966, E3.

122. Sloane, "Sales of War Toys Decline," B209. As Sloane reported, "one of the more noticeable trends is that military toys are not selling as well as they did in recent years."

123. Mary Cassal, "East," Marketing Trends, TN, April 1, 1966, 32.

124. Daisy ad, "Our experts have some hot ideas," TN, March 1, 1966, 157, and PT, April 1966, 107.

125. For a discussion of the war toys still on the market, see William Honan, "Christmas (Ka-Pow!) Again," *New Republic*, December 17, 1966, 7.

126. Mattel Marauder ad, TN, May 1, 1967, 51.

127. See the monthly Marketing Trends report in *Toys and Novelties* during these years.

128. See the ads for Monogram's new Fighting Boats of Viet Nam line, in TN, August 15, 1967, 77, and TN, September 1, 1967, 14.

129. Associated Press, "This Day in Sacramento," *Los Angeles Times*, March 7, 1967, 30.

130. On the Pentagon march and the shift in public opinion, see Young, *The Vietnam Wars*, 200–201, 210–11.

131. "The Case for War Toys," THW, May 6, 1968, 18.

132. Libby Frank, Report on Relevant Education, WILPF Annual Meeting, June 28–July 2, 1968, Series A4, Box 2, Folder: Committee on Childhood Education 1967–68, WILPF/US Records.

133. "THINK before You Buy a Toy of Violence!" (Parents for Responsibility in the Toy Industry flyer, 1968), Series A4, Box 2, Folder: Committee on Childhood Education 1968–69, WILPF Records.

134. "1,000 Pupils in Queens Scrap Toys of Violence," NYT, June 15, 1968.

135. Press photograph by Jack Lenahan for the *Chicago Sun-Times*, June 14, 1968, author's collection.

136. Andreas, "War Toys and the Peace Movement," 86–87.

137. "Bank Offers Dime for Each Toy Gun," *Chicago Tribune*, August 11, 1968, S10, 7; and "Kids, Turn in the Guns and Take Two Free Rides," *Rolling Meadows Herald*, August 9, 1968, 4. A couple of weeks after announcing the toy-gun drive, the president of the Chicago bank behind the initiative reported having received hundreds of them. See Jerry Shnay, "Fight about Guns Often Backfires," *Chicago Tribune*, August 22, 1968, S2A, 13.

138. The Editors, "What Women Can Do to End Violence in America," *McCall's*, July 1968. The editors initially mailed a copy of the article to all their readers and published it as an advertisement in the *Washington Post* on June 20, 1968. See *Crime and Violence*, 57–59.

139. "What You Can Do to Stop Violence—an Expert's View," *Family Circle*, October 1968. The quotation from the article comes from a PRITI flyer, November 1968, Series A4, Box 2, WILPF/US Records.

140. Benjamin Spock, "The Need to Control Aggression in Young Children," *Redbook*, November 1968.

141. Roy Harris, "Toy Business Changing Policy on Weapon Items," *Los Angeles Times*, July 7, 1968, F1.

142. Ted Erikson, "Toy Guns Are in for a Beating," *PT*, July 1968, 45.

143. Daisy ad, "Toy guns need not take a beating," *PT*, September 1968, 36.

144. See Reader's Forum, *PT*, October 1968, 6.

145. See Hendershot, *Saturday Morning Censors*, chap. 1.

146. Register's trip is mentioned in Ripley, "'Peace' Toymaker Urges Creativity."

147. Frank Gavitt quoted in "Look Who's Playing with Toys," *Forbes*, December 15, 1971, 29.

148. Mattel rep quoted in "Toy Industry Booming Even in the Face of Hard Times," *Los Angeles Times*, December 20, 1970, 3.

149. Boulding described the WILPF campaign as the War/Peace Toys Project in Childhood Education Memo, October/November 1965, Series A4, Box 2, Folder: Childhood Education Committee 1965, WILPF/US Records.

150. Elise Boulding to Walt Disney, January 5, 1965, Series A4, Box 2, Folder: Childhood Education Committee 1965, WILPF/US Records.

151. Boulding to Branch Chm. and Chm. Childhood Education Committee, September/October 1964.

152. "We've Updated G.I. Joe," in "3rd TMA Sales and Marketing Seminar Report," *PT*, October 1968, 47.

153. "We've Updated G.I. Joe."

154. "Failing War Toy Succeeds as Peaceful Adventurer," *NYT*, March 27, 1969.

155. K. Hall, "A Soldier's Body." For details on all these changes to the G.I. Joe brand, see Michlig, *GI Joe*.

156. See Engelhardt, *The End of Victory Culture*, 175–80.

157. Boulding, "Toys, Tots, and Terrors."

Chapter Three. Integrating the Doll Shelves

1. "The Advent of Soul Toys," *Ebony*, November 1968, 165.

2. On the history of Black stereotypes in toys, see Wilkinson, "Racial Socialization through Children's Toys"; and Bernstein, *Racial Innocence*, chap. 1. On the commercial uses of Black stereotypes, see Kern-Foxworth, *Aunt Jemima, Uncle Ben, and Rastus*; Goings, *Mammy and Uncle Mose*; and Hale, *Making Whiteness*.

3. On the National Negro Doll Company, see Mitchell, *Righteous Propagation*, 182–83; Halliday, *Buy Black*, 8–9; and Bernstein, *Racial Innocence*, 230–31. On Berry & Ross, Inc., see Mitchell, *Righteous Propagation*, 184, 188, 191, 195; Halliday, *Buy Black*, 10; and Forman-Brunell, *Made to Play House*, 150.

4. Mitchell, *Righteous Propagation*, chap. 6. For images and advertisements of these companies' dolls and other commercially made Black dolls of this era, see Garrett, *The Definitive Guide to Collecting Black Dolls*; and Perkins, *Black Dolls*. As the historian Michele Mitchell notes, some Black parents' preferences for Black dolls in the early twentieth century reflected concerns over interracial marriage as much as an interest in promoting racial pride; giving Black baby dolls to Black girls, they maintained, reinforced the expectation to marry a Black husband, whereas giving white dolls—representations of lighter-complexioned babies—opened up interracial marriage as a plausible aspiration.

5. *Tide*, March 7, 1947, cover image, reproduced in Chambers, *Madison Avenue and the Color Line*, 56.

6. Garrett, *The Definitive Guide to Collecting Black Dolls*, 18. Collector and doll historian Debbie Behan Garrett's blog, *Black Doll Collecting* (https://blackdollcollecting.blogspot.com), is an invaluable resource and image archive for the commercial and cultural history of Black dolls.

7. Garrett, *The Definitive Guide to Collecting Black Dolls*, 24.

8. Thomas, "Sara Lee"; G. Patterson, "Color Matters."

9. Garrett, *The Definitive Guide to Collecting Black Dolls*, 18, 24. The Patty-Jo doll is one of three hundred Black dolls that can be seen up close at the Philadelphia Doll Museum—founded, curated, and run by doll collector and historian Barbara Whiteman.

10. Asherbranner, "Toys as an Agent of Change," 97. In the previous decade, only during the 1952 and 1955 Christmas seasons did Sears offer a Black doll of any kind for sale (Asherbranner, "Toys as an Agent of Change," 48).

11. *TN*, Directory Issue, 1963. The industry continued to use the terms *Negro version* and *Colored version* interchangeably through the end of the decade. See, for instance, the news item about Ideal's Crissy doll, "Crissy Doll a Top Seller in New York Area," *PT*, August 1969, 26.

12. "Review of New Toys and Trends at the 61st Annual Toy Fair," *PT*, April 1964, 53.

13. Marcus, *Minders of Make-Believe*, 235–36.

14. "Mattel's 7 New Items for Spring '62," *PT*, November 1961, 85; see also Sears Christmas catalog, 1962, 407.

15. Asherbranner, "Toys as an Agent of Change," 97.

16. "The Way It Was," *TN*, April 1968, 142.

17. *PT*, May 1968, 26; *PT*, June 5, 1968, 75.

18. "1969 Toy Fair Makes Clear Industry's Professionalism," *THW*, April 7, 1969, 8.

19. "1969 Toy Fair Makes Clear Industry's Professionalism."

20. "Play Money Credit Card," *Oakland Tribune*, February 25, 1969, 24E.

21. For Colored Francie, see *Mattel Toys 1967*, 15, SDOTCC. On the origins of the Francie and Colored Francie dolls, see Halliday, *Buy Black*, 52–53.

22. For Talking Christie, see *Mattel Toys 1968*, 93, SDOTCC.

23. For Julia, see *Mattel Toys 1969*, 32, SDOTCC. See also DeWein and Ashabraner, *The Collectors Encyclopedia of Barbie Dolls and Collectibles*. On the significance of the Julia doll, see Halliday, *Buy Black*, 53–55.

24. "Juro Adds 'Lester' to Ventriloquist Line," *PT*, March 1969, 299.

25. Asherbranner, "Toys as an Agent of Change," 97.

26. See the 1969 Sears Christmas catalog, 587, 590, 592, 595, 599, 601.

27. See, for example, the Black and white Baby Precious dolls from the manufacturer Horsman, pictured side by side in the 1968 Sears Christmas catalog, 586.

28. "Integration Is Gaining on Doll Counters, Too," *NYT*, December 18, 1969, 56.

29. "Black Doll Business," *Stevens Point Daily Journal*, November 26, 1969, 22.

30. "Remco Has a TV Salesman, 'Ethnically Correct' Dolls," *PT*, March 1969, 246–47.

31. "Retailing: Black Christmas," *Newsweek*, December 9, 1968, 81.

32. "Marketing Trends," *TN*, February 1970, 105.

33. "The Untapped Market," *TN*, October 1968, 56.

34. Remco ad, "We're spending 5 ½ million dollars on color TV this year," *PT*, June 1969, 7.

35. "Black Doll Business," 22.

36. "The Advent of Soul Toys," 165.

37. Chambers, *Madison Avenue and the Color Line*, 47. See also Weems, *Desegregating the Dollar*, 70–79. On the beauty industry's race consciousness during this era, see Walker, "Black Is Profitable."

38. R. P. Finn, "What's Behind Retail Trends?," *PT*, August 1963, 76, 148; Leonard Sive, "The Negro Market—Rich, Complex, Neglected," *THW*, April 20, 1964, 16; Frank Seymour, "A Look at the Negro Market," *TN*, April 1966, 62, 44; R. P. Finn, "What's behind Retail Trends?," *PT*, April 1966, 99.

39. "Vast, 'Untapped' Nonwhite Market," *PT*, September 1968, 112.

40. "1969 Toy Fair Makes Clear Industry's Professionalism," *THW*, April 7, 1969, 8.

41. See Cohen, *A Consumers' Republic*, especially 370–85.

42. On the long history of consumerist strategies in the Black freedom struggle, see Chambers, "Equal in Every Way."

43. The trend is noted in "Economy Reflects New Negro Pride," *Tri-City Herald* (Richland, WA), December 14, 1967, 35; "The Advent of Soul Toys," 165; and "Boys Want Spacemen: Girls Still Prefer Dolls," *Ebony*, November 1969, 75. See also Weems, *Desegregating the Dollar*, chap. 4.

44. On Malcolm X's impact, see Van Deburg, *New Day in Babylon*, 3–8. On the goals of the Black Arts movement from one of its leaders, see Larry Neal, "Any Day

Now: Black Arts and Black Liberation," *Ebony*, August 1969, 54–58, 62. For starting points into the diverse history of the movement, see K. Jones, *South of Pico*; Zorach, *Art for People's Sake*; and Smethurst, *The Black Arts Movement*.

45. On Fanon's special influence, see Van Deburg, *New Day in Babylon*, 57–61. For a global perspective on these theoretical currents, see Wilder, *Freedom Time*.

46. Weems, *Desegregating the Dollar*, chap. 4.

47. "The Advent of Soul Toys," 165.

48. Seymour, "A Look at the Negro Market," 62, 64.

49. "Black Doll Business," 22.

50. "Black Doll Business," 22.

51. "Sales of Negro Dolls Skyrocket," *Chicago Defender*, December 23, 1967, 4.

52. "The Advent of Soul Toys," 165.

53. Robbins quoted in Helen Hennessy, "Black Doll Looks Like . . . the Real Item," *Edwardsville Intelligencer* (IL), December 23, 1968, 12, widely syndicated by the Newspaper Enterprise Association. On the origins of Remco, see Margalit Fox, "Isaac Heller, Toymaker to a Generation, Dies at 88," *NYT*, March 12, 2015, A21.

54. "Remco: Negro Girls Want 'Realistic' Dolls," *PT*, July 1968, 50. Forty years later, Robbins reiterated this point in an interview. Saul Robbins, phone interview by author, August 10, 2009.

55. That *A Healthy Personality for Every Child* was the title of the official report of the 1950 White House Conference on Children and Youth, written by the leading childhood experts of the time, is just one illustration of the term's central place in the era's psychological thought. See Hulbert, *Raising America*, chap. 7.

56. Scott, *Contempt and Pity*, 89. See also Herman, *The Romance of American Psychology*, chap. 7.

57. Herman, *The Romance of American Psychology*, 184.

58. Cherry, "Kenneth B. Clark and Social Psychology's Other History," 21. See also Bergner, "Black Children, White Preference."

59. Bernstein, *Racial Innocence*, 235–36.

60. Herman, *The Romance of American Psychology*, 194. Herman attributes the impact of the Clarks' work to their "ability to personalize the consequences of racism in a vulnerable group—children—and to do so in the name of empirical, scientific research" (194).

61. On the special place of psychology in the NAACP's legal strategy, see Schmidt, "The Children of *Brown*." As Schmidt notes, "An awareness of psychology played a central role in the creation of the entire worldview in which the NAACP created their case and in which the justices decided it" (177).

62. Clark, *Dark Ghetto*, 65.

63. These studies are discussed in the important group of articles collected in R. Jones, *Black Psychology*. The book symbolized the launch of what contributors called the "new black psychology."

64. Douglas Sirk, dir., *Imitation of Life* (Universal City, CA: Universal Studios, 1959). For an illuminating discussion of the film in the context of midcentury psychology and the history of racist stereotypes of Black women, see Russworm, *Blackness Is Burning*, chap. 3.

65. H.L.R. to the Editor, *Los Angeles Times*, November 28, 1967, B4.

66. "Black Dr. Spocks," *Time*, July 28, 1975.

67. Comer and Poussaint, *Black Childcare*, 11.

68. Comer and Poussaint, *Black Childcare*, 11.

69. Comer and Poussaint, *Black Childcare*, 25. See the similar statement by the child psychiatrist Francis Welsing in Jacqueline Trescott, "What a Black Doll Can Do for a Child," *Star-News*, November 30, 1974, A13, clipping file in Black Toys for Christmas, 1975, Silver Anvil Award Records, Public Relations Society of America, Wisconsin Historical Society, Madison, WI.

70. "The Advent of Soul Toys," 165; Remco official quoted in Leonard Sloane, "Toy Industry Talking of Profit and Sociology," *NYT*, March 10, 1968, F1.

71. Payton and Reade, *You, the Church, and Race*. According to the guide's third edition, it went through three printings in just over a year, with two thousand copies purchased by religious and secular groups across the country (4).

72. Payton and Reade, *You, the Church, and Race*, 34.

73. "For Negro Dolls," *PT*, May 1968, 8; "Church Group Asks Stores to Display Negro Dolls," *THW*, June 3, 1968, 18.

74. Schmidt, "The Children of *Brown*," 180. On trends in the social scientific study of race during the middle third of the century, see Gordon, *From Power to Prejudice*.

75. Perillo, "White Teachers and the 'Black Psyche,'" 159. The notion that anti-Black prejudice had damaging effects on white psyches was discussed by child advocates as early as 1930; see Selig, "The Whole Child."

76. Jackson, *Gunnar Myrdal and America's Conscience*.

77. Granger quoted in Marcus, *Minders of Make-Believe*, 220.

78. James P. Comer and Alvin F. Poussaint, "What White Parents Should Know about Children and Prejudice," *Redbook*, May 1972, 123.

79. Comer and Poussaint, "What White Parents Should Know about Children and Prejudice," 62.

80. "3-D Yarn Art Going Well in Los Angeles," *PT*, December 1969, 20.

81. "Marketing Trends," *TN*, February 1970, 105.

82. That company was Shindana Toys, the subject of chapter 4. The sales figures are from Harshe-Rotman & Druck, Inc., Shindana Toys Press Kit (ca. 1974–75), courtesy of Kirk Hallahan.

83. "Robbins Sees Black Dolls as 'Saleable' Good Toys," *THW*, May 19, 1969, 16.

84. On King's strong take on the dangers of affluence and materialism, see Horowitz, *The Anxieties of Affluence*, 177–88.

85. "Crissy Doll a Top Seller in New York Area," 26; "Profitable Growth: The Goal at Ideal Toy," *PT*, September 1969, 72.

86. See "The Untapped Market," 56.

87. Helen Hennessy, "Artist Designs Black Dolls with Negroid Features," *Iowa City Press-Citizen*, November 28, 1968, 8.

88. Hennessy, "Artist Designs Black Dolls with Negroid Features."

89. "The Advent of Soul Toys," 165.

90. "Photo-Beat," *PT*, May 1968, 26.

91. See G. Patterson, "Color Matters." Print media covering the Sara Lee story at the time used the term *anthropologically correct* to describe the doll's intentionally Black-coded features. See "Dolls for Negro Children: New Toy Which Is Anthropologically Correct Fills an Old Need," *Life* magazine, December 17, 1951, 62.

92. Sive, "The Negro Market—Rich, Complex, Neglected," 16, emphasis mine.

93. "Remco: Negro Girls Want 'Realistic' Dolls," 50.

94. Remco official quoted in Sloane, "Toy Industry Talking of Profit and Sociology," F1.

95. Hennessy, "Artist Designs Black Dolls with Negroid Features." Versions of Hennessy's article, syndicated by the Newspaper Enterprise Association, appeared in hundreds of newspapers across the country, usually with a headshot of McBurrows. The only article at the time to note that McBurrows was hired to supervise the new line's development is Sally Ryan, "New Toys Are Appearing," *Lincoln Journal Star*, March 4, 1968, 6.

96. "Playland Job Is Tailored to His Talents," Newspaper Enterprise Association story in *Sherbrooke Daily Record* (Quebec), December 19, 1968, 10.

97. The new division is noted in Sloane, "Toy Industry Talking of Profit and Sociology," F1; and "Doll Wins Praise of Black Community," *Los Angeles Times*, November 1969, 368.

98. "The Advent of Soul Toys," 165. My description of Tippy Tumbles is based on the 1968 Remco trade catalog. See Remco Industries, *Up and Up and Away We Go with REMCO in '68*, SDOTCC.

99. McBurrows quoted in "Remco: Negro Girls Want 'Realistic' Dolls," 51.

100. Remco ad, *Ebony*, October 1968, 173; "The Untapped Market," 56.

101. Kincaid quoted in Jenkins, "Introduction," 9.

102. On the participation of children and the politics of childhood in the civil rights movement, see King, *African American Childhoods*, chap. 10; and de Schweinitz, *If We Could Change the World*.

103. "The Advent of Soul Toys," 173.

104. On the exclusion of African American children from the middle-class ideology of childhood innocence, see Bernstein, *Racial Innocence*.

105. Box for Winking Winny doll, Remco Industries, 1968, author's collection.

106. Remco ad, "We're spending 5 ½ million dollars on color TV this year."

107. Remco ad, "We're spending 5 ½ million dollars on color TV this year."

108. Remco ad, "We're spending 5 ½ million dollars on color TV this year."

109. Remco ad, "We're spending 5 ½ million dollars on color TV this year."

110. Remco's advertising director attributed the company's move to the "vast, untapped market" for "ethnically correct" Black baby dolls. See "The Untapped Market," 56. See also "Robbins Sees Black Dolls as 'Saleable' Good Toys," 16.

111. "Remco Reports Record Year," *PT*, April 1969, 16.

112. "Remco Has a TV Salesman, 'Ethnically Correct' Dolls," 246–47.

113. Remco Industries, *Take Giant Step into '70*, 7, SDOTCC.

114. "Horsman Accents New Packaging—Sound, Action Dolls," *THW*, March 3, 1969, 149. Mattel's Talking Christie, introduced at the same 1968 Toy Fair as Remco's new line, also appeared to have a new head mold with racialized facial features like those of the Remco dolls. Yet despite the obvious effort toward Black representation,

Mattel never called attention to the new design, and both the trade press and commercial media overlooked it. See *Mattel Toys 1968*, 93, SDOTCC.

115. T. J. Rakstis, "Debate in the Doll House," *Today's Health*, December 1970, 66.

116. Fisher-Price, Merchandising Packet, 1974, 2, SDOTCC.

117. "Fisher Price would like you to meet our girls," color poster in Fisher-Price Merchandising Packet, 1974, 3, copy in author's collection. The statement was also printed on the doll boxes.

118. On Fisher-Price, see Cross, *Kids' Stuff*, 105–6, 108, 145, 161, 169.

119. The paragraphs that follow are based on my discussion with Donner. Karen Donner, phone interview by author, July 1, 2009.

120. See Fisher-Price catalogs for these years in the SDOTCC.

121. Donner interview.

122. "Rap: Henry H. Coords, President of Fisher-Price Toys," *Toys*, August 1974, 31.

123. Donner interview.

124. See Ford, *Liberated Threads*, especially chap. 4.

125. Ford, *Liberated Threads*; Walker, "Black Is Profitable."

126. Donner interview.

127. See Fisher-Price Merchandising Packet, 1974.

128. Elizabeth doll, Fisher-Price, 1974, author's collection.

129. Donner interview.

130. Fisher-Price, *Fisher-Price Toys 1974*, SDOTCC.

131. Elizabeth doll box, 1974, Fisher-Price, author's collection.

132. Fisher-Price ad, *PT*, April 1974, 54.

133. Fisher-Price ad, *PT*, June 1974, 78.

134. Donner interview.

135. "Inside the Doll Market," *Toys*, May 1975, 27.

136. "Black Doll Market Share," chart in Harshe-Rotman & Druck, Inc., Shindana Toys Press Kit (ca. 1974–75), courtesy of Kirk Hallahan.

Chapter Four. Black Power in Toyland

1. See "Case 11: Shindana Toys," in J. Brown and Lusterman, *Business and the Development of Ghetto Enterprise*, 78.

2. W. Martin, *No Coward Soldiers*, 3–9, 68–71, 82–131. See also W. Martin, "'Be Real Black for Me.'"

3. That celebration took shape across a wide range of cultural venues. See Collins and Crawford, "Introduction," 11.

4. "Shindana: Black Toymakers of Watts," *Sepia*, February 1971, 43. For other discussions of Shindana, see Halliday, *Buy Black*, 55–60; Hester, "Shindana Toys"; "The Legacy of Shindana Toys"; Gould, "Toys Make a Nation," chap. 5; Lord, *Forever Barbie*, 160–71; duCille, "Dyes and Dolls"; and Ellis, *People Making Places*, chap. 1.

5. The unemployment rate comes from Ogbar, *Black Power*, 127. On the Avalon neighborhood, see Ellis, "Operation Bootstrap," 74–75. On the Watts Rebellion, see Horne, *Fire This Time*.

6. Widener, "Writing Watts," 670; Robin D. G. Kelley, "Watts: Remember What They Built, Not What They Burned," *Los Angeles Times*, August 11, 2015.

7. "Interview with Lou Smith," 198–99. The other two workers were James Chaney and Andrew Goodman.

8. On N-VAC, see Ellis, "Operation Bootstrap," 76–84; and Smethurst, *The Black Arts Movement*, 295.

9. On the War on Poverty, see J. Patterson, *America's Struggle against Poverty in the Twentieth Century*, 122–52. On the War on Poverty in LA, see Bauman, *Race and the War on Poverty*.

10. Carmichael and Hamilton, *Black Power*, 2.

11. Rich, "The Congress of Racial Equality and Its Strategy," 117, quoted in Ellis, "Operation Bootstrap," 73–74. On the shift in national CORE's strategy, see Ellis, "Operation Bootstrap," 70–75; and Sugrue, *Sweet Land of Liberty*, chap. 11. As the historian Thomas J. Sugrue has noted, "CORE led the way in bridging community organizing and Black power" (*Sweet Land of Liberty*, 370).

12. On these trends, see, for example, Sugrue, *The Origins of the Urban Crisis*; and Cohen, *A Consumers' Republic*. On the ways these trends facilitated the turn to Black Power, see Self, *American Babylon*.

13. See references to the events of August 1965 in *Operation Bootstrap: Learn, Baby, Learn* (packet, n.d., ca. 1967), 6, 9, Box 30, Folder 22 ("Operation Bootstrap, 1967–1968, 1973"), TCOF.

14. On the significance of self-help to Black Power community development initiatives, see Hill and Rabig, *The Business of Black Power*. For different perspectives on the diverse Black Power movement, see, for example, Farmer, *Remaking Black Power*; Davies, *Mainstreaming Black Power*; and Joseph, *Waiting until the Midnight Hour*.

15. On the formation and early development of Operation Bootstrap, see Ellis, "Operation Bootstrap," 85–157; William Russell Ellis Jr., phone interview by author, July 15, 2009; and Davies, *Mainstreaming Black Power*, chap. 2. See also "Shindana Toy Company: Changing the American Doll Industry."

16. Maggie Bellows, "Watts Suffers—after 2 Long Years," *Chicago Defender*, May 27, 1967, 28.

17. Ellis, "Operation Bootstrap," 93. On Leon Sullivan's Opportunities Industrialization Center, see Countryman, *Up South*, 112–14.

18. Ellis, "Operation Bootstrap."

19. See *Operation Bootstrap: Learn, Baby, Learn*, 10.

20. Lou S. Smith to Friend, April 29, 1968, Box 30, Folder 22, TCOF. Smith also discussed his strong views on government support in "Interview with Lou Smith."

21. Operation Bootstrap's perspective on community partnerships is discussed in *Operation Bootstrap: Learn, Baby, Learn*, 2–10. On community nationalism, see R. Brown and Shaw, "Separate Nations," 26–30.

22. Elenore Child quoted in *Black Journal*, episode 17 (New York: WNET, October 1969). For more on *Black Journal*'s impact, see Heitner, *Black Power TV*, chap. 3.

23. Lou Smith quoted in "Shindana Discovers the 'Together' Dolls," *Black Enterprise*, December 1970, 25. For an in-depth discussion of Smith's political ideology and conception of social change, see Ellis, "Operation Bootstrap," 164–204.

24. On the long history of these strategies, see Nembhard, "Cooperative Ownership."

25. Price, *Dreaming Blackness*, 85.

26. Child quoted in *Black Journal*.

27. "The Following Courses Are Now Being Offered at No Charge" (Operation Bootstrap flyer, n.d.), Box 30, Folder 22, TCOF; Smith to Friend, April 29, 1968.

28. "Interview with Lou Smith," 201. In the early 1960s, Smith and Malcolm X appeared together on a radio show. See "Audio of Philadelphia CORE Chairman Louis Smith and Malcolm X," WDAS Radio, ca. early 1960s, The CORE Project, http://www.thecoreproject.org/omeka/items/show/78.

29. Ellis, "Operation Bootstrap," 114. See also "A Self-Help Program Stirs a Negro Slum," *Business Week*, March 25, 1967, clipping file, Box 30, Folder 22, TCOF. On the ways the therapeutic ethos informed the era's grassroots antipoverty efforts, see Germany, *New Orleans after the Promises*. On the Johnson administration's psychologization of poverty, see Steigerwald, *Culture's Vanities*, chap. 6.

30. Bellows, "Watts Suffers—after 2 Long Years."

31. "Black Dolls Help Change Image," *Philadelphia Inquirer*, November 16, 1973, clipping file, Black Toys for Christmas, Silver Anvil Award Records, Public Relations Society of America, Wisconsin Historical Society, Madison.

32. Bellows, "Watts Suffers—after 2 Long Years."

33. On the Black Arts movement in Los Angeles, see K. Jones, *South of Pico*. Black Power activist Maulana Karena, who created the African American holiday of Kwanzaa in 1966, was also based in LA. See Austin, *Achieving Blackness*, 73–109; and S. Brown, *Fighting for US*.

34. See "A Self-Help Program Stirs a Negro Slum"; and *Operation Bootstrap: Learn, Baby, Learn*.

35. See clippings in Box 30, Folder 22, TCOF.

36. Ellis, "Operation Bootstrap," 111–12, 154–55; Bellows, "Watts Suffers—after 2 Long Years." According to Lou Smith, Shriver offered OB $3 million of federal funding, which Smith and Hall immediately declined on principle. See "Interview with Lou Smith," 205.

37. Ellis, "Operation Bootstrap," 111.

38. Smith to Friend, April 29, 1968.

39. Smith to Friend, April 29, 1968.

40. Loewen, *Sundown Towns*, 23, 333.

41. On the Test Program, see J. Brown and Lusterman, *Business and the Development of Ghetto Enterprise*.

42. See Kotlowski, "Black Power—Nixon Style." The belief that corporate-run jobs programs, rather than federal ones, could adequately address poverty and economic stress would gain traction in the Richard Nixon administration. Nixon was the only US president to publicly endorse Black Power.

43. Lord, *Forever Barbie*, 159.

44. Spear quoted in "Helping Your Competitor," News of the Industry section, *TN*, December 1968, 31; "Shindana Discovers the 'Together' Dolls," 24–25.

45. "Case 11," 77; "Shindana Discovers the 'Together' Dolls," 24–25. As Spear stated at the time, "it was Elliot [Handler's] idea that what we could do that was unique was to teach somebody to make toys" (quoted in "Case 11," 77).

46. Lord, *Forever Barbie*, 165.

47. Spear quoted in "Shindana Discovers the 'Together' Dolls," 25.

48. "Case 11," 78.

49. "Case 11," 77, 79; "Helping Your Competitor," 31. On the Bank of Finance, see Mallard, "The (Los Angeles) Bank of Finance (1964–81)."

50. "Case 11," 78–79, 94.

51. Howard Neal, phone interview by author, March 13, 2019. A sales rep for area stores, Neal was invited by his supervisors to participate in the first Mattel–OB meetings in spring 1968, where plans for the toy division were first hatched. Given the status of his position relative to the executive managers heading up the initiative, Neal attributed the invitation to his being Black and recalled that other Black Mattel employees were also invited to join the planning, regardless of their position.

52. Gertrude Wilson, "Black Toy Manufacturer," *New York Amsterdam News*, November 15, 1969, 15. Shindana also intended to institute a profit-sharing plan for staff, although the plan never materialized.

53. Spear quoted in "Shindana Discovers the 'Together' Dolls," 25. There is some discrepancy among different sources about the amount of Mattel's financial gift to OB. *Ebony's* feature story on Shindana, for instance, reported that "over a nine-month period, Mattel invested $475,000 in cash and another $175,000 in equipment" ("Black Firm Joins the Toy Industry," *Ebony*, December 1969, 84). Lou Smith explained the nature of the partnership between OB and Mattel at a 1970 conference on community development corporations. "Most people don't believe it," Smith said, "but all of it was a gift from them to us." Smith quoted in *Information Exchange*, 8.

54. "Open Letter to Black Power Organizations" (n.d.), quoted in Ellis, *People Making Places*, 103. On the relationship of Black Power politics to white corporate America, see Fergus, *Liberalism, Black Power, and the Making of American Politics*.

55. Smith quoted in "Shindana Discovers the 'Together' Dolls," 24.

56. That the idea for producing a line of Black dolls originated with Handler comes from Smith's remarks at a 1970 conference of community organizers. Lou Smith quoted in *Information Exchange*, 8. See also "Helping Your Competitor," 31; and "Case 11," 78.

57. *Information Exchange*, 8.

58. Smith quoted in Susan Sherman Fadem, "He's Cornering the Black Doll Market," *St. Louis Globe-Democrat* (ca. 1974), clipping file in Black Toys for Christmas, 1975, Silver Anvil Award Records, Public Relations Society of America, Wisconsin Historical Society, Madison.

59. Lord, *Forever Barbie*, 167. A photograph of the ceremony was taken by Edward J. Pearson, copy in author's collection, courtesy of William Russell Ellis Jr.

60. Neal interview. According to Neal, Bootstrap's Herman Thompson originally proposed "Shindana" not for the company name but for the name of the first doll.

61. "Case 11," 77.

62. "Industry Joins Hands with Black Community," *PT*, November 1968, 79; "Helping Your Competitor," 31; "Retailing: Black Christmas," *Newsweek*, December 9, 1968, 79–81. See also Gould, "Toys Make a Nation," chap. 5.

63. Lord, *Forever Barbie*, 160.

64. "Shindana Black Dolls Make Toy Fair Debut," *THW*, April 7, 1969, 25; "Baby Nancy Made Big News in December," *PT*, March 1969, 179–80.

65. "Shindana Discovers the 'Together' Dolls," 24.

66. Baby Janie box, Shindana Toys, 1969, author's collection.

67. Wanda Career Girl box, Shindana Toys, 1972, author's collection.

68. On the regional sales offices, see "Valley of the Black Dolls," *New York Sunday News, Coloroto Magazine*, October 3, 1971, 8. For the retailers that carried Shindana products, see the Shindana ad in *New York Amsterdam News*, December 4, 1971, C11.

69. Betti Logan, "Black Toys, Black Pride," *Newsday*, November 11, 1974, A4.

70. Yale Eason, "A Real Doll: She's a Toy with a Beautiful Soul," *Chicago Tribune*, December 22, 1973, A2; J. I. Adkins Jr., "Black Toy Company Creates Black Pride," *Daily Defender*, November 14, 1974, 18; Art Carter, "Dolls Fulfill a Dream," *Chicago Defender*, December 28, 1974, B8.

71. Shindana ad, "Brother and sister dolls made by brothers and sisters," *New York Amsterdam News*, December 4, 1971, C11, and *Chicago Defender*, December 4, 1971, 17. In Shindana's first two years, Mattel provided free marketing services through its public relations firm, Carson/Roberts (see "Case 11," 80). The firm would have worked closely with Herman Thompson, Shindana's marketing director, according to Kirk Hallahan, who managed a pro bono public relations account in the mid-1970s for Shindana through his employer, Harshe-Rotman & Druck, Inc. Hallahan recalled Thompson as a collaborator rather than just a client; their coproduction of a 1974 national promotional campaign won Harshe-Rotman & Druck the coveted Silver Anvil Award from the Public Relations Society of America (Kirk Hallahan, phone interview by author, March 5, 2007). The historian Jason Chambers has noted that "African Americans in the advertising industry were in the unique position of being creators and interpreters of Black life and culture. In these roles they actively defined the meaning of 'Black consumer' for both prospective clients and the public" (Chambers, *Madison Avenue and the Color Line*, 15). Thompson deserves to be counted among those pioneering creators and interpreters of Black life and culture of this era.

72. Shindana ad, "Brother and sister dolls made by brothers and sisters."

73. Smith quoted in "Shindana: Black Toymakers of Watts," 43; see also "Black Firm Joins the Toy Industry," 91.

74. Smith quoted in "Retailing: Black Christmas," 81. See also "Toy Safety: It's More Than Just a Physical Problem," *Chicago Defender*, December 20, 1975, 9.

75. Shindana ad, "Brother and sister dolls made by brothers and sisters."

76. Logan, "Black Toys, Black Pride."

77. Smith quoted in Fadem, "He's Cornering the Black Doll Market."

78. Robert Bobo quoted in Jean Tyson, "Give Black Children Toys," *Atlanta Journal*, October 22, 1974, emphasis added, clipping file, Box 30, Folder 22, TCOF.

79. "Case 11," 78; and Wilson, "Black Toy Manufacturer."

80. "Black Toy Factory Tells Gains," *Chicago Daily Defender*, November 26, 1969, 10.

81. "Helping Your Competitor," 31. As *Playthings* reported in November 1968, the dolls were "designed to be a correct reflection of true Negro features, rather than a dark counterpart of a white doll." See "Industry Joins Hands with Black Community," PT, November 1968, 79.

82. "Shindana Discovers the 'Together' Dolls," 26.

83. "Shindana Discovers the 'Together' Dolls," 26.

84. Shindana news item, PT, April 1969, 54.

85. "Baby Nancy Made Big News in December," 179.

86. James Toatley quoted in *Black Journal*. Toatley became a noted sculptor after leaving Shindana.

87. Smith quoted in *Information Exchange*, 8.

88. Shindana ad, "Brother and sister dolls made by brothers and sisters."

89. Shindana ad, "Brother and sister dolls made by brothers and sisters."

90. Shindana ad, "Brother and sister dolls made by brothers and sisters."

91. "Black Firm Joins the Toy Industry," 90; Maultsby, "Soul," 278.

92. On the meaning of soul in the context of Black Arts and Black Power, see Van Deburg, *New Day in Babylon*, 195–96. For deeper investigations of soul in relation to music and the Black freedom struggle, see Lordi, *The Meaning of Soul*; Neal, *What the Music Said*; and Ward, *Just My Soul Responding*. On the uses of soul iconography in 1970s children's TV, see Serlin, "From Sesame Street to Schoolhouse Rock."

93. "Shindana: Black Toymakers of Watts"; "Shindana Discovers the 'Together' Dolls."

94. "Black Firm Joins the Toy Industry," 90.

95. "Shindana Discovers the 'Together' Dolls," 26.

96. "Baby Nancy Made Big News in December," 179–80; Baby Nancy doll (Pretty Pigtails), Shindana Toys, 1968, and Baby Nancy doll (Shorty Curls), Shindana Toys, 1969, both in author's collection.

97. "Shindana Discovers the 'Together' Dolls," 26.

98. "Shindana Discovers the 'Together' Dolls," 26.

99. Box for the Coochy doll, Shindana Toys, 1969, author's collection.

100. *Shindana Toys: Dolls Made by a Dream*, 1970 trade catalog, 2, SDOTCC.

101. *Shindana Toys: Dolls Made by a Dream*, 2.

102. *Shindana Toys: Dolls Made by a Dream*, 2.

103. See *Mattel Toys 1969*, 30, and *Mattel Dolls '71*, 24–25, both in SDOTCC. Other new Black fashion dolls included Hasbro's Soul and Kenner's Skye. See Hasbro's 1972 catalog, *Dolls*, and Kenner's 1976 catalog, *Kenner '76*, both in SDOTCC.

104. Mattel news item, PT, March 1970, 221; *Shindana Toys: Dolls Made by a Dream*, 2; Malaika doll, Shindana Toys, 1970, in original box, author's collection.

105. *Shindana Toys: Dolls Made by a Dream*, 2.

106. On the special role of style in the era's internationalist vision of Black woman-hood, see Ford, *Liberated Threads*.

107. As Ford writes, Makeba "became an icon of black diasporic militancy and African inspired fashion" (*Liberated Threads*, 13). Thanks to Tshepo Masango Chéry for bringing the song and its significance to my attention.

108. *Shindana Toys: Dolls Made by a Dream*, 1.

109. "Shindana Discovers the 'Together' Dolls," 26.

110. Tamu doll, Shindana Toys, 1970, author's collection.

111. *Shindana Toys: Dolls Made by a Dream*, 1.

112. "Shindana: Black Toymakers of Watts," 43.

113. On Black vernaculars and jive, see Abrahams, *Talking Black*; and L. Green, *African American English*. On jive's use in this period and its appropriation by mainstream white culture as the language of hipness, see Van Deburg, *New Day in Babylon*, 216–24.

114. See the 1970 Sears Christmas catalog, 24; and Mattel's Black and white Baby Drowsy dolls, 1971, author's collection.

115. Smith quoted in Jean Murphy, "Black Self-Help Project Keys on Dolls," *Mans-field News Journal* (OH), January 4, 1970, 10.

116. Cade, "On the Issue of Roles," 109.

117. Shindana was the first national toy manufacturer to use the term *Black* consis-tently for its Black dolls, reflecting larger cultural shifts in Black American preferences for racial identifiers. See B. Martin, "From Negro to Black to African American."

118. See Ringgold et al., *Black Dolls*. Thanks to Dominique Jean-Louis of the New-York Historical Society for sharing her vast knowledge of this subject during a tour of the *Black Dolls* exhibit that she curated at the Historical Society in the spring of 2022.

119. Wilky, Sis, Natra, and Coochy dolls, all from Shindana Toys, 1971, in original boxes, author's collection. Shindana later added other dolls to the Li'l Souls line, including the Jo-Jo and Rhonda dolls.

120. *Li'l Souls Story Coloring Book*, Shindana Toys, 1971, 1, author's collection.

121. *Li'l Souls Story Coloring Book*, 3.

122. *Li'l Souls Story Coloring Book*, 4.

123. *Li'l Souls Story Coloring Book*, 6.

124. *Li'l Souls Story Coloring Book*, 5.

125. *The Negro Family*, 8.

126. Stack, *All Our Kin*. Another important study was Billingsley, *Black Families in White America*.

127. Stack, *All Our Kin*, 73.

128. Stack, *All Our Kin*, 66.

129. Stack, *All Our Kin*, 89.

130. At the time of the Li'l Souls release, the only company that produced a set of Black dolls or figures that were identified as a family was Creative Playthings, which sold its Bendable Rubber Families in white and Black versions. See the Creative Playthings ad, *New Yorker*, October 16, 1965, 207. The next manufacturer to create a Black family set was Mattel. In 1975, it introduced the Happy Family, a brown-colored

and black-haired version of the original white Sunshine Family (1972), three nine-inch figures representing a mother, father, and baby.

131. Stack, *All Our Kin*, 22.

132. On the important place of migration narratives in African American literature, see Griffin, *Who Set You Flowin'?* On the impact of the Great Migration on the Black communities of Los Angeles, see K. Jones, *South of Pico*, 1–22.

133. *Li'l Souls Story Coloring Book*, 10.

134. *Li'l Souls Story Coloring Book*, 12.

135. Wanda Career Girl doll, Shindana Toys, 1972, original box, author's collection.

136. Wanda Career Girl box.

137. "Wanda Career Girl Brochure," Shindana Toys, 1972, author's collection.

138. *Mattel Toys 1968*, 93, SDOTCC.

139. "Wanda—the Dream Builder," *Shariki Ana* 23 (March–April 1973): 1, Box 30, Folder 22, TCOF.

140. Logan, "Black Toys, Black Pride."

141. "Wanda—the Dream Builder," 1.

142. Logan, "Black Toys, Black Pride"; Fadem, "He's Cornering the Black Doll Market."

143. For an overview of the Moynihan Report and the racialization of poverty in the 1960s, see Katz, *The Undeserving Poor*, 9–23. As the historian Michael Katz wrote, "Moynihan turned Black women's strengths and accomplishments into evidence that they had subverted the natural order of gender relations" (21).

144. Logan, "Black Toys, Black Pride."

145. Ladner, *Tomorrow's Tomorrow*, 1.

146. Ladner, *Tomorrow's Tomorrow*, 201.

147. On Malibu Barbie's popularity, see *Toy & Hobby World*'s monthly Toy Hit Parade feature throughout 1972.

148. Disco Wanda doll, Shindana Toys, 1978, original box, author's collection. See also Shindana Toys, *Shindana Toys 1978*, SDOTCC.

149. Wanda Career Girl box.

150. See the Shindana trade catalogs from the years 1973–76, SDOTCC.

151. Slade Super Agent doll, Shindana Toys, 1976, original box, author's collection.

152. Between 1964 and 1974, sales of action figures roughly tripled, from less than 3 percent to nearly 9 percent of the toy market. See "On the Brink of a Shakedown," *Toys*, June 1975, 55–59; and "Dolls: Big Figures from Fantasy," *Toys*, June 1977, 23–26.

153. On the origins and evolution of this critical debate, see Quinn, "'Tryin' to Get Over.'" See also Van Deburg, *Black Camelot,* 131–34; and Guerrero, *Framing Blackness*, chap. 3. Also helpful to my thinking about the history of Black filmmaking, including during this era, was Reid, *Black Lenses, Black Voices*.

154. Slade Super Agent box.

155. *Shindana Toys 1976*, 7, SDOTCC.

156. Slade Super Agent box.

157. Slade Super Agent box.

158. *Shindana Toys 1976*, 7.

159. For excellent starting points into the history of the Black Panther Party in Oakland and beyond, see Spencer, *The Revolution Has Come*; Bloom and Martin, *Black against Empire*; and Williams and Yazerow, *In Search of the Black Panther Party*.

160. *Shindana Toys 1976*, 7; Slade Super Agent box.

161. I learned about Edwards's military service from Phil Hatten, who was hired by Shindana to design its trade catalogs in the second half of the 1970s. Phil Hatten, phone interview by author, January 3, 2022.

162. On Black Americans' changing attitudes about military service during the mid to late twentieth century, see Mottle, "'We Resist on the Grounds We Aren't Citizens'"; and Boehm, *War! What Is It Good For?*

163. Scott, *Contempt and Pity*, 88–89, 142–43. See also Herman, *The Romance of American Psychology*, 192; and Metzl, *The Protest Psychosis*.

164. *Shindana Toys: Dolls Made by a Dream.*

165. While one major manufacturer previously made a doll with stereotypically East Asian features, it was not a typical hug-and-hold baby or toddler doll. In 1966, Remco Industries introduced Jan, a five-and-a-half-inch fashion doll, to its Pocketbook Doll line. Marketed as a "Japanese Playmate" for Heidi, the white character at the center of the line, Jan wore a jumper with "love" printed on it in Japanese and came with a kimono. Thanks to Stephen Higa for the translation.

166. See the Little Friends foldout in *Shindana Toys 1977*, courtesy of Phil Hatten. Two years later, Shindana would introduce another ethnically correct Hispanic doll, and outside the Little Friends collection. "A Hispanic doll with true Hispanic features!" began the catalog description of the new Mi Niña doll (*Shindana Toys 1978*, 16, author's collection). Unfortunately, for all the company's interest in not reproducing stereotypes, the Little Friends could be said to have done just that with its representation of a Native American child in 1978, a new addition to the Little Friends. Reflecting the white-defined romanticized image of Indigenous style popularized by the 1960s counterculture, the doll wore a culturally inaccurate headband and a buffalo-hide-style dress. By contrast, the Asian and Hispanic dolls were dressed in the typical, commercially mainstream styles of the time.

167. Original box for Little Friends Asian Boy, Shindana Toys, 1976, author's collection.

168. DuCille, *Skin Trade*, 17. DuCille's discussion of Black dolls in *Skin Trade* was originally published as a journal article; see duCille, "Dyes and Dolls." For an excellent discussion of ethnically correct toys and the ways children make sense of these objects' racial dimensions through play, see Chin, "Ethnically Correct Dolls."

169. W. Martin, "'Be Real Black for Me,'" 261. The term *strategic essentialism* was coined and developed by the theorist Gayatri Chakravorty Spivak in a 1984 interview with Elizabeth Grosz. See Grosz, "Criticism, Feminism and the Institution." On the concept of strategic essentialism in the specific context of Black cultural production, see Gates, *Double Negative*.

170. Weems, *Desegregating the Dollar*, 70, 76–77. This is not to say Shindana marketers did not actively capitalize on the popular iconography of Blackness to sell toys. In fact, they were among the first Black professionals to do so, pioneering the strategies

of the "soul sale" in part by calling attention to their company's Black identity and experience.

171. "Shindana Opens New Showroom," *Toys*, July 1974, 64; "Shindana Opens New York Showroom," *PT*, July 1974, 14.

172. Thompson quoted in "Shindana Opens New Showroom."

173. Logan, "Black Toys, Black Pride." For the toys, see *Shindana Toys 1974*, SDOTCC. Soular launched its first product in 1970; see "Black Is Business-ful," *TN*, May 1970, 26. By this point, the Jackson Five had already been the subjects of a children's cartoon series that ran on the ABC network from 1971 to 1972.

174. Ellis, *People Making Places*, 104.

175. Ellis, *People Making Places*, 104.

176. Harshe-Rotman & Druck, Inc., Shindana Toys Press Kit (ca. 1974–75), courtesy of Kirk Hallahan.

177. "Shindana Hits African Markets," *THW*, September 1974, 9.

178. Shindana Toys, *Shindana Toys 1972*, cover, SDOTCC.

179. Original box for Baby Nancy (Shorty Curls), Shindana Toys, 1969, author's collection.

180. Original box for Dreamy Dee Bee, Shindana Toys, 1969, author's collection.

181. DuCille, *Skin Trade*, 35–36.

182. Amanda Parker, "Learn, Baby, Learn: A Look at Operation Bootstrap," 5, paper submitted to UCLA History Department, May 29, 1974, Box 1, Folder 12, David L. Clark Los Angeles Oral Histories Collection, 1974–1982, collection number 2080, Department of Special Collections, UCLA Charles E. Young Research Library, Los Angeles, CA.

183. Ellis, *People Making Places*, 105.

184. "Shindana Toys Reorganizes Its Corporate Structure," *PT*, September 1976, 85.

185. See "Minutes of the Meeting of the Loan Committee of the Board of Directors of The Equitable Life Community Enterprises Corporation held on July 7, 1976," Box 9 (1996–044), Folder: "Equico Capital Corporation, Vol. I, Board of Directors, 4/2/71–12/16/80," RG6 Subsidiaries, Equitable Investment Corporation, Equitable Life Insurance Company Archives, New York; and Ellis, *People Making Places*, 104. The company also received financial assistance during the mid-1970s from one of Sears, Roebuck's social investment programs (Ellis, *People Making Places*, 104).

186. Steve Harvey, "Shintana Toy Co.: Blues for the Brown-Eyed Dolls," *Los Angeles Times*, August 26, 1983, 25. The article's misspelling of Shindana is from the original. See also Lord, *Forever Barbie*, 170.

187. A. Green, *Selling the Race*, 79.

188. J. Davis, *From Head Shops to Whole Foods*, 3.

Chapter Five. Equal Play

1. The following paragraphs are based on my interview with Montaperto. Nicki Montaperto, phone interview by author, February 14, 2020.

2. Letty Cottin Pogrebin, "Toys for Free Children," *Ms.*, December 1973, 48.

3. Pogrebin, "Toys for Free Children," 48.

4. The groups known to have carried out the toy consumer research came from Howard County NOW and Montgomery County NOW, both in Maryland; Boston NOW; and Union County NOW in New Jersey. Two Yale University sociologists, Janet Lever and Lou Wolf Goodman, also conducted a study in 1972, for which they and their research assistants spent thirty hours in toy stores tallying gender typing and observing consumer behavior. The different toy surveys were reported in several sources, and my discussion of the results is drawn from them. See Union County NOW, "Initial Report on Toy Campaign," *Union County NOW Newsletter*, December 1972, reel 2, in *Herstory: Microfilm Collection*; Howard County NOW, "National Action against Sexism in Toys" (flyer, n.d.), 2, Box 1, Folder 9, PACT Records; Nancy Lyon, "A Report on Children's Toys: Toys and Socialization to Sex Roles," *Ms.*, December 1972, 57; and Pogrebin, "Toys for Free Children," 50.

5. "Little Girls Make Big-Time Gourmets," *PT*, April 1972, 113.

6. "Age Group Guide to Toys," *TN*, November 1968, 69–79.

7. Sears Christmas catalog, 1967, 564; Sears Christmas catalog, 1970, 482.

8. Millett, *Token Learning*, pamphlet of the NOW-NYC educational committee, quoted in Linden-Ward and Green, *American Women in the 1960s*, 87.

9. Boston Women's Health Collective, *Our Bodies, Ourselves*, 11. On the collective, see Morgen, *Into Our Own Hands*, 3–40.

10. On the significance of psychological frameworks to the women's liberation movement, see Herman, *The Romance of American Psychology*, 276–303, and on socialization in particular, 294–96. To be sure, feminists of the 1960s and 1970s were not the first to conceive of women's oppression in personal, psychic terms. But the enhanced cultural influence of psychology after World War II, and the rise of humanistic psychology in particular, nourished a more pronounced therapeutic ethos throughout the many sectors of the diverse second wave.

11. Paris, "Happily Ever After," 534. Ruth Rosen notes the source of feminist interest in role socialization as a 1964 article published by the sociologist Alice Rossi in *Daedalus*. See Rosen, *The World Split Open*, 76–77.

12. Swinthe, *Feminism's Forgotten Fight*, 33.

13. Chodorow, "Being and Doing," 192.

14. Chodorow, "Being and Doing," 193.

15. Chodorow, "Being and Doing," 185.

16. Gornick and Moran, introduction to *Woman in Sexist Society*, xi.

17. By the early 1970s, writes the historian Alice Echols, liberal feminism "moved closer to radical feminism as it embraced the idea that the personal is political and the practice of consciousness-raising—both of which it had earlier rejected" (*Daring to Be Bad*, 11).

18. On second-wave feminism's interest in child socialization, see Paris, "Happily Ever After." On feminist views on toys during this era, see Lovett, "Child's Play." References to "culture and personality" school concepts, from the cross-cultural analysis of Mead and Benedict to the psychoanalytic tradition of Karen Horney, abounded in the sex-role socialization theory in the late 1960s and 1970s. On Chodorow, see Herman, *The Romance of American Psychology*, 295–96.

19. See Women on Words and Images, *Dick and Jane as Victims.*

20. Paris, "Happily Ever After," 524.

21. On NOW's campaign to reform *Sesame Street*, see Morrow, *Sesame Street and the Reform of Children's Television*, 155–57. The emphasis on children's media cultures also drew inspiration from parallel feminist media-reform campaigns. See Perlman, "Feminists in the Wasteland"; and Howard, "Pink Truck Ads."

22. See Paris, "Happily Ever After"; and Lovett and Rotskoff, *When We Were Free to Be.*

23. "Feminists Picket Toymakers," NOW press release, February 26, 1973, Box 2, Folder 4, PACT Records.

24. Nadine Brozan, "Using Toys to Free Children from the Roles Society Dictates," *NYT*, May 12, 1971, 38; "Women's Lib Group Seeks More 'Integrations' of Toys," *THW*, June 7, 1971; Montaperto interview. Some of these developments are reported in Pogrebin, "Toys for Free Children"; and Nancy Lyon, "More Than Child's Play," *Ms.*, December 1972, 54–59, 98.

25. Bradley, *Mass Media and the Shaping of American Feminism*, 38–40.

26. The Alliance's Ruth Abram estimated that the organization received five thousand letters. See Ruth Abram, "Introduction" (typescript, October 1976), 1, delivered at the First National Conference on Non-Sexist Early Childhood Education, Series II, Box 125, Folder 14, WAA Records. The quotes come from Barbara Sprung, "Non-Sexist, Multi-Racial Child Development Project Proposal for Funding" (typescript, n.d.), 1, Series II, Box 117, Folder 4, WAA Records. As the NCDP's founding director, Sprung was responsible for writing all major documents, such as grants and curriculum guides, in the initiative's first few years. Barbara Sprung, interview by author, March 25, 2022, New York, NY.

27. Carol Shapiro to Valerie Harms Sheehan of Norwalk, CT, March 29, 1972, Series III, Box 260, Folder 6: Child Care, 1971–1986, WAA Records.

28. On the origins of the Non-Sexist Child Development Project, see Ruth Abram, "Introduction," 2; and "Women's Action Alliance Breaks New Ground in Child Care," *The Spokeswoman*, December 1973, clipping file, Series II, Box 117, Folder 4, WAA Records.

29. Sprung interview, November 24, 2009.

30. The article was actually first printed in late 1971 as part of the *Ms.* preview supplement—a select forty pages of the magazine's first full issue that were included as an insert in *New York Magazine*. See Letty Cottin Pogrebin, "Down with Sexist Upbringing," *Ms.* supplement, in *New York Magazine*, December 20, 1971, 110, 114–18; and Letty Cottin Pogrebin, "Down with Sexist Upbringing," *Ms.*, Spring 1972.

31. The term comes from a Women's Action Alliance press release (n.d., ca. 1974), Box 2, Folder 10, PACT Records.

32. Allenna Leonard, phone interview by author, November 15, 2008.

33. Victoria Reiss, phone interview by author, October 29, 2008.

34. Patricia Powers, phone interview by author, October 5, 2006.

35. Ronald Smothers, "New Coalition to Press for Safer Toys," *NYT*, February 27, 1973, 75.

36. PACT pamphlet (n.d.), Box 2, folder titled "PACT Program Efforts, undated," PACT Records.

37. PACT pamphlet.

38. It is worth noting that the involvement of a prominent group like ACT, which lobbied Congress in favor of children's TV regulation throughout the 1970s, ensured that PACT's message reached even larger and less partisan organizations like the American Academy of Pediatrics and National Association for Young Children, both of which were ACT affiliates. Information on the origins and evolution of PACT is from interviews with Powers, Leonard, and Reiss.

39. Public Action Coalition on Toys, *Guidelines for Choosing Toys for Children* (Public Action Coalition on Toys, 1976), 4, Foundation for Child Development Records, Series 4, Subseries 4, Subject File: Public Action Coalition on Toys, 1974–1982, Rockefeller Archive Center, Sleepy Hollow, NY. The inside cover noted that the booklet had been a group effort: "Prepared for PACT by Myron Kaplan, Todd Boressof and Barbara Sprung with the collaboration and assistance of Victoria Reiss, Pat Powers and Minnie P. Berson."

40. The post–World War II era witnessed more frank discussions of sexuality, reflecting a middle-class parenting style that stressed the importance of embracing and fostering children's natural curiosity about all things. Early childhood masturbation, for instance, long viewed as indecent, deviant behavior requiring strict discipline or even psychiatric intervention, was increasingly accepted by progressive child professionals as part of normal play. And if a little girl or boy was curious about the other's body parts, experts like Benjamin Spock and Selma Fraiberg now suggested that parents should not make the subject taboo but naturalize it as part of life. See Jenkins, "The Sensuous Child."

41. Barbara Sprung, "Guide to Non-Sexist Early Education" (typescript, 1974), 43, Series II, Box 125, Folder 7, WAA Records.

42. Leonard quoted in Peter B. Gallagher, "This 'Living Doll' Is Raising Some Eyebrows," *St. Petersburg Times*, July 28, 1975, D1.

43. "End Toy Sexism" (flyer, 1974), 3, NOW-NYC and Parents for Responsibility in the Toy Industry, Box 1, Folder 9, PACT Records.

44. Pogrebin, "Toys for Free Children," 50.

45. See Union County NOW, "Initial Report on Toy Campaign"; Howard County NOW, "National Action against Sexism in Toys"; and Pogrebin, "Toys for Free Children."

46. "Toys That Don't Care," *PT*, August 1971, 58.

47. Howard County NOW, "National Action against Sexism in Toys."

48. Letty Cottin Pogrebin, phone interview by author, December 1, 2009.

49. "Kenner Wins NOW Award," *Toys*, June 1975, 10.

50. Judy Klemerud, "Award-Winning Toys: Nonsexist, Nonracist—and Peaceful," *NYT*, February 19, 1975, 56.

51. "Reply to TMA," press release, February 18, 1974, Box 1, Folder 9, PACT Records.

52. "Reply to TMA."

53. On Langdon's role in the Works Progress Administration, see Arboleda, *Educating Young Children in WPA Nursery Schools*. Langdon's credentials are also mentioned in the industry booklet *Marketing Toys*, 77–78.

54. Quote from "Give American Toys," promotional insert, American Toy Institute, in *Life*, November 23, 1953, 142.

55. See, for instance, "Give American Toys," 142–54.

56. "Give American Toys," 142.

57. Byrne, *They Came to Play*, 59.

58. "Reply to TMA," brackets in the original.

59. See "Toymakers, Child Experts, Hold Breakthrough Dialogue," *THW*, April 3, 1972, 1, 27–28.

60. PACT pamphlet (n.d., ca. 1974), Box 2, Folder 4, PACT Records.

61. Barbara Sprung, "A Brief Introduction to the Non-Sexist Child Development Project," (typescript, n.d.), 61, Series II, Box 112, Folder 17, WAA Records.

62. Sprung, "A Brief Introduction to the Non-Sexist Child Development Project," 61.

63. "End Toy Sexism."

64. Women's Action Alliance press release (n.d.), Box 2, Folder 10, PACT Records.

65. "A Good Toy is good for a girl or a boy, a Bad Toy isn't good for either" (flyer, n.d.), NOW-NYC and Parents for Responsibility in the Toy Industry, Box 1, Folder: Parents for Responsibility in the Toy Industry 1966–73, PACT Records; "End Toy Sexism."

66. National Organization for Women, "Statement of Purpose," 97.

67. Howard County NOW, "National Action against Sexism in Toys."

68. "A Good Toy is good for a girl or a boy, a Bad Toy isn't good for either."

69. "A Good Toy is good for a girl or a boy, a Bad Toy isn't good for either."

70. Barbara Sprung quoted in "Rearing Children for Freedom via Educational Materials," *Hyde Park Herald*, November 21, 1973, file clipping, Series II, Box 117, Folder 4, WAA Records.

71. "End Toy Sexism."

72. Howard County NOW, "National Action against Sexism in Toys."

73. Firestone, *The Dialectic of Sex*, quoted in Schneir, *Feminism in Our Time*, 247. In the late 1960s, Firestone was a founding member of New York Radical Women, Redstockings, and New York Radical Feminists.

74. Reber quoted in Brozan, "Using Toys to Free Children from the Roles Society Dictates," 38.

75. Sprung, "A Brief Introduction to the Non-Sexist Child Development Project," 27.

76. Sprung, "Guide to Non-Sexist Early Education," 156.

77. Sprung, "Guide to Non-Sexist Early Education," 42.

78. Sprung, "A Brief Introduction to the Non-Sexist Child Development Project," 28.

79. Felicia George to Editor of *New York Sunday News*, December 18, 1974, Series II, Box 104, Folder 16, WAA Records. It is worth noting that dolls for boys, known as "action figures" ever since Hasbro coined the term in 1964, had become a major category by the 1970s. In fact, from 1964 to 1974, sales of action figures roughly tripled, from less than 3 percent to nearly 9 percent of the toy market. See "On the Brink of a Shakedown," *Toys*, June 1975, 55–59; and "Dolls: Big Figures from Fantasy," *Toys*, June 1977, 23–26.

80. Pogrebin, "Toys for Free Children," 50.

81. Martin Abramson, "Toys That DO Care," *Chicago Daily News*, December 6, 1971, clipping, Box 2, Folder 10, PACT Records.

82. Brozan, "Using Toys to Free Children from the Roles Society Dictates."

83. Grant, "'A Thought a Mother Can Hardly Face,'" 118.

84. *The Brady Bunch*, season 1, episode 6, "A Clubhouse Is Not a Home," directed by John Rich, aired October 31, 1969 (Los Angeles: Paramount Television).

85. See, for example, Rekers and Yates, "Sex-Typed Play in Feminoid Boys versus Normal Boys and Girls." In 1973, the DSM-IV, the handbook of psychiatric diagnosis, removed the longtime classification of homosexuality as a mental illness, an event that LGBTQ rights advocates rightly celebrated as an important cultural victory. But, as Eve Kosofsky Sedgwick argued, in the wake of that decision, childhood gender identity disorder, or gender variance, assumed practically the same function: labeling gender nonconforming boys as psychologically abnormal and proto-gay. See Sedgwick, "How to Bring Your Kids Up Gay."

86. Spock quoted in Albin Krebs, "Agnew Takes Aim at Democrats," *NYT*, November 18, 1971, 55; Dr. Benjamin Spock, "Male Chauvinist Spock Recants—Almost," *New York Times Magazine*, September 12, 1971, 98, 100–101.

87. Farrell, "Attention to Difference," 49.

88. Letty Cottin Pogrebin, "Gifts for Free Children," *Ms.*, December 1974, 64.

89. Pogrebin, "Toys for Free Children," 49.

90. Letty Cottin Pogrebin, "Gifts for Free Children," *Ms.*, December 1976, 59.

91. Pogrebin, "Toys for Free Children," 49.

92. Pogrebin, "Toys for Free Children," 53. Whether Barbie in particular was guilty of being a "narcissistic spendthrift," as Pogrebin called the doll at one point, readers could of course decide. See Letty Cottin Pogrebin, "Bad News / Good News," *Ms.*, December 1975, 60.

93. See Carol Troy, "Little TV Doll, Who Made You? (And What, Exactly, Did He Have in Mind?)," *New York Magazine*, December 13, 1971, 51–54, 56, 59–60, 62, 65–66; and "New Fashion Dolls Take on Barbie," *THW*, July 1975, 19.

94. Pogrebin, "Gifts for Free Children, December 1976," 60.

95. Pogrebin, "Toys for Free Children," 49.

96. On some of the ways that second-wave feminists challenged, disrupted, and repurposed ideologies of motherhood in the 1970s, see Umansky, *Motherhood Reconceived*.

Chapter Six. Feminist Toys

1. Benjamin Spock, "What Toys Mean to Children," *Redbook*, December 1963, 121.

2. "Lionel TV Ad Recommends Electric Trains for Girls," *THW*, December 1973, 6. See also Rotskoff, "'Little Women's Libbers' and '*Free to Be* Kids,'" 106–7. Also present at the press conference was a child psychologist, ostensibly invited by Lionel to help field questions and symbolize its commitment to developmental understandings of play.

3. "Lionel TV Ad Recommends Electric Trains for Girls," 6. While I could not locate the date of Pogrebin and Steinem's meeting with Lionel executives, it seems

highly unlikely that they would have done so *after* the announcement, which, after all, was exactly what they were asking Lionel to do. In a sign that Lionel's TV campaign was not a one-time experiment, the company's 1974 catalog, introduced a few months later, featured pictures of girls on the cover for the first time in its history. *Lionel 1974*, author's collection.

4. Randolph P. Barton quoted in June Anderson Almquist, "Sexist Toys: Some Comments," *Seattle Times*, February 24, 1974, G6, clipping file, Box 1, Folder 9, PACT Records. See also the toy-industry official quoted in "Johnny Got His Gun," *Chelsea-Clinton News*, March 2, 1972, 1, 10, clipping file, Box 1, Folder 5, PACT Records; and TMA official Ted Erikson's remarks in "New Toys Reflect Bicentennial Spirit," *Modesto Bee*, November 27, 1975, D9.

5. Barton quoted in Vicky Reiss to Allenna and Pat, March 9, 1974, Box 1, folder "PACT Fundraising Efforts," PACT Records.

6. Denton Harris, "PACT Attacks All Areas of Industry," *THW*, March 5, 1973, 4.

7. Details about the PR campaign are from "TMA Woos Consumers in P.R. Campaign," *PT*, February 1975, 57; Sutton-Smith, "Play Theory," 105; and Jesse Rotman, phone interview by author, April 30, 2009. As Rotman, who ran the account for Harshe-Rotman & Druck, recalled, his first move was to hire Brian Sutton-Smith, chair of the Department of Psychology at Columbia University, to be the industry's official expert in residence. By the 1970s, Sutton-Smith's cautious position on the effects of toys on child development, mentioned in chapter 1, was well known in the field. To him, adults had a misguided tendency to impose their own interpretations of play onto the fantasy world of children without acknowledging the huge gap between adult understandings and child understandings of what that play means; he and a colleague called this the "idealization of play" (Sutton-Smith and Kelly-Byrne, "The Idealization of Play"). Not surprisingly, this analysis, which threw into doubt adult claims about what a war toy or a Barbie "did" to a child, had great appeal to the industry. And so, for three years, HR&D flew Sutton-Smith around the country as the face of the industry, participating in radio and TV spots, newspaper interviews, and press conferences. The campaign also included the placement of articles in hundreds of newspapers as well as the creation of informational handouts with Sutton-Smith's answers to questions such as "Do war toys encourage violence?" and "Do girls and boys play differently?" The campaign went on to receive the Silver Anvil Award from the Public Relations Society of America ("Public Affairs for the Toy Manufacturers of America, Inc.," Silver-Anvil Awards Records, Public Relations Society of America Records, Wisconsin Historical Society, Madison). One additional indication of the trade's worries about public image in this new age of protest was the TMA's 1974 decision to make the position of association president into a full-time salaried job, this after a half century of it being a volunteer post held by a current toy executive. As Fisher-Price president Henry Coords explained the change, "a volunteer president has to run his company. He can't give the time really to cope with the increased responsibility of that position. With the great rise in consumerism, government regulations of all kinds, and a greater feeling of professionalism in the TMA, we felt that a full-time spokesman for the TMA was necessary" ("Rap: Henry H. Coords, President of Fisher-Price Toys," *Toys*, August 1974, 34).

8. See Spruill, "Gender and America's Right Turn." Few observers could deny that the feminist awakening had gained a level of legitimacy in the American political mainstream that was unimaginable a decade earlier. In 1972, the Equal Rights Amendment to the Constitution won overwhelming congressional approval, and by mid-decade was just four states away from the thirty-eight required for ratification. The Supreme Court had expanded women's reproductive rights in *Roe v. Wade* (1973), and the Equal Economic Opportunity Commission charged ahead with antidiscrimination suits that opened new doors to female employment across the labor force. And yet these gains were accompanied by an aggressive antifeminist backlash that, through the efforts of activist traditionalists like Phyllis Schlafly, resounded far beyond the New Christian Right.

9. The activist was Joan Nicholson, National Coordinator of NOW's Task Force on the Image of Women. See "TMA Meet: Energy Crunch Was Overriding Topic," *PT*, January 1974, 74–75. As *Playthings* reported, TMA officials went so far as to send copies of Nicholson's speech to every TMA member who was unable to attend.

10. "New Fashion Dolls Take on Barbie," *THW*, July 1975, 19.

11. Quoted in "New Fashion Dolls Take on Barbie," 19.

12. Cross, *Kids' Stuff*, 174.

13. "New Fashion Dolls Take on Barbie," 19; Carol Troy, "Little TV Doll, Who Made You? (And What, Exactly, Did He Have in Mind?)," *New York Magazine*, December 13, 1971.

14. "New Fashion Dolls Take on Barbie," 19.

15. Quoted in "You Choose the Toys: A Consumer's Right to Influence Government and Industry" (typescript, n.d.), 11, Box 1, Folder 8, PACT Records.

16. My description is based on Dusty doll, Kenner Products, 1974, in original box, author's collection; and catalog images of Dusty in *Kenner '74*, SDOTCC. See also Buccola, "Dusty, the Dyke Barbie," 230.

17. On Billie Jean King, see Pipkin, "Life on the Cusp."

18. Schneir, "Phyllis Graber," 390–91.

19. Woolum, *Outstanding Women Athletes*, 18.

20. Buccola, "Dusty, the Dyke Barbie," 228.

21. Pogrebin, "Gifts for Free Children," *Ms.*, December 1974, 64.

22. Kenner Dusty comic-book ad, tear sheet (n.d.), author's collection.

23. Buccola, "Dusty, the Dyke Barbie," 231, 233–34.

24. *Kenner '76*, 32, SDOTCC.

25. "Kenner Wins NOW Award."

26. Ideal Toy Company, *Ideal 1974*, 36, SDOTCC.

27. "Ideal Toy Introduces First Female Action Figure," *PT*, September 1974, 35. In the actual play of children, of course, the boundaries separating the girl's doll and the boy's action figure have always been more fluid than the industry has formally acknowledged. As Heather Hendershot has written, "To be sure, children often ignore such institutional categories, placing a G.I. Joe action figure in a baby carriage or putting Barbie behind a machine gun, but the industry adamantly opposes representing

or suggesting such placement in television advertisements, packaging, print ads, and cartoons." Hendershot, *Saturday Morning Censors*, 114.

28. Ideal Toy Company, *Ideal 1974*, 1.

29. Derry Daring advertisement, comic-book tear sheet, ca. 1974, author's collection.

30. Ideal Toy Company, *Ideal 1974*, 39.

31. Ideal ad for Derry Daring, tear sheet (n.d.), author's collection.

32. Ideal Toy Company, *Ideal 1974*, 36.

33. "Debbie Lawler: The Pain and Payoff of Jumping over Cars," *People*, May 13, 1974.

34. Hendershot, *Saturday Morning Censors*, 113; Scalzo, *Evel Knievel and Other Daredevils*, 115.

35. Hendershot, *Saturday Morning Censors*, 113.

36. Derry Daring doll, Ideal Toy Company, 1974, original version from Trick Cycle set, author's collection.

37. Helen Reddy, "I Am Woman," comp. Helen Reddy and Ray Burton, from *I Am Woman* (Capitol Records ST-11068, 1972), LP.

38. Derry Daring doll and Trick Cycle, author's collection.

39. Scalzo, *Evel Knievel and Other Daredevils*, 117.

40. Derry Daring listing, Sears Christmas catalog (ca. 1974), tear sheet, author's collection.

41. Stewart Sims quoted in "Ideal Toy Introduces First Female Action Figure," *PT*, September 1974, 35.

42. For an excellent discussion of the New Woman on 1970s network TV, see Levine, *Wallowing in Sex*, chap. 4. Other interesting studies of TV's relationship to the social upheaval of the 1960s and 1970s include Ozersky, *Archie Bunker's America*; and Bodroghkozy, *Groove Tube*.

43. Ideal Toy Company, *Ideal 1974*, 36.

44. Derry Daring listing, Sears Christmas catalog, 1974.

45. Union County NOW, "Initial Report on Toy Campaign," *Union County NOW Newsletter*, December 1972, reel 2, in *Herstory: Microfilm Collection*.

46. Buccola, "Dusty, the Dyke Barbie," 231.

47. Skye doll, Kenner Toys, 1975, in original box, author's collection. Skye does not appear in the 1974 Kenner catalog with Dusty. On Skye's meaning within the Dusty brand, see Buccola, "Dusty, the Dyke Barbie."

48. Pipkin, "Life on the Cusp," 59.

49. According to the journalist Carol Troy, as early as 1971, Hasbro, too, had considered the potential appeal of a new kind of female fashion doll that tapped into feminist ideals. "With all the talk of women's liberation," reported Troy at the time, "[Hasbro] thought surely there was a place on the market for an 'action girl' who did adventuresome things like skydiving." Troy, "Little TV Doll, Who Made You?," 65.

50. "Three Firms Market 'Anatomically Correct' Baby Dolls," *THW*, April 1976, 21.

51. Barbara Wyden, "Little Brother Comes to America," *NYT*, October 29, 1967, 77–79.

52. Bette Benedict, phone interview by author, November 14, 2008.

53. Muriel Brown quoted in Ted J. Rakstis, "Debate in the Doll House," *Today's Health*, December 1970, 66.

54. Letty Cottin Pogrebin, "Bad News / Good News," *Ms.*, December 1975, 60.

55. Ted Judith Serren, "Doll World Now Has Real Boys," *Detroit Free Press*, July 14, 1976.

56. Mattel ad, *Good Housekeeping*, May 1977, author's collection.

57. Baby Brother Tender Love box, Mattel, Inc., 1976, author's collection.

58. "Three Firms Market 'Anatomically Correct' Baby Dolls," 21.

59. See Gitlin, *Inside Primetime*, chap. 10.

60. "Three Firms Market 'Anatomically Correct' Baby Dolls," 21.

61. Toy Products listing, *Toys*, May 1976, 23; Li'l Ruthie doll, Horsman Dolls, 1976, in original box, Toy and Game Collection, The Strong, Rochester, NY.

62. Ruth Abram, "Introduction" (typescript, October 1976), 2, Series II, Box 125, Folder 14, WAA Records. See also "Sex in the Preschools," *Saturday Review*, March 10, 1973, 48.

63. See Fisher-Price catalogs from these years in SDOTCC.

64. Barbara Sprung quoted in "Women's Action Alliance Breaks New Ground in Child Care," *The Spokeswoman*, December 1973, clipping file, Series II, Box 117, Folder 4, WAA Records.

65. Barbara Sprung, "Non-Sexist, Multi-Racial Child Development Project Proposal for Funding" (typescript, n.d.), 12, Series II, Box 117, Folder 4, WAA Records; Barbara Sprung, phone interview by author, November 24, 2009.

66. Sprung quoted in "Rearing Children for Freedom via Educational Materials," *Hyde Park Herald*, November 21, 1973, clipping file, Series II, Box 117, Folder 4, WAA Records.

67. Sprung interview, November 24, 2009.

68. Barbara Sprung to Director of Product Development, November 1, 1972, Series II, Box 104, Folder 9, WAA Records.

69. Murray, "Free for All Lesbians."

70. Sprung, "Non-Sexist, Multi-Racial Child Development Project Proposal for Funding," 11.

71. Sprung, "Non-Sexist, Multi-Racial Child Development Project Proposal for Funding," 11.

72. Sprung, "Non-Sexist, Multi-Racial Child Development Project Proposal for Funding," 11.

73. "Sex in the Preschools."

74. Maureen H. to Women's Action Alliance, March 8, 1973, Series II, Box 112, Folder 10, WAA Records.

75. Julie H. to Women's Action Alliance, March 17, 1973, Series II, Box 104, Folder 10, WAA Records.

76. Ann C., unaddressed letter, July 22, 1973, Series II, Box 104, Folder 10, WAA Records.

77. Barbara Sprung to Terri Moore, December 28, 1973, Series II, Box 104, Folder 11, WAA Records.

78. Ron Weingartner, phone interview by author, January 15, 2010.

79. Weingartner interview. See the inside of the boxes of My Family and Our Helpers, both originally published by Milton Bradley Company in 1974, author's collection. Ron Weingartner estimates that initial sales for My Family and Our Helpers likely numbered in the thousands at minimum, for otherwise the company would not have reprinted them. It appears that Milton Bradley kept both sets in print through the end of the decade. This means that, even with a low estimate, it is probable that more than ten thousand units were sold in the 1970s, and maybe several times that. With each unit representing a classroom of anywhere from twenty to thirty children, it is likely that hundreds of thousands of children played with the toys during these years.

80. All the quotations come from the Alliance's questionnaires filed in Series II, Box 125, Folder 4, WAA Records.

81. Klemerud, "Award-Winning Toys."

82. Certificate of Commendation blank template, Box 2, Folder: Programmatic Efforts: Pamphlet, PACT Records.

83. Klemerud, "Award-Winning Toys."

84. Letty Cottin Pogrebin, phone interview by author, December 1, 2009. Information on Pogrebin's role is from Victoria Reiss, phone interview by author, October 29, 2008.

85. On all the award winners, see Eleanor Bader, "Making the Top Ten," *Majority Report* 5, no. 9 (September 6, 1975), photocopy, Box 1, Folder: Public Action Coalition on Toys: Programming Efforts, 1975: Awards, PACT Records. Milton Bradley celebrated the achievement in its company newsletter. See "MB Product Wins First PACT Award," *Milton Bradley News*, April 1975, 1, clipping, Box 1, Folder: Public Action Coalition on Toys: Programming Efforts, 1975: Awards, PACT Records.

86. "PACT Cites 11 Firms for Making 'Life-Enhancing' Toys," *THW*, April 1976, clipping, Box 1, Folder: Public Action Coalition on Toys: Programming Efforts, 1976: Awards, PACT Records.

87. Quoted in Klemerud, "Award-Winning Toys."

88. Box for Baby Brother Tender Love (Black doll), author's collection; box for Baby Brother Tender Love (white doll), author's collection. I have viewed numerous images of Baby Brother Tender Love dolls in the original box on eBay and other online auction websites, and only one of them did not have the PACT logo and commendation.

89. See the letters in Box 1, Folder: Public Action Coalition on Toys: Programmatic Efforts, 1977, PACT Records; and Box 2, Folder: Public Action Coalition on Toys: Programmatic Efforts, 1979, PACT Records.

90. See the documents in Box 1, Folder: PACT–Fundraising Efforts, PACT Records. The Rockefeller grant, awarded in 1980, is noted in the Meeting of the Board of Directors, December 4, 1980, 11, https://storage.rockarch.org/6496b906-dcd5-41e9-adf4 -108a89925246-FCD001_010_00368.pdf.

91. Major media coverage included Nadine Brozan, "Nonsexist Child Rearing: One Advocate's Projection," *NYT*, February 13, 1981, A17.

92. The lotto set, published in 1980, was called First Reading about My Family. On the opening page of the early-reader booklet that came with the lotto boards, Sprung wrote this introduction: "Dear Children: This is a book about all kinds of families. It tells about the things they do together. Some families have one child. Some have many. Some families have one parent, and some have two. All the people in this book like being part of their family." Author's collection.

93. David Firestone, "While Barbie Talks Tough, G.I. Joe Goes Shopping," *NYT*, December 31, 1993, A12.

94. On Olmec, see Chin, "Ethnically Correct Dolls"; and "Inspiration, Inclusion, and the Making of a Multicultural Toy Company."

Epilogue

1. "L.A. Fills, Seals Time Capsule," *Los Angeles Times*, September 10, 1976, B2.

2. "Mattel Dolls to Reappear at Tricentennial," photograph item, *PT*, December 1976, 34.

3. "Mattel Dolls to Reappear at Tricentennial."

4. See Mechling, "Gun Play"; "LEGO Pulls Back Police Playset Affiliate Marketing amid George Floyd Protests," *ToyBook*, June 2, 2020, https://toybook.com/lego-pulling-back-potentially-sensitive-product-amid-george-floyd-protests/; Afdhel Aziz, "The Power of Purpose: Mattel Launches Creatable World to Celebrate Inclusive Play for All Kids," *Forbes*, September 25, 2019, https://www.forbes.com/sites/afdhelaziz/2019/09/25/the-power-of-purpose-mattel-launches-creatable-world-to-celebrate-inclusive-play-for-all-kids/; "Breaking Down Gender Stereotypes in Media and Toys so that Our Children Can Explore, Learn, and Dream without Limits," White House Office of the Secretary, press release, April 6, 2016, https://obamawhitehouse.archives.gov/the-press-office/2016/04/06/factsheet-breaking-down-gender-stereotypes-media-and-toys-so-our.

5. Benjamin, "The Cultural History of Toys," 116 (originally published in *Frankfurter Zeitung*, May 1928). My thanks to Andy Bush for bringing this article to my attention.

Bibliography

Archival, Digital, Library, and Museum Collections

David L. Clark Los Angeles Oral Histories Collection, 1974–1982. Department of Special Collections. UCLA Charles E. Young Research Library, Los Angeles, CA.

Equitable Investment Corporation. Equitable Life Insurance Company Archives, New York.

Foundation for Child Development Records. Rockefeller Archive Center, Sleepy Hollow, NY.

Free Library of Philadelphia, Philadelphia, PA.

Independent Voices Collection. Reveal Digital / JSTOR. https://www.jstor.org/site /reveal-digital/independent-voices/.

Newspapers.com.

Philadelphia Doll Museum Collection, Philadelphia, PA.

Public Action Coalition on Toys Collected Records. Swarthmore College Peace Collection, Swarthmore, PA.

Railroad, Business, and Labor Collections. Thomas J. Dodd Research Center. University of Connecticut at Storrs.

Silver Anvil Award Records. Public Relations Society of America Records. Wisconsin Historical Society, Madison.

Stephen and Diane Olin Toy Catalog Collection. Brian Sutton-Smith Library and Archives of Play. The Strong, Rochester, NY.

Toy and Game Collection. The Strong, Rochester, NY.

Twentieth Century Organizational Files. Southern California Library for Social Studies and Research, Los Angeles, CA.

Women's Action Alliance Records. Sophia Smith Collection. Smith College, Northampton, MA.

Women's International League for Peace and Freedom Records. Swarthmore College Peace Collection, Swarthmore, PA.

Women Strike for Peace Records. Swarthmore College Peace Collection, Swarthmore, PA.

Books, Articles, and Other Sources

A. J. Wood Research Corporation and Toy Manufacturers of the U.S.A. *Toy Buying in the United States: A One Year Study: Prepared for Toy Manufacturers of the U.S.A., Inc.* New York: Toy Manufacturers of the U.S.A., 1965.

Abrahams, Roger D. *Talking Black.* Rowley, MA: Newbury House, 1976.

Adorno, Theodor, Else Frenkel-Brunswick, Daniel J. Levinson, and Nevitt R. Sanford. *The Authoritarian Personality.* New York: Harper and Row, 1950.

Almqvist, Birgitta. "Educational Toys, Creative Toys." In *Toys, Play, and Child Development*, edited by Jeffrey H. Goldstein, 46–66. New York: Cambridge University Press, 1994.

Alonso, Harriet Hyman. "Mayhem and Moderation: Women Peace Activists during the McCarthy Era." In *Not June Cleaver: Women and Gender in Postwar America*, edited by Joanne Meyerowitz, 128–50. Philadelphia: Temple University Press, 1994.

Alonso, Harriet Hyman. *Peace as a Women's Issue: A History of the U.S. Movement for World Peace and Women's Rights.* Syracuse: Syracuse University Press, 1993.

Anderson, Jervis. *Guns in American Life.* New York: Random House, 1984.

Andreas, Carol R. "War Toys and the Peace Movement." *Journal of Social Issues* 25, no. 1 (1969): 83–100.

Appadurai, Arjun, ed. *The Social Life of Things: Commodities in Cultural Perspective.* Cambridge: Cambridge University Press, 1986.

Arboleda, Molly Quest. *Educating Young Children in WPA Nursery Schools: Federally-Funded Early Childhood Education from 1933–1943.* New York: Routledge, 2019.

Asherbranner, Wesley Anderson. "Toys as an Agent of Change: A Historical Survey of the Sears Christmas Wish Book, 1940–2000." Master's thesis, University of Regina, 2002.

Attfield, Judy. "Barbie and Action Man: Adult Toys for Girls and Boys, 1959–93." In *The Gendered Object*, edited by Pat Kirkham, 80–89. Manchester: Manchester University Press, 1996.

Austin, Algernon. *Achieving Blackness: Race, Black Nationalism and Afrocentrism in the Twentieth Century.* New York: New York University Press, 2006.

Barron, Frank X. *Creativity and Psychological Health: Origins of Personal Vitality and Creative Freedom.* Princeton, NJ: Van Nostrand, 1963.

Barthes, Roland. *Mythologies.* Selected and translated from the French by Annette Lavers. New York: Noonday Press, 1972.

Bauman, Robert. *Race and the War on Poverty: From Watts to East L.A.* Tulsa: University of Oklahoma Press, 2008.

Beatty, Barbara. *Preschool Education in America: The Culture of Young Children from the Colonial Era to the Present.* New Haven, CT: Yale University Press, 1995.

Beatty, Barbara, Emily D. Cahan, and Julia Grant, eds. *When Science Encounters the Child: Education, Parenting, and Child Welfare in 20th-Century America.* New York: Teachers College Press, 2006.

Benjamin, Walter. "The Cultural History of Toys." In *Walter Benjamin: Selected Writings*, vol, 2, pt. 1, *1927–1930*, edited by Michael W. Jennings et al. and translated by Rodney Livingstone et al., 113–16. Cambridge, MA: Harvard University Press, 1999.

Bergner, Gwen. "Black Children, White Preference: *Brown v. Board*, the Doll Tests, and the Politics of Self-Esteem." *American Quarterly* 61, no. 2 (2009): 299–332.

Bernstein, Robin. *Racial Innocence: Performing American Childhood from Slavery to Civil Rights.* New York: New York University Press, 2011.

Best, Joel. "Too Much Fun: Toys as Social Problems and Interpretation of Culture." *Symbolic Interaction* 21, no. 2 (1998): 197–212.

Billingsley, Andrew. *Black Families in White America.* Englewood Cliffs, NJ: Prentice Hall, 1968.

Binkley, Sam. *Getting Loose: Lifestyle Consumption in the 1970s.* Durham, NC: Duke University Press, 2007.

Blackwell, Joyce. *No Peace without Freedom: Race and the Women's International League for Peace and Freedom, 1915–1975.* Carbondale: Southern Illinois University Press, 2004.

Bloom, Joshua, and Waldo E. Martin Jr. *Black against Empire: The History and Politics of the Black Panther Party.* Berkeley: University of California Press, 2016.

Bodroghkozy, Aniko. *Groove Tube: Sixties Television and the Youth Rebellion.* Durham, NC: Duke University Press, 2001.

Boehm, Kimberley Phillips. *War! What Is It Good For? Black Freedom Struggles and the U.S. Military from World War II to Iraq.* Chapel Hill: University of North Carolina Press, 2012.

Boston Women's Health Collective. *Our Bodies, Ourselves: A Course by and for Women.* Boston: New England Free Press, 1970.

Bourdieu, Pierre. *Distinction: A Social Critique of the Judgement of Taste.* Translated by Richard Nice. Cambridge, MA: Harvard University Press, 1984.

Bradley, Patricia. *Mass Media and the Shaping of American Feminism, 1963–1975.* Jackson: University Press of Mississippi, 2003.

Brandow-Faller, Megan, ed. *Childhood by Design: Toys and the Material Culture of Childhood, 1700–Present.* London: Bloomsbury, 2018.

Braunstein, Peter, and Michael William Doyle. "Introduction: Historicizing the American Counterculture of the 1960s and '70s." In *Imagine Nation: The American Counterculture of the 1960s and '70s*, edited by Peter Braunstein and Michael William Doyle, 5–14. New York: Routledge, 2002.

Brick, Howard. *Age of Contradiction: American Thought and Culture in the Sixties.* Ithaca, NY: Cornell University Press, 2000.

Brown, Constance W. "Selma Fraiberg." *Jewish Women's Archive.* Accessed December 11, 2022. http://jwa.org/encyclopedia/article/fraiberg-selma.

Brown, James K., and Seymour Lusterman. *Business and the Development of Ghetto Enterprise.* New York: Conference Board, 1971.

Brown, Robert, and Todd Shaw. "Separate Nations: Two Attitudinal Dimensions of Black Nationalism." *Journal of Politics* 64, no. 1 (2002): 22–44.

Brown, Scot. *Fighting for US: Maulana Karenga, the US Organization, and Black Cultural Nationalism.* New York: New York University Press, 2003.

Buccola, Regina. "Dusty, the Dyke Barbie." *Children's Literature Association Quarterly* 29, no. 3 (Fall 2004): 228–52.

Buhle, Paul. *From the Lower East Side to Hollywood: Jews in American Popular Culture.* New York: Verso, 2004.

Byrne, Christopher. *They Came to Play: 100 Years of the Toy Industry Association.* New York: Toy Industry Association, 2016.

Cade, Toni, ed. *The Black Woman: An Anthology.* New York: New American Library, 1970.

Cade, Toni. "On the Issue of Roles." In *The Black Woman: An Anthology*, edited by Toni Cade, 101–10. New York: New American Library, 1970.

Cahan, Emily D. "Toward a Socially Relevant Science: Notes on a History of Child Development Research." In *When Science Encounters the Child: Education, Parenting, and Child Welfare in 20th-Century America*, edited by Barbara Beatty, Emily D. Cahan, and Julia Grant, 16–34. New York: Teachers College Press, 2006.

Capshaw, Katharine. *Civil Rights Childhood: Picturing Liberation in African American Photobooks.* Minneapolis: University of Minnesota Press, 2014.

Carmichael, Stokely, and Charles V. Hamilton. *Black Power: The Politics of Liberation in America.* New York: Vintage Books, 1967.

Chambers, Jason. "Equal in Every Way: African Americans, Consumption and Materialism from Reconstruction to the Civil Rights Movement." *Advertising and Society Review* 7, no. 1 (2006). doi:10.1353/asr.2006.0017.

Chambers, Jason. *Madison Avenue and the Color Line: African Americans in the Advertising Industry.* Philadelphia: University of Pennsylvania Press, 2009.

Cherry, Frances. "Kenneth B. Clark and Social Psychology's Other History." In *Racial Identity in Context: The Legacy of Kenneth B. Clark*, edited by Gina Philogene, 13–33. Washington, DC: American Psychological Association, 2004.

Chin, Elizabeth J. "Ethnically Correct Dolls: Toying with the Race Industry." *American Anthropologist* 101, no. 2 (1999): 305–21.

Chodorow, Nancy. "Being and Doing: A Cross-Cultural Examination of the Socialization of Males and Females." In *Woman in Sexist Society*, edited by Vivian Gornick and Barbara K. Moran, 173–97. New York: Basic Books, 1971.

Chudacoff, Howard. *Children at Play: An American History.* New York: New York University Press, 2008.

Clark, Kenneth B. *Dark Ghetto: Dilemmas of Social Power.* New York: Harper and Row, 1965.

Clark, Kenneth B. *Prejudice and Your Child.* Boston: Beacon, 1955.

Cohen, Lizabeth. *A Consumers' Republic: The Politics of Mass Consumption in Postwar America.* New York: Knopf, 2003.

Cohen-Cole, Jamie. "The Creative American: Cold War Salons, Social Science, and the Cure for Modern Society." *Isis* 100, no. 2 (2009): 219–62.

Collins, Lisa Gail, and Margot Natalie Crawford. "Introduction: Power to the People! The Art of Black Power." In *New Thoughts on the Black Arts Movement*, edited by Lisa Gail Collins and Margot Natalie Crawford, 1–22. New Brunswick, NJ: Rutgers University Press, 2006.

Comer, James P., and Alvin F. Poussaint. *Black Childcare: How to Bring Up a Healthy Black Child in America.* New York: Simon and Schuster, 1975.

Cook, Daniel Thomas. *The Commodification of Childhood: The Children's Clothing Industry and the Rise of the Child Consumer.* Durham, NC: Duke University Press, 2004.

Coontz, Stephanie. *The Way We Never Were: American Families and the Nostalgia Trap.* New York: Basic Books, 1992.

Countryman, Matthew. *Up South: Civil Rights and Black Power in Philadelphia.* Philadelphia: University of Pennsylvania Press, 2006.

Crime and Violence: Hearing before a Special Investigating Subcommittee of the Committee on the District of Columbia, House of Representatives, Ninetieth Congress, 2nd session, August 1, 1968. Washington, DC: US Government Printing Office, 1968.

Cross, Gary. *Cute and the Cool: Wondrous Innocence and Modern American Children's Culture.* New York: Oxford University Press, 2004.

Cross, Gary. *Kids' Stuff: Toys and the Changing World of Childhood.* Cambridge, MA: Harvard University Press, 1997.

Davies, Tom Adam. *Mainstreaming Black Power.* Berkeley: University of California Press, 2017.

Davis, Joshua Clark. *From Head Shops to Whole Foods: The Rise and Fall of Activist Entrepreneurs.* New York: Columbia University Press, 2017.

DeBenedetti, Charles. *An American Ordeal: The Antiwar Movement of the Vietnam Era.* Assisting author, Charles Chatfield. Syracuse: Syracuse University Press, 1990.

De Schweinitz, Rebecca. *If We Could Change the World: Young People and America's Long Struggle for Equality.* Chapel Hill: University of North Carolina Press, 2011.

DeWein, Sybil, and Joan Ashabraner. *The Collectors Encyclopedia of Barbie Dolls and Collectibles.* Paducah, KY: Collector Books, 1993.

Douglas, Mary, and Baron Isherwood. *The World of Goods: An Anthropology of Consumption.* London: Allen Lane, 1979.

Doyle, David. *Standard Catalog of Lionel Trains, 1945–1969.* Iola, WI: Krause, 2006.

DuCille, Ann. "Dyes and Dolls: Multicultural Barbie and the Merchandising of Difference." *differences: A Journal of Feminist Cultural Criticism* 6, no. 1 (1994): 47–67.

DuCille, Ann. *Skin Trade.* Cambridge, MA: Harvard University Press, 1996.

Echols, Alice. *Daring to Be Bad: Radical Feminism in America, 1967–1975.* Minneapolis: University of Minnesota Press, 1989.

Ellis, William Russell. "Operation Bootstrap: A Study in Ideology and the Institutionalization of Protest." PhD diss., University of California at Los Angeles.

Ellis, William Russell. *People Making Places: Episodes in Participation, 1964–1984.* Berkeley: Institute for the Study of Social Change, 1987.

Engelhardt, Tom. *The End of Victory Culture: American Triumphalism and the Disillusioning of a Generation.* New York: Basic Books, 1995.

Estepa, Andrea. "Taking the White Gloves Off: Women Strike for Peace and 'the Movement,' 1967–1983." In *Feminist Coalitions: Historical Perspectives on Second-Wave Feminism in the United States,* edited by Stephanie Gilmore, 84–122. Champaign: University of Illinois Press, 2008.

Fanning, Colin. "Building Kids: LEGO and the Commodification of Creativity." In *Childhood by Design: Toys and the Material Culture of Childhood, 1700–Present,* edited by Megan Brandow-Faller, 89–109. London: Bloomsbury, 2018.

Farber, David. "The Counterculture and the Antiwar Movement." In *Give Peace a Chance: Exploring the Vietnam Antiwar Movement,* edited by Melvin Small and William D. Hoover, 7–21. Syracuse: Syracuse University Press, 1992.

Farber, David, ed. *The Sixties: From Memory to History.* Chapel Hill: University of North Carolina Press, 1994.

Farmer, Ashley. *Remaking Black Power: How Black Women Transformed an Era.* Chapel Hill: University of North Carolina Press, 2017.

Farrell, Amy. "Attention to Difference: *Ms.* Magazine, Coalition Building, and Sisterhood." In *Feminist Coalitions: Historical Perspectives on Second-Wave Feminism in the United States,* edited by Stephanie Gilmore, 48–62. Urbana: University of Illinois Press, 2008.

Fass, Paula S. *The End of American Childhood: A History of Parenting from Life on the Frontier to the Managed Child.* Princeton, NJ: Princeton University Press, 2017.

Fergus, Devin. *Liberalism, Black Power, and the Making of American Politics, 1965–1980.* Athens: University of Georgia Press, 2009.

Firestone, Shulamith. *The Dialectic of Sex: The Case for Feminist Revolution.* New York: Morrow, 1970.

Ford, Tanisha C. *Liberated Threads: Black Women, Style, and the Global Politics of Soul.* Chapel Hill: University of North Carolina Press, 2015.

Forman-Brunell, Miriam. *Made to Play House: Dolls and the Commercialization of American Girlhood.* Baltimore, MD: Johns Hopkins University Press, 1998.

Fraiberg, Selma H. *The Magic Years: Understanding and Handling the Problems of Early Childhood.* New York: Charles Scribner's Sons, 1958.

Frank, Thomas. *The Conquest of Cool: Business Culture, Counterculture, and the Rise of Hip Consumerism.* Chicago: University of Chicago Press, 1996.

Gabler, Neal. *An Empire of Their Own: How the Jews Invented Hollywood.* New York: Doubleday, 1989.

Garrett, Debbie Behan. *The Definitive Guide to Collecting Black Dolls.* Grantsville, MD: Hobby House Press, 2003.

Gates, Racquel J. *Double Negative: The Black Image and Popular Culture.* Durham, NC: Duke University Press, 2018.

Geertz, Clifford. *The Interpretation of Cultures*. New York: Basic Books, 1973.

Germany, Kent B. *New Orleans after the Promises: Poverty, Citizenship, and the Search for the Great Society*. Athens: University of Georgia Press, 2007.

Gilbert, James. *Cycle of Outrage: America's Reaction to the Juvenile Delinquent in the 1950s*. New York: Oxford University Press, 1986.

Gitlin, Todd. *Inside Primetime*. New York: Pantheon Books, 1983.

Glickman, Lawrence B. *Buying Power: A History of Consumer Activism in America*. Chicago: University of Chicago Press, 2009.

Goings, Kenneth W. *Mammy and Uncle Mose: Black Collectibles and American Stereotyping*. Bloomington: Indiana University Press, 1994.

Goossen, Rachel Waltner. "Disarming the Toy Store and Reloading the Shopping Cart: Resistance to Violent Consumer Culture." *Peace and Change* 38, no. 3 (July 2013): 330–54.

Gordon, Leah. *From Power to Prejudice: The Rise of Racial Individualism in Midcentury America*. Chicago: University of Chicago Press, 2015.

Gornick, Vivian, and Barbara K. Moran, eds. *Woman in Sexist Society*. New York: Basic Books, 1971.

Gould, Sarah Zenaida. 2010. "Toys Make a Nation: A History of Ethnic Toys in America." PhD diss., University of Michigan.

Graebner, William. "The Unstable World of Dr. Benjamin Spock: Social Engineering in a Democratic Culture." *Journal of American History* 67, no. 3 (December 1980): 612–29.

Grant, Julia. *Raising Baby by the Book: The Education of American Mothers*. New Haven, CT: Yale University Press, 1998.

Grant, Julia. "'A Thought a Mother Can Hardly Face': Sissy Boys, Parents, and Professionals in Mid-Twentieth-Century America." In *Modern American Queer History*, edited by Allida Mae Black, 117–30. Philadelphia: Temple University Press, 2001.

Green, Adam. *Selling the Race: Culture, Community, and Black Chicago, 1940–1955*. Chicago: University of Chicago Press, 2006.

Green, Lisa J. *African American English: A Linguistic Introduction*. New York: Cambridge University Press, 2002.

Grieve, Victoria M. *Little Cold Warriors: American Childhood in the 1950s*. New York: Oxford University Press, 2018.

Griffin, Farah Jasmine. *Who Set You Flowin'? The African American Migration Narrative*. New York: Oxford University Press, 1996.

Grosz, Elizabeth. "Criticism, Feminism and the Institution: An Interview with Gayatri Chakravorty Spivak." *Thesis Eleven* 10/11 (1984–85): 175–87.

Guerrero, Ed. *Framing Blackness: The African American Image in Film*. Philadelphia: Temple University Press, 1993.

Hale, Grace Elizabeth. *Making Whiteness: The Culture of Segregation in the South, 1890–1940*. New York: Pantheon Books, 1998.

Hall, Karen. "A Soldier's Body: G.I. Joe, Hasbro's Great American Hero and the Symptoms of Empire." *Journal of Popular Culture* 38, no. 1 (August 2004): 34–54.

Halliday, Aria S. *Buy Black: How Black Women Transformed US Pop Culture.* Urbana: University of Illinois Press, 2022.

Harding, James M., and Cindy Rosenthal, eds. *Restaging the Sixties: Radical Theaters and Their Legacies.* Ann Arbor: University of Michigan Press, 2006.

Hartley, Ruth M., and Robert M. Goldenson. *The Complete Book of Children's Play.* Rev. ed. New York: Thomas Crowell, 1963.

Hartman, Andrew. *A War for the Soul of America: A History of the Culture Wars.* Chicago: University of Chicago Press, 2015.

Hečlo, Hugh. "The Sixties' False Dawn: Awakenings, Movements, and Postmodern Policy-Making." *Journal of Policy History* 8, no. 1 (1996): 34–63.

Heitner, Devorah. *Black Power TV.* Durham, NC: Duke University Press, 2013.

Hendershot, Heather. *Saturday Morning Censors: Television Regulation before the V-Chip.* Durham, NC: Duke University Press, 1998.

Henricks, Thomas. "The Nature of Play: An Overview." *American Journal of Play* 1 (Fall 2008): 157–80.

Henry, Jules. *Culture against Man.* New York: Random House, 1963.

Herman, Ellen. *The Romance of American Psychology: Political Culture in the Age of Experts.* Berkeley: University of California Press, 1995.

Herstory: Microfilm Collection. Berkeley, CA: Women's History Research Center, 1972.

Hester, Yolanda. "Shindana Toys: Dolls That Made a Difference." PBS SoCal, November 26, 2019. https://www.pbssocal.org/shows/lost-l-a/shindana-toys-dolls-made-difference.

Higonnet, Anne. *Pictures of Innocence: The History and Crisis of Ideal Childhood.* New York: Thames and Hudson, 1998.

Hill, Laura Warren, and Julia Rabig, eds. *The Business of Black Power: Community Development, Capitalism, and Corporate Responsibility in Postwar America.* Rochester, NY: University of Rochester Press, 2012.

Hilton, Matthew. "Consumer Movements." In *The Oxford Handbook of the History of Consumption*, edited by Frank Trentmann, 505–20. Oxford: Oxford University Press, 2012.

Hoberman, J., and Jeffrey Shandler, eds. *Entertaining America: Jews, Movies, and Broadcasting.* Princeton, NJ: Princeton University Press, 2003.

Hogan, Kirsten. *The Feminist Bookstore Movement: Lesbian Antiracism and Feminist Accountability.* Durham, NC: Duke University Press, 2016.

Horne, Gerald. *Fire This Time: The Watts Uprising and the 1960s.* Charlottesville: University of Virginia Press, 1995.

Horowitz, Daniel. *The Anxieties of Affluence: Critiques of American Consumer Culture, 1939–1979.* Amherst: University of Massachusetts Press, 2004.

Howard, Ella. "Pink Truck Ads: Second Wave Feminism and Gendered Marketing." *Journal of Women's History* 24, no. 10 (Winter 2010): 137–61.

Hulbert, Ann. *Raising America: Experts, Parents, and a Century of Advice about Children.* New York: Alfred A. Knopf, 2003.

Hutchinson, Braden. "Fighting the War at Home: Voice of Women and War Toy Activism in Postwar Canada." In *Worth Fighting For: Canada's Tradition of War Resistance from 1812 to the War on Terror*, edited by Lara Campbell, Michael Dawson, and Catherine Gidney, 147–58. Toronto: Between the Lines, 2012.

Information Exchange: A Conference on Community Based Economic Development. Cambridge Institute, Occasional Bulletin 2. Cambridge, MA: Cambridge Institute, June 1970.

"Inspiration, Inclusion, and the Making of a Multicultural Toy Company: An Interview with Yla Eason." *American Journal of Play* 13, nos. 2/3 (Winter 2022): 170–83.

"Interview with Lou Smith." In *Good Times: An Oral History of America in the Nineteen Sixties*, edited by Peter Joseph, 198–205. New York: Morrow, 1974.

Isserman, Maurice, and Michael Kazin. *America Divided: The Civil War of the Sixties.* New York: Oxford University Press, 2000.

Jackson, Walter A. *Gunnar Myrdal and America's Conscience: Social Engineering and Racial Liberalism, 1938–1987.* Chapel Hill: University of North Carolina Press, 1990.

Jacobson, Lisa. *Raising Consumers: Children and the American Mass Market in the Early Twentieth Century.* New York: Columbia University Press, 2004.

Jenkins, Henry. "Introduction: Childhood Innocence and Other Modern Myths." In *The Children's Culture Reader*, edited by Henry Jenkins, 1–37. New York: New York University Press, 1998.

Jenkins, Henry. "The Sensuous Child: Benjamin Spock and the Sexual Revolution." In *The Children's Culture Reader*, edited by Henry Jenkins, 209–30. New York: New York University Press, 1998.

Jones, Kellie. *South of Pico: African American Artists in Los Angeles in the 1960s and 1970s.* Durham, NC: Duke University Press, 2017.

Jones, Reginald R., ed. *Black Psychology.* New York: Harper and Row, 1972.

Joseph, Peniel E. *Waiting until the Midnight Hour: A Narrative History of Black Power in America.* Philadelphia: Temple University Press, 2006.

Kamp, David. *Sunny Days: The Children's Revolution That Changed America.* New York: Simon and Schuster, 2020.

Karp, Jonathan. "The Roots of Jewish Concentration in the American Popular Music Business, 1890–1945." In *Doing Business in America: A Jewish History*, edited by Hasia Diner, 123–44. West Lafayette, IN: Purdue University Press, 2018.

Katz, Michael B. *The Undeserving Poor: America's Enduring Confrontation with Poverty.* Rev. ed. New York: Oxford University Press, 2013.

Kelsen, David. "The Life and Times of Malvina Reynolds, Long Beach's Most Legendary (and Hated) Folk Singer." *OC Weekly*, August 31, 2016. https://www.ocweekly.com/the-life-and-times-of-malvina-reynolds-long-beachs-most-legendary-and-hated-folk-singer-7474438/.

Kennedy, John F. "Address to the UN General Assembly." September 25, 1961. John F. Kennedy Presidential Library and Museum. https://www.jfklibrary.org/learn/about-jfk/historic-speeches/address-to-the-united-nations-general-assembly.

Kern-Foxworth, Marilyn. *Aunt Jemima, Uncle Ben, and Rastus: Blacks in Advertising, Yesterday, Today, and Tomorrow*. Westport, CT: Greenwood, 1994.

Kerstens, Elizabeth Kelley. *Plymouth's Air Rifle Industry*. Charleston, SC: Arcadia, 2013.

King, Wilma. *African American Childhoods: Historical Perspectives from Slavery to Civil Rights*. New York: Palgrave Macmillan, 2005.

Kirk, Andrew G. "The *Whole Earth Catalog*, New Games, and Urban Environmentalism." In *Cities and Nature in the American West*, edited by Char Miller, 242–54. Reno: University of Nevada Press, 2010.

Kline, Stephen. *Out of the Garden: Toys and Children's Culture in the Age of TV Marketing*. London: Verso, 1993.

Kotlowski, Dean. "Black Power—Nixon Style: The Nixon Administration and Minority Business Enterprise." *Business History Review* 72, no. 3 (1998): 409–45.

Ladner, Joyce. *Tomorrow's Tomorrow: The Black Woman*. Garden City, NY: Doubleday, 1971.

Lange, Alexandra. *The Design of Childhood: How the Material World Shapes Independent Kids*. London: Bloomsbury, 2018.

Lareau, Annette. *Unequal Childhoods: Class, Race, and Family Life*. Berkeley: University of California Press, 2003.

"Legacy of Shindana Toys: Black Play and Black Power: An Interview with David Crittendon, Yolanda Hester, and Rob Goldberg, The." *American Journal of Play* 13, nos. 2/3 (2022): 135–46.

Levine, Elana. *Wallowing in Sex: The New Sexual Culture of 1970s American Television*. Durham, NC: Duke University Press, 2007.

Linden-Ward, Blanche, and Carol Hurd Green. *American Women in the 1960s: Changing the Future*. New York: Twain, 1993.

Loewen, James. *Sundown Towns: A Hidden Dimension of American Racism*. New York: New Press, 2005.

Lofland, John. *Polite Protesters: The American Peace Movement of the 1980s*. Syracuse: Syracuse University Press, 1993.

Lord, M. G. *Forever Barbie: The Unauthorized Biography of a Real Doll*. New York: Morrow, 1994.

Lordi, Emily J. *The Meaning of Soul: Black Music and Resilience since the 1960s*. Durham, NC: Duke University Press, 2020.

Lovett, Laura. "Child's Play: Boys' Toys, Women's Work, and 'Free Children.'" In *When We Were Free to Be: Looking Back at a Children's Classic and the Difference It Made*, edited by Laura Lovett and Lori Rotskoff, 111–26. Chapel Hill: University of North Carolina Press, 2012.

Lovett, Laura, and Lori Rotskoff, eds. *When We Were Free to Be: Looking Back at a Children's Classic and the Difference It Made*. Chapel Hill: University of North Carolina Press, 2012.

Lyons, Paul. *People of This Generation: The Rise and Fall of the New Left in Philadel-phia.* Philadelphia: University of Pennsylvania Press, 2011.

Mallard, Natalie. "The (Los Angeles) Bank of Finance (1964–81)." BlackPast.org, August 15, 2018. http://www.blackpast.org/african-american-history/los -angeles-bank-of-finance-1964-1981/.

Marcus, Leonard S. *Minders of Make-Believe: Idealists, Entrepreneurs, and the Shap-ing of American Children's Literature.* New York: Houghton Mifflin, 2008.

Marketing Toys. Chicago: Toys and Novelties, 1949.

Martin, Ben L. "From Negro to Black to African American: The Power of Names and Naming." *Political Science Quarterly* 106, no. 1 (Spring 1991): 83–107.

Martin, Waldo E., Jr. "'Be Real Black for Me': Representation, Authenticity, and the Cultural Politics of Black Power." In *The Cultural Turn in U.S. History: Past, Present, Future,* edited by James W. Cook, Lawrence B. Glickman, and Michael O'Malley, 243–66. Chicago: University of Chicago Press, 2008.

Martin, Waldo E., Jr. *No Coward Soldiers: Black Cultural Politics and Postwar Amer-ica.* Cambridge, MA: Harvard University Press, 2005.

Maultsby, Portia K. "Soul." In *African American Music: An Introduction,* edited by Mellonee V. Burnim and Portia K. Maultsby, 277–98. 2nd ed. New York: Routledge, 2015.

May, Elaine Tyler. *Homeward Bound: American Families in the Cold War Era.* New York: Basic Books, 1988.

McBride, David. "Death City Radicals: The Counterculture in Los Angeles." In *The New Left Revisited,* edited by John McMillian and Paul Buhle, 110–38. Phila-delphia: Temple University Press, 2003.

McClintock, Inez, and Marshall McClintock. *Toys in America.* Washington, DC: Public Affairs Press, 1961.

Mechling, Jay. "Gun Play." *American Journal of Play* 1, no. 2 (Fall 2008): 192–209.

Mergen, Bernard. "Made, Bought, and Stolen: Toys and the Culture of Child-hood." In *Small Worlds: Children and Adolescents in America, 1850–1950,* edited by Elliot West and Paula Petrik, 86–106. Lawrence: University Press of Kansas, 1992.

Mergen, Bernard. *Play and Playthings: A Reference Guide.* Westport, CT: Green-wood, 1982.

Metzl, Jonathan. *The Protest Psychosis: How Schizophrenia Became a Black Disease.* Boston: Beacon, 2010.

Meyerowitz, Joanne. "'How Common Culture Shapes the Separate Lives': Sexuality, Race, and Mid-Twentieth Century Social Constructionist Thought." *Journal of American History* 96, no. 4 (March 2010): 1057–84.

Michlig, John. *GI Joe: The Complete Story of America's Favorite Man of Action.* San Francisco: Chronicle Books, 1998.

Mickenberg, Julia. *Learning from the Left: Children's Literature, the Cold War, and Radical Politics in the U.S.* New York: New York University Press, 2006.

Mickenberg, Julia. "The Pedagogy of the Popular Front: 'Progressive Parenting' for a New Generation, 1918–1945." In *The American Child: A Cultural Studies*

Reader, edited by Caroline Field Levander and Carol J. Singley, 226–45. New Brunswick, NJ: Rutgers University Press, 2003.

Mintz, Steven. "The Changing Face of Children's Culture." In *The Reinvention of Childhood in Postwar America*, edited by Paula S. Fass and Michael Grossberg, 38–50. Philadelphia: University of Pennsylvania Press, 2012.

Mintz, Steven. *Huck's Raft: A History of American Childhood*. Cambridge, MA: Harvard University Press, 2004.

Mintz, Steven, and Susan Kellogg. *Domestic Revolutions: A Social History of American Family Life*. New York: Free Press, 1987.

Mitchell, Michele. *Righteous Propagation: African Americans and the Politics of Racial Destiny after Reconstruction*. Chapel Hill: University of North Carolina Press, 2004.

Mollin, Marian. *Radical Pacifism in Modern America: Egalitarianism and Protest*. Philadelphia: University of Pennsylvania Press, 2006.

Morgen, Sandra. *Into Our Own Hands: The Women's Health Movement in the United States, 1969–1990*. New Brunswick, NJ: Rutgers University Press, 2002.

Morrow, Robert W. *Sesame Street and the Reform of Children's Television*. Baltimore, MD: Johns Hopkins University Press, 2006.

Mottle, Lauren. "'We Resist on the Grounds We Aren't Citizens': Black Draft Resistance in the Vietnam War Era." *Journal of Civil and Human Rights* 6, no. 2 (Fall/Winter 2020): 26–52.

Murray, Heather. "Free for All Lesbians: Lesbian Cultural Production and Consumption in the United States during the 1970s." *Journal of the History of Sexuality* 16, no. 2 (May 2007): 251–75.

Myrdal, Gunnar. *An American Dilemma: The Negro Problem and Modern Democracy*. New York: Harper, 1944.

National Organization for Women. "Statement of Purpose." In *Feminism in Our Time: The Essential Writings, World War II to the Present*, edited by Miriam Schneir, 95–102. New York: Vintage Books, 1994.

Neal, Mark Anthony. *What the Music Said: Black Popular Music and Black Public Culture*. New York: Routledge, 1999.

Negro Family: The Case for National Action, The. Washington, DC: Office of Planning and Policy Research, US Department of Labor, 1965.

Nelson-Rowe, Shan. "Ritual, Magic, and Educational Toys: Symbolic Aspects of Toy Selection." In *Troubling Children: Studies on Children and Social Problems*, edited by Joel Best, 117–31. New York: Walter de Gruyter, 1994.

Nembhard, Jessica Gordon. "Cooperative Ownership in the Struggle for African American Economic Empowerment." *Humanity and Society* 28, no. 23 (August 2004): 298–321.

Newcombe, Horace. "From Old Frontier to New Frontier." In *The Revolution Wasn't Televised: Sixties Television and Social Conflict*, edited by Lynn Spigel and Michael Curtin, 287–305. New York: Routledge, 1997.

Ogata, Amy F. "Creative Playthings: Educational Toys and Postwar American Culture." *Winterthur Portfolio* 39, no. 2 (2004): 129–56.

Ogata, Amy F. *Designing the Creative Child: Playthings and Places in Midcentury America.* Minneapolis: University of Minnesota Press, 2013.

Ogbar, Jeffrey O. G. *Black Power: Radical Politics and African American Identity.* Baltimore, MD: Johns Hopkins University Press, 2005.

Ostrofsky, Kathryn A. "Taking *Sesame* to the Streets: Young People's Interactions with Pop Music's Urban Aesthetic in the 1970s." *Journal of Popular Music Studies* 24, no. 3 (September 2012): 287–304.

Ozersky, Josh. *Archie Bunker's America: TV in an Era of Change, 1968–1978.* Carbondale: Southern Illinois University Press, 2003.

Paris, Leslie. "Happily Ever After: *Free to Be . . . You and Me*, Second-Wave Feminism, and 1970s American Children's Culture." In *The Oxford Handbook of Children's Literature*, edited by Julia Mickenberg and Lynne Vallone, 519–38. New York: Oxford University Press, 2011.

Patterson, Gordon. "Color Matters: The Creation of the Sara Lee Doll." *Florida Historical Quarterly* 73, no. 2 (October 1994): 147–65.

Patterson, James T. *America's Struggle against Poverty in the Twentieth Century.* Rev. ed. Cambridge, MA: Harvard University Press, 2009.

Patterson, James T. *Grand Expectations: The United States, 1945–1974.* New York: Oxford University Press, 1996.

Payton, Hughston R., and Lynne Reade. *You, the Church, and Race: A Study/Action Guide on White Racism.* 3rd ed. Los Angeles: Synod of Southern California, United Presbyterian Church of the U.S.A., 1969.

Perillo, Jonna. "White Teachers and the 'Black Psyche': Interculturalism and the Psychology of Race in the New York City High Schools, 1940–1950." In *When Science Encounters the Child: Education, Parenting, and Child Welfare in 20th-Century America*, edited by Barbara Beatty, Emily D. Cahan, and Julia Grant, 157–74. New York: Teachers College Press, 2006.

Perkins, Myla. *Black Dolls: An Identification and Value Guide, 1820–1991.* Paducah, KY: Collector Books, 1995.

Perlman, Allison. "Feminists in the Wasteland: The National Organization for Women and Television Reform." *Feminist Media Studies* 7, no. 4 (2007): 413–31.

Petigny, Alan. *The Permissive Society: America 1941–1965.* New York: Cambridge University Press, 2009.

Pipkin, James. "Life on the Cusp: Lynda Huey and Billie Jean King." In *Impossible to Hold: Women and Culture in the 1960s*, edited by Avital Bloch and Lauri Umansky, 43–64. New York: New York University Press, 2005.

Plant, Rebecca Jo. *Mom: The Transformation of Motherhood in Modern America.* Chicago: University of Chicago Press, 2010.

Pogrebin, Letty Cottin. *Growing Up Free: Raising Your Child in the '80s.* New York: Bantam, 1981.

Price, Melanye T. *Dreaming Blackness: Black Nationalism and African American Public Opinion.* New York: New York University Press, 2009.

Pugh, Allison J. *Longing and Belonging: Parents, Children, and Consumer Culture.* Berkeley: University of California Press, 2009.

Pugh, Allison J. "Selling Compromise: Toys, Motherhood, and the Cultural Deal." *Gender and Society* 19, no. 6 (December 2005): 729–49.

Quinn, Eithne. "'Tryin' to Get Over': *Super Fly*, Black Politics, and Post–Civil Rights Film Enterprise." *Cinema Journal* 49, no. 2 (2010): 86–105.

Rand, Erica. *Barbie's Queer Accessories*. Durham, NC: Duke University Press, 1995.

Regan, Patrick M. "War Toys, War Movies, and the Militarization of the United States, 1900–85." *Journal of Peace Research* 31, no. 1 (1994): 45–58.

Reid, Mark A. *Black Lenses, Black Voices: African American Cinema Now*. Lanham, MD: Rowman and Littlefield, 2005.

Rekers, George A., and Cindy E. Yates. "Sex-Typed Play in Feminoid Boys versus Normal Boys and Girls." *Journal of Abnormal Psychology* 4, no. 1 (1976): 1–8.

Rhodes, Joel P. *Growing Up in a Land Called Honalee: The Sixties in the Lives of American Children*. Columbia: University of Missouri Press, 2017.

Rhodes, Joel P. *The Vietnam War in American Childhood*. Athens: University of Georgia Press, 2019.

Rich, Marvin. "The Congress of Racial Equality and Its Strategy." *The Annals* 357 (January 1965): 113–18.

Richards, Ruth. "Frank Barron and the Study of Creativity: A Voice That Lives On." *Journal of Humanistic Psychology* 46, no. 3 (July 2006): 352–70.

Ringgold, Faith, Frank Maresca, Margo Jefferson, and Lyle Rexer. *Black Dolls: From the Collection of Deborah Neff*. Santa Fe, NM: Radius Books, 2015.

Rosen, Ruth. *The World Split Open: How the Modern Women's Movement Changed America*. New York: Basic Books, 2004.

Rossinow, Doug. "'The Revolution Is about Our Lives': The New Left's Counterculture." In *Imagine Nation: The American Counterculture of the 1960s and '70s*, edited by Peter Braunstein and Michael William Doyle, 99–104. New York: Routledge, 2002.

Rossinow, Doug. *Visions of Progress: The Left-Liberal Tradition in America*. Philadelphia: University of Pennsylvania Press, 2007.

Rotskoff, Lori. "'Little Women's Libbers' and 'Free to Be Kids': Children and the Struggle for Gender Equality in the United States." In *When We Were Free to Be: Looking Back at a Children's Classic and the Difference It Made*, edited by Laura Lovett and Lori Rotskoff, 92–110. Chapel Hill: University of North Carolina Press, 2012.

Rupp, Leila J. "The Survival of American Feminism: The Women's Movement in the Postwar Period." In *Reshaping America: Society and Institutions, 1945–1960*, edited by Robert H. Bremner and Gary W. Reichard, 33–65. Columbus: Ohio State University Press, 1982.

Russworm, TreaAndrea M. *Blackness Is Burning: Civil Rights, Popular Culture, and the Problem of Recognition*. Detroit: Wayne State University Press, 2016.

Sammond, Nicholas. *Babes in Tomorrowland: Walt Disney and the Making of the American Child, 1930–1960*. Durham, NC: Duke University Press, 2005.

Scalzo, Joe. *Evel Knievel and Other Daredevils*. New York: Grosset and Dunlap, 1974.

Schmidt, Christopher W. "The Children of *Brown*: Psychology and School Desegregation in Midcentury America." In *When Science Encounters the Child: Education, Parenting, and Child Welfare in 20th-Century America*, edited by Barbara Beatty, Emily D. Cahan, and Julia Grant, 175–94. New York: Teachers College Press, 2006.

Schneider, Cy. *Children's Television: The Art, The Business, and How It Works.* New York: NTC Business Books, 1987.

Schneidhorst, Amy C. *Building a Just and Secure World: Popular Front Women's Struggle for Peace and Justice in Chicago during the 1960s.* New York: Continuum, 2011.

Schneir, Miriam, ed. *Feminism in Our Time: The Essential Writings, World War II to the Present.* New York: Vintage Books, 1994.

Schneir, Miriam. "Phyllis Graber: Discrimination in High School Sports." In *Feminism in Our Time: The Essential Writings, World War II to the Present*, edited by Miriam Schneir, 390–92. New York: Vintage Books, 1994.

Schor, Juliet B. "In Defense of Consumer Critique: Revisiting the Consumption Debates of the Twentieth Century." *Annals of the American Academy of Political and Social Science* 611 (May 2007): 16–30.

Schulman, Bruce J. *The Seventies: The Great Shift in American Culture, Politics, and Society.* New York: Free Press, 2001.

Scott, Daryl Michael. *Contempt and Pity: Social Policy and the Image of the Damaged Black Psyche, 1880–1996.* Chapel Hill: University of North Carolina Press, 1997.

Sedgwick, Eve Kosofsky. "How to Bring Your Kids Up Gay." *Social Text* 29 (1991): 18–27.

Seiter, Ellen. *Sold Separately: Children and Parents in Consumer Culture.* New Brunswick, NJ: Rutgers University Press, 1993.

Seiter, Ellen. "Toys Are Us: Marketing to Parents and Children." *Cultural Studies* 6, no. 2 (1992): 232–47.

Self, Robert O. *American Babylon: Race and the Struggle for Postwar Oakland.* Princeton, NJ: Princeton University Press, 2003.

Selig, Diana. "The Whole Child: Social Science and Race at the White House Conference of 1930." In *When Science Encounters the Child: Education, Parenting, and Child Welfare in 20th-Century America*, edited by Barbara Beatty, Emily D. Cahan, and Julia Grant, 136–56. New York: Teachers College Press, 2006.

Serlin, David H. "From Sesame Street to Schoolhouse Rock: Urban Pedagogy and Soul Iconography during the 1970s." In *Soul: Black Power, Politics, and Pleasure*, edited by Richard Green and Monique Guillory, 105–20. New York: New York University Press, 1998.

Sherry, Michael S. "Death, Mourning, and Memorial Culture." In *The Columbia History of Post–World War II America*, edited by Mark Christopher Carnes, 155–77. New York: Columbia University Press, 2007.

"Shindana Toy Company: Changing the American Doll Industry." *Lost LA*, season 4, episode 6. Los Angeles: KCET, 2019.

Smethurst, James. *The Black Arts Movement: Literary Nationalism in the 1960s and 1970s*. Chapel Hill: University of North Carolina Press, 2006.

Spencer, Robyn C. *The Revolution Has Come: Black Power, Gender, and the Black Panther Party in Oakland*. Durham, NC: Duke University Press, 2016.

Spigel, Lynn. *Make Room for TV: Television and the Family Ideal in Postwar America*. Chicago: University of Chicago Press, 1992.

Spigel, Lynn, and Michael Curtin, eds. *The Revolution Wasn't Televised: Sixties Television and Social Conflict*. New York: Routledge, 1997.

Spock, Benjamin. *Baby and Child Care*. 3rd ed. New York: Hawthorn Books, 1968.

Spock, Benjamin. *The Commonsense Book of Baby and Child Care*. 2nd ed. New York: Duell, Sloan, and Pearce, 1957. Orig. pub. 1946.

Spock, Benjamin. *Dr. Spock Talks with Mothers: Growth and Guidance*. Boston: Houghton Mifflin, 1961.

Spock, Benjamin, and Mary Morgan. *Spock on Spock: A Memoir of Growing Up with the Century*. New York: Pantheon Books, 1989.

Spruill, Marjorie J. "Gender and America's Right Turn." In *Rightward Bound: Making America Conservative in the Seventies*, edited by Bruce J. Schulman and Julian E. Zelizer, 71–89. Cambridge, MA: Harvard University Press, 2008.

Sprung, Barbara. *Non-Sexist Education for Young Children: A Practical Guide*. New York: Citation Press, 1975.

Stack, Carol B. *All Our Kin: Strategies for Survival in a Black Community*. New York: Harper and Row, 1974.

Steigerwald, David. *Culture's Vanities: The Paradox of Cultural Diversity in a Globalized World*. Lanham, MD: Rowman and Littlefield, 2006.

Stephenson, Carolyn M. "Women Leaders in the Peace/Antiwar Movements." In *Gender and Women's Leadership: A Reference Handbook*, vol. 1, edited by Karen O'Connor, 279–89. London: SAGE, 2010.

Stern, Sydney Landensohn, and Ted Schoenbaum. *Toyland: The High Stakes Game of the Toy Industry*. New York: Contemporary Books, 1990.

Strickland, Charles E., and Andrew M. Ambrose. "The Baby Boom, Prosperity, and the Changing Worlds of Children, 1945–1963." In *American Childhood: A Research Guide and Historical Handbook*, edited by Joseph M. Hawes and N. Ray Hiner, 533–85. Westport, CT: Greenwood, 1985.

Sugrue, Thomas J. *The Origins of the Urban Crisis*. Princeton, NJ: Princeton University Press, 1995.

Sugrue, Thomas J. *Sweet Land of Liberty: The Forgotten Struggle for Civil Rights in the North*. New York: Random House, 2008.

Sutton-Smith, Brian. "Play Theory: A Personal Journey and New Thoughts." *American Journal of Play* 1, no. 1 (2008): 80–123.

Sutton-Smith, Brian. "The Role of Play in Cognitive Development." *Young Children* 22, no. 6 (September 1967): 361–70.

Sutton-Smith, Brian. *Toys as Culture*. New York: Gardner, 1986.

Sutton-Smith, Brian, and Diana Kelly-Byrne. "The Idealization of Play." In *Play in Animals and Humans*, edited by Peter K. Smith, 305–22. Oxford: Blackwell, 1984,

Swerdlow, Amy. "Ladies' Day at the Capitol: Women Strike for Peace versus HUAC."
    Feminist Studies 8, no. 3 (Autumn 1982): 493–520.

Swerdlow, Amy. *Women Strike for Peace: Traditional Motherhood and Radical Politics in the 1960s.* Chicago: University of Chicago Press, 1993.

Swinthe, Kirsten. *Feminism's Forgotten Fight: The Unfinished Struggle for Work and Family.* Cambridge, MA: Harvard University Press, 2018.

Thomas, Sabrina Lynette. "Sara Lee: The Rise and Fall of the Ultimate Negro Doll."
    Transforming Anthropology 15, no. 1 (2008): 38–49.

Torres, Sasha. *Black, White, and in Color: Television and Black Civil Rights.* Princeton, NJ: Princeton University Press, 2003.

Toys in Wartime: Suggestions to Parents on Making Toys at Wartime. Washington, DC: US Department of Labor, Children's Bureau, 1942.

Turner, Fred. *The Democratic Surround: Multimedia and American Liberalism from World War II to the Psychedelic Sixties.* Chicago: University of Chicago Press, 2013.

Umansky, Lauri. *Motherhood Reconceived: Feminism and the Legacies of the Sixties.* New York: New York University Press, 1996.

Van Deburg, William L. *Black Camelot: African American Culture Heroes in Their Times, 1960–1980.* Chicago: University of Chicago Press, 1997.

Van Deburg, William L. *New Day in Babylon: The Black Power Movement and American Culture, 1965–1975.* Chicago: University of Chicago Press, 1992.

Vogel, David. *The Market for Virtue: The Potential and Limits of Corporate Social Responsibility.* Washington, DC: Brookings Institution Press, 2006.

Walker, Susannah. "Black Is Profitable: The Commodification of the Afro, 1960–1975." In *Beauty and Business: Commerce, Gender, and Culture in Modern America,* edited by Philip Scranton, 254–77. New York: Routledge, 2000.

Ward, Brian. *Just My Soul Responding: Rhythm and Blues, Black Consciousness, and Race Relations.* Berkeley: University of California Press, 1998.

Weems, Robert E. *Desegregating the Dollar: African American Consumerism in the Twentieth Century.* New York: New York University Press, 1998.

Wertham, Fredric. *A Sign for Cain: An Exploration of Human Violence.* New York: Macmillan, 1966.

West, Mark. *Children, Culture, and Controversy.* Hamden, CT: Archon Books, 1988.

Widener, Daniel. "Writing Watts: Bud Schulberg, Black Poetry, and the Cultural War on Poverty." *Journal of Urban History* 34, no. 4 (May 2008): 655–87.

Wilder, Gary. *Freedom Time: Negritude, Decolonization, and the Future of the World.* Durham, NC: Duke University Press, 2015.

Wilkinson, Doris. "Racial Socialization through Children's Toys: A Sociohistorical Examination." *Journal of Black Studies* 5, no. 1 (September 1974): 96–109.

Williams, Yohuru, and Jama Yazerow, eds. *In Search of the Black Panther Party: New Perspectives on a Revolutionary Movement.* Durham, NC: Duke University Press, 2006.

Women on Words and Images. *Dick and Jane as Victims: Sex Stereotyping in Children's Readers.* Princeton, NJ: Women on Words and Images, 1972.

Woolum, Janet. *Outstanding Women Athletes: Who They Are and How They Influenced Sports in America*. Phoenix: Oryx, 1998.

Young, Marilyn. *The Vietnam Wars 1945–1990*. New York: HarperCollins, 1991.

Zeiger, Susan. "The Schoolhouse vs. the Armory: U.S. Teachers and the Campaign against Militarism in the Schools, 1914–1918." *Journal of Women's History* 15, no. 2 (Summer 2003): 150–79.

Zorach, Rebecca. *Art for People's Sake: Artists and Community in Black Chicago, 1965–1975*. Durham, NC: Duke University Press, 2019.

Zuckerman, Michael. "Dr. Spock: The Confidence Man." In *The Family in History*, edited by Charles Rosenberg, 179–207. Philadelphia: University of Pennsylvania Press, 1975.

Index

Page locators in italics refer to figures.